STORIES OF JOSEPH

STORIES OF JOSEPH

Narrative Migrations between Judaism and Islam

Marc S. Bernstein

Wayne State University Press
Detroit

ISBN: 978-0-8143-2566-7 (pbk.)

Library of Congress has cataloged the hardcover edition as follows:

Bernstein, Marc Steven.
Stories of Joseph : narrative migrations between Judaism and Islam / Marc S. Bernstein.
p. cm.
Included bibliographical references and index.
ISBN 0-8143-2565-3 (cloth : alk. paper)
1. Joseph (Son of Jacob) in rabbinical literature. 2. Midrash-History and criticism. 3. Qissit Sayyidna Usuf il-Siddiq. 4. Joseph (Son of Jacob)—Folklore. 5. Legends, Islamic-History and criticism. 6. Intercultural communication in folklore. 7. Intertextuality. I. Title.
BM518.J68B47 2006
296.1'9—dc22 2006014048

Published with the assistance of a fund established by Thelma Gray James of Wayne State University for the publication of folklore and English studies.

♾ The paper used in this publication meets the minimum requirements of the American National Standard for Information Sciences—Permanence of Paper for Printed Library Materials, ANSI Z39.48–1984.

For Natalie, Emily, Joshua, Lianna . . . and Jenny

Great seas cannot extinguish love; no river can sweep it away . . .

Song of Songs 8:7

While the "other" may be perceived as being either LIKE-US or NOT-LIKE-US, he is, in fact, most problematic when he is TOO-MUCH-LIKE-US, or when he claims to BE-US. It is here that the real urgency of a "theory of the other" emerges. This urgency is called forth not by the requirement to place the "other," but rather to situate ourselves. It is here, to invoke the language of a theory of ritual, that we are not so much concerned with the drama of "expulsion," but with the more mundane and persistent processes of "micro-adjustment." This is not a matter of the "far," but preeminently, of the "near." The problem is not alterity, but similarity—at times, even identity. A "theory of the other" is but another way of phrasing a "theory of the self."

Jonathan Z. Smith,
"What a Difference a Difference Makes"

Le désir de l'homme est le désir de l'Autre.

Jacques Lacan, *Écrits*

Contents

Preface xi

Abbreviations xix

Introduction: Written in Gold on Sheets of Silver 1

I. *The Story of Our Master Joseph the Righteous*

Translator's Foreword 47

A Translation of *The Story of Our Master Joseph the Righteous* 56

II. The Most Beautiful of Stories

1 A Pearl in the Dust 137

2 Joseph, His Father, and His Brothers 157

3 Joseph and Zulaykhā 205

4 Between the Pit and Mrs. Potiphar 243

Appendix: The *Sūrah* of Joseph 257

Notes 265

Bibliography 289

Index 305

Preface

> In the name of the Lord, the eternal God, may we be successful in what we do. We shall now begin *The Story of Our Master Joseph the Righteous*. . . .
>
> *Joseph,* 1

The history of Jewish life under Islam is often envisaged—both by scholars and in the popular imagination—as conforming to one or the other of two stereotypical conceptions. In the one view, it was an ecumenical, symbiotic utopia in which the Jews, as a protected "People of the Book," flourished in an environment characterized by a large degree of autonomy and creative interchange with the majority culture. In the other, opposing view, this history is read as a dark tale of unmitigated repression in which the Jewish minority was often the target of religious intolerance and persecution. In my work, I seek to interrogate these two polarized caricatures through the prism of literature: in particular, through the body of popular tales that treats characters sacred to both traditions.[1] The present study, then, consists of a critical discussion of the cross-cultural patterns evidenced in the Judaic and Islamic scriptural and exegetical traditions surrounding the figure of Joseph son of Jacob. The analysis revolves around a Judeo-Arabic retelling of the story of Joseph titled *The Story of Our Master Joseph the Righteous*. The particular manuscript studied is contained in a codex that belonged to the nineteenth-century Karaite community of Cairo.

Key to our analysis is that corpus of Jewish scriptural exegesis known as midrash. This Hebrew term designates the discursive mode that "seeks out" (the underlying connotation of the word's consonantal root) meanings from the core text of the culture—the Hebrew Bible—in an effort to keep *the* Text perpetually relevant. This is primarily accomplished through an investigation on the level of the individual verse, but attention is often drawn to even smaller units—a turn of phrase, a single word—all the way down to the form of a particular letter; in any case, the practice of midrash is typically an enterprise of discrete analysis. However, a related body of popular works is one that is referred to (rather inelegantly) in the scholarly literature as "retellings." These consist of expansions of biblical stories that are based on the verse-bound interpretations of midrash, as well as on material borrowed from other cultures; here, however, as opposed to the disconnected interpretations offered by the Midrash, the motifs are strung together and interrelated in order to form a continuous and relatively seamless narrative. While midrash, in general, is characterized by a hermeneutic that allows for multiple, at times even contradictory interpretations of Scripture, it remains integrally connected to the source text and limited by ideological constraints. Retellings of biblical stories, on the other hand, exhibit greater narrative freedom and more clearly reflect the popular and religious culture of the period in which they were composed or were current; moreover, they represent a genre that is doubly open—to parallel but distinct interpretations of Scripture and also to influences that may come even from outside the tradition.

In the present study, I expand the metatextual discourses of midrash and retelling to incorporate the parallel genre in the Islamic tradition: "The Stories of the Prophets." These are homiletic stories of biblical and other pre-Islamic figures featured in the Qurʾān and considered prophets in Islam. Because the primary medium for cross-denominational conversation between Muslims and Jews concerning these personages was the Arabic language, a fruitful avenue of inquiry into their intercultural connections is an analysis of such retellings of biblical narratives composed in Judeo-Arabic—the Arabic language spoken and written by Jews in various forms throughout the Arab world from the period before the advent of Islam until today. Of particular interest are those narrative expansions of the biblical text that deal with biblical characters revered within both the Jewish and Muslim communities. In both communities, this work was often the creation of a hybrid category of typically anonymous writers best described as "folk authors."

Remarkably, *The Story of Our Master Joseph the Righteous,* seemingly a retelling for a Jewish audience of the biblical Joseph story rooted in the midrashic tradition, is simultaneously an adaptation of cognate Islamic material contained in "The Stories of the Prophets" literature. Making matters more complex, the body of quranic and extraquranic literature is itself beholden to earlier Jewish midrashic traditions; these, in turn, have correspondingly borrowed from ancient Near Eastern and Hellenistic literatures. While the process of the absorption of Jewish and Christian scriptural and exegetical traditions into Islam has been well documented by scholars, *Joseph* takes the process one step further. Here we have a fascinating example of this phenomenon of cultural borrowing coming full circle: a Jewish text has seemingly taken its form from an Islamic prototype, which in turn was derived from the Jewish literary mode of scriptural interpretation known as midrash. It would be difficult to overestimate the significance of such an example of buried cross-connections to the understanding of the mechanisms involved in the transfer of cultural artifacts. That this should constitute a desideratum for further research has been highlighted by one leading contemporary scholar of midrash: "In future studies, it will be important to deal with the ways that midrash has been occulted in the Jewish-Christian-Moslem polysystem, and to discern the underground channels within this system in which it was kept alive as well."[2] It is precisely these subterranean conduits—those submerged trends and peripheral (albeit canonical) genres—that I hope to explore in this analysis of cross-cultural interchange in religious, folk literature.

This book establishes a context for this sharing of material and employs analytical tools drawn from the fields of comparative religion, folklore, Semitic philology, and psychoanalytic and literary theory. In the introduction, "Written in Gold on Sheets of Silver," we will begin with a consideration of general issues surrounding the absorption of Jewish biblical and extrabiblical material within the Islamic tradition and trace the evolution of Jewish/Islamic cross-cultural contacts. Not wishing to ignore the history of polemics that were also part of this history, we will examine issues of competition between the two cultures over claims to this material and the consequent limits to interchange. The emphasis here is on the creative possibilities and relative "openendedness" latent within the midrashic system of exegesis and its tolerance for, indeed, its fostering of multiple interpretations when confronting essentially "gapped" but sacred texts. In this section, I will also highlight the implications of this intertextual toleration of polysemy for the significant cross-cultural and cross-linguistic patterns evidenced in Judeo-Arabic midrashic works.

At the core of this study lies the Judeo-Arabic tale, *The Story of Our Master Joseph the Righteous*. Thus, after a brief foreword, part 1 consists of a translation of this romance or novella based on several nineteenth-century manuscript versions. Annotations to the text will point out the significant parallels to scriptural and exegetical material in both Jewish and Islamic tradition. (A critical edition and transcription of the Arabic text is also in the works but owing to practical considerations will necessarily be published separately.)

The second part of this volume consists of a close reading of the narrative of *The Story of Our Master Joseph* that integrates an eclectic variety of theoretical and generic concerns. In the context of this discussion I present a comparative analysis of this text, both with the biblical and quranic scriptural accounts as well as with the vast body of legendary literature about Joseph composed by Jewish and Muslim exegetes and preachers over the centuries. In chapter 1 we will begin by surveying the midrashic adumbrations of those ethical and physical qualities that combine to make Joseph the hero in Jewish and Islamic retellings of his story, including *The Story of Our Master Joseph the Righteous*. These traits will come into play in the exegetical traditions surrounding both Joseph's interactions with his brothers and his relationship with al-ʿAzīz and Zulaykhā (the biblical Potiphars). The midrashic accounts of each of these interactions respectively, then, shall in turn be the focus of the following two chapters of this section. The analysis here will involve not only an examination of the ways in which particular stories or motifs function as narrative expansions of Scripture, but also an exploration of the manner in which these innovations were passed back and forth between both religio-literary traditions. In our discussion we will also explore the limitations to such cross-cultural interchange that in the final analysis preclude one from equating the two traditions. In the final chapter of the book we will consider the linkages between the two sub-narratives of Joseph and his family and Joseph and the Potiphars in *The Story of Our Master Joseph the Righteous,* as well as a brief meditation on the tale's resonances with the existential condition of Jewish life in exile.

The genesis of this study was a search for cross-cultural influences in the intertextual patterns evidenced by "The Stories of the Prophets" literature in the Islamic tradition, on the one hand, and the Midrash in Judaism, on the other. While there has been much written on the topic, historically scholars have often sought to argue for the ultimately Jewish—or, alternatively, Christian—sources of the material included in the Islamic scriptural, exegetical, and popular traditions about characters and events that also appear in the Hebrew Bible and the New Testament. This in turn has elicited in recent times a decidedly vociferous defense of the independence and integrity of the Muslim accounts. While in this book I present a case study of one such example of cross-cultural intertextuality, I am decidedly not interested in tracing ultimate sources. This would not only be an endeavor of forbidding complexity—given the intricate and often effaced map of interactions between the traditions—but also one fraught with a long history of polemicism. If we have learned anything from postmodern theory, such a "searching after origins" is largely beside the point given the essential intertextuality inherent to all text (ancient Jewish sources included); however, perhaps more significantly, such an agenda is antithetical to the ecumenical and nonproprietary atmosphere that should drive scholarship in these areas.

My intention here is rather to integrate philological techniques within a comparative literary analysis so as to refine our understanding of the mechanisms involved in the transfer of cultural artifacts. The discussion will emphasize ways in which the use of allusion and nuance indicate knowledge of other texts even across denominational lines. Throughout our discussion, however, I will not lose sight of cultivating a broader aesthetic appreciation for the various and variegated *stories* of Joseph, the plethora of variations on and expansions of—in the words of the Qurʾān—this "finest of tales." Thus, the book proceeds simultaneously along three trajectories of inquiry: it is at one and the same time a broad examination of the patterns of Jewish-Muslim intercultural exchange; a focused analysis of the workings of a specific text and its range of intertextual patternings; and an exploration of the creative use made of such materials toward an aesthetic aim. While posing a steep and at times vertiginous challenge for the reader, it is my hope that such a diversity of perspectives will enrich our appreciation for this story and "problematize" our understanding of the dynamics of intercultural exchange between majority and minority populations, as well as "complicate" our view of the forces of *intra*cultural continuity and innovation.

This work has taken a long and circuitous path toward publication, and along the way I have incurred many debts to friends and colleagues. My mentor, William M. (Ze'ev) Brinner, originally suggested "The Stories of the Prophets" literature as a fertile area for research into the intersection of Islamic and Jewish cultures, and I am grateful for his ongoing support and guidance over many years. In an act of true generosity toward a young scholar, Haggai Ben-Shammai spent many hours going over with me the Judeo-Arabic text of the Joseph story upon which this study is based. At a crucial juncture in the work, I benefited greatly from the editorial assistance of my dear friend Rita Kohl, a true "writer's reader," whose insightful comments dramatically improved the book. Reuven Firestone read the entire manuscript more than once and gave freely of his scholarly advice to aid me in its revision. Eli Yassif suggested important parallel texts and key concepts from the realm of folk literature. An anonymous reader for Wayne State University Press also made many fruitful suggestions for changes. Jacob Lassner made the initial connection with the Press and offered encouragement along the way. For help in providing access to the original Judeo-Arabic manuscript, I wish to thank Jane Levy and Seymour Fromer, former librarian, and emeritus director, respectively, of the Judah L. Magnes Museum in Berkeley, California. For providing material assistance during the period of writing, I am grateful to the University of California, Phi Beta Kappa, the Koret Foundation, the Fulbright Program, the Memorial Foundation for Jewish Culture, and the National Foundation for Jewish Culture, the National Endowment for the Humanities, and the institutional support of Michigan State University. I wish to thank my copyeditor Tammy Rastoder and also my editors at Wayne State University Press, who did wonderful work on a complicated project: Carrie Downes, production editor; Kristin Harpster Lawrence, managing editor; Kathryn Wildfong, acquiring editor; Jane Hoehner, director; as well as Arthur Evans, director emeritus.

Finally, but most significantly, this book would never have seen the light of day without the assistance, understanding, and commitment of—in the words of the anonymous poets responsible for the Song of Songs—"my Beloved" *and* "my Friend," Jenny Lewis. In addition to providing unending encouragement and unstinting support, she read over the manuscript countless times and her many astute suggestions, like those of the anonymous authors and tradents whose contributions have been seamlessly interwoven into *The Story of Our Master Joseph the Righteous,* have become an integral and inseparable part of the final product. She and our children—Natalie, Emily, Joshua, and Lianna—have uncomplainingly borne up under the demands of this project and it is thus to them that I humbly dedicate this work: I know it is but a small token of gratitude, but it comes from the innermost recesses of my heart. To all the others who have long-sufferingly awaited its appearance in print, including my parents, Norma Tarrow and Alfred Bernstein, Bernard Lewis and Teddie Pincus; my brothers, Art and Jon; and my dearest friend, Nir, I can do no better than cite the words of Joseph's father Jacob in the Qurʾān: "Fair patience!" (*fa-ṣabr*^{un} *jamīl*^{un}, Q 12:18, 83).

Of course, all errors of commission or omission remain my own responsibility. Apt here is the dictum of ʿAnan ben David, the eighth-century putative founder of the Karaite sect from which the particular manuscript edition of

The Story of Our Master Joseph the Righteous studied here derives: "Search well in the Torah and do not rely on my opinion."[3]

Some technical matters: The system employed for the transliteration of Arabic and Hebrew terms follows for the most part standard practice (as, for example, that employed in *The Encyclopaedia of Islam* and *The Encyclopedia Judaica,* respectively), although given its Egyptian provenance, citations from the Judeo-Arabic work, *The Story of Our Master Joseph the Righteous,* will phonetically transcribe the definite article, which in Classical form of the language is *al,* as *il,* except in the case of common Islamic names and terms. Other changes from standard pronunciation will be similarly reflected in the transcription (for example, the Classical *jīm* will be recorded as [g] in accord with the local dialect). Arabic case endings will be marked as such by their placement in superscript. References to the tale itself will be abbreviated in citation within the body of this book to *Joseph.* The Arabic title of this tale—*Qiṣṣit sayyidnā yūsuf il-ṣiddīq* (abbreviated to QSY)—with an accompanying superscript numeral will be used in the footnotes when referring to a specific textual variant (thus, QSY^1, QSY^2, and so on). All page references to *Joseph* will be keyed to the internal pagination of the manuscript contained in the Karaite Collection of the Judah L. Magnes Museum (QSY^1) unless otherwise noted. Scriptural passages, whether biblical or quranic, when embedded within a particular exegesis will be indicated by the use of italic type. Translations of passages from the Torah and from the Prophets and Writings are taken respectively from Robert Alter's *The Five Books of Moses* and the second edition of the new Jewish Publication Society translation of the Tanakh (the Hebrew Bible), with the exception of those cases in our discussion in which I seek to highlight a particular lexical nuance.[4] Unless otherwise specified, all additional translations from the Hebrew and Arabic are mine, including the translation of the Joseph *sūrah* from the Qurʾān found in the appendix.

In these times when an American Jew by the name of Joseph can aspire to the position of leader of the world's most powerful country and the Muslim community in the United States can grow to unprecedented proportions, such a tale as ours might have additional relevance for the most prosperous, powerful, and self-confident Jewish and Muslim Diasporas in history. In its openness to cultural influences *The Story of Our Master Joseph* bespeaks a time when Jewish-Muslim relations could engender a discourse and dialogue, even in the context of competition over control of sacred characters and texts. Contemporary events in the Middle East have precipitated a plunge to a new nadir in Jewish-Muslim relations (including the despoiling of the traditional tomb of Joseph in Shechem/Nablus), reminding us of those pits of despair and violence into which our protagonist sunk so long ago. We can only pray that, as in the story of Joseph and his brothers, the voices of reconciliation and peace will prevail and both peoples will deliver themselves and each other from the abyss and maybe even come to recognize their fraternal link. Such a hope is reflected in the words of Joseph Lieberman to a group of Detroit area Arab-Americans: "I am Joseph, your brother" (Gen. 45:4).

Abbreviations

A	Arabic
AH	*Anno Hegira* [L: "year of the Hijrah"]
AM	*Anno Mundi* [L: "year of Creation"]
b.	*ibn* (A) or *ben* (H): "son of"
BCE	Before the Common Era
Behnstedt-Woidich	Peter Behnstedt and Manfred Woidich, *Die ägyptisch-arabischen Dialekte: Glossar*
BR	*Bereishit raba*
BT	Babylonian Talmud
CE	(of the) Common Era
Dozy	Reinhart Pieter Anne Dozy, *Supplément aux Dictionnaries Arabes*
EI	*Encyclopaedia of Islam* (second edition)
EJ	*Encyclopedia Judaica*
EQ	*Encyclopedia of the Qurʾān*
G	Greek
H	Hebrew
Hinds-Badawi	Martin Hinds and El-Said M. Badawi, *A Dictionary of Egyptian Arabic: Arabic-English*
JT	Jerusalem Talmud
Joseph	*The Story of Our Master Joseph the Righteous*
JA	Judeo-Arabic
L	Latin
Lane	E. W. Lane, *Arabic-English Lexicon*
PRE	*Pirqei de-rabbi eliʿezer*
Q	Qurʾān
QSY^n	*Qiṣṣit sayyidnā yūsuf* (superscript numeral refers to specific manuscript)
R.	Rabbi
Spiro	Socrates Spiro, *An Arabic-English Vocabulary of the Colloquial Arabic of Egypt* (first edition)

Introduction: Written in Gold on Sheets of Silver

The issue is not influence but interaction.
David Biale, "Challenging the Boundaries"

This book is a study of the two-way migration of textual traditions between Judaism and Islam that takes as its particular focus the story of Joseph son of Jacob, the biblical patriarch and quranic prophet. The discussion of these patterns of interchange will be anchored in a detailed presentation and consideration of a Judeo-Arabic retelling of the tale recorded in a manuscript from nineteenth-century Cairo titled *The Story of Our Master Joseph the Righteous* (*Qiṣṣit sayyidnā yūsuf il-ṣiddīq*). The central point of the investigation is to highlight and illuminate the ways in which this text constitutes a remarkable example of the flow of literary artifacts between Jewish and Muslim cultures.[1] In doing so, my methodology, mirroring the eclectic nature of the text itself, will draw from diverse perspectives and fields. While this may be somewhat disorienting to anyone seeking a single thread of analysis, the shifting among different theoretical and methodological frameworks will, aside from its discursive utility, serve to jar us from accepting simplistic notions of cultural influence and textual history. Moreover, this approach will help highlight some of the profound ambiguities of the tale and the complex patterns of borrowing that it exhibits.

That the character of Joseph is the locus of significant cross-cultural exchange perhaps should not on initial reflection be surprising given his prominence in each of the Jewish and Muslim traditions. As merely a first-order approximation, the centrality of this figure may be gauged by the space and pride of place he occupies in each community's foundational texts. In the biblical Book of Genesis, the Joseph cycle takes up the full final third of this book of the Jewish people's origins (chapters 37–50); while the descent to Egypt of Jacob's household, which his story occasions, sets the stage for the Exodus and the Sinaitic revelation—the pivotal events in the formation of the Jewish people. In the Qurʾān, Joseph's tale comprises an entire chapter, or *sūrah,* bearing his name.[2] It is, moreover, the only instance of a "complete" and continuous narrative surrounding one of the many biblical protagonists who figure in the Muslim scripture. On the symbolic level, within Jewish tradition the vicissitudes faced by Joseph have come to stand as the prototype of the people's experience in Exile; while in Islam, the quranic Joseph, along with Abraham and Moses, served as a model for Muḥammad, exemplifying for him the difficulties the Arabian prophet had to overcome in gaining acceptance for his mission. Each of these scriptural accounts subsequently provided a springboard for rich traditions of exegesis and narrative elaborations that date all the way back to each canon's period of crystallization, and which formed the lifeblood of both communities' engagement with text that extends over the centuries and continues down to the present day.

While there thus arose two distinct bodies of traditions of the tale in postbiblical and postquranic literature, respectively, there were also significant points of connection and opportunities for cross-fertilization. Naturally, given the later date of composition of the Qurʾān, in terms of the scriptural accounts, the influence could necessarily be but one-way—the incorporating and adapting of Jewish (as well as Christian) biblical and postbiblical written and oral traditions within the Scripture of the younger sister-religion. (This, of course, doesn't negate the fact of earlier Near Eastern influences on the formation of the biblical canon itself.) However, with respect to developments in both traditions *after* the advent of Islam, the pattern of intertextual relations extended in both directions. While at times the pressures for isolation between the two communities were strong, particularly in the realm of religious law valorized by the cultural elites, nonetheless, there were many occasions for interaction, most notably in the spheres of legend and popular literature, where sectarian boundaries could often be traversed with relative impunity.

Throughout centuries of close contact in a wide variety of geographic locales—almost entirely characterized by the presence of a Jewish minority within the hegemonic Islamic state—there were myriad opportunities for the borrowing of cultural motifs. Narrative expansions[3] of the scriptural tales were a particularly fertile field in which such cross-pollinations could occur. The upholders of sectarian and doctrinal purity exerted little control over their development, which is perhaps not unconnected to their perception of these tales as comprising inferior, if not vulgar, fanciful entertainments. Nevertheless, despite periodic efforts to suppress their diffusion, such expanded retellings of narratives from the Bible and Qur'ān served as a major creative outlet for the folk imagination.

It is in the realm of such popular traditions surrounding scriptural figures revered by both Jews and Muslims that we may productively look for examples of fluid movement across religious boundaries. This legendary material typically had its origin in the hermeneutic systems of the respective communities. Within Jewish tradition, the archetype for this practice was known as midrash, and this will be a focal paradigm employed in the current study. Here, however, I will invoke the term to name a general condition of metatextuality, applying it not just in its more limited, technical sense to the discrete, verse-bound interpretations of the Bible from the Rabbinic period but also to expanded narrative retellings of biblical accounts; in addition, I extend its use to the parallel Islamic discourse recorded in the Stories of the Prophets literature. According to this conception, midrash implies more a *mode* than a specific genre, one that sought (and continues to seek) to make the foundation texts of the respective communities perpetually relevant by engaging in a never-ending dialectic with the scriptural tradition. By doing so, this process thereby ensured unity of the community and continuity with the past.

Oftentimes, such expansions were transmitted orally within the Jewish tradition by the preacher, the *darshan* or *magīd,* in the context of the sabbath homily of the synagogue. Within the Islamic milieu, the *quṣṣāṣ,* or popular storytellers, played a major role in the propagation of these tales. Together with written texts, these oral traditions made up the actual treasure trove of folklore that was both a primary vehicle for popular culture and a legacy that could be transmitted from generation to generation. At times, this literature was also the means by which marginalized or heterodox notions could creep into the discourse. Significantly, the informality and nondoctrinal basis of these expansions led to their relative openness to "foreign" and diachronic influences. A most fruitful locus of inquiry for the analysis of such cross-cultural patterns is the tradition of Judeo-Arabic retellings of biblical stories. While our primary focus will be the intersection and sharing of traditions, at the same time, contention over ownership of these traditions has also been part of this intertextual history. Thus, while we will typically not be concerned with establishing the ultimate derivation of individual motifs, we shall give attention to polemical disputations regarding claims to the unique possession of the true or authentic Joseph story, as well as other limits to this borrowing.

My hypothesis, then, is that Judeo-Arabic midrashic narrations of biblical tales such as *The Story of Our Master Joseph the Righteous,* coming from a milieu in which there was a great degree of cross-cultural interchange, reflect the influence of Islamic hagiographic material. In particular, I am interested in the corpus of diverse texts that treat the pre-Islamic biblical and extrabiblical figures and events represented in the Qurʾān. From the earliest date, this material was considered by Muslim scholars to have a Jewish or Christian root, related either by informants who remained within the fold of those communities or introduced by converts to Islam. This literature was designated by the generic rubric, *isrāʾīliyyāt,* and was incorporated within the classical universal histories as well as quranic exegesis. An important example of the former is the introduction and pre-Islamic portions of the history composed by al-Ṭábarī (d. 923 CE) entitled *Tāʾrīkh al-rusul w'al-mulūk.*[4] The corpus of quranic commentary, the *Tafsīr,* also contains much relevant information—the most significant for our concerns will be the work of the same al-Ṭabarī, as well as the exegetical traditions collated by al-Bayḍāwī (d. between 1282–1291 CE—or perhaps as late as 1316).[5] Finally, these stories were subsequently anthologized and presented in the form of a continuous narrative in collections referred to as "The Stories of the Prophets" (*qiṣaṣ al-anbiyāʾ*). Among the most famous collections of these tales is the *Kitāb ʿarāʾis al-majālis fī qiṣaṣ al-anbiyāʾ* ("The Book of the Brides of Sessions on the Stories of the Prophets") by Abū Isḥāq Aḥmad al-Tháʿlabī (d. 1035 or 1036 CE).[6] There are also various versions of a collection attributed to a certain Muḥammad b. ʿAbdállāh al-Kisāʾī.[7] Finally, Sufi works that sought in the lives of these 'saints' examples of mystical union and expressions of the esoteric meanings of faith are an additional repository of such traditions.[8] Such retellings retain a wide appeal to the current day, and contemporary anthologies in a variety of popularized forms are still readily available in the urban centers of the Arabo-Islamic world, for example, in the bookstores of today's downtown Cairo.

Collectively, the roots of this diverse body of material reach back to pre-Islamic Arabia, where knowledge of the legends of the Bible and apocrypha was ostensibly transmitted to the Arabs by the Jewish and Christian communities in the Peninsula, as well as through the work of Christian missionaries in the region.[9] In particular, it can be assumed that Muḥammad would have interacted with those Jews who lived in Yathrib, an oasis north of Mecca and the major Jewish town of the Hijāz.[10] Although the manner in which this material was disseminated is still a matter of debate, there can be no doubt that biblical and legendary material is preserved widely in the Qurʾān and Islamic traditional literature. However, it is also clear that this material subsequently underwent a separate trajectory of development within the orbit of Islamicate civilization. What will be of interest to us is tracing this development and investigating the continued presence of these henceforth bilateral intertextual relationships.

The narrative surrounding Joseph that stands at the center of the analysis is but one example of an entire genre of Judeo-Arabic retellings of biblical and postbiblical stories, which are based on midrashic and folk literature but have been drawn together and creatively reshaped according to the dictates of the adapters' imaginations. Books or chapbooks of this sort were composed primarily for "the simple folk"—that is, those whose Hebrew and Aramaic literacy was limited and did not have in their possession the books of the Jewish canon—and manuscript versions of the individual tales were typically bound together in a single codex. Besides Joseph, among the biblical figures to become the subject of such works were Abraham, Moses, King Saul, King David, King Solomon, and Queen Esther. Jewish figures from later times also had tales composed in their honor, most notably Hannah and her seven sons, Rabbi Akiva, Judith, Bustanai, and Maimonides.

The particular version of the story of Joseph which we treat here is one variant of a tale that had a wide circulation throughout the Jewish communities of the Arab East. It is found in many manuscripts and was printed several times amongst Iraqi Jews in Baghdad, Jews of Iraqi descent in the cities of India, in Aden, and in North Africa.[11] The tale is noteworthy for its length and the abundance of narrative detail; in particular, the attempted seduction of Joseph by his master's wife commands special attention. As is typical of midrash, and popular traditions in general, the tale cannot be identified with any known author, but instead was the product of an anonymous folk-author who collated and integrated diverse traditions.[12] What *is* clear, however, is that the narrative is highly dependent on both Jewish and Islamic material—with the boundaries between the two often elided. Indeed, the most dramatic feature of this Jewish text is the extent to which its author—consciously or not—incorporates Islamic material drawn from the literature of the Stories of the Prophets. Simultaneously, at crucial junctures the narrative departs from, and even vehemently rejects, certain Islamic narrative expansions that were deemed objectionable. Such nodes of strong *re-* or *mis-*reading of these source materials reflect the dialectic tensions involved in cross-cultural borrowing and the competition over cultural space and icons.

From the standpoint of language, the *Joseph* text is highly colloquial, reflecting popular traditions that are very likely oral in derivation and transmission. Although Judeo-Arabic was typically written in Hebrew script, the commonality of a shared spoken language made it much more likely for elements to pass between these cultures despite the different orthographic traditions. The story's narrative structure and plot are also reflective of its heterogeneous provenance: cast in the form of a Hellenistic romance or a medieval novella, the tale highlights the permeability of temporal and spatial boundaries among Ancient Near Eastern, Greek, Jewish, and Islamic literatures.[13]

Israelite "Stuff": Adoption and Adaptation

In order to understand better the dynamic whereby Jewish material was incorporated into Islamic texts, we need to set out the *Sitz im Leben*—the social setting—for early Muslim interactions with the two other Abrahamic traditions. Reuven Firestone has offered an evolutionary account of the Islamic absorption of what he refers to as "biblicist" material; that is, that material stemming from the Jewish and Christian biblical and extrabiblical traditions.[14] Such an understanding of this process is based on the premise that by the sixth century of the Common Era, in the period immediately prior to the advent of Islam, Jews and Christians were well assimilated into life in Arabia. There is much internal evidence in the Qurʾān itself for the degree of this integration, including striking correspondences with biblical laws and customs, the identity of scriptural protagonists, and even the incorporation of borrowed vocabulary and calques. These parallels were noticed already in the first Islamic century, marking the beginning of a polemic that has continued to this day. On the one hand, Jews and Christians, aware of the anterior position of the Bible and threatened by Muslim claims to political and cultural hegemony, viewed the Islamic scripture condescendingly as comprising a flawed copy of biblicist material. In their view, divergences and discrepancies from the "original" dispensation were due to Muslim error.[15] Muslims, on the other hand, uncomfortably cognizant of the temporal priority of the sister religions, argued that while both the Hebrew Bible and the Gospels derived from the same eternal heavenly scripture (*umm al-kitāb*) as the Qurʾān, the Jews and Christians had engaged in distortion (Arabic: *taḥrīf*) of their revelations.[16]

In the modern period as well, this bias has tainted research in these areas and even the work of ostensibly sympathetic scholars has been plagued by attempts to identify putative Ur-texts that would support a claim for chronologic precedence. An interesting counterphenomenon of the post-Enlightenment era has been the tendency of Jewish orientalists—influenced by the spirit of liberalism and confidence in positive societal evolution—to overcompensate in their treatment of this material and to perceive the relationship between

Jews and Muslims as being marked by high levels of synergism and symbiosis.[17] What is significant in either case—both that of the polemicist and that of the apologist or accomodationist—is the overdetermined nature of the discussion surrounding such shared material. The legacy of this highly charged discourse should be a warning to all who dare tread in these domains.

In analogous fashion, the history of Jewish life in the Arabo-Islamic world is one that has been subjected to relatively high doses of religious polemic and inflammatory apologetics. One of two polar perceptions of this history would have the Jews enjoying a near-utopian existence as a respected "People of the Book" (*ahl al-kitāb*—those peoples esteemed by Islam for possessing a revealed religion, primarily Jews, Christians, and Samaritans, but later this status was extended to Zoroastrians and Hindis), protected contractually under the terms of *dhimma*. This social compact safeguarded adherents of these religions in exchange for observance of certain discriminatory statutes of varied inconvenience or severity, application of which fluctuated greatly over time and place.[18] The contrasting negative view—influenced on the one hand by the relatively rare anti-Jewish fanatic outbreaks as well as the harsh polemic of some quranic passages, and on the other by what Salo Baron famously termed "the lachrymose conception of Jewish history"—views Jewish existence under Islam in martyrological terms, with Jews being given the choice between the Book or the Sword. The "truth"—as close as can be approximated—was much more subtle, and there were great divergences in tolerance depending on the historical context.

Recently, efforts have been focused on achieving a more nuanced perception of the history of minority populations living under Muslim rule.[19] While there were outbreaks of persecution, what can be stated unequivocally is that Jews within the Islamic world suffered far less than their coreligionists in Christendom. Although the Qurʾān itself records antipathy towards the Jews, it is typically akin in tone to the chagrin and anger of a spurned suitor. Muḥammad had early hopes of engaging the Arabian Jewish and Christian communities and convincing them that he was the bearer of a new dispensation, which, despite its innovations, was syncretistic in its essence and decidedly continuous with the Jewish and Christian revelations. While he did enjoy a modicum of success in persuading some to convert, the overall Jewish communal reception was cool, if not overtly hostile, to his claims. Much of the resentment directed towards those who refused to recognize his mission is preserved in the later, so-called Medinan passages of the Qurʾān where Muḥammad inveighs against the Jews. Unfortunately, such statements have served as ready fodder for anti-Jewish polemics throughout the centuries, including, in its most extreme formulation, hostile and violent expressions from a rejectionist, radical Islam engaged in *jihād* against all non-Muslims.

Still, all in all, within "normative" Islam the Jews as a "People of the Book" did not face religious compulsion. This fundamental precept of religious tolerance is expressed in the Qurʾān: "There shall be no compulsion in religion" (*lā ikrāha fī al-dīn*) (Q 2:256). While discrimination was built into the *dhimma* system of protection, outright persecution and acts of violence against Jews were the exception down to the modern era. Even the notorious statutes encoded in the infamous Pact of ʿUmar were enforced mostly in the breach.[20] While we should in no way attempt to whitewash the history of Jews under Islam, we should not embrace either of these extreme and all too facile conceptions. It should be assumed that despite official pronouncements and warnings to the contrary, interactions on a popular level continued unabated; indeed it is likely that clerical inveighing against such contact is a marker of its relative ubiquity.

A more productive, comparativist approach requires us to bear in mind the permeable cultural boundaries that characterized early Islam in its expansive mode during the first and the beginning of the second centuries after its founding. During this time period of explosive growth of the empire, from 622 CE through the latter part of the eighth century, as Muslims came into contact with Jewish and Christian populations, they were actively encouraged by the religious establishment to learn more from their sources about the biblicist figures mentioned in the Qurʾān. The quranic text assumed background knowledge not always readily available to the growing community of believers—especially in the far-flung reaches of the new empire. Moreover, the nearly unmitigated, exhortative tone of the Islamic scripture generates relatively little narrative flow and continuity, and this too made the anthologizing of stories from outside sources a desideratum.

Indeed, those traditions treating pre-Islamic biblical and extrabiblical characters came to be referred to by Muslim scholars as *isrāʾīliyyāt,* literally, Israelite "material," or "stuff"; in other words, literature about the *bánū isrāʾīl* ("the Children of Israel"). The name of this genre highlights the open acceptance and acknowledgment of originally biblicist traditions, introduced by Jewish or (to a much lesser extent) Christian informants, or by actual converts to Islam. These materials, in addition to native pagan elements indigenous to tribal religions of the Arabian Peninsula, were the basis for the construction of the Islamicate concept of the so-called "Age of Ignorance" (*al-jāhiliyyah*), the era of pre-Islamic history. Although these borrowings were sometimes viewed as suspect and at times even proscribed, the general attitude of openness in this early period is reflected in the well-known edict of the Prophet: "Narrate [traditions] from the Children of Israel for there is nothing objectionable in that." This *ḥadīth*, or report from the Prophet Muḥammad, is first cited in the *Risālah* of al-Shāfiʿī (d. 204 AH). M. J. Kister examined the widely divergent opinions of Muslim scholars surrounding this saying and the attempts to limit its application, attempts that ultimately failed. As he concludes: "The saying *ḥaddithū ʿan banī isrāʾīla wa-lā ḥaraja,* attached to various other traditions, became widely current among Muslims in the first half of the second century. This permission to narrate stories about the Children of Israel caused the door to be opened widely to Jewish lore and traditions transmitted by Muslim scholars."[21]

The breadth of the borrowing from both Jewish and Christian material and its conformity to orthodox practice are attested to by the system set up to classify the relative "soundness" of a particular tradition:

> The term *isrāʾīliyyāt* is actually used in classical and more recent Islamic terminology, not merely for the specifically Jewish elements which entered the science of Qurʾānic *tafsīr* but [also] for the Christian and other non-Muslim extraneous elements. The use of the *isrāʾīliyyāt* for elucidating certain aspects of Qurʾānic and *ḥadīth* texts, or for amplifying vaguenesses in them, was regarded as legitimate; hence Ibn Taymīya classifies *isrāʾīliyyāt* under the headings *ṣaḥīḥ* ["sound"], *kadhib* ["unsound"], and *maskūt ʿanhu* ["those about which it is not possible to validate or invalidate"].[22]

This pattern of condoned, cultural absorption applies to the Umayyad and early ʿAbbasid periods, the period before the "gates of collection" were to close and the term *isrāʾīliyyāt* acquired its largely derogatory sense within "official" Islam.[23] The formal process of the gathering of such tales came to an end in the latter half of the eighth century when the *ulamāʾ* (religious scholars) began to forbid the transmission of traditions that were considered to be of foreign origin. The purging of foreign material was ideologically consistent with the perception that Islam had first gained dominion over, and then supplanted and superseded, all other religious communities—a perception that was seemingly validated and reinforced by the wildly dramatic success of the Islamic territorial expansion. Such a dynamic may be rooted in an essential "anxiety of influence" whose origins reside in a conscious or subconscious awareness of the antecedent position of the earlier tradition. This uneasiness could have been held in abeyance during the period of Islam's spread and consolidation, but afterwards the existence of earlier traditions could have constituted an unavoidable irritant.[24]

However, while the term *isrāʾīliyyāt* did eventually come to carry a pejorative sense and was often grounds for exclusion of a tale labeled as such from canonical texts, in actuality, many of these traditions were *not* excluded. This was for the simple reason that the background information these tales provided was required if Muslims were to make intelligible and accessible the otherwise obscure events surrounding the biblicist characters as they are depicted in the Qurʾān, as with the marked exception of Joseph, these figures are alluded to only sparingly or haphazardly in the Islamic Scripture. However, even more to the point, the ubiquity of these traditions surrounding the pre-Islamic prophets, and the favor they found in folk culture, made their complete eradication impossible. In practice, and despite the admonitions of the religious establishment, most of the Israelite material was not expurgated, and such borrowing continued on the popular level. Moreover, while in the prestigious area of Islamic law (*al-sharīʿah*) the insistence on the exclusion of "foreign" material was rather strict, legendary material had less bearing on state and religious affairs, and consequently such pressures for its sanitizing were less intense. Additionally, by the time foreign lore had become an issue, much of the material had already evolved to be compatible with Islamic ideology and had gained acceptance within the canonical tradition and generated in turn its own subsequent body of tradition. The result of this process of transformation and harmonization is that those tales called *isrāʾīliyyāt* do not correspond exactly with Jewish aggadic sources. From the perspective of intertextuality, then, these traditions, no matter what their ultimate derivation, have undergone a process of textual formation of their own and therefore can be said to represent a truly authentic Islamic literature.

As mentioned then, these elements—adopted and adapted—were to serve as the major foundation for the Islamicate concept of pre-Revelatory history, and to a very large extent, by the tenth century the Muslim historical narratives treating this period are based on the *isrāʾīliyyāt* collections. Indeed, the people involved in the recording and transmission of these traditions are portrayed as consciously aware of their foreign provenance. In this manner, even foreign materials could be brought to corroborate the truth and ascendancy of Islam. In fact, their very foreignness was often deliberately retained in order to reinforce the unimpeachable credentials of such outside evidence. This notion is given further cogency when one considers that this testimony often was attributed to former or present adherents of the subsumed religions of Christianity and Judaism. This is demonstrated explicitly in the traditions that have Jews confirm the prophecy of Muḥammad, or the many traditions related back to originally Jewish tradents who had adopted Islam.

Central to the acceptance and authority of a particular tradition was its claim to an early date and reliable source. In the chains of transmission that precede individual traditions and establish their authority, the *asānīd* (singular: *isnād*), many of the tales are traced back to the tradents ʿAbdallāh b. Salām, Kaʿb al-Aḥbār and Wahb ibn Munabbih, early Jewish converts to Islam.[25] Modern critical study of Islam has questioned the historical reliability of these chains, but what is significant for our purposes is that the authenticity of such traditions was in fact affirmed by apostate Jews. Thus, it becomes clear that this sphere provides us with an example of open and acknowledged sharing of tradition.[26]

In this early expansive period, then, the success of the Islamic conquests lent credence to the claims for the truth and priority of Islam, and Jews and their traditions were not perceived as a threat; on the contrary, given this context, *isrāʾīliyyāt* were a legitimate, even the most credible, source of information. In those limited areas where there arose conflicts with Islamic sensibilities, most notably the question of the infallibility of the prophets (*ʿisma*), there was ready the notion of the older traditions' "falsification" (*taḥrīf*) or "alteration" (*tabdīl*) of the revelation vouchsafed to them. This was a particularly effective "work-around" that allowed Islam to base itself on ancient traditions and at the same time undermine its rivals' truth claims and bolster its own.

The Story of Our Master Joseph the Righteous

One particularly revealing window into the transfer of cultural artifacts between Judaism and Islam from the realm of Judeo-Arabic literature is the folk narrative that is the focus of this book. This tale, *Qiṣṣit sayyidnā yūsuf il-ṣiddīq* (*The Story of Our Master Joseph the Righteous*), exists in many different adaptations representing somewhat different traditions. The extant versions, which date primarily from the late eighteenth through the early twentieth centuries and vary in completeness, are housed in manuscript collections throughout the world. The present study is based on a manuscript from the Karaite community of Cairo, copied in 1836, which is now located in the Karaite Collection of the Judah L. Magnes Museum in Berkeley, California. In the discussion that follows I will refer to this particular version as *Joseph*—or QSY[1] when contrasted with other versions. For purposes of comparison and clarification of obscure sections, I will refer in particular to three other versions of this Joseph text, also of Egyptian provenance, in the Ḥanān Collection of the Institute for Microfilmed Hebrew Manuscripts at the Jewish National and University Library in Jerusalem. Two of these—QSY[2] and QSY[3]—parallel the account as recorded in QSY[1], while QSY[4] represents a distinct alternative tradition. I will also have recourse to several other texts when they can illumine our understanding of the Magnes text, or offer a contrasting tradition of interest. That this particular manuscript was recorded by a Karaite scribe and was in the possession of the Karaite community in Cairo seems to have had little direct bearing on the content. Although one could argue that Karaites, being typically less isolated from the majority population in Egypt, had more direct access to Islamic material, the sectarian provenance of this particular manuscript seems irrelevant, as the text is extant in nearly identical form in Rabbanite manuscripts. Thus, while in itself a fascinating topic, we will not venture here into the history of the Karaite community in Egypt or Jewish intercommunal relations.[27]

The Story of Our Master Joseph enjoyed a wide circulation among Jews in the Islamic world; a catalogue of the Firkovich collection in St. Petersburg lists some dozen and a half versions.[28] In its lengthier versions, the tale comprises the entire cycle of the story of Joseph. Such works belong to a genre of literature consisting of retellings of biblical narratives by folk authors. This type of literature differs from midrash proper in the sense that the metatext has become text in its own right. That is to say, although the particular expansions may have had their origin in some particular idiosyncrasy within the biblical text, they are no longer verse-bound; instead, they have assumed an independent status, and have been joined together by the author or storyteller intent on presenting a continuous and relatively seamless narrative. During the medieval period, this form of Jewish literature gained momentum—under the influence of models such as the Alexander Romance—and tales about cultural icons provided a forum for Jews to foreground the exploits of their heroes. As such, they were an authentic form of literary pursuit, and one that, with parallels in Hellenistic literature and medieval romances, comprises a precursor to the modern novel.

The *Tasbīḥ*—A Declaration of Narrative Independence

That *Joseph* is a self-consciously discrete narrative is made evident from the tale's outset. Within the introductory section known in Arabic as the *tasbīḥ*—literally, the "praising" of God, which was traditionally inserted at the beginning of a literary work—are presented in encapsulated verse many of the elements that serve to distinguish and define this text. While the title of this work, given simply as *The Story of Our Master Joseph the Righteous,* could be taken as a simple declarative statement, it also allows for the possibility of reading that initial definite article as proprietary, as laying out the claim for *Joseph* to be *the* story relating the events in the life of this character to the exclusion of all others. Moreover, the proem begins by emphasizing that the tale of Joseph is presented here "in all completeness and perfection": implicitly, the author makes the claim that his tale, in its exhaustiveness and accuracy, is superior to all other versions. Moreover, he makes clear that it is an eclectic work, championing it as one in which the various expansions of the story over the ages have been gathered and incorporated in encyclopedic fashion. The authenticity of this method is vouched for again at the conclusion of this brief preface: "And this is what happened, words of perfect exactness."[29]

Given its title, it is readily apparent, therefore, that, unlike the Joseph cycle in Genesis, which is enmeshed within the biblical narrative and plays a pivotal role in the formation of the Jewish people, the story as presented here is an independent work in which attention is to be placed on the main character. In the manner of a bildungsroman, the narrative highlights the major events in the development of Joseph as he grows to manhood and rises in power. He accomplishes this while overcoming hardship and trials, as one who, in evocation of a well-established theme in religious, didactic literature, "came by relief after distress."[30] With all focus on the one character, it is a tale in which many of the biblical *intra*textual references present in the Genesis story of Joseph have been effaced; absent as well is any sense of the context of Israelite tribal history. Most significant from an aesthetic standpoint, however, is the process of "sanitization" the tale has undergone, whereby much of the moral ambiguity surrounding the biblical characters and their actions is removed. Instead, the didactic purpose of the work (which by definition cannot allow for moral vagueness) becomes paramount and is here explicitly spelled out by the narrator.

In its seeking to harmonize many of the apparent logical inconsistencies of the Bible, *Joseph* brings about a reduction in the open-ended nature of the biblical narrative, whose ambiguities allow for multiple and nuanced readings of the story. Thus, somewhat paradoxically, despite the expansion that the tale has undergone, Joseph appears in *The Story of Our Master Joseph* as a less complex and individuated character, more of a romance hero than his biblical counterpart. The Joseph of Genesis, while generally fitting readers' notions of a valorized ancestor—as one who was Jacob's favorite son and who benefited from Divine providence—can also at significant junctures be portrayed through the oblique critique of the reticent biblical narrator as diverging from the figure of the paragon of consummate piety. In contrast, Joseph in this Judeo-Arabic retelling does not depart from "the straight and narrow"; if he errs, it is unintentional. As a result he remains throughout a flat and somewhat predictable character. If the biblical Joseph has agency and evolves from a self-involved, insensitive youth to a mature leader of his people and Egypt, the protagonist of *Qiṣṣit sayyidna yūsuf* is an instrument through whom God will achieve His ends.

Within the context of *The Story of Our Master Joseph,* then, the didactic purpose of the work has gained the upper hand; in this set piece, it is God who, with perfect omniscience and omnipotence, manipulates all events and characters as described in this preamble: "The Living Eternal One, Who from His abode in Heaven executes His designs, Who puts an end to all evil and brings relief; He raises up and brings low. The Mighty One, there is none like Him: Who does as He wills, Who makes the poor prosper and impoverishes the prosperous, distances the near and brings close the distant" (*Joseph,* 1). We are given here already in the *tasbīḥ,* in effect, a characterization of the story as one in which all proceeds according to God's decree: the Brothers' evil plot will be confounded, and Joseph and Jacob will be freed of their hardship; the Brothers and Zulaykhā will be displaced from their superior positions, while Joseph will be master of his brethren and in Egypt; Zulaykhā will lose her riches, while Joseph will come into wealth; Joseph will be separated from his beloved father, but in the end he will be put out of Zulaykhā's reach and brought together again with his family. That this section is indeed a précis is made explicit by the phrase that concludes the *tasbīḥ*—"as happened to Master Joseph"—and marks the shift into the story proper and the time dimension of the narrative present.

Of Plots Narrative and Conspiratorial

This convention of the *tasbīḥ,* this synopsis at the story's outset, creates expectations for the audience, while simultaneously emphasizing the overarching, instructive purpose of the narrative. The presence of such a prefatory abstract may strike modern readers as being somewhat akin to the (unsolicited) giving away of the plot of a movie or novel, the punch line of a joke, or the answer to a riddle; however, focus on the story's didactic purpose served to arouse the anticipation of the audience, well familiar with the general story and now reminded of its bare-bones outline, as to what might be the particular concatenation of events to ensue within the confines of this very broad sketch. Moreover, as we have just noted, the listeners or readers are guaranteed that that which is being proffered is the full and authentic version. A formal structure is thus created that actually serves to enhance the narrative tension critical to maximizing audience interest and enjoyment.

Immediately following this prologue, the narrative commences with the words: "The Sages, peace upon them, said. . . ." This rubric, *qālū al-ʿulamāʾ* (echoing the parallel Hebrew expression *amru rabanan*) serves in *The Story of Our Master Joseph* to mark off sections of the story. However, it is also a vestigial remnant of the exegetical base of the tale and a reminder of its origins in the separate commentary of unnamed scholars that the narrator cites with only this generic attribution.[31] In contrast to any clearly defined chain of transmission, this static expression—in its very anonymity—occludes any concrete connection to a specific exegete or school, to any particular midrashic work, or, for that matter, to any exclusive denominational tradition. By this means, the various traditions are melded together to form a narrative covering the period of Joseph's life from his youth to his death. Yet in spite of this glossing-over of sources, the tale remains anchored to those traditions, indistinct though they may be, while simultaneously focusing the reader's attention squarely on the events and drama of the narrative.

The story proper begins by supplying some basic background on Jacob's family and the privileged status of Rachel and Joseph within the family unit. The child Joseph naively relates to his brothers and father his dreams of the sheaves of grain and the celestial bodies that bow down before him. These are readily interpreted by them as auguring his future dominance. Such portents further heighten the envy the Brothers already feel toward him for the favor he enjoys in their father's eyes. Thus, the true plot of the story commences with precisely that: a "plot" by his older siblings to be rid of Joseph (*Joseph,* 1–4).

Jacob, concerned that the older brothers have been delayed in the pasture, sends Joseph to find them. Ironically, they, in the meantime, are planning their younger brother's demise. When, with the help of a stranger, he eventually tracks them down, they are initially intent on his murder and heedless of the boy's pleas. In the end, however, the Brothers are convinced by the pragmatic arguments of Reuben to cast Joseph into a well (4–10). In response to Joseph's cries, God dispatches the angel Gabriel to this pit to keep him company, while the Brothers return to Jacob with a bloodied garment and the tale that a wolf has killed Joseph. Jacob, deprived of his prophetic powers, believes them and is beside himself with grief. However, when he grasps the stained tunic, he becomes suspicious as to why neither Joseph's scent nor any marks of tearing are present, and he requires his sons to bring before him the perpetrator if they are indeed telling the truth (11–16).

The sons go out and hunt down a wolf, but when he is brought before Jacob, the wolf speaks and maintains his innocence. Jacob, now disbelieving his sons, can only resort to patience in God's providence and subsequently sinks into a deep state of mourning (16–22).

In accordance with Divine plan, after Joseph has been in the pit for three days, the Brothers sell Joseph as a slave to a certain Malik, part of a caravan of traders on its way to Egypt that has happened upon the well. The caravan sets off after obtaining a deed and being warned by the Brothers that Joseph is untrustworthy. However, upon passing his mother's tomb, Joseph falls from his camel and offers up pleas to Rachel. When Joseph's master notices the boy's absence, he returns to beat him. In punishment for this assault on a prophet, God brings on a series of "natural" cataclysmic events that abate only when Malik begs for Joseph's intercession with God (22–42).

Egypt is described as being in a state of social and economic decline at that time; Joseph's arrival, however, is the occasion for dramatic improvements in the country's fortunes. These transformations are attributed to God's desire that the native population come to love Joseph. Meanwhile, all those who view the youth are overcome with amazement at his beauty. Malik takes Joseph to his palace and secludes him under a veil of curtains so that none may see him. However, a group of Egyptian merchants comes to Malik to find out what he has brought back from Syria. He reticently reveals to them that he has purchased a young man from the sons of Jacob the Prophet but declines to show him to them. Nevertheless, the merchants extract from Malik a promise that he will offer Joseph up for sale at auction (42–50).

On the day of the auction, the merchant makes elaborate preparations to best display Joseph's beauty, and the people gather from all parts of the kingdom. After initial bids from a group of Ethiopian slave-traders, and then by a foreign queen named al-Qurᶜā, a local dignitary, al-ᶜAzīz, purchases Joseph at the urging of his wife, Zulaykhā. Al-ᶜAzīz, who, the text notes, doesn't care for women, entrusts Joseph into his wife's custody and then departs for his own town (51–68).

At this point, the narrative elaborates at great length on the strategies Zulaykhā employs in her (nearly successful!) attempts to seduce Joseph. In doing so, she provides him luxurious garments, food, drinks, and jewelry; she brings Joseph into a lush garden and sends her servants to entertain him and put him in the appropriate mood—but she is unable to sway him. She attempts to spend the night with him and pursues him relentlessly, but he refuses to look at her and departs from her presence. She runs after him and, in grabbing his gown, scratches his chest. In response, Joseph delivers Zulaykhā a kick that knocks her to the ground and causes a huge contusion to swell up on her back (68–81).

Undaunted, Zulaykhā brings him into a series of five houses and offers him a life of ease, but Joseph continues to put her off. Zulaykhā then enlists the support of her mother and her husband in order to build "A House of Honor" for Joseph. She brings him into the Dome Room of this structure, but still he refuses to acquiesce to her demands. Zulaykhā even offers to poison her husband in order to be rid of his claim upon her. Joseph asks about some curtains in the room, and Zulaykhā explains that behind it is the idol she worships and before whom she is ashamed to commit adultery. Joseph rebukes her, and she offers to give alms unto Joseph's god, but Joseph explains that such impure acts are not acceptable unto the Divine. She proceeds to praise various physical features of Joseph, but he counters by pointing out their ephemeral nature, describing in macabre terms their postmortem state. However, Zulaykhā's great beauty and her allure as a virgin threaten to overwhelm even Joseph's immunity to her charms. In order to maintain his continence he is compelled to tie knots in the waistband of his trousers in the name of biblical heroes (81–104).

Finally, an old Coptic woman advises Zulaykhā to place images of herself in all the directions that Joseph might turn. God also intervenes at this point, casting a powerful lust within the two protagonists. Joseph becomes confused and desires her; he places his leg on hers and sits on the bed untying the knots in his pants. As he comes to the second and third knots he has visions of a hand upon which are inscribed the punishments for adultery. When he comes to the fourth knot, a herald announces that should he succumb he will be erased from the Book of Prophecy. The angels protest to God, and He sends Gabriel, who appears before Joseph in the image of Jacob. Even so, Joseph is unable to restrain himself; he unties the fifth knot and is saved from sin only by falling unconscious. Coming to, he breaks down the door and flees from Zulaykhā, while she grabs his garment and tears it from behind. As Zulaykhā pursues Joseph out the door, they come upon al-ʿAzīz. He believes his wife's claim that Joseph sought to seduce her, and Joseph is taken off to prison to be tortured. However, Gabriel inspires Zulaykhā's newborn nephew to call for an examination of the torn shirt and Joseph is vindicated and released from prison (105–14).

Al-ʿAzīz punishes his wife by keeping Joseph from her for many days. She pines away and abstains from all pleasure until she is secretly able to bring Joseph to herself. Seven Egyptian princesses criticize her love for the servant boy; in self-justification, Zulaykhā sends for them. She adorns Joseph, and provides the ladies delicacies, including citrons and knives with which to cut them. When Joseph is summoned, so entranced are the women by his beauty that they all slice their hands instead of the fruit. As Joseph draws near, Zulaykhā recites a series of garden poems describing her lovesickness. The women, having seen Joseph's beauty, now condone Zulaykhā's behavior. When they ask Joseph why he doesn't accede to his mistress's demands, he responds that he would prefer imprisonment (114–22).

These words provide God the pretext for having Joseph jailed once more. While thus incarcerated, Joseph prays to God, but his physical condition deteriorates. However, two of the king's servants—his chief cupbearer and chief baker—are also detained there. Seeking to have some fun at Joseph's expense, they each fabricate a dream and come before Joseph to have their visions elucidated. Upon receiving his interpretation, they reveal their ruse, yet Joseph's words are confirmed: the cupbearer is returned to his position, while the baker is crucified. Joseph asks the cupbearer to remember him before Pharaoh (122–26).

Present along with them in prison is a North African, whom, because of his unruliness, al-ʿAzīz decides to transfer to Mesopotamia. As he is led through the Valley of Canaan, his escort comes upon Jacob, who calls for the prisoner and asks him about Joseph. When the prisoner reports that he believes Joseph is dead, Jacob loses consciousness, but the Angel of Death comes to him and reports that Joseph is actually alive and well. Meanwhile, Zulaykhā remains in a state of mourning that wastes her body (126–29).

After seven years, God decides that it is time for Joseph to be released. The Egyptian ruler, King Diyān, holds his decennial festival on the banks of the Nile. Falling asleep on his throne, he dreams of seven healthy cows that are devoured by seven grotesque, lean cows; then he sees seven golden and purple shoots of corn that are swallowed by seven withered stalks. Not one of his wise men is able to interpret the dream, but the cupbearer, who has until this time forgotten Joseph's request, is jarred into remembering Joseph and is given the king's leave to fetch him. He comes to Joseph and relating to him Pharaoh's dream, pretends that it was he who had the vision. Joseph is able to discern his mendacity and initially refuses to provide an interpretation. Only when the cupbearer invokes Jacob's name is Joseph moved to tell him that the vision means seven years of plenty will be followed by seven years of famine (129–34).

The cupbearer returns to the king, initially pretending that it is he who came up with the interpretation. The king bids Joseph to come, but he refuses to do so until he is publicly exonerated. Diyān thus calls for Zulaykhā and the women who had been with her in order to conduct an inquiry; the latter maintain Joseph's innocence, but Joseph's mistress keeps silent until God makes her speak the truth. Upon his release from prison, all are overjoyed, but Gabriel reminds Joseph that without God's intervention he would have fallen into sin. The king orders al-ʿAzīz to decorate the royal plaza and appoints Joseph Grand Vizier. Joseph rules adeptly and administers the food supplies to avoid the ravages of the drought (134–40).

The famine erupts and spreads beyond Egypt, and Joseph, anticipating that his brothers might arrive to purchase food, orders the gatekeepers to maintain lists of all who enter through the capital city's twelve gates. Their resources depleted, Jacob does indeed send all the Brothers (except for Benjamin), cautioning them to enter via different gates in order to avoid the evil eye. When their arrival is noted, Joseph sends for the Brothers but keeps his identity secret from them. He accuses them of being conspirators: Why else would they have entered from separate gates, and how otherwise to account for their presence in the district of the prostitutes? (140–47)

Joseph imprisons the Brothers, and they begin to castigate each other, assuming that the current predicament is owing to what they did to Joseph. Reuben chastises them, while Joseph listens from behind the door. Bringing them before him once more, Joseph gives them provisions but orders that to confirm their truthfulness one of the Brothers must fetch the youngest brother. He decides to imprison Simeon and sends the others on their way, but not before ordering that the Brothers' silver be surreptitiously placed back in their packs. En route they discover the returned silver and are distraught. When they reach Canaan, they relate to their father what has transpired and tell him of the "king's" demand. Initially, Jacob is adamant that he will not send Benjamin with them; however, when the food runs out he has no choice but to assent and accept Judah's guarantees to safeguard Benjamin (147–57).

When the Brothers arrive back in Egypt and come before the Vizier, Benjamin is able to divine that he is none other than Joseph his brother. Joseph then reveals to his younger brother his plot to plant a silver arrow in Benjamin's sack. Inviting the Brothers to a banquet, to their amazement Joseph is able to seat them all according to their ages. After they leave once more to return to their father, Joseph sends after them, and their packs are searched until the arrow is found in Benjamin's sack. Joseph informs them that in punishment Benjamin must remain behind as his slave. Judah volunteers to take the place of Benjamin, but Joseph refuses, so Judah threatens to destroy the city, sending Naphtali to survey its defenses (157–60).

Joseph now turns to his brothers and asks why they did not act so protectively when Joseph was being sold. Judah grows enraged and draws his sword. His shout brings about a variety of natural disasters, and Joseph signals to his son Manasseh to pacify him. Joseph then clears the room of Egyptians and informs his brethren that he is indeed their long-lost brother, showing them his circumcised penis in proof. All rejoice at being reunited, and Joseph distributes gifts. (Here, the narrator mentions that Seraḥ, daughter of Asher, has continually told Jacob that Joseph survives, but he did not believe her; in reward, she is one of the very few individuals admitted by God to the Garden of Eden while yet alive.) The Brothers are instructed to return with their father, but they worry that their guilt will now be revealed before Jacob (160–62).

Meanwhile, back in Syria, Gabriel appears before Jacob to tell him that Joseph is alive, but Jacob has had his prophetic powers restored and preempts the angel's announcement. Jacob then sets out with his joyous household to greet his returning sons. When the Brothers hear the celebration, they fail to understand its cause until they reach Jacob and he tells them he knows already of Joseph's being alive. They beg his forgiveness for what they have done, but Jacob responds that it has all turned out as he had told them: God will requite the steadfast with blessings. The entire clan descends to Egypt, and the famine comes to an end upon Jacob's entry into the land (162–67).

The account now backtracks to the fifth year of the famine, relating how the entire Egyptian populace became slaves in return for food. Zulaykhā's health, in the meantime, has deteriorated, and she dwells alone in a hut. When Joseph passes by, she grabs hold of his horse, but Joseph will not look at her until she announces her belief in God and breaks her idol. The next time Joseph passes by she announces her conversion, and Joseph instructs his servants to bring the old woman to his house. When he returns there he asks if she has any requests; she replies that she asks to have her sight returned, that she be made a twelve-year-old girl again, and that Joseph marry her. At this, Joseph informs her that he is now free to treat her as she deserves, and he dispatches her with his sword (167–69).

The denouement describes how Jacob lived in comfort and honor for another seventeen years. Before he dies, he instructs Joseph not to bear any grudge against his brothers and asks to be buried in the ancestral grave of Abraham and Isaac back in Canaan. Concerned about the legitimacy of Joseph's children, Ephraim and Manasseh, after Joseph produces a marriage certificate, Jacob blesses them. He then bids farewell to his children in the form of a poem (169–72).

After Jacob's death, Joseph does as his father requested and does not punish his brothers, but still they are worried that now that the father is gone Joseph will exact vengeance. Joseph responds that while it is true they had intended him evil, God had made things work out for the best. As a coda, Seraḥ takes up a musical instrument and sings verses relating how it was the Brothers conspired against the unsuspecting Joseph. The narrative concludes by mentioning that Joseph lived another seventy years until the ripe old age of one hundred and ten, and that from the time he died until Moses ascended with the Israelites he was mourned by all Egypt (172–75).

Joseph between Judaism and Islam

While the narrative expansions contained in *Joseph* are to a large extent based on the well-known Jewish midrashic interpolations found in such compilations as *Bereishit raba* and *Midrash tanḥuma,* what is most fascinating about the text are the ways in which its incorporation of particular motifs also reflects familiarity with the Islamic material surrounding Joseph. Indeed, there are a variety of specific allusive elements that indicate that what we have before us is a Judeo-Arabic rendition of a largely Islamic work. The following will serve merely as examples (all page references are to the internal pagination of the QSY[1] manuscript as presented in the translation that follows this chapter).

Actual quranic verses are cited—albeit paraphrased in colloquial Arabic. The verses in question concern the punishments meted out for adultery and depart totally from the sanctions imposed according to Jewish law. They appear at a juncture in the story when Joseph is about to succumb to Zulaykhā's advances; as he undoes the knots he has tied to prevent himself from yielding to temptation, he sees these verses inscribed on the palm of a hand. Thus, upon untying the second knot he sees: "[As for] the adulteress: her satisfier shall not be other than the adulterer and polytheist in that which is forbidden (*il-zāniya mā mūrḍihā illā zānī wa-mushrik fī il-ḥarām*)" (*Joseph,* 108). Compare this with the quranic verse outlining the conjugal restrictions placed on an adulterer: "As for the adulteress: none but an adulterer or an idolater may marry her. True believers are forbidden such [marriages] (*w'al-zāniyatu lā yankiḥuhā illā zānin aw mushrikun wa-ḥurima dhālika ʿalā al-muʾminīn*)"

(Q 24:3). When Joseph loosens the third knot he sees written upon a hand: "[As for] the adulteress and the adulterer: each one will be beaten one hundred times with a lash of fire (*il-zāniya w'il-zānī yuḍrabū kull wāḥid minhum mīt ḍarba bi-ṣōt min il-nār*)" (*Joseph,* 108). This reflects the verse that in the Qurʾān immediately precedes the one cited above: "[As for] the adulterer and the adulteress: give each one of them a hundred lashes (*al-zāniyatu w'al-zānī fa-jlidū kulla wāḥidin minhumā miʾata jaldatin*)" (Q 24:2).

That the language employed here is a paraphrasing in colloquial Arabic of the quranic verses is itself highly significant. While it certainly is indicative of a permeability of boundaries between Jewish and Islamic tradition, at the same time it is a clear indication of the distance of the author from the original text. Given the Islamic view of the miraculous nature of the Qurʾān and the inimitable eloquence of its Arabic, a Muslim would certainly have taken care to cite the sacred scripture accurately.[32] And yet the very fact that these verses had penetrated in any form into Judeo-Arabic is a stunning indication of the consanguine interrelationship of the Muslim and Jewish traditions.

Much of the nomenclature in *Joseph* is in accordance with Islamic traditions, and there are as well allusions to quranic or extraquranic (and nonbiblicist) personages or events. Thus, for example, the main protagonists are given as *Yūsuf il-ṣiddīq* (Joseph the Righteous), al-ʿAzīz, and Zulaykhā. Joseph's grandfather, in an allusion to his near immolation at the hands of his father, Abraham, is referred to as "Isaac your Sacrifice" (*dhabīḥak; Joseph,* 113)—a form of association and specification not found in Jewish sources. Basing itself on the name of a prominent Arabian tribe—one known for its meritorious relations with Muḥammad, *The Story of Our Master Joseph* gives the name of the merchant or king who first purchases Joseph as Ibn Rāʿ al-Khuzāʿī (*Joseph,* 23, 31, 53).[33] At the auction following Joseph's arrival in Egypt, one of the competing bidders for Joseph is al-Qurʿa, Queen of ʿĀr. In accordance with Islamic traditions, she is referred to as a descendant of al-Shaddād, who built her Ramzat al-ʿImrān (*Joseph,* 60–64). Jacob's land is referred to as "the Land of Syria" (*al-Shām*), the common Muslim designation for the Holy Land (*Joseph,* 22; 46; 48–49; 53; 55; 141; 145).

Rhymed Arabic verse is recited by Joseph (*Joseph,* 37), followed by a series of love and garden poems recited by Zulaykhā describing the beloved's effect on the lover (*Joseph,* 119–21); and at the text's conclusion, Seraḥ bat Asher recites a poem summarizing the story of Joseph and his brethren up to the point of his sale to the merchant caravan (*Joseph,* 173–74). The poetry, by virtue of its rhyme and metrical pattern, certainly reflects an original Arabic composition and not a translation. Moreover, several of the motifs contained in poems are absent from—or even contradict—the account given in the prose portions of the text and thus would seem to represent wholesale importation of extant verse traditions.[34]

An *argumentum ex silencio* arising out of the text is the relative paucity of Hebrew or Aramaic terms, part of the Jewish cultural patrimony that would otherwise typically be present in a Judeo-Arabic literary work. These would include elements drawn from biblical and rabbinic sources, as well as from the vocabulary of Jewish daily life, liturgy, and ritual observance. While the text does indeed begin with the call to God in Hebrew—"In the name of the Lord, the everlasting God, may we be successful in what we do" (*Joseph,* 1)—this could very well have been affixed to the tale. Such a line of reasoning would also be supported by the presence here in other versions of the cognate traditional Islamic formula of the *basmallah*—"In the name of the Merciful Compassionate One"—that is drawn from the "Opening" chapter of the Qurʾān, *al-fātiḥah.* The final Hebrew lines of the text—"And peace on all of Israel. Amen. Thus may it be Thy will. Amen Selah. And peace upon all Children of Scripture" (*Joseph,* 176)—could similarly be a case of a later scribal addition to an essentially Islamic text.

In contrast, there is sprinkled throughout the body of the text a preponderance of Islamic theological and legal concepts, which are given in Arabic. For example, the contract signed by the Brothers for the sale of Joseph (*Joseph,* 31) begins with the very same text of the *basmallah* just mentioned. In addition, "the Day of Resurrection" is rendered in Arabic—*yawm al-qiyāmah*—as opposed to its Hebrew correlate, *yom ha-din* (*Joseph,* 25; 31; 103; 148; 154). While both these examples are not necessarily exclusively Islamic and may appear in other Judeo-Arabic texts that bear no such direct Islamic influence, they seem to confirm the general pattern.[35]

Similarly, the narrative is consistent with Islamic cultural, religious, and legal notions. Joseph, for example, upon his arrival in Egypt performs the ritual ablutions before prayer (*Joseph,* 43). Muslim piety requires that the devout wash their hands, feet, and face before each of the five daily prayers. In her attempts to woo Joseph, Zulaykhā builds him a small mosque (JA: *zuwāya; Joseph,* 92). Joseph and Jacob are repeatedly referred to as prophets (*anbiyāʾ*) as they are considered in Islam but not in Jewish tradition. The Brothers are themselves referred to by their father as "children of the prophets" (*awlād al-anbiyāʾ; Joseph,* 17), while at the point at which Joseph is tying knots in his waistband (*Joseph,* 101–2), David is called a prophet. Moreover, at the same juncture Abraham is called "The Friend of God" (JA: *al-khalīl*) while Moses is referred to as "the Messenger" (JA: *al-rasūl*)—the traditional Muslim epithets applied to these figures.

On a thematic level, forbearance and patience (A: *al-ṣabr*) are emphasized with regard to both Joseph and Jacob. While belief in the ultimate redemption of the oppressed righteous figure is also consonant with Jewish mores, it resonates even more fully with Muslim notions of surrender to God's will—the literal meaning of *islām*. A few examples of this (among many others) may be cited: Joseph is resigned to his fate after pleading with his brothers to release him—"that which God wants will be" (*Joseph,* 7); Jacob expresses his disbelief in the Brothers' story of Joseph being eaten by the wolf—"You are mocking me and laughing at me, but my patience is with the Generous One and we will seek His help" (*Joseph,* 15); Reuben reassures Joseph in the pit, that "[God] will reward the patient with good" (*Joseph,* 18).

These elements will be discussed further in part 2 of this book, but for now they should suffice to establish the hybrid nature of this text as one that liberally incorporates traditions deriving from both Islamic and Judaic traditions, and relates in continuous fashion a whole constellation of elements taken from biblical and extrabiblical, quranic and extraquranic works. What is also fascinating and enlightening for our discussion of the limits of cross-cultural patterns are the ways in which the story explicitly rejects Islamic motifs. In this way, it departs from late midrashic works such as *Sefer ha-yashar* that also incorporated Islamic material.

The Story of Yusuf

While the author and the date of composition of *Joseph* remain unknown, its relationship to an Islamic *Vorlage* is established by the existence of a sixteenth-century Spanish text that is nearly identical in content. Within an anthology of narratives surrounding the Joseph story from Golden Age Spanish literature, Michael McGaha includes a translation of a text he calls *The Story of Yusuf, Son of Yaᶜqub.*[36] Only one manuscript is extant, codex number 5292 in the Biblioteca Nacional in Madrid, but it reveals an antecedent tradition which very closely resembles the Judeo-Arabic version we are considering, and at times parallels *Joseph* exactly. The text is an example of the type of literature known in Spanish as *Aljamiado* (from the Arabic *al-ᶜajamiyyah,* "foreign"). This form of literature is somewhat analogous to Judeo-Arabic in that it consists of Spanish texts written in Arabic or Hebrew script. This text also contains a considerable amount of loan words from Arabic—mostly reflecting Islamic cultural or religious vocabulary—as well as Arabic words that have been "Iberianized" and inflected according to the rules of Spanish.

The primary difference (other than language and script) between this text and *Joseph* is the incorporation of direct citations from the Qurʾān into the story, which thereby shape its contours. Thus, the tale as it is presented conforms much more closely to the quranic version and follows its story line. It does not contradict that account but, in the manner of midrash, generously interposes material to illuminate obscurities or fill out the bare-bones outline of the scriptural tale. Indeed, the narrative expansions overwhelm the skeletal quranic framework; the narrative can proceed for pages in between citations of scriptural verses. Unlike *Joseph,* in which the narrative sections are typically introduced by the generic formula ("The Sages, peace upon them, have said"), the overwhelming majority of the traditions here are cited in the name of the specific tradent, Wahb ibn Munabbih, who we have mentioned above. In order to provide an idea as to the close correspondence of this text to *Joseph,* I will list below the chapter headings, which have been assigned by McGaha in order to divide the text into its narrative sections:

Yusuf's Birth
The Tree and the Rods
Yusuf's Dreams
Yusuf's Brothers Plot to Kill Him
Yahuda (Judah) Intervenes
Yusuf in the Cistern
The Brothers Return to Yaʿqub (Jacob)
Allah's Promise to Yusuf in the Cistern
The Brothers Sell Yusuf to the Merchant
Yusuf's Lament at His Mother's Grave
Allah Protects Yusuf with a Storm
Arrival in Misra (Egypt)
Malik Sells Yusuf to the King
Yusuf and the Arab
Zalikha Falls in Love with Yusuf
She Attempts to Seduce Him
Zalikha Falsely Accuses Yusuf
An Infant Testifies for Yusuf
Women Gossip about Zalikha

Yusuf Goes to Prison
The Cupbearer and the Baker
The King's Dream
Yusuf Is Released from Prison
Yusuf Becomes King
The Aged Zalikha Becomes a Slave
Yusuf Marries Zalikha
Yusuf's Brothers Go to Misra
Yusuf Receives His Brothers
The Brothers Return to Yaᶜqub
The Brothers Go Back to Misra with Yamin (Benjamin)
Yusuf Reunited with Yamin
Yamin Accused of Theft
The Brothers Return to Yaᶜqub
Yusuf Tests His Brothers
Yusuf Reveals Himself
The Brothers Go to Get Yaᶜqub
Yusuf Receives Yaᶜqub in Misra

The Story of Yusuf is written in the Aragonese dialect, although the language has been Castilianized, and has has been dated on the basis of phonetic idiosyncrasies to the sixteenth century. On the basis of the flawed nature of the extant manuscript, McGaha proposes that it may have been derived from an original work dating from up to a century earlier. In any case, it is clear how the flowering of knowledge and the cultural cross-pollination that typified much of Andalusian life could have generated a text as eclectic as *Yusuf* or *Joseph.* While the Aljamiado text is evidently a precursor to the nineteenth-century Judeo-Arabic manuscripts under study, this, of course, does not preclude the possibility that *Yusuf* itself was based on an Arabic original.[37]

As far as literary genre, both *Yusuf* and *Joseph* fit into the category of the romance, whose roots may be traced back to Hellenistic literature and through the chivalric novels of medieval Europe. McGaha has utilized Northrop Frye's discussion of this genre in his introduction to *Yusuf* and it bears reiterating here.[38] According to Frye, the romance is typically comprised of three stages: the *agon* (G: "conflict"), or the stage of the perilous journey and the preliminary challenges; the *pathos* ("the death struggle"), in which the foe or the hero must be eradicated; and the *anagnorisis,* (G: "discovery") or exaltation of the hero. As McGaha points out, in the romance of Joseph, the pattern is actually doubled due to the dual nature of the struggle with which Joseph must contend—the conflict with his brothers and his confrontation with Zulaykhā.

We can see how this pattern correlates with the events recorded in *Joseph:* the *agon* stage comprises the favorite son's early rivalry with his brothers and then Zulaykhā's first mild attempts at enticement; the *pathos* phase consists of Joseph's being cast into the cistern to die and extends into the danger he faces when he confronts alone the Brothers' wrath. With regard to Zulaykhā, this most dangerous juncture consists of the full-out frontal attempts to seduce Joseph, followed by his being thrown into prison. Finally, *anagnorisis* corresponds to Joseph's release from prison and his elevation to a position so exalted that "by the throne alone" is Pharaoh greater than him. In the family context, the terms of Joseph's joyous reunion with his brothers and father are confirmation of the truth of his childhood dreams in accord with God's will. This pattern of reiteration of the three stages results in a more complicated, overarching, narrative network that will be the focus of the final chapter of the present study.

Intertextuality

The textual history of *The Story of Our Master Joseph,* gapped though it is, presents an interesting case of the migration of narrative traditions. Looking at the text from the vantage point of intertextuality, that is, the web of textual connections and associations that govern the composition and our understanding of all text, we can distinguish between a macro and a micro level. Regarding the former, this text simultaneously exhibits two modes of intertextual relations. On the one hand, the tale constitutes a broad palimpsest of literary allusions to Jewish traditions from the Bible onward, woven together in the form of a romance with Joseph cast as the hero. On the other hand, the text also exhibits a high degree of Islamic influence, so much so that it appears to be largely an adaptation of a Muslim text. As noted above, Muslim traditions surrounding biblical figures and events in the Qurʾān served as a filter of biblical and midrashic traditions before evolving into a distinct literature. This was the case not just for Joseph but also for many other biblicist characters, who in contrast to the favorite son of Jacob, are mentioned in the Islamic scripture only on an ad hoc basis. However, while *Joseph* incorporates a great deal of Islamic material, it retains its independence from these traditions, both by its rejection of certain motifs and its use of the Hebrew script, a convention that constituted an orthographic barrier to Muslim access to texts composed in Judeo-Arabic.

If viewed from the remove of a different culture, this narrative is a conglomeration of Jewish/Hebraic and Muslim/Arabic motifs. However, looking at this text from the internal subjective experience of Judeo-Arabic culture—from the outlook of the audience for whom these texts or oral narratives were intended—these texts were not copies, translations, or adaptations of Hebrew or Arabic "originals"; rather, they existed independently, without the mediation of their sources. Thus, from a point of view internal to Judeo-Arabic culture, and given the linguistic barrier dividing Arabic-speaking Jews from Hebrew culture and Muslims from Judeo-Arabic tradition, *The Story of Our Master Joseph* functioned as an independent text.

In these ways the text exhibits the progression of a metatext (that is, scriptural exegesis) developed through a network of intertextual patternings to the point where it becomes a text in its own right. This is then an illustration of the common intertextual tendency toward the blurring of the boundaries between metatext and text, an effacing contingent upon historical circumstance.[39] An added and fascinating dimension of this fluidity between the "original" texts and the later alluding text are the instances in which the allusions traverse lines of ethnicity, with or without the conscious intent of the "author." This dual or ambiguous intertextual relationship of Hebraic and both oral and written Arabic cultures is a further reflection of the tensions, as well as the productive dynamic, that characterized the minority Judeo-Arabic language community living within the Islamic orbit.

This notion of intertextuality helps focus attention on the ways in which meaning is constructed through associations with antecedent texts. However, beyond this truism, it is more difficult to apply this concept analytically to concrete texts. This framework can only be honed into an effective tool if we focus on the actual allusive mechanisms employed—the "micro" level of textual analysis referred to above. In our consideration of these tales about Joseph, it will thus be important to point out the exact nature of intertextual relations by examining specific elements within the text and tracing their origin. It bears repeating that this is not with the end of establishing the original claim by one or the other tradition of a particular motif but for the purpose of teasing out something of the processes involved in these cross-cultural intersections. It is precisely this type of analysis that will be carried out in part 2 of this study. However, in order to provide a context for our consideration of this narrative system, we will first examine the roots of the tale of Joseph as laid out in the Bible and Qurʾān that were to serve as the basis for its exegetical and midrashic elaborations.[40]

The Biblical Joseph

The Joseph who looms so large in the Midrash differs markedly from the Joseph of Genesis, and we will shortly discuss some of the surprising ways in which the story has evolved within Jewish tradition. In seeking to understand the reasons for these changes, we need to recognize the biblical tale's likely original etiological purpose of providing an explanation as to how and why the Israelites came to sojourn in Egypt—this despite God's oft-repeated promise to the Patriarchs that their descendants will inherit the land of Canaan. Following the settlement of Israel in the Land, Joseph's name became equated with all the tribes that made up the Northern Kingdom. Thus, the text is simultaneously seeking to establish a story to account for the historical ascendancy of the tribes of Joseph (that is, those bearing the names of his sons, Manasseh and Ephraim) within the tribal federation. However, from a relatively early juncture, the Assyrian conquest and the fall of the Northern Kingdom in 722 BCE rendered moot these historicizing and etiological purposes. And yet, given the prominence of the Joseph tale within the foundation story of the Jewish people, such an interpretive vacuum could not long continue to exist. This historical superfluity freed the interpreters to seek out more universal themes that could be gleaned from the narrative. By virtue of its perennial efforts to make Scripture relevant, this was a task for which midrash was ideally suited. Moreover, the experience of Exile under Babylonian rule made the Joseph tale ripe for recycling as both the proto- and archetypical tale of exilic experience.

While these external historical factors freed up the tale for reinterpretation, of equal importance in the recycling of the narrative lay the recognition within the culture of the intrinsic literary merit of the Joseph story in Genesis. This appreciation was based on the length of the Joseph cycle within the book, its development of themes and characters, and its sustained focus on several narrative strands throughout the story—strands which are eventually woven together at the tale's conclusion. (While such recognition of the story's worth has typified the comments of exegetes over the ages, one contemporary example is the frequent allusion to the story made by Robert Alter in his study of the aesthetics of biblical prose in *The Art of Biblical Narrative,* where a check of the index shows that a discussion of the Joseph tale appears on fifty-six of the one hundred eighty-nine pages of the volume.[41])

Indeed, it is this very literariness that has been cited by biblical critics as evidence of its nonhistorical origins—evidence used to support the claim that Joseph's name has been artificially attached to a preexisting tale.[42] Additional corroboration for this argument comes from the fact that Joseph in the Genesis narrative bears little resemblance to his portrayal in other parts of the Bible. Joseph outside of Genesis is simply the progenitor of the two tribes of Ephraim and Manasseh which resided in the North during much of the biblical period. This is reflected already in the so-called "Blessing of Jacob" that marks the end of the first biblical book, where the dominance of Joseph's descendants is laid out in terms of fertility and agricultural productivity:

> From the God of your fathers, may He aid you,
> Shaddai, may He bless you—
> blessings of heavens above,
> blessings of the deep that lies below,
> blessings of breasts and womb . . .
> May they rest on the head of Joseph,
> on the brow of the one set apart from his brothers.
>
> Gen. 49:25–26[43]

Such *realia* might be the origin of the Joseph story in Genesis, with the natural endowments that the character Joseph enjoyed in the Genesis narrative standing in metonymic relation to the blessings his descendants will enjoy in the land they inherit. This "success"—to extend this line of reasoning—was perhaps the envy of the other tribes, a jealousy that in Jungian terms either mirrored or was interpolated within the earlier archetypal tale of fraternal strife.

With the aforementioned fall of the Northern Kingdom to the Assyrians in the eighth century BCE, reference to Joseph's name becomes eclipsed in the Bible; he is referred to only sparingly as emblematic of some sort of desperate hope for the unification of the North and South. The exception that perhaps proves the rule in this regard is the allusion to Joseph in Psalm 105 that gives a cursory account of his being sold into slavery. Within this context, Joseph's enslavement is part of the Psalmist's overview of the everlasting covenantal promise God has made to the Patriarchs, a promise that will culminate in the Exodus:

> [The Lord] called down a famine on the land,
> destroyed every staff of bread.
> He sent ahead of them a man,
> Joseph, sold into slavery.
> His feet were subjected to fetters;
> an iron collar was put on his neck.

Until his prediction came true
the decree of the Lord purged him.
The king sent to have him freed;
the ruler of nations released him.
He made him the lord of his household,
empowered him over all his possessions,
to discipline his princes at will,
to teach his elders wisdom.
Then Israel came to Egypt;
Jacob sojourned in the land of Ham.

Psalms 105:16–23

One might think that with the exile of the Jews to Babylonia, the diasporic resonances with the Joseph story in Genesis would become clear. However, although the associations with Joseph were maintained in the biblical exegesis of the Samaritans who saw him as their direct ancestor, within Jewish tradition proper Joseph is not immediately rehabilitated in the wake of that cataclysmic event. In the postexilic book of Chronicles, seemingly a full recapitulation of Israelite history, the story of Joseph and the account of the Exodus are somewhat astonishingly omitted. This might be explained by the Chronicler's ideological commitment to emphasize the perennial connection of the People of Israel to the Land of Israel (*Eretz Yisra'el*) and to avoid making too explicit a connection with this tale of exile from that land. In any event, it is likely that this break with any historical connection with Joseph in the minds of the "returning remnant"—those Jews who came back from Babylon in the wake of the Edict of Cyrus II in 538 BCE—opened up the possibilities for (re)interpretation of the Joseph of Genesis.[44]

The insights offered by "rubbish theory"—an evolutionary and dialectic account of the assigning of worth to cultural artifacts—might be useful here in understanding the process by which the Joseph story eventually came to be recycled.[45] According to this notion, cultural artifacts are either "durable"—that is, they possess long-term value in the culture—or they are "transient." However, even durable artifacts eventually become divested of worth or relevance within the culture because of changing circumstance; yet, as "durables," having at one time possessed a value that is deeply encoded in the cultural system, they may potentially be rehabilitated through a process of reinterpretation or reassigning of worth. But there is a paradox involved in this process: those "durables" that pass out of vogue and decrease in value need to pass through a stage of possessing no value—of becoming "rubbish"—before they may be reclaimed. This is necessary in order that room can be created for an innovative interpretation that can exploit other elements that would otherwise be excluded or contradicted by the old interpretation. To bring an analogy from an entirely different realm, this process is somewhat akin to the kabbalistic notion of *tzimtzum,* in which God, whose essence initially filled the entire universe, voluntarily undergoes a "contraction" in order to allow room for human endeavor; so too, interpretive space must be created by such a shrinking of meaning in order for the new meaning to be invested in the artifact.

In the case of the story of Joseph, the interpretations of the biblical and late biblical period were no longer based in the reality of the hegemony and economic and agricultural productivity of the northern tribes. Thus, the biblical tale was voided of its value for the culture and threatened with obsolescence. However, the Bible is the cultural durable par excellence—a fact that is the driving force behind all midrashic innovation. The devaluation of the old interpretation by its lack of connection to contemporary reality freed the text from the sway of this original interpretation. The interpreters were then obliged to look anew at the account in Genesis and to come up with innovative associations in order to make it relevant once more. With the return from exile, there was a need for reinterpretation that would take into account the events of the dispersion.

This process of the rehabilitation of the Joseph story began in the extra-biblical writings that came to be known as the Apocrypha and Pseudepigrapha. These works, in particular *The Testament of Joseph, Joseph and Aseneth,* and *Jubilees,* provide key evidence of the ways in which the Bible was being interpreted from the third century BCE to the second century CE. With the geopolitical associations of Joseph now a distant memory—and, along with them, the regional political and economic realities that his name represented—what now loomed in the foreground was the Joseph of the Genesis narrative as *dramatis persona.* It was these works that also opened the gates for the later exegetical traditions of the Midrash.

The Quranic Joseph

Joseph, along with Abraham and Moses, is one of the biblical characters accorded a central role in the foundation text of Islam. Al-Thaʿlabī, in his introduction to his collection of tales about the pre-Islamic prophets, enumerates five reasons the Islamic sages give for transmitting stories about the prophets: that they are a manifestation of Muḥammad's prophethood, in that though he was illiterate, through a miracle they were revealed to him; that they served as a model for the Prophet and an example for the people to avoid the transgressions of previous peoples; that they comprise a confirmation of the nobility of the Prophet and his followers in that God relieved them from the trials of earlier peoples and eased the strictures of their laws; that they provide instruction and guidance in behavior to the people; that they ensure that the legacy of the prophets would continue down through posterity.[46]

While the Prophet Muḥammad consciously modeled himself in particular after Abraham and Moses—the founder of monotheism, and the liberator who overcame oppression and the naysayers in his community—the trials Joseph faced were also viewed as antecedents for the struggles of the founder of Islam. A further connection drawn between Joseph and Muḥammad in Islamic tradition was their sharing great physical beauty. Beyond these associations, however, the literary treatment of Joseph is unique among the biblical characters appearing in the Qurʾān in that the major events of the story as related in the Bible and elaborated in the Midrash are recounted at length. In fact, the whole twelfth chapter of the sacred book (aptly titled "The *Sūrah* of Joseph") is given over to the telling of his story. As opposed to the other biblical and extrabiblical forebears who are mentioned in scattered places in the Qurʾān, the Joseph narrative is a complete (if pithy) story.

One reason for the minimal development of the other biblical characters in the Islamic scripture may be that their tales were widely known. If this was the case, the author/narrator could assume that any allusion would be readily understood by the audience and, as part of a living oral tradition, would require no further elaboration. As I have spelled out above, knowledge of these tales might very well have been communicated to the Arabs in the Peninsula by their contact with the Jewish and Christian communities present there, as well as by the work of Christian missionaries in the region. As the empire expanded and the memories of biblicist material receded, however, there arose a need to cull the traditions for information about these figures and record them in a form that was compatible with Islamic tenets. It was this necessity that gave rise to the great quranic commentaries and the "Stories of the Prophets" literature. In general, the Qurʾān is not interested in relating all the details of the biblical tale or its midrashic expansions but rather, in the interest of moral instruction, divests it nearly entirely of narrative flow. Again, the Joseph story constitutes the exception; it might very well have avoided such sporadic allusion precisely because its literary nature was appreciated and was viewed as being consonant with the didactic message of the tale.

In the span of less than one hundred verses—Qurʾān 12:4–101—the whole of the tale is concisely related. The *sūrah* itself contains internal evidence for the appreciation of the special nature of this story (as well as support for its existence as a discrete narrative): "*We relate unto you the finest of tales* (*aḥsan al-qaṣaṣ*) *in revealing to you this Recitation* (*qurʾān*)" (Q 12:3). As al-Bayḍāwī points out in his exegesis of the words "this *qurʾān,*" the Joseph chapter served as the archetype for "*the* recitation," the Qurʾān itself, a name that came to be assigned to the whole of the Islamic scripture. Islamic tradition interpreted the tale's being called "the finest of tales" as a comment on its completeness or, alternatively, its aesthetic worth.

Additionally, it was also seen as "the finest of tales" in its presentation of the moral virtue of the protagonist. What is stressed here is the chapter's didactic function, as is borne out by the way in which the Qurʾān concludes its version of the tale: "Our story is not one that could be invented, but a confirmation of what has come before it, an explanation of everything, and a right guidance and a mercy for a believing people" (Q 12: 111). This summary formulation does not negate the role of literary artistry; on the contrary, such artistry would serve to enhance the tale's role as a tool for moral education. These two aspects—the aesthetic and the didactic—are combined in al-Bayḍāwī's interpretation of verse 3: "[Either it is] 'the best sort of storytelling' because it is related in the finest of styles; or it is 'the best kind of thing related' because it includes marvels and aphorisms and signs and instructive examples"[47] (*Commentary on Sūrah 12,* 1–2). It is clear that the virtues of Joseph emphasized in the Qurʾān are his steadfastness (and for that matter, that of Jacob, as well) in the face of tribulation and his ability to withstand temptation and overcome "the guile of women." The theme overarching all of these mortal dealings is God's providential role as the omniscient architect of human affairs.

The quranic story of Joseph is also unique in the dominance of literary principles that govern its exposition. Mustansir Mir has demonstrated how the plot development of the quranic story is organized around the Arabic literary-rhetorical device of "involution and [then] evolution in reverse" (*al-laff w'al-nashr ʿalā al-ʿaks*).[48] According to this principle, tension is created in the bulk of the narrative but then quickly proceeds to unravel as these same tensions are resolved in chiastic fashion. This structure generates in turn its own aesthetic balance and progression toward a satisfying sense of closure for the reader who anticipates and is eventually rewarded with solutions to the various "problems." Mir has outlined *Sūrat Yūsuf* according to the following schema:

(a) Joseph's dream (vv. 4–6);
(b) The Brothers' plot against Joseph (8–18);
(c) The attempt by the wife of al-ᶜAzīz to seduce Joseph (23–29);
(d) A similar attempt by Egyptian ladies (30–31);
(e) Joseph's imprisonment (35);
(f) The king's dream (43–44).

The ensuing action represents the resolution of all these tensions in reverse order:

(f') The interpretation of the king's dream (45–49);
(e') Joseph's release from prison (50);
(d') The confessions of the Egyptian ladies, followed by
(c') The confession of the wife of al-ᶜAzīz (51);
(b') The lesson learned by the Brothers (58 ff.); and finally,
(a') The fulfillment of Joseph's dream (100).

As this basic structure is also preserved in expanded form in *The Story of Our Master Joseph* and in the other traditions of the Stories of the Prophets, it is another way in which this text indeed reflects the determinant influences of the Islamic tradition.

Claims to Ownership

Much of Western scholarship up to the present has regarded the version of the Joseph story in the Qurʾān as a pale imitation of the versions in the Hebrew Bible and associated midrashic works, and in general has viewed the Qurʾān's divergences from the older Jewish and Christian Scriptures as the result of an imperfect process of copying and collating. Such a perspective is inherently flawed, and recent attempts have focused on the authenticity of Islamic accounts as an independent tradition. (The very same may be said for attempts to trace ancient Near Eastern parallels for biblical motifs that have the aim of somehow discrediting the originality of the biblical text or destroying its organic unity.) As John Renard has argued in his discussion of the story:

> Non-Muslim readers may be tempted to interpret the story primarily as a retelling of the biblical account in Genesis 37–46. Comparative study can indeed shed important light on both traditions, but ceding authority or definitive form to the earlier tradition may diminish the value of the later. The two

> accounts arise out of very different circumstances, differ in tone, and communicate different messages; each must be read on its own terms.[49]

I discussed above the process of adoption and adaptation of biblicist material within Islam, a process that culminated in the eventual rejection of such "Israelite" material (in theory if not in practice) and an assertion of the independence of Islamic narrative tradition. Such an evolution can clearly be seen in the case of the story of Joseph where the centrality that Joseph assumes in Islam led to an intercultural struggle for control over the text. Paradoxically, there existed two somewhat contradictory trends within Muslim exegesis of the Joseph tale: on the one hand, the Islamic commentators were interested in demonstrating the sublime quality of the story, even adducing as evidence the reverence with which the Jews regarded it. Thus, al-Kisāʾī concludes his version of the story of Joseph: "It is said that because of its greatness, the Jews used to write the story of Joseph with gold ink on silver sheets and suspend them in their tabernacles" (*Tales of the Prophets,* 192). Moreover, in the same context, al-Kisāʾī also has a tradition, related in the name of Wahb, that God, whenever He would send a prophet, would tell him the story of Joseph as He did to Muḥammad.[50] Thus, there is no claim made that the tale is an original one; on the contrary, the veneration of the story by the Jews is brought as evidence of its timelessness and universality.

On the other hand, there was also a need for Islam to stake out a proprietary claim of its own to the story. Al-Thaʿlabī, in his discussion of the same quranic verse that introduces the Islamic scriptural version of the Joseph tale—"*We relate unto you the finest of tales*"—provides various opinions as to its meaning. One of the traditions he brings interprets the verse in a polemical mode: "According to Muqātil, Saʿīd ibn Jubayr said that the Companions of the Messenger of Allah gathered around Salmān al-Fārisī and said, 'Salmān, tell us what is the best of the Torah.' Whereupon God revealed, '*We relate unto you the finest of tales,*' by which He meant that the stories in the Qurʾān are better than those in the Torah" (Al-Thaʿlabī, 181). Al-Bayḍāwī has a version of this tale in his comment on the first verse of the *sūrah,* based on the interpretation that reads "*These are the verses of the Elucidating Book*" (*tilka āyāt al-kitāb al-mubīn*) as "the *sūrah* which makes plain to the Jews that which they asked": "For in regard to this last explanation it is recorded that their learned men said to the chiefs of the polytheists, 'Ask Muḥammad why Jacob's family moved from Syria to Egypt, and about the story of Joseph,' whereupon this *sūrah* was revealed" (*Commentary on Sūrah 12,* 1).

Another tradition, brought by al-Thaᶜlabī in the name of Ibn ᶜAbbas, relates a tale wherein Muḥammad is tested by the Jews regarding the whole of the Joseph tale and shows that he possesses a more complete version (in other words, one that includes the midrashic narrative expansions!) than that in the Bible.[51] Al-Kisāʾī, echoing a common theme in the contest waged over textual ownership, relates that God had given the chapter to every prophet but that the Jews suppressed it; its miraculous revelation to Muḥammad served then as proof of his prophethood. Moreover, according to this tradition, it is the Jews themselves who explicitly connected Muḥammad with Joseph through their acknowledgment of his truthfulness:

> The people of the Torah used to conceal the story of Joseph. When God sent Muḥammad as a prophet, the Jews came to him, among them ᶜAbdallāh ibn Salām and many of the tribe of Aḥbār, and said to him, "Muḥammad, if you be a prophet, tell us the story of Joseph and his brethren." And he began to recite it, sometimes raising his voice and sometimes lowering it. The Jews wept and said, "Muḥammad has been given more of the story of Joseph than is in our Torah." Then they asked him, "Where did you learn this, Muḥammad, for we conceal this chapter?" Muḥammad said, "My Lord has revealed it to me."—"You speak the truth (*ṣadaqta*), Muḥammad," they said. (*Tales of the Prophets,* 192)

We see then that the recourse for some Muslim commentators who sought at the same time to uphold the sanctity, antiquity, and authenticity of the tale, and yet to insist that they possessed it in its best version, was to attribute a campaign of its suppression to the Jews. Thus, Muḥammad's knowledge of the tale becomes additional proof of his prophetic mission. Both al-Thaᶜlabī and al-Bayḍāwī cite the tradition from Jābir b. ᶜAbdallāh, wherein a Jew (in al-Thaᶜlabī he is given the name Nistār, meaning "hidden" in Hebrew) came to Muḥammad and challenged him to give the names of the stars alluded to in Joseph's childhood dreams. The Prophet kept silent until Gabriel came down and informed him of their names. Muḥammad then calls for the Jew and asks him if the latter will accept Islam if Muḥammad is able to name them, whereupon Muḥammad succeeds in giving their names.[52]

In a similar polemic vein, the twelfth-century Baghdadi preacher, al-Jawzī, in his defense of the discredited practice of preaching, enumerates six reasons why the "pious ancestors" despised storytelling. The second of these concerns the Israelite traditions' unreliability. (The reference to David and Uriah concerns the famous events narrated in 2 Samuel chapter 11, in which

David, covetous of Uriah's wife, Bathsheba, arranges for him to die on the battlefield):

> The stories *(akhbār)* of the ancient peoples were seldom authentic, especially those that were related concerning ancient Israel, while at the same time the Revelation given to us was fully adequate. ʿUmar b. al-Khaṭṭāb once told some excerpts from the Torah to the Prophet whereupon the latter responded: "Rid yourself of them, ʿUmar, especially in view of the ridiculous things that are known in Judaism: such as their teachings that David sent Uriah out in order that he might be killed and then married his wife, and that Joseph unloosed his garments in the presence of Zulaykhā!" Now the Prophets are above preposterous acts such as these. When the ignorant person hears such things breaking [God's law] becomes a trivial matter, and he says to himself: "After all, my sin is really nothing new!"[53]

This polemic extends into debate even over the linguistic origins of Joseph's name. As al-Thaʿlabī records:

> There are various views about the meaning of the name Joseph. The majority of scholars have held that it is a Hebrew name and therefore does not follow the rules of Arabic; others have said that it is an Arabic name. I have heard the learned Abū al-Qāsim al-Ḥabībī say that his father said about Abū al-Ḥasan al-Aqṭaʿ the Wise, when he was asked about "Joseph," he said, "In (our spoken) language *asaf* is sadness, and *asīf* is a slave (or worshipper); now, both of those meanings came together in him, and therefore he is called Yūsuf [Joseph]." (Al-Thaʿlabī, 182)

In support of an Arabic etymology, al-Thaʿlabī also brings a tradition from Kaʿb al-Aḥbār according to which God had his descendants appear before him one after the other. When Joseph appears, Adam is struck by his splendor and, clasping him to his breast, exclaims: "My son, do not be sad (*taʾasaf*) for you are Joseph (*Yūsuf*)." According to this tradition, Adam was the first one to call him Joseph (ibid., 183). However, al-Bayḍāwī (who tends to linguistic interpretations), claiming to represent the opinion of "the majority of scholars," deduces that Yūsuf is a Hebrew word from the fact that it is not fully declined and therefore is not derived from the Arabic verb, *āsafa.* It is likely that what lies here behind al-Bayḍāwī's comment is an alternative Arabic form of Joseph's name, Yūsif, more proximate to the Hebrew and without the assimilation of the second vowel to the first, that has been handed down traditionally since the third Meccan period. This name offers the further advantage of being a putative participial form of the Arabic IVth form verb.[54] This semantic connection has intriguing parallels with the double etiology established by the biblical narrator for Joseph's name: "And God remembered Rachel and God heard her and He opened her womb, and she conceived and bore a son, and she said, 'God has taken away (*asaf*) my shame.' And she called his name Joseph (*yosef*), which is to say, 'May the Lord add (*yosef*) me another son'" (Gen. 30:22–24).

Transcending these claims to ownership of the narrative is the notion that Joseph himself was a Muslim. The Qurʾān itself makes it clear that none of the earlier prophets accepted by the new faith were to be considered either Jewish or Christian; rather, the followers of these faiths concealed aspects of the divine revelation and were now rendered superfluous:

> Or do you say that Abraham, Ishmael, Isaac, Jacob, and the Tribes were Jews or Christians? Say: Are you more knowing or is God? Who is more unjust than he who hides a testimony he has from God? But God is not unaware of what you people do.
>
> That community has already passed away. It has what it has earned and you have what you have earned. You shall not be questioned about what they would do. (Q 2:140–41)

In common with Jewish tradition that traces its origins to the monotheistic faith of Abraham, an Abrahamic faith is posited, one whose followers believe in the previous prophets. The adherents of this new religion will submit themselves solely to the authority of God, from whence the rubric "Muslim" originates:

> Say [O Muḥammad]: "By no means! They have said: 'Be Jews or Christians in order to be rightly guided.' Abraham was a monothesist (*ḥanīf*) by faith and no idolater (*mushrik*)."
>
> Say [O Muslims]: "We have come to believe in God and that which was brought down to us; in what was brought down to Abraham, Ishmael, Isaac, Jacob, and the Tribes; and that which was given to Moses and Jesus; and that which was given to the prophets by their Lord. We make no distinction among any of them, and to Him we have surrendered ourselves (*muslimūn*)." (Q 2:135–36)

Thus, in al-Kisāʾī, for example, we find the following in relation to Joseph: "Joseph ceased not to call the people of Egypt to be faithful until many of them did believe. Some others, however, complained to their king, Rayyan, who called Joseph and said, 'O Plenipotent, you know that the people of Egypt have loved you greatly for calling them to Islam'" (*Tales of the Prophets,* 191).

The heated question of origins is taken up by Thomas Mann in the "Prelude" to *Joseph and His Brothers* (subtitled, without his intent of course, in a manner that could serve to symbolize the contested ownership over the tradition: "Descent into Hell"!). Here Mann is able to point out succinctly the relative nature of our plumbing the depths of "the well of the past": "Thus there may exist provisional origins, which practically and in fact form the first beginnings of the particular tradition held by a given community, folk or communion of faith; and memory, though sufficiently instructed that the depths have not actually been plumbed, yet nationally may find reassurance in some primitive point of time and, personally, and historically speaking, come to rest there" (*Joseph and His Brothers,* 3).

Midrash, Multiple Meanings, and Innovation

The Story of Our Master Joseph, a Judeo-Arabic retelling of the biblical and quranic tales of the favorite son of Jacob, is seemingly an adaptation of a Muslim narrative. However, it is simultaneously—both directly and obliquely—derived from the midrashic discourse that we have discussed above. While midrash originally comprised verse-centered interpretations of biblical material, the rabbinic comments *inter alia* served to expand the biblical narrative, developing themes that were either somehow latent within the text or, more commonly, elicited from its silences. At times, these interpretations had a legal justification, both functioning as a prooftext for a specific halakhic ruling and establishing its antiquity and biblical origin; frequently they had a didactic purpose, imparting to the audience some moral lesson; alternatively they served a literary-aesthetic end, filling in or supplementing where interpretation could add to the pleasure of the audience. Moreover, it was not uncommon that these purposes overlapped. Once these interpretations had been formulated, they were often gathered together in midrashic compilations that formed a running commentary to the biblical books.

In a further second-order evolution, these discrete expansions could be consolidated by a typically anonymous folk author within a continuous narrative surrounding a particular biblical character or event. In so doing, these now integrated motifs assumed an independent existence as a more elaborate *retelling* of the biblical tale. Such retellings are eclectic by nature and are typically constructed to suit a popular audience; however, despite their folk origins, they exhibit a unique literary artistry and often bespeak an oral, "storytelling" source. The relative independence of these works from the particular exegetical raison d'être of their component parts is key to the cross-sectarian transferability of this material. Midrash will thus be seen to be a mode that is equally trenchant in the Islamic context, and one particularly congenial to the migration of material over cultural borders. At its most fluid, the midrashic impulse gave rise to a discourse surrounding a shared pool of traditions and techniques. Such considerations are of especial relevance to the sort of cross-cultural interaction manifested in *The Story of Our Master Joseph.*

In accord with this essential temporal and generic heterogeneity, Daniel Boyarin offers a positivistic definition of midrash that borders on tautology, namely the practice as it is named and characterized by the relevant cultural community, or, in his words, "the type of biblical interpretation which is found in the Jewish biblical commentaries which the Jews call midrash." According to his conception, the two criteria necessary for a text being considered midrash are its status as a form of metatextuality (a text commenting on another antecedent text), and its recognition as such by its creators and audience—the Jewish community whose members alternately compose, recite, hear, transmit, or read these texts.[55] In the current study, we will further extend the limits of such metatextual discourse to take in another religio-cultural tradition that has evolved a central and living practice of scriptural commentary. This view allows for a dynamic and cross-cultural model of midrash.

The dialectical struggle to maintain the relevance of the founding texts of the community was an ongoing one. Such a perspective is particularly cogent to a discussion of the readiness of the midrashic innovators to look beyond their own denominational walls for homiletical material that could reinvigorate tradition or invest it with new meaning for the believer. While often condemned by the upholders of orthodoxy for their popular nature and their divergence from doctrine, aggadic material in particular was a source of dynamism and vitality within the tradition. A similar tension may be observed within Islamic tradition. Following the expansion and integration of "foreign" elements within the Islamic canon, over the course of the ensuing centuries the Muslim religious establishment often sought to suppress those *isrāʾīliyyāt* most objectionable to their religious sensibilities. And yet, these popular forms continued to be the living site for the integration and evolution of these tales.

The Rabbis who created the Aggadah had a two-fold purpose in mind: on the one hand, since it was assumed that the Torah had multiple meanings, they sought to explore the full range of these semantic possibilities with the goal of moral and religious instruction and the derivation of eternal truths. Conversely, since it was assumed that the Bible held all answers, the *aggadot* were used to highlight the explicit—and flesh out the implicit—answers that Scripture held to contemporary and future problems confronting the Jewish community. Such a perspective on Torah study is recorded in the Mishnah in the immortal words of Ben Bagbag: "Turn it over and turn it over again, for everything is in it" (*Pirqei avot* V 22). This process had its origins in the discord between rabbinic religion and the text from which it was derived and claimed legitimization, a dissonance between the unitary message of Scripture and fragmented, quotidian reality. While the notion that Israel's God is a god of history has become commonplace, in fact, historical thinking was present in Israel's contemporary surroundings, while biblical thought also includes notions deriving from a cyclic worldview.[56] However, despite the inaccuracies inherent in such a generalization, the Israelite linear view of God's actions in history does contrast with paradigms that maintain the cyclical nature of existence. Accordingly, the seeking after knowledge (that core meaning of the biblical root *d-r-sh*) as to how past events have shaped the present becomes an obsession for Israel.[57]

Such a mechanism of self-glossing is at least as evident within Islamic culture. The essential discontinuity of the Qurʾān necessitated recourse to outside material to fill in a text whose gaps threatened to completely overwhelm the coherence of the whole. This problem was exacerbated in the wake of the conquests and the diffusion of Islam on a massive scale to peoples without background knowledge necessary to making sense of events in the Islamic Scripture. This process can clearly be seen in a retelling such as *Joseph:* here, in a highly evolved iteration of the story, the gaps and background knowledge have been filled in to make explicit the values the narrator sought to convey.

In similar fashion, the Islamic community attempted to interpret current events in terms of the quranic (including, necessarily, its biblicist component) past. This applies as well to Muḥammad's conception of his role as analogous to the pre-Islamic prophets, identifying his struggles with those of his precursors and reading his own experience back into their biographies. Muḥammad was certain that God would deal with him as He had dealt with the previous prophets, a point of view that is confirmed in God's words to Muḥammad in the chapter that immediately precedes the Joseph tale: "And all that We relate unto you of the tidings of the Messengers is so that thereby We may make firm your heart" (Q 11:120). A similar viewpoint on continuity with previous revelations is present in the Joseph *sūrah*'s final admonition as to the merit of the story: "Our story is not one that could be fabricated, but a confirmation of what has come before it, an explanation of everything and a right guidance and a mercy for a believing people" (Q 12:111).

For Jews, during the period of the Exile and afterward, within the context of intercommunal disputes and the appearance of self-appointed prophets, the divine word was increasingly to become a text. These texts were seen as powerful and as requiring interpretation in order for their deeper meanings to be revealed. As a result of this turmoil the true word became remote and hope grew for restoration of true prophecy. But with the discrediting of claimants to new prophecy, the interpreters of these texts—the Rabbis—became the heirs to the prophets. As those who reveal the esoteric meaning behind the words of the text, they were seen as guided by something approaching divine inspiration.[58]

Within Islam, such a conception of prophecy is relevant with regard to the self-positioning of Muḥammad vis-à-vis his predecessors, who served as precursors for Muḥammad, both in terms of their behavior and with regard to the resistance they encountered from disbelievers. Islam, in its syncretism, regarded biblicist figures as prophets and bearers of a divine message; thus their lives, as presented in narrative form in the Stories of Prophets, are of the utmost importance in filling out the sketchy mention made of them in the Qur᾽ān. As Muḥammad represents the ideal of human perfection, his biography, the *Sīrah,* and his way of life as communicated in the *ḥadīth* reports of the *Sunnah,* became a model for the community of believers to emulate. As in the case of rabbinic hermeneutics, analogous concepts of exoteric (*ẓāhir*) and esoteric (*bāṭin*) meaning also exist in Islam, and these hidden inner meanings of gnosis are particularly developed in Sufi circles for whom the story of Joseph and Zulaykhā was seen as a core expression of union with the divine.[59] Postquranic Islamic tradition also adheres to a principle of multiple meanings. Thus, the varying traditions are recorded, each with a chain of transmission, and typically with no attempt to harmonize or reach a conclusive decision. Here, too, while the approach is decidedly multivocal, there are constraints on the interpretation; not everything is fair game, and those interpretations that contradict Islamic norms or doctrine are taboo. An example of these boundaries is the notion of the infallibility of the prophets (*ʿisma*) through which Islamic tradition calls into question biblicist accounts for positing that the prophets were capable of "preposterous acts."

At the risk of going out on a fragile psycho-sociological limb, such a difference in outlook between Jewish and Islamic exegesis may in fact point up a contrast between Judaism and Islam in terms of cultural gestalt. The nuanced perception of progenitors present in the biblical text, often containing at least an implicit critique of patriarchs, the children of Israel, and even the most revered monarchs, encouraged a tendency toward self-critique. This tendency carries over into midrash; although the opposite sanitizing tendency is also present, the Rabbis are often not shy about exploiting clues or submerged subterranean critical streams in order to point out the waywardness even of biblical heroes. Some of this may have to do with the divergent processes of textual formation. Islam, possessing as it does a second-order version of the biblical tales, often presents its heroes in a flatter, one-dimensional fashion and in an unremittingly positive light. Significant exceptions to this may be seen in the critical attitude towards Joseph's brothers or in the Israelites' rebelliousness towards Moses, and yet, this may be explained by the fact that these figures are conceived as being outside of the community of believers. Muslim notions of subversiveness are directed outward, mostly at other communities, which was the prerogative of a superordinate Islam. Even in its period of waning, that memory of glory was ever present, manifested to this day in the anti-Western stance of many traditional Muslims. Rabbinic tradition, on the other hand, owing perhaps to the discrepancy between Jews' position as an often oppressed minority and their status as the chosen people of a just God, had developed a theology according to which the suffering of the community was divine punishment for their sins. Such cognitive dissonance may have engendered an exaggerated tendency toward self-criticism, and by extension, enabled critique even of biblical heroes.

Be that as it may, *The Story of Our Master Joseph the Righteous* constitutes a wonderful example of the multivocality of the popular Judeo-Arabic traditions. While based in midrashic interpretations, it also incorporates Islamic motifs surrounding the figure of Joseph. This latter material, while having a basis in the midrashic expansions and Hellenistic versions of the tale, followed its own path of evolution. Within *Joseph,* much of the discrete nature of these interpretations has been erased, as have the boundaries that separated Jewish from Muslim traditions of exegesis, homiletics, and storytelling. It therefore represents the openness of such popular traditions through its fusion of ancient Near Eastern, Jewish, Hellenistic, Persian, and Islamic motifs. And yet at significant junctures it engages these interpretations polemically in order to stake its own claim for control of the text. It is therefore most decidedly not a totally open-ended text, and there are linguistic, theological, and broader ideological limits to its range of interpretation—of which more anon in part 2 of this work. For the present, let us proceed to the story itself.

I

THE STORY OF OUR MASTER JOSEPH THE RIGHTEOUS

Translator's Foreword

For men are tales—it is said that no man dies but mention of him revives him.

Al-Thaʿlabī, *Lives of the Prophets*

The Joseph story is a remarkable test case for the study of the intersection of Jewish and Islamic cultures through the nexus of text. The specific Judeo-Arabic version that is the focus of this study, *The Story of Our Master Joseph the Righteous* (JA: *Qiṣṣit sayyidnā yūsuf il-ṣiddīq*), is a particularly rich instantiation of the flow of artifacts back and forth across denominational lines. The tale was a common one in Judeo-Arabic literature, found throughout the Arabic-speaking world, and versions of it survive in many manuscript collections. The translation that follows is of a nineteenth-century copy found in the Karaite Collection of the Blumenthal Library at the Judah L. Magnes Museum in Berkeley, California. This collection consists of approximately forty-six codices, both printed and handwritten—as well as assorted fragments—formerly belonging to the Karaite community of Cairo. Most of this material dates from the eighteenth and nineteenth centuries.[1] The *Joseph* text is complete, and is 177 pages in length. The volume in which it appears also contains a story of Joseph in verse; another Judeo-Arabic midrashic work, *The Great Story of Our Master the Messenger Moses;* and another shorter version of the Moses tale. While the date of Joseph's actual composition remains unknown, in the colophon, the scribe—one Joseph Ha-Levi, son of Abraham Ha-Levi, son of Moses Ha-Levi—gives the date of its transcription as 5597 AM/1252 AH, corresponding to 1837 on the Gregorian calendar.[2] He also invokes there a blessing upon "all Children of Scripture," a designation for the Karaites, clearly marking the story's circulation within that community. At the end of the story it is recorded that the text was purchased by "Issac . . .

son of Rabbi Joseph, Head of the Community . . . son of Elisha the Cantor." This same name is embossed in gold on the leather cover of the codex. The orthography is for the most part a very clear, square Egyptian script; however, there is a change in hand at page 91 through the first four lines of page 92; then from the fifth line of page 92 until the end of the manuscript a third hand takes over. The first scribe maintains a consistent sixteen lines to a page. The lines are straight, justified at each margin with the words evenly spaced on the line. There are regular section headings that until page 15 consist of the formulaic: "The Sages, peace be upon them, have said" (*qālū il-ʿulamāʾ ʿaleihim il-salām*). Afterwards, this first hand demarcates other divisions in the narrative with headings recorded in larger-size script that often are centered on the line. These text divisions are typically preceded by a colon—the only punctuation to appear in the text. There are catchwords at the bottom of the right-hand pages indicating the first word to appear on the facing page. The brief interlude of the second hand is marked by a much coarser script, with no attempt to justify lines, and includes a rather clumsy crossing-out of several words. The third hand is more regular, but somewhat more cramped and less even than the first hand: the text is not always centered vertically on the page, the number of lines varies from between fifteen to eighteen, and the lines meander slightly up and down. In contrast to the first hand, there are catchwords on each page, both verso and recto.

I have furthermore relied on two manuscripts contained in the Ḥanān Collection, also from Cairo, and now part of the collection at the Institute for Microfilms of Hebrew Manuscripts at the University and National Library at the Hebrew University in Jerusalem. The first, given the internal reference number of 97, and below designated as QSY², dates from 1851, while a second similar version dating from 1848 and assigned the number 42 will here be cited as QSY³. These texts present a narrative nearly identical to QSY¹, and will be referred to in the translation in cases of unclear reading. Item 66 in the Collection represents a second textual tradition, and is cited as QSY⁴ when it offers an alternative midrashic motif. At the Institute I was able to examine other manuscripts, some of which are only fragments, and these too will be compared when warranted. I have also had the opportunity to view other Judeo-Arabic Joseph manuscripts at the Firkovich Collection housed in the State Library in St. Petersburg. Paul Fenton, in his hand-list of this Collection, records some eighteen items under the rubric *Qiṣṣit sayyidnā yūsuf;* most of these are short fragments, with the exception of item 932, which contains forty leaves and is cited below as QSY⁹³².[3] Finally, I have utilized as well two printed editions of the story, one published in Baghdad in 1914, which is cited here as QSYBaghdad, and another text from Tunis dating from 1910, to which I assign the rubric QSYTunis.[4]

Judeo-Arabic

An obvious but most significant feature of the transmission of cultural artifacts between Judaism and Islam is the fact that the primary conduit for this interchange was the Arabic language. Our text, *The Story of Our Master Joseph,* is written in Judeo-Arabic, that form of the language used for centuries by Jews living in the Arabic-speaking world. Judeo-Arabic is another manifestation of the connections between Muslim and Jewish communities. At the same time, and analogous to the existence of parallel Jewish and Islamic extrascriptural material, its usage reflects the tensions extant within the Judeo-Arabic sociolinguistic community, on the one hand, and between it and the dominant Muslim Arabic community, on the other. Judeo-Arabic belongs to the larger category of Jewish languages, the major, but by no means sole, examples of which are Yiddish (Judeo-German), Judeo-Persian, Judeo-Spanish, and Judeo Neo-Aramaic. There has been a significant amount of polemic directed to the question of whether Judeo-Arabic constitutes an independent language or should be more accurately termed a "sociolect" or "ethnolect"—that is, a subordinate form of a particular language (here, Arabic) limited to a distinct social or ethnic minority community. Yet, the independent nature of this form of the language is brought out by the fact that over the course of time it came to be thought of as a literary language in its own right, employed even by Jewish authors competent in Classical Arabic.[5]

The use of Arabic by Jews has a long history. There is some evidence that Jews residing in the Arabian Peninsula before the advent of Islam spoke some form of differentiated Arabic dialect known as *al-yahūdiyyah* ("Jewish-ese"). The influence of Jewish concepts on the wider peninsular community would account for the presence in the Qurʾān of some Hebrew and Aramaic lexical items that were loan words in this dialect. However, the period of Classical Judeo-Arabic can be said to commence with the career of Saʿadya ha-Gaʾon (882–942 CE), whose translation of the Bible exerted great influence upon the written forms of the language and served to standardize Judeo-Arabic orthography. Judeo-Arabic culture flourished over the course of the next few centuries and was the medium for remarkable achievements in the fields of linguistics, belles lettres, philosophy, and medicine.[6] After the fifteenth century, and continuing down to the nineteenth century, a growing rift between the Jewish minority and Muslim majority gave rise to a radical new character for Judeo-Arabic, one that reflected class distinctions and the shifting cultural affinities of the Jewish elites. Neo-Arabic (colloquial) features became more prominent in the language, which was used more and more by the less educated, while the Hebrew used by elites was eventually to be supplanted by European languages associated with the colonial powers.

Along with Muslim and Christian Arabic, Judeo-Arabic is considered a division of Middle Arabic. Joshua Blau, the doyen of Judeo-Arabic studies, has used the rubric "Middle Arabic" to denote both the later lingual type of Arabic, and the mixed languages of Jewish and Christian Arabic.[7] In recent works, Blau opposes Old Arabic to Neo-Arabic and has restricted the sense of the term "Middle Arabic" to describe the linguistic register that combines elements of both. This latter term refers to that form of Arabic that evolved from the Classical Arabic within a linguistic setting defined by "diglossia." Diglossia (literally, "two tongues") describes a bipolar linguistic situation within a particular speech community: one pole consists of a formal variety of the language that is transmitted largely through formal education, is often more complex grammatically, and is the vehicle for a large, respected—or even revered—body of literature. The other pole comprises the colloquial form of the language, which is employed mostly for ordinary speech, is characterized morphologically by a weakening and alteration of vowels, and is more analytical in its grammar. ("Synthetic"—as opposed to "analytic"—refers to a grammar characterized by the expression of a complex notion by a single compounded or complex word or morpheme—instead of by a number of distinct elements.) Moreover, this form of the language typically lacks a "high cultural" tradition.[8]

In actuality, these two forms constitute the extreme ends of a continuum that encompasses an infinite number of possible intermediate and intersecting realizations in any given communicative act. For that reason, one scholar has introduced the term "multiglossia," arguing that it more accurately reflects the existence of more than two varieties of the language.[9] However, this term also has its disadvantages in that it occludes the bipolar nature of the continuum, as well as the shifting proportions of formal versus colloquial elements on the level of the individual speaker. Perhaps a term such as "heteroglossia" would better convey something of the fluid and overlapping nature of the varieties of the language—a notion of continuum along with a sense of the shifting bounds of the particular admixture of formal and colloquial elements. However, any attempt to locate specific types of languages is at its core flawed and overstates the discrete nature of levels of the language. Beyond such semantics, what *is* clear is that Middle Arabic consists of a range of options for the speaker stretching between two poles.

The dynamism of such a system is generated by the different status of the two poles within the culture, and the linguistic choices the speaker/author makes in the context of a specific language act. These choices are conditioned by the function of the act, the topic engaged, and the audience addressed—in addition to the competence of the speaker or author in the formal language. Within the Arabic diglossic system or polysystem, the two poles in Arabic are represented by Classical Arabic (*al-fuṣḥā*), that form of the language frozen in form by the Qurʾān and standardized through the work of early grammarians, and the colloquial (*al-ʿāmmiyyah*), used primarily in speech and varying widely by region, with the range of intermediate options designated by the term Middle Arabic (*al-lúghah al-wúsṭā*).

Middle Arabic arose in the wake of the Arab conquest of the Middle East during the seventh century of the Common Era; or according to another conflicting view, this evolved form already existed prior to Islam's spread. In either case, the rapid expansion of the empire greatly accelerated the evolution of this process, as many subject peoples adopted Arabic as their primary medium of communication. Arabic, perhaps due to its relative physical isolation in the Peninsula up to the advent of Islam, had until that point retained many "archaic" features. Many of these were reflected in "synthetic" elements that had been discarded in other Semitic languages. (We will leave aside the question as to how these supposedly archaic features ever evolved to begin with—if it is assumed that natural and inexorable processes of linguistic evolution would lead to their evanescence and a more analytic form of expression.)

Most significant in this regard was the near-total loss in other Semitic languages of the flexional system—the change of word ending in conjugation and declension. Other languages in the new Islamic orbit had already lost these endings, and according to Blau, the indigenous populations encountered difficulties in adjusting to this and other complexities of the Arabic system. Of course, perhaps it was not simply due to the inability of non-Arabs to master the details of the grammar but rather that the contact with such "evolved" forms of language merely accelerated processes already latent in Arabic. Be that as it may, the end result was the evolution of grammatical structures devoid of these endings. This process was in itself facilitated by the presence of such non-inflected variants in the pausal form (that form of the word occurring at the end of a spoken breath group) even in "normative," that is, Classical, Arabic.

One of the outstanding characteristics of Middle Arabic is the presence of pseudoclassical features, referred to in the scholarship as "pseudocorrections." These are items "corrected" because of the author's desire to write in a more elevated style—that is, one that more closely approximates the "prestigious" Classical variety. Such pseudocorrections manifest themselves in two ways. In the case of "hypocorrections" the changes that are implemented go only part way toward achieving a form attested in the Classical (in other words, they "under"-correct), while in the case of the more common "hypercorrection," the user in effect overshoots the mark and derives forms that do not exist in the Classical language. In this latter type, the author paradoxically refrains from using forms that are correct according to Classical Arabic owing to their prevalence in the dialect. Assuming the dialectical features to be incorrect, the author replaces them with a form that, while correct in certain contexts in the Classical, is wrong in the given situation. (A simple analogy drawn from English grammar would be the erroneous substitution of forms of the personal pronoun, as in "She likes Jim and I.")

Middle Arabic is thus a heterogeneous linguistic system that incorporates Classical Arabic, dialectical features, and such pseudocorrections. Of course, these so-called pseudocorrections could, within a particular social grouping, eventually assume a normative character within the linguistic system, notwithstanding their origin as "mistakes."

Jews in the Arabic orbit in the wake of the Islamic conquests rather rapidly forsook their sacred Hebrew and Aramaic, sister Semitic languages of Arabic. This might prima facie be surprising given the long history and prestige within the cultural system of the languages of the Bible and Talmud. (Also worth noting is the different linguistic result that obtained for Jews under Christendom, in which there was a far greater degree of linguistic separation from the dominant culture.) An explanation for this phenomenon of linguistic diffusion may be found in the case of Aramaic itself. In the fifth and sixth centuries prior to the Common Era, in the wake of the spread of the Babylonian Empire, this language had already developed into a lingua franca, a hegemonic, international tongue of the Middle East. As Aramaic a thousand years later gradually lost ground to Arabic, Jews—not unlike other indigenous populations—adopted the language of the conquerors. In rather short order, then, Jews were using Arabic for a wide range of communicative activities.

A well-known exception to this Arabizing trend was the continued use of Hebrew in poetry, which has typically been attributed to Jews' lack of command of the nuances of Classical Arabic. According to this conception, as Jews were not bound by conformity to the lofty ideal of pristine Arabic, *al-ʿarabiyyah,* they felt less compelled to master its intricacies. The use of Hebrew and Aramaic in religious contexts also served to limit the degree of mastery of the language of the majority culture. In addition to the linguistic barriers, cultural barriers (including the valorization of Bedouin norms) would have also posed an obstacle. On the other hand, the existence of a tradition of Hebrew liturgical poetry that had stretched uninterrupted through the Aramaic period in Palestine would also have contributed to its continued use. Furthermore, Jewish poets, by opting to use Hebrew, were thus able to assert cultural independence from the majority culture, as well as to express the intrinsic prestige of their own linguistic legacy.

In addition to the features in common with Christian and Muslim Middle Arabic (again, comprising the fusion of elements from Classical Arabic, the local vernacular, and pseudocorrections), Judeo-Arabic also has two distinctive features: incorporation of Hebrew and Aramaic words, and the predominant use of Hebrew script. What is most striking about the use of Hebrew and Aramaic lexical items is the extent to which the Arabic base fully absorbed and assimilated these loan words, this despite the "sanctity" of the source languages. Their insertion (which can be especially pervasive in religious or legal texts) did not alter the underlying deep structure of the language. These lexemes have been adapted to the grammar of Arabic, and this meant that the influence of Hebrew on Arabic was mostly superficial. Interestingly, even within the same text, the author can switch back and forth between the synonymous Hebrew and Arabic terms. A more specialized phenomenon, of special relevance in our discussion of the *Joseph* text, however, is the use of words that are cognate in both languages but have different nuances of meaning. In such cases it is often quite difficult to discern what is the intent of the author. We will discuss below such an example, the Semitic root *ṣ-d-q,* whose bilingual ambiguity determines much of the direction and "spin" of Arabic retellings of the Joseph story.

As a rule, Jews preferred writing in Hebrew script, although there was a tendency for Karaites to employ Arabic script, a fact that is reflective perhaps of their greater degree of absorption into Arabic culture. (There are even early Karaite manuscripts that contain portions of the Hebrew Bible transliterated in Arabic characters).[10] The use of Hebrew characters in Judeo-Arabic texts has several important ramifications. An examination of the orthographic conventions can reveal underlying morphological shifts within colloquial usage that might be occluded in the standardized texts. *Joseph* exhibits some of these idiosyncratic elements. As an example, the speech of Egyptian Jews from the twelfth century on belonged to the broader Maghrebine family. Thus the presence in our text of such elements may indicate that Muslim dialects in Egypt of this time were Maghrebine as well and that this shift may have been assimilated through migration of Jews of higher social status from the Maghreb. Even to this day, in Egypt dialects of the Maghrebine-type have coexisted with dialects of the Cairene-type.[11] Perhaps the best-known feature peculiar to the former type is the use of the *nqtl* and *nqtlū* verbal paradigm to denote the imperfect first-person singular and plural, respectively, this idiosyncrasy being "a veritable shibboleth of this dialect group."[12]

All of this dialectal interplay notwithstanding, the general use of Hebrew script is a concrete reification of the walls that separated the bulk of the Jewish population from Arabo-Islamic culture. True, the "cultural symbiosis" of Jews and Arabs was very pervasive, unmatched in some respects until our own day.[13] "Nevertheless," Blau points out, "it was the symbiosis of two separate cultures, which remained separate despite their basic similarity and mutual contact." After warning of the danger of retrojecting the experience of Western individualism, he continues: "The cultural symbiosis of medieval Jews and Arabs was, as a rule, not the achievement of individual Jews and Muslims, but of Jewish and Arab social groups. Therefore, generally speaking, the barriers between the two cultures remained."[14] Such an observation can serve as an important corrective to a flattening of cultural distinction and to idyllic fantasies of unhindered interpersonal contact between members of the minority and majority communities.

In the literary analysis of *The Story of Our Master Joseph* that follows the translation and constitutes the second part of this study, we will examine the development of the character of the protagonist and trace the two principal subplots which came to dominate the narrative expansions in the midrash—that of Joseph's interactions with his brothers, and that of Joseph's relationship with the wife of Potiphar. We shall also be interested in those elements that transcend these sectional divisions. We will explore the ways in which *Joseph* relies on *midrashim* generated by the Bible and Qur'ān but is also simultaneously an independent work, in which the origins and ad hoc nature of these underlying interpretations are now concealed in an attempt to create a continuous narrative. In addition to a general analysis of metatextual elements within the story—that is, the midrashic expansions of the biblical and quranic story contained within the various midrashic accounts—I will also be highlighting the intertextual relationship of *The Story of Our Master Joseph* to other Jewish and Islamic traditions surrounding the story. Thus, the analysis will proceed on two fronts: by exploring the ways in which gaps in the Bible motivated certain interpretations, I will be attempting where possible to recover the "lost origins" of these midrashic expansions (especially with reference to *The Story of Our Master Joseph*). At the same time, by considering the pattern of borrowing that ensued in Jewish and Islamic works, I will be seeking to better understand the nature of the byways along which these narrative elaborations traveled.

If the metaphor we have chosen to employ in this work is one of migration, translation itself is another form of journey. Symbolic of the nonauthoritative and subjective nature of all attempts to render an original work in another language, I have titled this effort "A Translation." In my recasting of text of *The Story of Our Master Joseph* in English, I have stayed as close as possible to a literal rendition, departing from this method only when compelled by reasons of clarity or style. The page numbers given in the margins follow those of the manuscript, and references in the notes will correspond to this internal pagination. One of the aims of this translation of *The Story of Joseph* is to make the tale available to a modern audience. As reflected in the epigraph to this foreword, the Muslim compilers of traditions about the prophets, as well as the Jewish midrashic innovators, were concerned about keeping the memory and legacy of their righteous forebears alive so that posterity might learn from their example. In part 2 of this study we shall proceed to consider the ways in which *The Story of Joseph* accomplished this task, while focusing on the specific ways in which the various Jewish and Islamic versions of the Joseph story interact with each other, as well as with their own internal scriptural and midrashic referents.

A Translation of *The Story of Our Master Joseph the Righteous*

[1] In the name of the Lord, the eternal God, may we be successful in what we do.[1] We shall now begin *The Story of Our Master Joseph the Righteous,*[2] peace upon him, in all completeness and perfection, in praise of God who is the One Lord; we have no god but Him. The Living Eternal One, Who from His abode in Heaven executes His designs, Who puts an end to all evil and brings relief; He raises up and brings low. The Mighty One, there is none like Him: Who does as He wills, Who makes the poor prosper and impoverishes the prosperous, distances the near and brings close the distant—as happened to Master Joseph the Righteous, who came by relief after distress.[3] And this is what happened, words of perfect exactness.[4]

The Sages, peace upon them, said[5] that there was among the prophets[6] one whose name was Jacob, peace upon him, who had four wives. And among these wives there was one more righteous[7] than the others. She was beautiful
[2] to behold and of elegant appearance,[8] and [Jacob] loved her greatly. And Jacob the Prophet had twelve righteous sons, saints of God,[9] two of whom were from that righteous woman. And one of them was more righteous[10] than his brothers, and his name was Joseph. And Jacob, peace upon him, loved Joseph

1. H: *bi-shem yy ʾel ʿolam naʿaseh ve-naṣlîʾaḥ.*
2. JA: *il-ṣiddīq.*
3. JA: *il-farag baʿda il-dīq.*
4. JA: *wi-hādā garā kalām taḥqīq bil-tamām.*
5. JA: *qālū il-ʿulamāʾ.*
6. JA and H: *nabīʾ.*
7. JA: *ṣāliḥ.*
8. JA: *ḥasanat il-manẓar dharīfat il-shakl.* QSY^2 reads . . . *dharīfat al-wagh*—"stunning of face."
9. JA: *itnāshar awlād ṣāliḥīn awliyāʾ allāh.*
10. JA: *ṣiddīq aktar.*

greatly, more than his brothers, due to Jacob's love for Joseph's mother, Lady Rachel, peace upon her. And Joseph was more righteous[11] than his brothers; moreover, he was perfect in beauty and handsomeness.[12] And there was no one like him in that generation, neither in all the other generations down to this very day.

One night, Joseph the Righteous had a vision in which his eleven brothers were gathered in the desert[13] harvesting wheat and binding [the sheaves] together. And Joseph the Righteous saw that they, the twelve of them, had set erect their sheaves[14] with Joseph's sheaf in the midst of them, and the
[3] eleven sheaves moved around in a circle and bowed down to Joseph's sheaf. Then morning came, and he went and told his brothers his dream. [When] they heard his dream, all of them treated it seriously because they understood [from it] that he would rule over all of them and it would be their destiny to bow down to him.[15]

Then, after that, [Joseph] dreamt a second dream in which the sun, the moon, and eleven planets were bowing down to him.[16] And he awoke, but did not tell his brothers anything because he knew that deceit and wickedness were in their hearts. So he went and told his father, who looked at him and said to him, "Conceal your dream from your brothers. There is no doubt but that you will attain a high station and all of us will come and kiss your hands; but do not let them know, for your brothers will rely upon this. O son, do not make me have to urge you to take care of yourself."[17]

11. JA: *aṣdaq min dūn* [*ikhwatu*]. (The text contains a scribal error, reading *ʾūkhtuhū* with an *alef* inserted above the line between the first *waw* and the *khaf.*) QSY² reads *wi-wāhīd minhūm ṣiddīq aktar min ikhwātū.*

12. JA: *kamal il-ḥusn w'il-gamāl.*

13. JA: *ṣaḥrah;* also so in Saʾadya. QSY² reads "in the field" (*fī al-ḥasīdah*), while QSY-Baghdad has "in the middle of the wilderness" (*fī wuṣṭ al-barīyah*).

14. JA: *farīṣah,* with the plural *farṣah.* Meaning uncertain. This word is also the one employed in QSY². The context here requires "bundles" or "sheaves" based on nearly all the Jewish and Islamic sources. The root, *f-r-ṣ,* according to Lane, means "to cut"; thus, the connotation could be "cuttings," or "gleanings." The related root, *f-r-z,* yields "to sort, arrange" (Behnstedt-Woidich; Spiro; and Wehr), or "to remove, set aside" (Lane). QSY⁴ reads *ḥizmah*—"bundle"—as does Baghdad. Saʾadya, in his translation of Genesis, has *jurzah,* meaning "bundle" (of hay, etc.).

15. See Genesis 37:5–8.

16. See Genesis 37:9; Q 12:4; al-Thaʿlabī, 185–87; al-Kisāʾī, 168.

17. JA: *mā taʿūz nuwāṣīk ʿála rūḥak.* QSY² reads "I am afraid for you." While the account in Genesis 37:9–11 does not provide any indication that Jacob interpreted these dreams as presaging Joseph's good fortune, this is included in the midrash and the Islamic accounts. See BR 84:12; PRE 38; *Antiquities* 2.15; Q 12:5; al-Kisāʾī, 167–68.

[4] *The Sages, peace upon them, said* that his brothers learned of the dream and interpreted it. And they drew inferences from that dream, and because of it they hated him greatly and no longer wished him peace.[18] Thus, when they went to tend their flocks in the pasture, they agreed on a thing that they would do to him in order to nullify the portents of his dream. And each one began to give his opinion about their brother, Joseph. When they went out to pasture, they tarried more than was their wont, and Jacob the Prophet, peace upon him, said to Joseph, "Why don't you go and see your brothers in the pasture because I fear for them; I pray that a catastrophe has not befallen them."[19]

The Sages, peace upon them, said that this fear that entered Master Jacob
[5] did not depart until he was reunited with Joseph; while the power of prophecy abandoned him from the time Joseph left his father's side. And when [Jacob] said to [Joseph], "Go see your brothers in the pasture," Joseph said to his father, "I hear and I obey, my father." So he set out; but he did not find them. Then he saw a man sitting [there] and he asked him, "O sir, have you seen Jacob's sons pass by?" The man said to him, "O son, I was in the village and they were there, and I heard them saying, 'Let us go back and graze at the head of the valley'; and if you walk on and trust in God you will find them there." So Joseph went and caught up to them, and he overheard them saying, "Joseph the Dreamer[20] has come to you. Let us take him and kill him, and we will be rid of him and his dreams, and we will see what good will come of his treacherous dreams."

[6] *The Sages, peace upon them, said* that Reuben, when he heard these words, said, "O brothers, if you seize him and kill him,[21] our father is endowed with prophecy and he will know that we have murdered him, and you will bear sin with him forever." And Joseph said to them, "O brothers, O masters, all who have said fire, their mouths will burn, but all who have said words [of truth] will flourish; indeed, this is a dream of falsehood."[22] And so they said to Joseph, "O Joseph, are you Rachel's son?" He said, "Yes indeed, O brothers."

18. See Gen. 37:4: "and they [the Brothers] hated him and could not speak peaceably to him."

19. See the Aramaic targum of Pseudo-Jonathan on Genesis 37:13 and *Sefer ha-yashar* 14. QSY^2 1b has Jacob say: "Do not go to see your brothers in the pasture because I fear for you."

20. JA: *ṣāḥib il-aḥlām*. A literal translation of Gen. 37:19: *báʾal ha-ḥalomot.*

21. Scribal error. Text reads *taqūlū* for *taqtūlū.*

22. JA: *kull man qāl nār ʾiḥtarak fūmū wa-kull man qāl kalām ṣaḥ wā-dā manām kadāb*. For this denial of the dream, see al-Ṭabarī, *Prophets and Patriarchs,* 150: "[The Brothers] said: 'Call on the sun, the moon, and the eleven stars to keep you company.' [Joseph] said, 'Verily, I did not dream that.'"

They said to him, "[Then] your murder is inevitable." And when he heard these words, he cried bitterly. But Reuben said, "By the truth of my Lord, there is no god but Him, not one of you shall raise his hand in the shedding of blood; let's throw him in a well instead."[23] They said to him, "O Reuben, find us a well in which we can throw him." At the moment Joseph heard these
[7] words, he cried bitterly, and he said to them, "May God's wrath be upon you if you do not relieve me from a thing to which I am not equal; for I cannot bear all of these matters: the first being that you will separate me from Jacob, my father; and the second, that you will ensnare him in sadness and will bring down the gray hair of your father in sadness to the Hereafter."[24] So they said to him, "O Joseph, that is something which cannot be—that you return to your father." He said to them, "That which God wants will be."

After that, they held and bound him, and they stripped him of his clothes. And he began looking at them, all the while crying bitterly and saying, "O brothers, have mercy on me! God, may He be praised and exalted, will have mercy on you." And one of them got up and said to him, "If you don't be quiet we will kill you[25] and torture you the most painful of tortures so that we see what good are your dreams." Then they came to him, stripping him of his
[8] clothes. And they threw him in the well, and he fell face down.[26] After regaining consciousness, he cried bitterly and called out from within the well and said, "O brothers, may you be pardoned by God! How I sit here hungry and thirsty in this well!" One of his brothers answered him and said to him, "You are the one who brought this upon yourself when you told your father the dream in which the sun and the moon and eleven planets bowed down to you. If you had intelligence you would not have met Jacob with these words, or if you had certain knowledge you would not have said 'I am hungry,' nor 'I am thirsty.'" And Joseph said, "My patience is with God, may He be exalted, the Generous One. May He reward the steadfast with benificence.[27] I say, I have been bound up, but I have repented unto God; He will accept my penitence. As for you, do not throw me into the pit—accept my penitence."

And Reuben answered him and said to him, "My brother Joseph, as long
[9] as I am alive and in good health, do not fear murder, but I fear that after I am

23. JA: *bīr.* See Gen. 37:21–22; Q 12:10. In al-Kisāʾī, it is Judah who suggests throwing him into the well.

24. See Gen. 37:35, 42:38, 44:29, 44:31.

25. JA: *mā taskūt wallā naqtūlak.*

26. QSY[2] adds that he became unconscious. See al-Thaʿlabī, 190.

27. JA: *laqad yuʿāwid il-ṣābirīn kheir.*

gone great sadness will afflict you. So do not bring upon yourself anything but good." And Joseph said to Reuben, "My brother, by the truth of God, may He be praised and exalted, do not inform your father and do not let him know what my brothers have done with me, that they have tortured me. But so long as I am alive, do not forget me and continue speaking to me from above the well until the time that I die. O Reuben, if you see a small child like me among the Brothers,[28] continue to cry for me; and if you see the old man Jacob sitting, may you be granted increase from God,[29] may He be praised and exalted, that you will remember me and cry for me. My brother Reuben, I adjure you by the Subduing One,[30] there is no one but He, to take care of my brother, the
[10] sad one, the orphan, Benjamin. And if you see my brothers gathered together, likewise remember me and cry for me. And I will not be afraid if I die today or tomorrow; as for what frightens me, it is only that Jacob, my father, will remain in great distress and sadness after I am gone[31] and that he will no longer have any patience after I am gone."

Then the Sages, peace upon them, [said]: Then Joseph's brothers came to Reuben and said to him, "O Reuben, say to Joseph, Rachel's son: 'Die of hunger in this well.' Get up and leave him. What concern did you have to answer him? And let us go to his father and say to him: 'Joseph was eaten by a wolf.'"

The Sages, peace upon them, said when night fell upon Joseph, he saw the
[11] darkness and yelled out to his brothers, but not one of them answered him. So he raised his eyes to the heavens and cried, and he called out in a loud voice, saying: "O God of Abraham, Isaac, and Jacob, on their account I pray to you to send me one of your saints[32] to keep me company in this well."[33] And upon doing so, the angels heard and said: "Our God, our Master, we hear the voice of an oppressed person crying in anguish: the crying is that of a boy, but the prayer[34] is that of a prophet." And God, may He be praised and exalted, said,

28. I.e., Benjamin.

29. JA: *īzḍād b'illah.*

30. QSY^2 reads "by the ineffable name" (*b'il-ism il-mūʿazām*); i.e., the Tetragrammaton.

31. JA: *min baʿadī.* A euphemism for death.

32. JA: *walī min awliyāk.*

33. Here, and at many other strategic nexuses in the tale, QSYTunis inserts lines of verse. An analysis of these poems is beyond the scope of the present study, but I hope to return to them in a later work.

34. JA: *il-dūʿā.*

"My angels, bearers of My throne[35] and those worthy of My honor, I am aware of this and nothing of it is hidden from Me and My power and My honor and My strength and My glory. Yet, I will not take Joseph out from the well until
12] three days have passed, and I shall judge him over his brothers and place control of Egypt in his hand."

Then He commanded the angel Gabriel, peace upon him, and said to him, "O Gabriel, go before[36] my servant Joseph and say to him: 'Your Lord extends His greetings to you, there is no god but Him—it was He Who saved your forefather Abraham the Friend [of God][37] from the fiery furnace.[38] I will take you out of this well after a period of three days and judge you over your brothers. And you shall rule Egypt and your brothers will fall conquered into your hand.'" Then the angel Gabriel, peace upon him, descended to Joseph the Righteous and called out to him, "Peace upon you." And Joseph responded likewise, and then said to him, "Who are you who have come to keep me company in this well? My brothers cast me away and did not have mercy upon me."

35. JA: *ʿarshī.* Thackston (*The Tales of the Prophets of al-Kisāʾī,* 337n. 3), however, provides an account of the architecture of the royal throne that differentiates between two parts of the throne: "While *ʿarsh* and *kursī* are often translated as 'throne' and 'footstool,' respectively, from what is known of Oriental thrones it is clear that two distinct parts are being referred to. The *kursī* is a raised platform upon which the ruler sits, while the *ʿarsh* is a vaulted canopy over the throne itself."

36. Reading JA: *beina yadayā,* where the second word has been omitted from the text. This reading is supported by QSY^{2}.

37. JA: *il-khalīl.* The traditional Muslim *laqab* (epithet) applied to Abraham. Cf. Q 4:125–26: "And who is finer with respect to religion than one who raises his face to God in submission (*aslam wajhahu li-llāh*)? He is a doer of good and has followed the faith of the true-believing Abraham, whom God chose to be his friend (*khalīl*)."

38. For the story of the tyrant Nimrod casting Abraham into the furnace (and his subsequent rescue), see *Bereishit raba* 49:1, itself apparently derived from the tale of Nebuchadnezzar and the preservation of the three young men in the fiery furnace (Daniel 3:24–25). Although like many protagonists, Nimrod does not appear by name in the Qurʾān, evidence for knowledge of the legend appears in Q 2:260 and 29:24. In the latter case, Muslim exegetes determined that Namrūd (or Namrūdh or Nimrūd as he is known in Arabic) is the anonymous interlocutor: *His people did not answer except by saying: "Kill him or burn him!" but God saved him from the fire.* For the treatments within the *isrāʾīliyyāt*, see: al-Ṭabarī's version of the tale in *Prophets and Patriarchs*, 58–61); al-Thaʿlabī, 131–34; and al-Kisāī, 131–150. Max Grünbaum was able to demonstrate (*Neue Beiträge zur semitischen Sagenkunde*, Leiden: Brill, 1892, 90–9, 125–32), that later Midrash, including *Pirqei de-rabbi eliʿezer, Tanna de bei eliyahu, Midrash haggadot, Sefer ha-yashar,* and *Sheiveṭ musar* of R. Eliyahu Ha-Kohen from Smyrna, drew heavily from the Muslim versions. See EI, s.v., "Namrūd"; EQ, s.v., "Nimrod."

[13] *The Sages, peace upon them, said* [Gabriel] said to him, "O Joseph, I am Gabriel, messenger of God,[39] may He be praised and exalted; I have come to keep you company in this well." At that time, Joseph got up and saw the angel Gabriel and his heart trembled, but he opened his mouth and said: "O Maker of every formed thing, O Restorer of all who are broken, O Vanquisher of all who are vanquished, O Forgiver of sins, O Subduer on behalf of all who have been subdued, O Companion to all, O Rewarder of good to the patient—I ask you to keep me company and place love for You in my heart in order that I will have no ruler other than You." And when Joseph the Righteous made this plea before God, may He be praised and exalted, God, may He be praised and exalted, accepted it and ordered all the angels to come to Joseph.[40]

As for his brothers: they took a goat-kid, slaughtered it, and stained
[14] Joseph's shirt with its blood—because the blood of goat-kids resembles the blood of a human.[41] Then they came to Jacob their father and they shouted together and began to cry until their voice rose in the air like thunder. And when the prophet Jacob heard their voice, he was distressed because of it, and he said, "A disaster has befallen my sons." Then they approached him and said to him, "O father, we went to water the flock and left Joseph behind, and a wolf came and ate him. And if you do not believe our speech and we are not trustworthy[42] in your view, then here is his shirt upon which is the blood." And they related to him the story of the wolf and took out for him Joseph's shirt, which was stained with blood.[43]

The Sages, peace upon them, said that at that time prophecy departed
[15] from Jacob, his father, peace upon him, and he believed them[44] and he shouted at the top of his lungs, letting out a great scream. Then he fell facedown upon the ground and was unconscious for three hours, so that they raised a hue and a cry thinking that he had departed this world. When he awoke from his fainting he cried bitterly and said, "O Joseph, I used to hold you close to my breast out of my fear for you, but none of that was of any benefit now that you are in the belly of the wolf. O that I were with you and what befell you had befallen

39. JA: *rāsūl allāh.* QSY[2] reads: "I am the angel (*malīk*) Gabriel."

40. See al-Thaʿlabī, 191.

41. See BR 84:19: "Why a he-goat? Because its blood is similar to human blood."

42. JA: *wi-in kān mā taṣada*[*q*]*t qawlana wa-lā iḥnah ṣādiq*[*īn*]. Cf. Q 12:17.

43. Cf. Q 12:16–18: "And they came weeping to their father in the evening. They said: 'Father, we went off to compete together and left Joseph behind with our belongings, and then the wolf ate him, but you don't believe us even though we're telling the truth,' and they brought forth his shirt with false blood."

44. JA: *fa-ṣaddaqahum.*

me instead." But Jacob took the shirt and smelled it and did not find Joseph's
scent in it, nor any ripping, nor any shredding.[45] And Jacob knew that this was
strange, and he said to them, "You are mocking me and laughing at me, but
my patience is with the Generous One and we will seek His help."[46]

Then he cried and said, "O wolf! O wolf! O wolf!" And Jacob shouted these
16] words three times, and he said to his sons, "God forbid[47] that the wolf ate Joseph;
rather, you have lied to me with these words. If you were being truthful,[48] you
would have hunted down the wolf."[49] Then they were afraid of their father, so
they said to each other, "What's stopping us? Let's go out and hunt down the
wolf that ate our brother." So they went out and hunted down a wolf.[50] And they
bound him up and brought him to their father, and they said to him, "O prophet
of God, the wolf is unable to stand before you[51] because he has eaten your son."
And Simeon and Levi turned him around, the one who would not come near.[52]

Then the wolf approached Jacob, and the wolf shouted and said, "Loosen
my fetters because I am wrongly accused." Then Jacob said to the wolf, "O
wolf, why did you eat my son? You have brought down upon me lasting sad-
17] ness." And the wolf said, "O prophet of God, by your gray hair, I have not
eaten any child of yours and I have not striven against you in his murder—the
children of the prophets have slandered the wolf."[53] And Jacob responded to

45. QSYTunis (6a) has here that it is the wolf's scent Jacob is unable to detect. Cf. al-Thaᶜlabī, 192: "When they told Jacob about Joseph, he wept greatly and said to them, 'Show me the shirt,' and they showed it. He said, 'By God, I have never before seen [a day] like this, nor a wolf with as little ferocity as this one, devouring my son without leaving the slightest rip in the collar or anywhere else in the shirt.' He cried out, then fell down in a faint and awoke only after a long time."

46. JA: *wi-lākin ṣabri ᶜalā allāh wa-bihu nastaᶜīn.* See Q 12:18: "He said: 'It isn't so! You yourselves have plotted something; but fair patience! In God may aid be sought against what you describe.'"

47. H: *ḥas ve-shalōm.*

48. JA: *ṣādiqīn.*

49. In QSYTunis (6b) the Brothers protest that they will not be able to identify the specific wolf that devoured Joseph.

50. In al-Kisāʾī (171), Jacob commands the animals in the wild to bring him the wolf that devoured Joseph. They return with a "foreign" wolf who denies committing any such crime.

51. JA: *mārtīkh.* QSY^1 has a corrupt reading that apparently considers this to be the wolf's proper name, based on a confusion of the letter *resh* for *yod.* I have emended the reading based on QSY^2 and QSY^4, which have *mā yatīq yūqaf* and *lam yaqdir yaqif,* respectively.

52. JA: *yankūsū aladhi lā yaqrab.* QSY^2 and QSY^3 have: "They held [the wolf] so that they could bring him closer to their father," while QSY^4 yields "they hit him" (*yaḍrabū*). QSYTunis has Simeon and Levi hold the wolf in order to prevent his escape.

53. For the episode of the slandered wolf that answers the charges against him, see al-Thaᶜlabī, 193.

them and said to them, "You have mocked me, but my patience is with God the Generous and in Him we will seek help."[54] Then he cried bitterly and said, "O Joseph, my child, I shall mourn for you my entire life." Then Jacob listened to[55] what had happened to [Joseph] and gave a shout and said, "My poor little one, my Joseph. You do not know what we do in the manner of sadness and crying after you." And he said to his sons, "What have you done to Joseph your brother?" And they said to him, "What we have told you is what happened."

Then Jacob built a house of wood and named it "The House of Mourning for Joseph,"[56] and around it the birds nested and the wild animals dwelled. In
[18] that location Jacob commenced to mourn and refrain from sleep; neither did he raise his head (which was between his knees) from the ground. And he abstained from food and drink, and sleep did not come upon him all the while he was mourning over Joseph. And he became weak, and his face became pale, and his body grew thin.

Then after that, Reuben went to the well where Joseph was and began to speak to him, saying, "O Joseph, be steadfast. When your Lord wants to, He will take you out of this well, for He is capable of anything." And he threw him food and said, "Eat, my child, and God, may He be praised and exalted, will reward the patient with good." And Joseph asked about the old man,[57] his father, and said, "What is he doing now that I am gone? I pray that he is alive in the world and in his patience for me. And how does he bear his grief?" And
[19] Reuben said, "O Joseph, since you have gone your father spends his nights crying and his days in mourning—in distress and sadness. And he has isolated himself alone in a house in the middle of the wilderness and named it 'The House of Mourning for Joseph.' And his head is between his knees; he does not ever lift it. And the birds have nested there. And he abstains from food and drink. And I could not remain because of the abundance of crying. Mothers have taken to not leaving their children alone out of fear that what befell you will befall them. And I swear, O Joseph, no sustenance has gone down into my stomach today, or any drink, and I withhold sleep from my eye. And you know who oppresses you, and I am innocent of what they did to you and had I not been present and saved you from their hand and acted with might and main [no good would have occurred].[58] And Joseph, by virtue of the pact

54. Cf. Q 12:18.
55. JA: *ṣnṭ* (from Dozy).
56. JA: *beit ḥuzn yūsuf.*
57. JA: *il-sheikh.*
58. The end of the sentence is missing here and has been supplied from QSY³.

[20] that is between you and me, do not invoke God against me,[59] because I did not oppress you. However, may God, may He be exalted, grant you patience."[60] And Joseph said to Reuben, "My brother, I do not invoke God against you nor against those who have harmed me; yet I do ask of God to take me out from this well." And Reuben cried as long as he saw Joseph in the well, but he could not take him out because the Brothers had taken a solemn oath,[61] and because of that he did not say anything to his father, but he was afraid that Joseph would die or be murdered. And Reuben brought Joseph food—lunch and dinner—in those three days during which he remained in the well.[62]

The Sages, peace upon them, said Joseph's brothers woke early to water
[21] the flocks. And when they came to the well where Joseph was, Zebulun called out and said, "O Joseph, O son of Rachel, have you not died yet?" And [Joseph] said, "My brothers, if you had any mercy, you would have shown mercy to me." And when they heard his words, they said, "Come let us smash him with stones. But you, Reuben, you do not allow us to do what we want to do." And Reuben said to them, "Has what you have already done not sufficed; must you also smash his skull?"

Then the Sages, peace upon them, said: Reuben was a merciful man and he loved Joseph dearly, and he did not depart from him during the day out of his fear for him lest they return with stones. And his efforts and his powers protected him from them. And when the three days had elapsed during which
[22] Joseph was in the well, God, may He be praised and exalted, appeared in His mercy and had pity on his tender age. And God sent to him in the well Nimrod's garment which [had belonged to] Esau,[63] and along with it the Angels of Mercy, who kept him company and did not leave him. Then the angel Gabriel, peace upon him, descended and said to him, "O Joseph, I have come to save you. Lo, here comes a caravan from Syria[64] on its way to Egypt." And when the caravaneers came to that site, there was pasturage in it, and they said to each other, "This place is good. Let us alight in it and graze and water the cattle, and we will eat lunch and then depart." And the people alighted close

59. JA: *lā tadʿī ʿalayya.*

60. JA: *yuṣbirāk.*

61. JA: *ʿahd.* See al-Thaʿlabī, 189: "When [the Brothers] were about to kill him, Judah, the son of Joseph's maternal aunt and the only brother with good intentions towards him, said to them, 'Have you not made an agreement with me that you would not kill him?'"

62. In al-Thaʿlabī (194), it is Judah who brings Joseph food. Josephus (*Antiquities* 2:21–31) has a much expanded account of Reuben's intercession, in which the oldest brother presents many arguments as to why the Brothers should not harm Joseph.

63. Reading from QSY^2 and QSYTunis: *alladhī kān ʿinda ʿeisav.*

64. JA: *il-shām.* In al-Thaʿlabī, the caravan is coming from Midian.

by the well where Joseph was. And when Joseph's brothers saw the people,
fear overtook them, [and] they came close to the well in order to give water to
[23] the caravan's people.[65] And the owner of this caravan was a king who went by
the name of Ibn Rāʿi al-Khuzāʿī.[66] And Jacob's sons said to him, "This place
is ours, O friends, and it is our pasturing place and the halting place of our
flocks. So depart from us without having to be forcibly expelled." And the
king said to them, "Dine with us, because we are about to eat lunch, and then
we will depart at once."

And when Joseph's brothers heard them mention food and the midday
meal, they consulted amongst themselves and said to each other, "O brothers,
no one should oppose them, for 'food gains the good will of the deceived.'"[67]
So Joseph's brothers sat with the people for the meal.[68] And after they had
eaten lunch together and gone to their flocks to water them, the Brothers gathered together and they said to each other, "It is inevitable that the people will
[24] water their flocks. However, we will not let them water from the well where
Joseph is so that they don't come upon him . . . what do you think?" And
Judah said to them, "Let us go and water our flocks at that well and when they
see us they won't come near to us." And Simeon and Levi said to them, "Why
don't you take our advice—that each one of us will take a stone, and we'll
come to the well and throw it, and we'll smash his skull." And Judah said,
"No, by God, may He be praised and exalted, there is no god like Him nor
anything worshipped but Him. Do not kill and adorn yourselves in [Joseph's]
blood. By God, if you do not accept my advice today, I will betray you to your
father, and he will wash his hands of you, and I will become an enemy to you

65. See Q 12:19.

66. The text actually reads: Ibn Dʿā al-Khuzʿī; however, this is apparently a scribal error reflecting confusion of the similarly formed letters *resh* and *dalet.* (It should be noted, in passing, that this is evidence that this particular manuscript was *not* copied directly from a text written in Arabic script as no such similarity exists between the corresponding graphemes.) The name al-Khuzāʿī is based on that of an Arabian tribal name. In al-Thaʿlabī, the name is given as Mālik b. Duʿar, who, in line with the quranic narrative (12:19), is sent to draw water from the well in which Joseph sits and discovers him, while in al-Kisāʾī (171), he is called Mālik ibn Dhuʿr the Khazaite, who together with his companions pulls Joseph up from the well. QSYTunis (9a) calls him "Ibn al-Khuzāmī, king of the merchants."

67. JA: *li'anna il-ṭaʿām yurāḍī kull maghbūn;* apparently an Arabic proverb.

68. See Gen. 37:25: "And they sat down to eat bread."

throughout my life.[69] *O brothers, if anyone did such a thing to a dog of yours,
[25] you wouldn't desist from him. All the more so, this is your brother, your flesh and blood, and he does not deserve that.*[70] And they said to him, "O Judah, he is not our [brother] but yours; you will not allow us to do to him what we want. Let's kill him and be rid of his false dreams and of him."

The Sages, peace upon them, said that Judah's temper was unlike any other mortal's ever, and that his temper resembled the Attribute of Justice.[71] And as soon as he would shout, two hairs from his breasts would rise up, and tear his clothes, and stick out from them—and each hair was like a double-edged sword.[72] And so his temper rose against his brothers, and the sword rose up and attacked them. And he said to them, "Woe unto you from God, may He be praised and exalted, because of [Joseph] on the Day of Resurrection.[73]
[26] There is no escape for you from that day on which you will be ashamed to face God—your Lord—and His punishment." And they said to him, "O Judah, tell us what you want us to do with him." And he said to them, "I'll advise you what to do regarding your brother. Is it not enough for you that you have separated him and Jacob his father? Indeed, murdering your brother is not proper, my brothers, nor is it sound. Let us go to this caravan and say to them, 'Our

69. Cf. al-Thaʿlabī (192):

> When Joseph's brothers arose on the morrow, they returned to their pastures and said to each other, "Now we see what has come of our lying to our father yesterday. If we want him to believe us and remove the blame from us, let us go to the pit, and let us take Joseph and separate his ribs from his flesh, then bring him to his father." But Judah said, "Brothers, what about the agreement between us? By God, if you do what you say, I shall tell Jacob what you have done to him. Then I shall be an enemy to you as long as I live."

70. *. . .* *law kān wāḥid fī* [. . .] *kalb min kilabhum mā kūntū turagiʿū ʿanhūm ʿanhū wi-khaṣā akhūkum.* The text here is defective, missing the word for "to do" (*faʿal*) and an incorrect pronoun following the word for "dogs." It has been emended according to QSY^2, QSY^3, and QSYTunis. In al-Thaʿlabī (189), the Brothers cast to the dogs the provisions Jacob had sent along with Joseph.

71. H: *mīdat ha-dīn.* Also QSY^2. One of the divine attributes; it describes the stringency of God's intolerance of evil and punishment of sin. Rabbinic literature is replete with discussions of the tensions that exist between this attribute (expressed by the divine name *elohim*) and that of compassion (expressed by the Tetragrammaton—the Hebrew letters *yod, heh, vav, heh*). Although the world depends on justice, it cannot continue to exist without being tempered by mercy (cf. *Sheimot raba* 30:15).

72. According to QSY^2 these hairs would burn the *ḥawāʾiz* (meaning uncertain).

73. JA: *yawm il-qiyāmah.*

slave was previously stolen,[74] and today marks three days that we have been searching for him, and we haven't been able to find him. And he will confirm to you his slavery.' So sell him and conceal the affair."[75] And so they accepted Judah's advice.

[Now] the caravan was in two parts. And Judah came to the merchant,
[27] and he told them about the matter, that he wanted to sell the slave. And the
merchant sent one of his slaves with Judah, and they came to the well. And
they let down the pail,[76] and Joseph put his foot and his hand on the thick
rope.[77] And their sight was confused, and they saw a thing that they had never
seen before, and they said, "This one is without a doubt one of the angels
of Heaven or of Paradise—a *jinn.* Indeed, we have never seen in this world
anyone like this one—neither with regard to his beauty nor his comeliness."[78]
And all those present in the caravan surrounded Joseph to see his beauty and
his comeliness. And when Joseph's brothers saw that the merchant had pulled
Joseph out[79] from the well, they knew.[80] And Jacob's sons approached the
merchant, and they saw Joseph sitting with the merchant. And the Brothers
[28] said to each other, "Praise be to God who returned our slave to us, for [he
has been a fugitive from us] for three days—we would never turn away from
him." And Joseph raised his eye[s] and looked at his brothers with the look of
one who fears his enemies.

Then the Sages, peace upon them, said he said to his brothers, "By God, if I did not fear you, I would be furious with you."[81] And Judah came to him and spoke to him in Hebrew and said to him, "O brother, O Joseph, I know the tale of you and the tale of your brothers—that they envied you and wanted to kill

74. JA: *sābiq surāq.* QSY[2] reads: "This is our slave and he stole" (*hādhā ᶜābdīnā wi-sārīq*). Al-Thaᶜlabī (194) has: "This is our slave, he ran away from us." QSYTunis (10a) has: "Our white slave is a fugitive thief."

75. Cf. Q 12:19: "And they concealed him as goods."

76. Cf. Q 12:19. In al-Thaᶜlabī (194), Mālik himself is the one dispatched to fetch water for the caravan and, in the process, comes upon Joseph in the well.

77. Reading *salabah* for the unmarked *sin/shin* in text.

78. JA: *ḥūsnuhū wi-lā fī gamalhū.* See Q 12:19: "And a company of travelers came, and they sent forth their waterdrawer who lowered down his pail. He said: 'What good news this lad is!'"

79. Reading *qaḍa* for *qada;* QSY[2] reads *tallaᶜū.* The verb reappears on page 46 of the manuscript, when God "removes" the tyrants from Egypt. QSY[932] also reads *qad.*

80. See Q 12:19: "They concealed him as goods."

81. JA: *nughdābkūm.* QSY[2] (6b) and QSYTunis (10b) read somewhat more probably *nukadhdhibukūm*: "I would expose you as liars," which is quite similar in terms of the graphemes. Interestingly, QSYTunis also notes here that the merchant told Joseph not to cry because he will adopt the youth as his son, adding, "If you steal from me, God will allow it."

you. And this caravan with which you are going is better for you, because otherwise I fear that you will be murdered. Therefore, O Joseph, by the gray hair of Abraham the Friend of God, our forefather, peace upon him, accept enslave-
29] ment to them as they have said to you, even though it shall pain me wherever I go. For I have been advising you already for two hours that they should sell you to this merchant—it is better for you than being murdered. And were it not for God, may He be praised and exalted, Who is capable of anything, you would not have remained alive to this day." And Joseph said to Judah, "My brother, I know that you are a faithful adviser in all that you say."

The Sages, peace upon them, said that when the merchant heard Judah saying these words to Joseph, the merchant got up at that time and alighted from his she-camel; he was not the remorseful one.[82] Then Simeon approached Joseph and said to him, "By God, if you do not confirm your slavery[83] we will
30] kill you."[84] And when Joseph heard Simeon's words, he bowed his head and cried. And the merchant said to them, "You are not telling the truth,[85] for if you were, he would not be crying." They said to him, "He doesn't desire to part from us, but we hate him." And with that, the people questioned Joseph and said to him, "Are you a slave?" He said, "Yes indeed, I am a slave."[86] And they did not ask him anything else. And the merchant said to them, "O sons of Jacob, will you sell us the youth?" They said, "Yes." The merchant said, "How much?" They said, "Whatever is of little importance to you, O

82. JA: *lays yikūn hādhā il-nādim.* Referring here to the merchant; i.e., that he was still interested in concluding the deal. See *Joseph,* 31, where the merchant, concerned that the Brothers will be remorseful (*yindimū*) and renege on the deal, requires them to sign over a deed of title. QSYTunis (11a) adds that the merchant was suspicious because Joseph and the Brothers were conversing in Hebrew.

83. JA: *tuqirr b'il-ᶜabūdiyyā.*

84. Cf. al-Thaᶜlabī (194): "But Joseph kept the truth to himself, fearing that they would kill him."

85. JA: *ṣiddiqīn.*

86. JA: *mamlūk.* A passive-participial form connoting "belonging to, owned or possessed by." The term came to denote a member of one of the armies of slaves imported to Islamic countries to serve as soldiers. Eventually, leaders of these armies were able to wrest control of the state apparatus by virtue of the military power that they wielded and assume control of several Muslim states during the Middle Ages.

The same exchange is recorded in al-Kisāʾī (171), but there it is added that Joseph meant by this that he was a "slave of God."

merchant, because we hate him."[87] Then the merchant reached his hand under his garment and began sorting out a few dirhams,[88] and they took them and divided them up while Joseph watched them. And each one's share was two
[31] dirhams.[89] And when Reuben reached out his hand for the price of his brother Joseph, Joseph said to him, "O Reuben, do not take any of my price, so that God, may He be praised and exalted, will not demand it of you[90] on the Day of Resurrection."[91] And Reuben did not take anything of his price out of consideration for Joseph, but his brothers grasped onto the money.

The Sages, peace upon them, said that the merchant said to them, "O sons of Jacob, I am afraid that there will come a time when you'll regret selling your youth; I insist that you write a deed for me and place it in my hand. And every one of you will place his signature on it so that you will not reconsider and regret your selling this youth." Then his brother[92] brought out ink and pen and wrote the following:

> *In the name of God, the Merciful and Compassionate,*[93] *this one, who was*
> [32] *bought by the son of King al-Khuzaʿi—possessor of the fame of Egypt—as a slave, is the convicted thief,*[94] *so-and so, son of so-and-so. He was sold from the hand of the sons of Jacob the Prophet, peace upon him, and the slave is called Joseph by name.*

And he took the deed and his scribe wrote "Simeon, son of [Jacob]"[95] and each of them placed his signature. And they had already obtained his price

87. Cf. Q 12:20: "And they sold him for a trivial price, for a few dirhams, and they cared little for him." For the disagreement amongst the Muslim commentators as to the exact number of dirhams (twenty, twenty-two, or forty), see al-Thaʿlabī, 195. In al-Kisāʾī (171), his price is given as eighty dirhams, although later in this retelling (187), when the Brothers come to Egypt and Joseph has the writ recording his sale read out loud, it states that he was sold for "twenty dirhams, the weight of which is eighteen drachmas."

88. JA: *khafīf il-darāhim.* QSY² and QSYTunis read "twenty dirhams."

89. See Q 12:20.

90. QSY² has "hold you to account."

91. JA: *yawm il-qiyāmah.*

92. The brother in question here is unnamed; however, QSYTunis (11b) specifies that it was Simeon who composed the document. QSY² reads "his brothers." In al-Kisāʾī (171), Judah is the brother whom Joseph warns not to take his share of the sale.

93. JA: *b'ismillāhi il-raḥmān il-raḥīm;* i.e., the first words of the *fātiḥah,* the "opening" chapter of the Qurʾān, cited traditionally by Muslims before commencing any important act. See EI, s.v. "basmallah."

94. JA: *sābiq surāq.* QSY² has *ʿabd sārīq;* i.e., that Joseph was "a thieving slave."

95. Scribal error. The text reads "Simeon son of Simeon." Corrected on the basis of QSY-Tunis (11b). Once more, by the simple act of singling out Simeon from the list of brothers who

from the king, twenty light dirhams in pharaonic Egyptian currency.[96] And not one of them looked at his comrade because of the paltriness of [Joseph's] price. And that is all. Then Jacob's children took the letter and affixed their signatures, and they sealed it and folded it up, and they handed it over to the merchant. And the merchant handed it to Joseph and said, "This deed is yours. Know that all that they have said about you is true."[97]

33] *The Sages, peace upon them, said* when the merchant sought to take leave, Jacob's children said to him, "O merchant, do not depart until we clarify a flaw for you." And the merchant said to them, "Tell me, O sons of Jacob, what is his flaw." They said to him, "We have sold our slave because he once stole; he is not trustworthy.[98] So be wary of him and do not convey him unless he is bound by his hands and his feet."[99] And the merchant said to them, "O sons of Jacob, clearly it shows on the face of this youth that he is one of the prophets; it would be a sin to torment him and bind him." Then they said to him, "We have warned you."

Then the king dressed [Joseph] in a woolen *gibba,*[100] and they bound his hands and feet with iron.[101] And Joseph said, "O sir, out of your grace and beneficence, please give me time in order that I may entrust my brothers and
34] place them in charge of my bereaved, orphaned brother Benjamin who is with them at home." So they loosened his foot for they pitied him. And he began to call to the Brothers, but they distanced themselves from him. And when Joseph saw that not one of them stopped for him, he quickened his gait, but he fell down upon his face. And Reuben turned around and saw that Joseph had

---

affixed their signatures, the narrator focuses attention on his role in the plot. The names are omitted from QSY^{2} and QSY^{932}.

96. See Popper, *Egypt and Syria Under the Circassian Sultans,* for values.

97. In QSYTunis (12a) the merchant hands the deed to Joseph and says, "Keep this document with you, my son, for I know that everything they say in it is false; however, if you don't retain the document with you, then I will know that all that they said about you is true." Al-Kisāʾī also has this account of a deed of sale; there (171) it is mentioned that Joseph retained this letter until his brothers came to him in Egypt.

98. JA: *ṣādiq.* QSYTunis (12a) has the Brothers maintain that Joseph is not trustworthy in his work.

99. See al-Thaʿlabī, 195: "When Mālik b. Duʿar and his friends were about to depart with Joseph, the Brothers, walking at their side, warned them: 'Beware of him, he is a runaway, a thief, a liar.'"

100. The *gibba* is a long outer garment, open in front, with wide sleeves, and apparently of coarse texture.

101. See Psalms 105:18: "His feet were subjected to fetters; an iron collar was put on his neck."

fallen. At that moment, he said to his brothers, "O sons of Jacob, for God's sake I ask that you stop for Joseph that he might make a request of you, and greet you, and enjoin you." They said to him, "O Reuben, we are grateful and thankful to God that we are relieved of him and of his dreams, and yet you insist on saying these words." At that time Reuben said to them, "My brothers, it must be that you do not regret what you have done with your brother; it is
[35] inevitable then that you will search for him and pay his weight in gold[102] and silver so that you see him."

The Sages, peace upon them, said that the Tribes,[103] when they heard these words from their brother Reuben, at that moment, halted until Joseph came to them. And when he approached them and saw them, he cried bitterly and said to them, "I beseech God, may He be praised and exalted, O brothers, that God, may He be praised and exalted, not punish you for your sin against me, and for all that you have done to me, and for how you have tormented me." And no one wanted to answer him. At that time Joseph said to them, "O my brothers, I have enjoined you, and my good will towards you shall be like the mercy of Heaven. And my brother Reuben, keep all that I have commanded you about my brother Benjamin, because he has no one save God, may He be praised and exalted, and may I not need to bid you a second time. And my brother Reuben, how can it be that my father, the elder, Jacob the Prophet, peace upon
[36] him, will remain without seeing[104] joy or happiness after I am gone. Yet my patience is with the generous God and in Him we will seek help,[105] O brothers." And that is all.

The Sages, peace upon them, said [that] then Joseph's brothers went on their way, but Joseph returned to the caravan. And when Joseph approached his master, his master took him and placed him bareback on a she-camel, and they set off with him. Then they passed by the grave of Lady Rachel, his mother. And Joseph saw the grave of his mother and he fell from off the camel, and threw himself to the sand, and began to roll in it, and say, "O mother, my condition has deteriorated after I departed from you. Loosen from your face

102. The word "gold" (*dhahab*) is not in the text proper but appears only in the catchword (an aid to the reader that provides in the margins the first word of the following page). This reading is indicated as well by the *waw* before the following word "silver" and is confirmed in QSY^{2} and QSY^{932}.

103. H (with prefixed Arabic definite article): *il-shevaṭīm*.

104. JA: *qāʿid wi-lā bi-yanẓūr.*

105. See Q 1:4.

the knot of happiness[106] and see the despair and travail that have befallen me since they sold me as a vanquished slave, and the tribulation that has afflicted
37] me. Have steadfastness, O mother, for what has overcome me . . .

For from my father Jacob they have separated me,
And my young age they did not pity me,
And with all the torments they tortured me;
They stripped his shirt from upon me,
And into the well they threw me,
And with rocks they stoned me,
And after beasts they dropped me.[107]
And they rejoiced while they despised me,
And peddled as a wretched slave they sold me.

"O my mother, would that I had gone after you on the day in which you left, then none of this distress or sadness would have befallen me. However, mother, entreat God, may He be praised and exalted, that He may unite us soon, for He is capable of all things."

The Sages, peace upon them, said that Master Joseph then heard a voice calling from Heaven saying, "O Joseph, son of Jacob, be patient, for your patience is in God, may He be praised and exalted, who created you, and
38] He will bring an end to your straitened circumstances and eliminate your misfortune."

After that, the merchant who had purchased [Joseph] inquired after him, saying, "Where is the youth Joseph?" Then he searched for him but did not find him, and so they shouted, saying, "The youth dismounted from off the back of the camel."[108] And he said, "Get up and bring him." Then they rushed off and found him by his mother's grave, and they brought him to the merchant. As soon as the merchant saw him, he looked him in the face and said, "Your masters said that you are a convicted thieving slave,[109] but we did not

106. JA: *ḥallī min waghik ʿuqdat il-riḍā*. I.e., cast off the veil of happiness that blinds her to his suffering.

107. I.e., they cast him into a well in which they had placed vermin.

108. QSYTunis (13a) specifies that the caravan travelled for two days before reaching Rachel's grave. There it is also related how the chief merchant descended from his mount in order to pray at the tomb, while the remainder of the caravan stood and waited for him to finish.

109. JA: *ʿabd sābiq sarāq*. QSYTunis (14b) has: "You are a fugitive thief."

believe it until we observed in you that all that they said is true; not one of us believed it until you ran away." Then Joseph answered him in the sweetest of words and said to him, "O master, do not be harsh with me and do not harm me because I remained by the grave of my mother. For when I found my mother's grave I remembered everything, and I threw myself upon her grave.
[39] And I jumped off the camel, and I fell unconscious for some time. And when I awoke, I did not find any of you, and so I continued to sit, crying on her grave. And I looked around but did not find you, O master."

And the merchant struck him on the face,[110] and Joseph cried and raised his eyes to Heaven and said, "O Lord of the Worlds, restore my rights because I am oppressed." And at that moment the earth shook and was filled with dust, and the lands burned fiercely,[111] and little stones descended,[112] and the rains fell, and the sun was eclipsed,[113] and the world was darkened. And no one could any longer see his companion. Then the caravan drivers said to each other, "Do we not know for what reason this calamity and this catastrophe has suddenly befallen us? O friends, one of you has sinned against his lord; offer up sacrifices so that he will forgive you your sin." Yet all the while the situa-
[40] tion was growing steadily worse. And with that, the merchant said to them, "I know for what reason—yet, O people of the caravan, I ask you not to punish me; for all that has befallen you is entirely because of me." And they said to him, "Why, O Malik, has all this happened?" He said to them, "Surely, because I struck the Hebrew youth on his face; afterwards I heard him beseeching God, may He be praised and exalted, regarding us, and at that time this thing happened. And what do you advise us to do, O elders?" And they said to him, "What we advise you is to sit before this youth, the prophet, and be blessed by him because he is a prophet of the generous God, and beseech him to forbear from you, because you, O Malik, have sought naught but our destruction."

Then the merchant came up to Joseph and said to him, "O Joseph, I have
[41] wronged you; O Joseph, I ask of your God that He not destroy me. However,

110. Both al-Thaʿlabī (195–96) and al-Kisāʾī (171) record this scene at Rachel's Tomb until this point but omit any account of what happens after the merchant strikes Joseph.

111. JA: *itgahgahīt* (from Lane). QSY[932] reads *itzaʿazaʿat.*

112. In QSYTunis these are described as hailstones that pursued the caravan—here referred to as Eqyptians.

113. JA: *ʾlʾūb*(?). The text has been emended here according to QSY[2]: *w'itkhafaḍat il-shams.*

O Joseph, I give you permission[114] to hit me a great blow on my face, harder than the one I dealt you, for this is permitted you.[115] Then He will have mercy on all creatures, because, O Joseph, we have been destroyed by your prayer." And Joseph said to him, "O merchant, O my prince, my master, my lord, I do not have authority to pardon for the blow to my face, but, O my masters, God has pardoned you." Then Joseph raised his hands to Heaven and said, "O my God, O my Master, do not punish them on account of their blame and sin concerning me, and have mercy on them because You are the most merciful of all upon anyone who has defied You." And with that, God, may He be praised and
42] exalted, raised the impediment and the torment from them. And the world was illuminated, and the sky cleared, and rains ceased, and the caravan had rest from the torment. Then the merchant said to Joseph, "You had only to alight at the resting place but there came comfort and relief."[116] And that was by the blessing of Joseph. And the merchant would hear the angels coming to Joseph and greeting him—evening and morning. And the merchant would hear this[117] and would see a sort of white cloud over Joseph's head.[118] And if the angels mentioned Jacob, Joseph's weeping would intensify.[119]

The Sages, peace upon them, said when the caravan reached Egypt and encamped on the Nile River,[120] the caravan inquired of the inhabitants of Egypt,

114. Meaning uncertain. QSY^{1} and QSY^{932} read *adeitak ragab:* "I have produced fear in you" or "I give you desire"(?). I have translated according to QSY^{2}: *wi-anah aᶜaṭik idhn.*

115. JA: *mubāḥ.* From the realm of Islamic law, this rubric is applied to actions that are neither punished nor rewarded but are merely permissible. QSYTunis (15b) does not contain the merchant's offer but has him explain that he was afraid Joseph would be eaten by wild animals. There, as well, Joseph in his prayer to God requests absolution for the merchant so that the caravan will recognize God's power and that His name will be sanctified.

116. JA: *rakhā w'il-farag.* Jacob's arrival in Egypt will also cause the land to be blessed and misery to vanish.

117. JA: *yaṣṭanaṭ.* Also found in QSY^{932}. QSY^{2} reads *yasmaᶜ:* "hear."

118. The angels and white cloud are recorded in al-Thaᶜlabī as well (196). This detail is absent from QSYTunis, but in its place (16a-b) there is an extended account of how the head merchant invited Joseph to spend the night with him in his tent. Joseph asks him how much longer will it take them to reach the city of Egypt. The merchant responds that they still have a ten-day journey before them, but Joseph tells his master that although he has never before left his town, he can smell Egypt and therefore it cannot be more than a half-day's journey away. At dawn of the next day Joseph proceeds to lead the caravan along a path heretofore unknown, they reach Egypt by noon, and the caravaneers are suitably amazed.

119. A very similar account of Joseph's travails on the road is contained in *Sefer ha-yashar* Va-yeishev.

120. JA: *nahr il-nīl.* QSY^{2} reads *baḥr il- nīl.*

saying to them, "O people of the land, are these the provinces of Egypt?"[121]
[43] [The people] said to them, "Yes indeed." And when Joseph saw the Nile, he removed his clothes from upon himself and stripped naked and, putting on his robe,[122] he descended and washed himself[123] and praised his Lord, immersing himself in the river because he was weary from the trip.[124]

The Sages, peace upon them, said [that] when he bathed in the river, he saw the fish rolling around on his belly and his chest, and they were embracing him and kissing him. And when Joseph came out of the water, the world was shining and appeared without clouds, and the sun rose. And all the people of Egypt were looking upon Joseph in his beauty and the glow of his countenance. And the Gates of Heaven opened, and the angels descended on Joseph, and the earth appeared verdant, and there was joy and happiness. And Joseph began to look like the moon on the fourteenth eve of the month.[125] Then Joseph put on the gar-
[44] ment with which the angel Gabriel had clothed him beforehand when he was in the well.[126] And the merchant was overjoyed with him and placed him on the best female riding-camel, which they had adorned[127] in gold and silver, and they dressed him in a green silken caftan and brought Joseph into the city of Egypt.[128] And Egypt became like unto the beauty of Joseph, and from between his eyes a light[129] that resembled Heaven shone upon the women in their houses and upon the men in their shops. And the world glowed in Joseph's light to the point that the people of Egypt were amazed and said, "This is the light of the sun and not the light of the moon, for [even] the clouds are revealed." And the people were astounded by such an extraordinary thing, the likes of which they had never seen before. And the merchant said to the people of Egypt, "O people of the land, this light is not any of the things you have said; rather, it is
[45] the light of the youth who has arrived. And if you lift your eyes, you will find him on the back of the camel."

121. JA: *il-dayār il-miṣriyyā.*

122. JA: *shālhu;* also in QSY[932]. Hinds-Badawi gives *shawāl* as "a plain loose dress."

123. JA: *itwaḍā.*

124. Al-Thaᶜlabī mentions merely that Mālik ordered Joseph to wash himself (196).

125. That is, the full moon in the lunar calendar of Jews and Muslims.

126. See al-Thaᶜlabī, 190.

127. JA: *mgrbs.* Meaning uncertain. Possible corruption of *muzarkash,* as it appears in QSY-Tunis (21a).

128. I.e., the capital city, which in pharaonic Egypt would have been Memphis. However, the author could be making an anachronistic reference here to modern Cairo founded in 969 by the Fāṭimids, who established it as their capital, or to the previous capital of Fuṣṭāṭ ("Old Cairo") founded in 641 by the Muslim conqueror of Egypt, ᶜAmr b. ᶜAṣṣ. See EI, s.v. "Miṣr."

129. The allusion here is to the ethereal glow ("nimbus") that according to Muslim tradition surrounds the prophets and that may be seen depicted in Islamic paintings.

Then the people of the land gathered from every corner and every place in order to see the beauty of this youth and his comeliness. Then the caravan entered [Egypt] and brought Joseph near. When they brought him to the palace of the merchant who was his master, he seated him there. Then the merchant came to him and said, "O Joseph, thank God for a safe conclusion to the trip and its travails," and he lowered the curtain over him in order that no one would see him or catch sight of him.[130] And prior to Joseph's entering Egypt, the country was in decline—its trees were barren of fruit, its prices were high, its kings were oppressive, and its houses were desolate. But when
46] Joseph entered that land, God, may He be praised and exalted, desired blessings for it in order that the people of Egypt would love him. So God, may He be praised and exalted, sent the Angels of Delight[131] to that country for Joseph's sake. And God, may He be praised and exalted, implored the Nile; on that night in which Joseph arrived, the Nile rose eleven cubits. And He caused a just king to rule over them, removed the tyrants, and the wrongdoers[132] were dismissed,[133] and the land was populated because of Joseph.

Then after that, the merchants of Egypt said to each other, "Let's go greet the merchant, the son of the king,[134] because he has come from Damascus with goods, and let us see what he has brought of the produce of Syria and see what he has about him." Then they approached him while he was seated in
47] his house, and they kissed his hands and greeted him, saying to him, "Peace upon you." And he responded to them, "Peace upon you, and the mercy of God and His blessing."[135] And he was seated on a throne of gold, inlaid with different manner of jewels and rubies. Then the king's son, who was Joseph's master, said to them, "Be seated, O merchants of Egypt." And they sat down upon rugs of silk and brocade, and he brought before them a table of gold and trays of metal and dishes of silver, and he set for them wine and food, and he fed them the finest of foods and poured them the finest of drinks. Then after
48] that, the merchant said to the merchants who were beside him, "What is your desire, O merchants of Egypt, O masters, O lords?" Then they said to him, "O

130. QSYTunis (16b) records that the reason for Joseph's seclusion was the merchant's fear of the evil eye.

131. JA: *malāʾikat il-riḍā.*

132. JA: *shayāshṭīn.* QSY[932] *sheiṭān.* Hinds-Badawi: *itshayṭan* "to behave naughtily" (based on the Arabic word for "Satan").

133. JA: *iṣrafat.* QSY[932] appears to be corrected to read *iṣqafat.* I have translated according to Hinds-Badawi, which gives this definition for *rafad,* with *rafat* as a variant.

134. Here the merchant is referred to as the king's son, as opposed to above, where he may be himself a king.

135. JA: *il-salām ʿaleikum wi-raḥmat allāh wi-barakatū.*

merchant, you have all that we desire, O Malik." And he said to them, "Whatever you desire I have. So speak and everything you mention of wine and fruit and nuts will be brought to your side." They said to him, "We are not [in need of][136] anything you have mentioned—not fruit and not nuts and not the fruits of Syria. We did not come but to see the goods that you brought from Syria, because all of the blessings in our land are due to your blessing." And he lowered his head to the ground and said, "Perhaps it is due to the blessing of Joseph."

[49] *The Sages, peace upon them, said* that the merchant who was Joseph's master began to take counsel of himself, and he said, "Shall I tell them?"[137] And the merchants said to the king, "Tell us what you are thinking about. You have some commodity: display it before us and we will buy it for the dearest price. However, if it is not with you, say to us 'I do not have it' and let us go immediately on our way." Then after that he kept silent a while, and he said to them, "I have a youth whose face is like the moon on the fourteenth night." And they said to him, "Where did you acquire him?" And he said to them, "I acquired him from the Land of Syria, from the Valley of Canaan, from the sons of the prophet Jacob, peace upon him." And the merchants said to him, "O king,[138] why don't you show us this youth so that we may purchase him from you. And if you do not wish to sell him, let us come to know his beauty
[50] and comeliness, because we have heard that the sons of the prophet Jacob are elegant of form and beautiful of stature. So bring him here and let us look upon his beauty and his comeliness so that we will know if all that you described of this youth is true." Then the merchant said to them, "Your viewing the youth today is not proper, but as for his sale, it is inevitable." And the merchants said to him, "O king, give us an appointment for a day in which you will bring the youth so that we will come and see him." Then the king promised them a day in which they would come. So they bade him farewell and he said to them, "Upon you peace."

When the merchants left from before the merchant who was Joseph's
[51] master, they rode off in a procession.[139] And Master Joseph remained in the

136. Scribal error. The manuscript includes here the superfluous "And he said. . . ."

137. JA: *in kan naqūl lahūm.* Note here the use of *nafʿal* form to denote the singular—a prototypically Maghrebine dialectical feature. QSY² reads "if he should tell them about this youth or not" (*in kān yukhbirhūm ʿalā hādhā il-ghulām am lā*).

138. JA: *l'il-malik.* Note the use here of the definite article, which would seem to indicate that *malik* refers here to the title of "king."

139. "They" apparently refers here to Malik and his entourage, as in QSYTunis (18b) it is recorded that he left for the slave market astride his charger and accompanied by servants and soldiers.

house alone; he did not have anyone working with him nor any companionship. And his master went down to the slave-market in order to make a place for Joseph so as to display Joseph's beauty and comeliness to the people on the day he wished to sell him to the merchants. Then he made a raised platform[140] of gold, and below the platform was a divan[141] encrusted with all manner of jewels and diamonds and rubies, and the top of the divan was neither high nor low, so that his face would be seen by only a minority of people of those who came—those whose vision was clear. And all the slaves, mamelukes, and servants surrounded him.

The Sages, peace upon them, said that God, may He be praised and exalted,
52] inspired the merchant, and placed in his mind the notion that he should elevate the site where Joseph would sit so that he would look out over the people, the entire population. So he made a platform of gold and braced the divan with columns of white alabaster, between which he placed marble columns. And he draped over the divan curtains of silk. And he lowered the curtains and installed within them a platform of sandalwood with four columns of gold. At the top [of this platform] was a peacock adorned in all its wings, and above the wings were jewels, while the tail was adorned with all other types of metal and rubies. And in the benches of the platform[142] were pillows of green brocade filled with musk and ambergris upon which Joseph would sit. And Joseph's master issued a proclamation to all the inhabitants of the provinces of
53] Egypt—the East and the West and the South and the North—that they should come to the slave-market on such-and-such a day in such-and-such a month to see the beauty of that youth whom the son of King Khuzaʿi had brought from the land of Syria.

Then the notables of Egypt came from the corners of all the provinces to the slave-market. And there came the appointed day, that which had been agreed upon by Joseph's master and the merchants and the notables of Egypt. And Joseph's master decreed that there should not remain any adult or any child in the land of Egypt, but that they should come and see this youth—his beauty

140. JA: *kūrsī.*
141. JA: *sarīr.*
142. JA: *ayādī il-kūrsī.*

and his comeliness. And the women and the men came . . . and al-ʿAzīz[143] sent
[54] after Zulaykhā and all her household and her slaves and her maidservants and her mamelukes. And they opened the gates and raised the curtains, and no one was kept in seclusion on that day. As for the wife of al-ʿAzīz (who was Zulaykhā): she had already drawn near, along with all of her women, in order to see Joseph. And they had adorned themselves with beautiful decoration, and they carried with them ground saffron and musk and raw ambergris. And al-ʿAzīz went out in his procession and his finery—the men standing on one side and the women on the other. And the merchants sent to the king, Joseph's master, and said to him, "The people have assembled[144] from [all] four directions—the East and the West and the South and the North." Then the merchant sent for the youth in order that the people might view him—his beauty, his comeliness, and his stature.[145] Then they went to the merchant and said to him,
[55] "Bring us Joseph."

After that, the merchant took Joseph and sat him down before him, and he held [Joseph's] head in his hands and said to him, "O Joseph, the people—the men and the women—have gathered in the marketplace in order to see your beauty and your comeliness and your stature. And you know, O Joseph, that it was I who acquired you from the land of Syria, from the children of the prophet Jacob, peace upon him." At that moment, Joseph said to the merchant, "O my master, my prince, my protector,[146] do not mention the sons of Jacob; I burn with anger for the trial and for all the manner of torture to which
[56] they subjected me." And he cried bitterly and said, "O merchant, you have acquired me—an oppressed, miserable, subjugated, mourning slave—and I am before you, O king, so do to me what you will. For this is harshness from God, may He be praised and exalted, who is my Lord and there is no god but He."[147] And the merchant was impressed by Joseph—by his intelligence, the sweetness of his tongue, and his authority.[148] Then the merchant said to him,

143. QSYTunis (19a) describes Al-ʿAzīz as Pharaoh's deputy, and that all sheep and cattle slaughtered in Egypt needed his stamp of approval. According to this version, his original name had been Potiphar, but after he was elevated by the king, the latter called him 'Al-ʿAzīz' (i.e., "the mighty one"). In addition, the text records there that Al-ʿAzīz sent the eunuch to summon Zulaykhā.

144. The text reads *inqasharat* as does QSY[932], apparently a scribal error. I have emended according to QSY[2] (JA: *inḥashareit*).

145. JA: *wi-ṣūrathu.*

146. JA: *yā sīdī wi-yā amīrī wi-yā mawlāya.*

147. JA: *huwa rabbī wi-lā illāh illā huwa.*

148. JA: *riyāsathu.*

"O Joseph, I have adorned you with decoration, and I will place you on high and overlooking all, and the people will see your beauty and comeliness."

Then he adorned him, dressing him in the finest of garments, incomparable in adornment. And the merchant clothed Joseph in a shirt of Mukal[149] silk, and he adorned his braids with mother of pearl and rubies, and he draped
57] over his head a strand of pearls and ruby, and placed on his head a fez[150] of red ruby. And he trimmed him with [. . .] of gold; each and every [. . .][151] was oval-shaped[152]—hanging from his head. And he placed on him an oval-shaped collar of gold, hanging[153] on his chest. And he placed on his hand rings of gold with stones of red ruby (for at that time, men and women would wear chains and necklaces like the women would wear). And he adorned him with a bracelet inlaid with gold and ruby and diamond and jewels and with all the metals. And he put on him royal anklets and dressed him in a sash of gold within
58] which were crystal stars, and he made streams of gold flow upon it. And with him were seventy Egyptian merchants who rode before Joseph. Then Joseph emerged riding, and the people were walking before him, step by step: on his right, seventy slaves, and also on his left, seventy slaves. And in front of Joseph was the king who was Joseph's master. As for al-ʿAzīz, he continued walking with the people following behind him.

And when the people saw [Joseph's] beauty and his comeliness and his stature—while he was in this great procession and this retinue and the people were in front of him—their hearts grew faint and their eyes were overwhelmed by his radiance. And they were unable to look at him, such that the people fell
59] on their faces and swooned on the ground for a long time, saying, "We have never seen anyone like this youth." And they brought him to the stand[154] and seated him in a domed edifice. And his master positioned two callers—one on his right and one on his left. And the two of them began calling out, saying, "Whoever will buy this youth—his price is that which is on him of gold crowns, pearls, precious metals, emerald, ruby, diamond, and turquoise; and trousers and the locks of hair[155] upon his [156] forehead; and the rings, gold chains,

149. JA: *il-mukala:* a seaport in southern Yemen.

150. JA: *ṭarbush.*

151. JA: The two missing words in this sentence are *qrqyt* and *qr,* plural and singular forms, respectively. QSY[2] employs the corresponding forms of *khālkhāl:* "anklet."

152. JA: *fī ṣūrah beiḍah;* literally, "egg-shaped."

153. JA: *khalāyiq.*

154. JA: *mawqif.*

155. JA: *msyāḥ.* Emended according to QSY[932], which reads *masāyiḥ.*

156. Text reads "their"—as does QSY[932].

and anklets that are on his feet, and all that is upon him." And all the kings went walking around him, and ground[157] saffron and musk and raw ambergris
[60] descended on him as if he were [. . .][158] in that parade and procession.

The Sages, peace upon them, said that there were in the land of Egypt seven steward-merchants[159] from the land of Ethiopia, and not one of them knew from whence his wealth poured forth.[160] And these steward-merchants were going to trade in the land of Ethiopia and they, those merchants of the Ethiopian kings, took with them, each one, ten loads of gold in order to buy with it goods from the land of Egypt. And these seven merchants came forward to buy Master Joseph.

Then a queen from the people of ʿĀr came forward, and she was called al-Qurʿā, daughter of Ṭīlōn, son of Quraysh, son of ʿĀr, son of ʿĀdīl, son of
[61] Shaddād,[161] who built her Ramzat al-ʿImār—there were nothing like them on [the face of the] earth. And she was called ruler in all the cities of Ethiopia. And so she came forward and said to the king, "I have already purchased this youth from you."[162] And he said to her, "Buy him." She said to him, "Expect from me obedience." And he said to her, "Your majesty,[163] bring what is comfortable for you." And she said to him, "I have bought him from you for his weight in gold, his weight in silver, his weight in jewels and precious stones and all the other metals and ruby and emerald and crystal; and a gazelle of gold whose head is of diamond, her eyes of crystal, her face of pearls, her ears
[62] of turquoise, her body of metals, her teats of jewels, her feet of red ruby and her tail of pearl; and my precinct[164] and my town upon the bank of the Nile." And she turned to her companion[165] and said to her, "Bring forth what you

157. JA: *sāyiq.* Emended on the basis of QSY^{2} and QSYTunis, which read *ṣāḥīq.*

158. JA: *fūlsān.* Also QSY^{932}. Meaning uncertain. QSY^{2} reads *fūrsān:* "horsemen," while QSYTunis (20a) reads "like the sultans on their day of coronation."

159. JA: *tuggār min il-qahramān min bilād il-ḥabash.* In QSYBaghdad, the merchants are described as being engaged in the purchase of black slaves (*ʿabīd sūd*), while each merchant is described as carrying seven loads of gold (QSYBaghdad, 17). In QSYTunis (20b), these merchants are described as being from "the land of al-Qarāmān, which is located above Ethiopia."

160. JA: *wi-lam aḥadan yaʿaraf tarīq mālū min ʾein.* Also QSY^{932}. QSY^{2} reads *wi-lam yaʿrifū akhīr mālhūm fein.* Meaning uncertain but is clearly descriptive of their inordinate wealth.

161. Al-Thaʿlabī (188) notes that this is the name of Benjamin in Arabic, and provides a suitable etiology: "Rachel bore him Joseph and Binyāmīn (Benjamin), who is called Shaddād in Arabic but was named Binyāmīn because his mother Rachel died in childbirth, and (Hebrew) *yāmīn* means 'complication' in Arabic."

162. In other words, he is no longer for sale to the Ethiopian steward-merchants.

163. JA: *ṣulṭana.*

164. JA: *ḍeifī.* Meaning uncertain.

165. JA: *rafīqathā.*

have." Her companion took out a silken purse decorated in gold and gave it to her. And al-Qurᶜa took it from her and pulled out from it a necklace of jewels that her forefather, al-Shaddād son of Mād, the one who had built for her Ramzāt al-ᶜImdān, had strung[166] for her. There was no one in Egypt who could afford the price of this necklace. She took it out of the purse and the world began to shine from that necklace—"like lightning at the time of rain"—as the
63] proverb goes.[167] It was the necklace of al-Qurᶜa, daughter of Ṭilōn, a relative by marriage of the king[168] who was Joseph's master. That necklace and the finery of the world[169] were before [the king], but he passed over all that she gave him and cast his eyes upon this necklace. And so he extended his hand, the king did, to take the necklace in the sale of Joseph.[170]

But when Zulaykhā saw that Joseph was about to be sold to al-Qurᶜa, daughter of Ṭilōn, she sent to al-ᶜAzīz, her husband, and said to him, "Buy Joseph for me." So al-ᶜAzīz, her husband, approached the merchant, Joseph's master, and said to him, "O king, I will buy this youth from you, and I will
64] give you for him one hundred times what al-Qurᶜa, daughter of Ṭilōn, gave you." Then al-ᶜAzīz summoned a scale, and he seated Joseph on it, and his weight came to one hundred *rotls*. (And every *rotl* of those days was equivalent to four *rotl* of our time.)[171] [Now] Joseph was seventeen years old. Then al-ᶜAzīz bought him for the amount he had mentioned, one hundred times what al-Qurᶜa, daughter of Ṭilōn, had offered. And al-ᶜAzīz loved [Joseph] because of his exceeding beauty and comeliness—he loved him dearly.

The Sages, peace upon them, said that when Joseph was sold to al-ᶜAzīz, Zulaykhā's husband, he had on his head a crown belonging to his previous
65] master. So [the merchant] said to al-ᶜAzīz, "Sir, I will take from you the price of this crown since it is upon Joseph's head." So al-ᶜAzīz said to him, "Take the money and the crown." After that, the king, Joseph's previous master, reached out his hand to take the crown from off of Joseph's head. However, once he extended his arm, he was unable to move it. Then Joseph said, "O my

166. Reading *naẓmū* for *laḍamū*. Behnstedt-Woidich, s.v. "l-ḍ-m," confirms this shift.

167. JA: *naṣīb il-malik.*

168. QSYTunis (21a) records the proverb as: "Do you have upon you the necklace of al-Qurᶜa, daughter of Ṭīlōn?"

169. JA: *zaneit il-dunyā.*

170. See al-Kisāʾi, 172. Al-Thaᶜlabī (197), offers an abbreviated account of Joseph's sale, mentioning that he generated a bidding frenzy until the price reached his weight in musk, silver, and silk, and that Potiphar bought him for this price.

171. A rotl is a unit of weight that in Egypt is equivalent to 449.28 grams. Thus, Joseph's weight (adorned in all the finery) came to nearly 180 kilograms.

Lord, with my whole heart[172] I ask You and You alone, O Lord of the Worlds, that you release the hand of my master." And al-ᶜAzīz said to him, "Joseph, I
[66] am your only master now." And Joseph said to him, "Sir, nevertheless, I ate of his bread and therefore he retains a claim upon me." With this, the merchant's hand was released. And after the merchant took the crown from off of Joseph's head, al-ᶜAzīz took Joseph by the hand and brought him to Zulaykhā's palace. And Joseph was sold to them as slaves are sold to their masters—but poor Joseph maintained his steadfastness in the judgment of his Lord.[173]

With that, *the Sages, peace upon them, said* that once Joseph was sold to al-ᶜAzīz, Zulaykhā's husband, al-ᶜAzīz got lost on his way home. He walked on and inquired, "Zulaykhā's house . . . ?" And the people began to say, "Al-
[67] ᶜAzīz, do you not know Zulaykhā's house? After all, she is your wife! . . . Go out this street and enter such-and-such a street, and you will see the palace of your wife, Zulaykhā." He went out in the trackless wilderness[174] with Joseph behind him. And al-ᶜAzīz raised his eyes and found himself in the open country, he and Joseph, and he began to cry, saying, "O my Lord, woe unto my queen.[175] What will become of me?" At that moment, al-ᶜAzīz looked up and saw the palace of his wife, Zulaykhā. When she made her appearance, al-ᶜAzīz winked at Joseph and said to him, "Kiss your mistress's hands," so Joseph arose and kissed her hand.[176] And [al-ᶜAzīz] said to her, "O Zulaykhā,

172. JA: *bi-kasr qalbī.* Also QSY[932]. Meaning uncertain. If the letter *sin* is read as a *taʾ* (in accord with Egyptian pronunciation) this yields "with all my heart."

173. At this point there follows in QSY Baghdad, QSY[2], and QSY[932] the tale of the Bedouin. The accounts vary, but to summarize the version given in the first of these, Joseph is out taking a walk when he comes upon a Bedouin astride a she-camel. When the camel sees Joseph, she wallows at Joseph's feet, sheds many tears, and refuses to move despite being beaten. The Arab is amazed and asks Joseph what relationship exists between them, and Joseph informs him that this is the very camel that carried him down to Egypt. It turns out that the Arab has come from the Valley of Canaan, and so Joseph asks him to bear a letter to his father. When the Arab arrives in Canaan, Bilhah directs him to the top of the mountain where Jacob sits in mourning. Jacob smells his hand, and, detecting Joseph's scent, is reassured that the Arab is telling him the truth. Jacob asks the Arab what reward he would like. The Bedouin tells him that although he is very rich and has twelve wives, he has no children, and this is what he prays for. He also asks that the camel be rewarded. In response to Jacob's prayers, the camel is granted a place in Paradise, within the year each of the Arab's wives bear him two children, and the Arab lives to see the seventh generation of his descendants. It is clear that such a tale comes to counter any critique of Joseph for making no effort to contact his father all the while he is in Egypt. The parallel in our text appears to be a story of the prisoner from the West (*Joseph,* 126–27), with the difference that this figure erroneously suggests to Jacob that Joseph has died in prison.

174. JA: *barrā il-tīh.* QSY[932] reads *il-barīyā.*

175. JA: *sulṭanatī.*

176. QSYTunis (22b) adds that Zulaykhā "winked at Joseph, and Joseph knew that by this wink she was saying to him, 'Welcome to my dear beloved.'"

honor this boy for me out of respect for me. He might prove useful to me;
68] we will treat him like our children."[177] [Now] al-ᶜAzīz did not love women at all,[178] and because of that he loved Joseph and took him as a child in place of his child, and he loved him dearly.[179]

The Sages, peace upon them, said [that] when al-ᶜAzīz departed from Zulaykhā's presence, he left Joseph with her and went to his kingdom.[180] Between his town and Zulaykhā's there was a journey of seven days. And when al-ᶜAzīz set out, bidding farewell to his wife and Joseph, God made the way easy for him: by the blessing of Joseph he traversed in two days and a night what usually took seven days and nights. And sustenance and good fortune
69] and delight came to al-ᶜAzīz. And al-ᶜAzīz said, "Clearly all this is due to the blessing of Joseph." And so he was overjoyed, and he sent a letter to his wife Zulaykhā, saying, "O Zulaykhā, I do not need to commit to your charge our child, Joseph, because he is a prophet. Do not give him work; this is our child and our beloved." And when Zulaykhā heard the words[181] of the letter she was overjoyed. And she said to herself, "Who is this boy about whom al-ᶜAzīz has sent me a letter with his seal entrusting him to me, instructing me not to give him work, and that through his blessing such-and-such will happen to me?"
70] Then she said, "Bring us Joseph so that we may see if his face is like mine."

So they brought Joseph to her, and when she saw him she turned her eyes away from his face and she was jealous of him. And she took a mirror and brought his face close to hers, and when she saw his face in the mirror it was like the moon on the fourteenth night.[182] And she reached out her hand to Joseph and took him and sat him down next to her and placed him on her lap and removed from him all that he was wearing. She brought him hot water and sat him down in it, and she dressed him in an Egyptian shirt belonging to al-ᶜAzīz and pants. And she adorned his braids with white pearl and red ruby,

177. Cf. Q 12:21: "And the one who bought him, an Egyptian, said to his wife: 'Provide him with worthy accommodations; he may be of use to us, or we may adopt him as our son.'"

178. QSYTunis (22b) does not mention here al-ᶜAzīz's dislike of women, only that he had no children and therefore sought to adopt Joseph. QSY² prefaces to this narrator's comment the statement that he *did* like children.

179. Al-Thaᶜlabī (197) records, in the name of Ibn Isḥāq, that "Potiphar did not lie with women, and that his wife, Raᶜīl was beautiful, and lived in comfort and luxury."

180. QSYTunis (22b) explains that Pharaoh had appointed al-ᶜAzīz ruler of Upper Egypt and commander of its troops, and for that reason he would not often come to the City of Egypt and thereby be absent from his kingdom.

181. JA: *il-ḥurūf;* literally, "the letters" (as in "letters of the alphabet").

182. QSYTunis (23a) adds that Joseph had by now recovered from his exhaustion and that his beauty had been restored.

and she placed rings of all the precious metals on his fingers. And she put
[71] bracelets on his arms and placed anklets around his legs, and she girded him. And she placed a crown on him, and she spread al-ᶜAzīz's bed for him. She fed him the best of foods, and she poured milk and honey for him in al-ᶜAzīz's cup and gave him to drink. She said to him, "O Joseph, did you not hear al-ᶜAzīz tell me, 'O Zulaykhā, honor this youth for me and love him dearly as an honor to me?' And I, O Joseph, by the life of al-ᶜAzīz, will honor you with the honor that I honor al-ᶜAzīz. So reside in his residence—it is the residence of kings—and I will love you a love of a great nature. And you and I, O Joseph, are [joined] in incomparable desire and sincere love. And if you desire, O
[72] Joseph, make me your wife for your sake." And when he heard these words from out of Zulaykhā's mouth, he cried bitterly and said to her, "I ask you, by God, not to love me and not to honor me in a way that would be a sin for me. O Zulaykhā, do not make me reside in the dwelling of licentiousness, because I am innocent of you and of your honoring and love."

And when Zulaykhā heard Joseph's words, she said to herself, "The words of a mameluke are merely words; such is the case with that which Joseph has said"—yet she was not able to turn his head. And so she said to him, "O Joseph, how can I not love you and not honor you, for you are equal
[73] to me." And he said to her, "O my lady, because of my father's love for me, my brothers envied me and sold me as a miserable slave to you and to others. O my lady, do not cause me to reside in the dwellings of licentiousness." [And Zulaykhā said,] "But I love you a great love, and I did not buy you as a slave to a master;[183] I did not buy you despised, but cherished; and you are surrounded by honor. And so I order you, O Joseph, to obey me and not to disregard my command and my word for indeed you are esteemed by me." And he said to her, "O my lady, slaves are bought for service. I ask of you to make use of me and tire me out until my brow perspires; I am not a person to whom honor is due." She said to him, "O Joseph, a king, when he buys slaves, does
[74] not make them serve him great servitude. O Joseph, I am rich beyond need of your service through the service of others beside you. On the contrary, I will be a servant unto you, and I will treat as an enemy whosoever shows enmity to you and I will place my hands upon you as a shield against those who would cast upon you swords and lances. So do not refuse to comply with accepting this honor." He said to her, "O Zulaykhā, honor me some other way, because I know that the consequence of this honor will not be to the good."

183. Scribal error. Text reads *wi-ana ishtareitak bi-ᶜabdan illa sīd,* as does QSY[932]. I have emended according to QSYBaghdad, 31: *mā ishtaraytak ᶜabd illa sayyid.*

A Description of the Garden

She said, "O Joseph, I have a garden. Arise so that you and I may go and look at it." And Zulaykhā had a garden without parallel anywhere, and its name
75] was "The Garden of the Followers"—within it were all kinds of flowers and trees and fruits. It was arranged row upon row, and between each row was one sort of tree; in it was a roaring river, while there lived within all sorts of aromatic plants and all sorts of birds and beasts. In the middle of the garden was a pool filled with milk and a pool filled with honey. And around that garden was erected a wall, and upon its guesthouse was a domed structure set upon columns of sandalwood, ivory, and ebony. And over the openings of this structure were curtains; while on its floor there were spread carpets of red silk. In [the garden] was an observatory within which were suspended lanterns of jewels hanging from chains of gold and silver. At each seat of this observatory
76] there were two hand-mills—a hand-mill to grind saffron and a hand-mill to grind nutmeg.

And when Zulaykhā wanted to come to the garden, she would send Joseph ahead, but she did not consent to go with Joseph; rather, she sent with him old and wizened maidservants and servant-men and slaves whom she ordered to jest[184] with him and laugh before him. And she said to them, "O my servants, if Joseph laughs with you, let me know and I will go to him; but if he doesn't laugh, let me know."[185] And when the maidservants went with Joseph to the garden, they sat down beside him and they danced and played and laughed
77] before him; but he did not turn around and he kept aloof from them and turned his face to the rear. And when the maidservants saw that he despised them, they were afraid for themselves. And a group of them went and informed Zulaykhā of that.

After that, Joseph said to the servants who remained with him, "O servants, I have a lord who created me and to whom destiny[186] belongs. Know that your mistress does not preserve you from torment. But you, if you repent your sins, you will be happy and be saved and gain recompense from God, the Granter of Forgiveness, the Serene, the Everlasting One." And they believed in him and in his words. When Joseph would give praise to God in the garden, the birds and the beasts and the trees would give praise with him. And the

184. Reading *ytmḥzūn* for *ytmzḥūn* (transposing of *ḥ* and *z*), which is confirmed in QSYBaghdad.

185. QSYTunis (25a) adds that Zulaykhā offered a reward of one thousand dinars to the one who would come to tell her about Joseph's receptive mood.

186. JA: *il-masīr*.

[78] maidservants gave praise with Joseph every day; at all times when Joseph would give praise, the maidservants would give praise with him. And they repented unto God, may He be exalted, on account of Joseph.

The Sages, peace upon them, said that every day Zulaykhā would send Joseph a tray filled with gold and all the precious metals. This tray was covered with an embroidered kerchief, and surrounding the tray were arranged cloth bundles of all types of jewels and rubies and emeralds. And Joseph, peace be upon him, would gather up the stones in his hand and place them in the tray and cover them with the kerchief and send them back to his mistress, Zulaykhā, in order that her heart would cease from its love for him.
[79] But Zulaykhā would continue to love him come what may. And when she longed to see Joseph she would don regal attire and put on a headdress of fine chains adorned with all types of stones and metals. And she would send the slaves and servants to sprinkle the path with rose-water and to cover the path from her house to the garden with carpet and with satin. And she ordered the mamelukes and the harem chamberlains to walk before her, and they traveled about[187] step by step. And so they opened the gates of the garden, and she went up to Joseph and said to him, "O Joseph, O face of the moon, God has glorified you with blessing. Tonight I will stay beside you and all this. . . ."[188] And poor Joseph remained silent; he did not want to answer her.

And she remained in the palace where Joseph was, and she ordered that the curtains be drawn and the lanterns be lit and silk carpets be spread out.
[80] And she sent and had the two hand-mills brought—the hand-mill to grind saffron and the hand-mill to grind sweet basil. And the water ran to her from the rivers, and she poured milk and honey into ruby cups. And she was not sated of looking at his face. So Zulaykhā asked him about herself,[189] but he did not want to answer her. And she talked to him, and he did not want to talk to her. She turned to face him, but he did not want to see her, so she said to him, "O Joseph, Joseph, speak to me, Joseph. Look at my face which is like unto the moon." And he did not give her any answer, but turned his face to his right. So she appeared to his right. And Joseph departed from her presence, and she ran after him and grabbed him by his gown. And she scratched him on his chest, and he let out a tremendous shout.[190] And her hands slipped away from

187. JA: *yatagalūn.*

188. JA: *wi-kull hādhah.* Euphemism.

189. QSYTunis (26a) has: "about himself."

190. JA: *min wisṭ rāsū*—literally, "from the middle of his head." QSYTunis (26a) has *min wisṭ kabdahu,* literally "from the middle of his liver." In either case, the intention seems to be that the scream came from the very depths of his being.

81] his chest, and he kicked her with his foot and threw her on her spine. And her back crumpled, and there arose on her a hump like that of a camel.

The Sages, peace upon them, said about that scratch which Zulaykhā scratched [Joseph, that when he shouted] the angels of Heaven heard him and blood spurted[191] from his breast. And Joseph was like unto his brother Judah in his temper, for when Judah would shout, the blood would spurt from his nipples, and similarly Joseph.

Zulaykhā departed from Joseph's presence, but when she went to her residence she said to herself, "How can Joseph kick me with his foot and I remain silent in the face of this perverseness, immorality, and fornication by which he has loathed me? I will play with his mind with these five houses of mine,
82] and I will restore my right of him by their furnishings." [Now] Zulaykhā had five houses[192] that were constructed of all types of jewels, silver, gold, pearl, ruby, emerald, and diamond, which al-ʿAzīz, king[193] of Egypt, had built. And she went to bring Joseph into these houses.[194] Among these houses were two houses—one of glass and the other of tin, and she named them "The Houses of Seclusion."

[The Description of the House of Gold][195]

Its[196] top and its bottom and its floors and its beds and its arches and its porticos and its stairs and its walls were of gold. Its doors were inlaid with all manner of jewels, and within it was a table of gold on which there were plates of silver and all the types of metal. She furnished the house and sent after Joseph
83] to come to it. And Joseph came, as he could not disobey.[197] And Zulaykhā saw him and welcomed him and said to him, "Greetings and welcome, beloved of my heart and light of my eye!" And she arose and showed him the chairs

191. JA: *bazz.*

192. In QSYTunis (26b) there are four houses: the House of Gold, the House of Silver, the House of Crystal, and the House of Tin.

193. In QSY² he is referred to as *ṣūlṭān.*

194. See BR 87:5: "[Joseph said to Potiphar's Wife,] 'I fear The-Holy-One-Blessed-Be-He.' She said to him, 'And if He doesn't exist?' He said [to her], '*Great is the Lord, and highly to be praised* (Psalms 48:2).' R. Abin said, 'She brought him in and out of rooms and from chamber to chamber. . . .'"

195. QSY² reads: "The first house was of gold and this is a description of it."

196. This house (as well as all those that follow) is referred to pronominally in the feminine.

197. QSYTunis (27a) adds that this fear was of her malevolence.

and the beds and the enclosures.[198] She brought before him good food and drink and liquor in bottles of ruby and a jeweled cup. She sat beside him and occupied the place of honor by him. And under her calf was a cloth sachet containing jewelry and a rose and a kerchief for Joseph.

A Description of the House of Silver

As for the House of Silver: Its doors and its walls were of silver and its beds and chairs were of jewels and rubies and emeralds and carnelian. In it was
[84] a silver bed and a silver table inlaid with jewels. She ushered Joseph in and brought him food and a jeweled drinking cup and bottles containing liquor. And she occupied the place of honor beside him. And she brought to Joseph under her calf a cloth bundle in which was a rose and jewelry and a kerchief.

A Description of the House of Glass

As for the House of Glass that belonged to Zulaykhā: Its top was of pure crystal. And its top and its bottom were of red glass and its walls of veined marble and its doors were of gold and its windows were detailed in gold and all types of jewels. In it was a gold table with jeweled plates. And she made ready for
[85] Joseph the drinking cup and good food and a cloth sachet under her calf in which were a kerchief and jewels and a rose.

A Description of the House of Tin

As for the House of Tin:[199] At the top of it was a tin pool and its walls were of tin. Then she brought rose water and she released it in the pool. And there was a fountain with flower-water and two or three fountains that she filled with [. . .] water.[200] And she placed perfume in them, and aromatic plants and fruits were floating in them. And in each fountain were fish.[201] And when she brought Joseph, she spread for him silken rugs and brocade, and at each gate she placed two ladies-in-waiting. And she suspended in each gate two lan-

198. JA: *aṣwārā.* Meaning uncertain.
199. JA: *qazrīr.*
200. JA: *mā khalāf.*
201. JA: *sardawān.* Meaning uncertain. Hinds-Badawi gives *sardīn* as a collective noun meaning sardine or a type of Nile fish.

terns—one on the right and one on the left—and they were made of jewels[202]
and their chains were of gold. And she set at each entrance a statue of herself
86] and a statue of Joseph. She placed in the ceiling stars of gold like the celestial
bodies. She sent the servants after Joseph, and they said to him, "O Joseph,
come speak to your mistress Zulaykhā." And he got up at once and went out
from the garden. And when he approached her, she said to him, "O Joseph, I
have invited you today to join me in my life of ease. As the proverb [goes]: 'A
slave must obey the order of his mistress and whatever his master desires he
must do for him.'"[203]

Then she took Joseph by the hand and brought him into the House of
Gold, and she sat him down on a bed and put jewelry on him and placed a cup
in his hands and said to him, "Drink the cup, O light of my eye, because al-
ʿAzīz sent instructions that you shall heed and be obedient of my command.
O Joseph, hearken unto what I order you." Joseph said to her, "Al-ʿAzīz did
87] not know that you invited me to the Forbidden. Praised be God, the Wise and
the Steadfast, who knows that which is secret and the openly proclaimed. Al-
ʿAzīz has more right to you than I. And you, O Zulaykhā, trust in God and
take me out of this house. I am already afraid that I will perish[204] because you
have invited me to the Forbidden, and you would love to drown me in the Sea
of Disobedience and the Seats of Torture. However, I am pure before my Lord
and know nothing about that." And Zulaykhā, when she saw Joseph's temper
rising because of her, began to gaze at him, but he turned his eye and could
not look at her; and she sought to seduce him,[205] but he did not consent, and
he trusted in God.

And with that, she took him out of the House of Gold and seated him
88] in the House of Silver. Then she sat him down upon a silver divan[206] (the
arms of which were of all the metals) with a pommel[207] at the head of the

202. JA: *wi-hūm il-gawāhir.* Note the use of the plural pronoun referring to a nonhuman noun. The word *min* is also missing from this construction but is clearly indicated by the following: *wi-sālsilhum min il-dhahab.*

203. JA: *ka-mathal il-ʿabd hādah ṭāʿa mawlātuh wi-yikūn kamā yashtahī khīdu yafʿal lu.*

204. JA: *fa-qad khasheit ʾan ʾahlak.* My thanks to Gavriel Rosenbaum for deciphering this phrase.

205. JA: *awrādatū ʿalā nafsihā.* Among the meanings that Wehr lists for the IV form verb of the root *rwd* is the sense of "to urge, induce, or prompt."

206. JA: *sarīr.*

207. JA: *dūmānah.* Meaning uncertain.

throne,[208] and she adorned him in jewelry. Then she placed the glass in his hand and said to him, "Drink," and he drank. And she filled it a second time and said to him, "You are with me in the residence of al-ʿAzīz—with me and more."[209] Then she began to gaze at him and began to jest with him, but he averted his eyes and did not consent to look at her. Meanwhile, she said to him, "O my beloved, by God, I love you a greater love than that which I bear al-ʿAzīz. So speak to me, O Joseph; talk to me, my master." And he said to her, "Trust in God and know that your bringing me into the houses of al-ʿAzīz will not be permitted you by God, for no one but he may enter his house." Then she sought to seduce him, whereupon he was fortified by God, may He be exalted.

And with that, she took him out of the House of Silver and brought him
[89] into the House of Tin and sat him down upon a tin throne. After that, she sat him upon the divan of al-ʿAzīz, and she adorned him in jewels, and she gave him the drinking-cup and said to him, "If the slave does the will of his master he will be fortunate, and he will be dear and beloved unto her." But he said to her, "You say how fortunate is the slave who does the will of his master and obeys her in a wicked thing—he is not beloved; rather, woe unto him and woe unto the slave if he neglects the memory of his lord." And he turned his face from her, and in the rest of the houses he did not look at her. She got up and left him, but after a while she came to him and said, "Come, let me show you the garden," and they went into the garden. And she did not speak to him and he did not speak to her,
[90] so she began to cry until her color and her shape and her beauty and comeliness changed due to the enormity of that which afflicted her.

Then Zulaykhā sent word to her mother, saying, "I want to build a house of honor for this youth."[210] Her mother's name was al-ʿAṭrifah, and she was a queen. Then she conveyed the letter to her mother al-ʿAṭrifah.[211] And when [al-ʿAṭrifah] read the letter in which her daughter Zulaykhā asked her to build a house for her, she sent her one hundred loads of gold and silver, and a hundred loads of jewels and brocade, and one hundred loads of metals, diamonds, rubies, emeralds, and agate. And she sent with them one thousand craftsmen

208. JA: *kursī.*

209. Euphemism.

210. QSYTunis (29a) provides the rationale for this new building project: The four houses into which she had brought Joseph belonged to al-ʿAzīz; now she will build a house in Joseph's name that wil be even grander.

211. In a different hand in the margin is added—"And she was a queen. Then she conveyed the letter to her mother al-ʿAtrīfa"—repeating information already given in the body of the text. The narrative here appears belabored and stumbling; I have emended the text to be readable.

to make her what she wanted. But what her mother sent her did not suffice for
91] her, so she sent[212] to al-ʿAzīz, her husband, saying to him, "O al-ʿAzīz, I want
to build a house of honor for this youth." So he sent her fifty loads of gold and
silver, and fifty loads of all the metals; and fifty engineers, and fifty builders,
and five hundred marble craftsmen, and one hundred carpenters to work in
sandalwood and ivory and ebony. He gathered for her musk and ambergris
and aloes and saffron and fine oil in order that they would build a house for
Joseph.

She arranged that they would build her a square house upon [four] marble
columns with four walls of marble.[213] And she placed an image of gold inlaid
with all manner of jewels between every two pieces of marble. And above
each piece of marble was a bull of gold, whose belly she filled with musk and
92] raw ambergris, and she made for it horns and eyes of jewel. And in each corner
of the house she placed a picture of Joseph and a picture of herself. She made
its ceilings of ebony and sandalwood,[214] and the beams (which numbered a
thousand) were of ivory; she placed in each one a ring[215] and [in] each ring
was a jeweled lantern whose chains were of gold and silver. And each lantern
[was hanging] by four ropes of chain—two of gold and two of silver. She
built for him[216] as well a small mosque[217] and painted it with the likenesses of
Joseph and herself. And she set up a bed of gold, and she erected in it a table of
sandalwood and amber [that was] decorated with [jewels].[218] Then she spread
out silk rugs and placed in the corners of the house statues of gazelles[219] in
silver and gold, and by each gazelle was a basin of alabaster. And they were
93] four gazelles: In the mouth of the first gazelle she placed pure water flowing[220]
into the middle basin. And she placed at each basin two handmaidens, and

212. Change in hand at this point in the text.

213. The syntax here is confusing. Emended according to QSYBaghdad and QSYTunis.

214. Another change in hand, making this the third and final scribe to record parts of this text. This scribe is less given to marking paragraph divisions.

215. JA: *khalqah.*

216. Text is difficult here.

217. JA: *zuwāyā.* QSYTunis (29b) reads: "Adjacent to the house she placed an entrance to a chapel [*bāb maqṣūrah*], in which was a 'chamber for purity' [*khaznah l'il-nazhah*]."

218. The word "jewels" is missing, but may be surmised based on the frequent occurrence in this text of the expression "all sorts of jewels."

219. The scribe here had initially written *ṣurat yūsuf* ("a statue of Joseph"), but has corrected it by placing a line over the second word.

220. JA: *ghāzlah.* Meaning uncertain. Emended on the basis of QSYTunis (29b), which gives the liquids flowing from the four gazelles as aged wine, honey with milk, rosewater, and pure water.

with them a cup, a drinking vessel,[221] a pitcher, a kerchief, and a censer of gold. [And the house's] columns were of alabaster and its dome of diamond, and she placed on its door a peacock of gold whose feet were of silver, its head of ruby, its beak of agate, and its tail of turquoise; and she filled its belly with musk and raw ambergris. And she placed to the right of the door a bull of gold, and whenever she sat on the throne, she would send a man into the belly of the bull and he would bellow and run around like a bull. And she placed to the left of the door a lion of gold, whose head was ruby and its claws jewels, and she placed within its belly a man who would run like a lion. And she made a flowing river scented with saffron, and she placed trees around the river. Then when she had finished the construction of the four houses[222] she said to him, "O Joseph, I am your mistress and now I have become your maidservant. And
[94] I have built for you four houses—of gold, silver, glass, and tin. And I will build for you a fifth house, and it will be entirely of ivory."

The House of Ivory

Its top and its bottom were of ivory and its doors and walls of ebony inlaid with all manner of jewels. In it she prepared for Joseph a drinking-cup, and she placed him upon a throne and brought him a sachet in which there was a rose and a kerchief and jewelry. Then she ordered built a dome thirty cubits in height.

A Description of the House of the Dome

And the dome was set on four corners of silver, and under each corner was a golden calf. And the top of the dome was of gold, and she hung in its interior curtains of silk that she used to conceal Joseph and herself. Then she ordered the craftsmen to fashion by the door of the house four mechanical mameluke statues; whenever Joseph would come and was present in the dome the mamelukes would bow down to him. And she ordered that they make for her four

221. JA: *ṭasat.* Wehr gives *ṭasah* as a round shallow drinking cup made of metal.

222. Textual difficulty, apparently a repetition or citation of a parallel source. In our text, it is mentioned that Zulaykhā had five houses built for her by al-ʿAzīz. However, this confusion is resolved in QSYTunis (30b), where the second set of five houses consists of the house proper (*al-bayt*), the treasury (*al-khaznah*), the chapel (*al-maqṣūrah*), the dome (*al-qubbah*), and the retreat (*al-khalwah*).

mechanical maidservants; if Joseph entered they would clap for him.[223] Afterwards, she paid the craftsmen handsomely[224] so that they were thankful when
95] they left her. Then Zulaykhā entered the dome, and she looked at it and cried. And her slave-girls and her maidservants said to her, "O mistress, why do you cry? What was made for you has never been done for a queen, neither before you nor after you." And she said to them, "Why shouldn't I cry? I made all this for Joseph, and yet he does not obey me."

Then Zulaykhā [sent] after al-ᶜAzīz and said to him, "Come see the houses that I have built for you and for your youth."[225] And when al-ᶜAzīz heard her words, he rode in a mighty procession—with his soldiers riding before him—from his town to Zulaykhā's. And when the soldiers and al-ᶜAzīz saw the houses that she had built, they were overjoyed, and al-ᶜAzīz and his troops began going in and out of the houses. Then al-ᶜAzīz said to Zulaykhā, "Call these houses the 'House of Victory and Happiness and Blessing and Relief.'" Then al-ᶜAzīz—he and his troops—left by degrees, and he went to his town.[226]

96] Then Zulaykhā sent after Joseph, and she brought him to those houses. And she dressed him in jewels and silk and sat him upon a throne. Then she sat down next to him and kissed him between his[227] eyes. She sent after her domestics and her slave-girls and seated them before Joseph, and she said to them, "Adorn him with fine embellishments and honor him and decorate him[228] with gold and silver, and do not leave off anything of the royal raiment[229] in your attiring him." And she said to him, "O Joseph, you are in the 'House of Freedom and Happiness and Reward.'" And she [spoke] to him again, saying, "Have you ever seen a mistress who did for her slave what I have done for you? Look at this house which I have built for you—finer than any other—and this dome which I have built for you, and know that kings cannot make such as this house; I have made it only for you." Then she lit

223. Seemingly, a description of mechanical dolls that might serve to date at least this section of the story as being from a relatively late period.

224. JA: *aḥsānat.*

225. In QSYBaghdad (43), Zulaykhā requests the building materials on the pretext that she is building the structure for the husband, although in this text she tells him outright that she is building the palace for the youth.

226. QSYTunis (30b) adds that alᶜAzīz and his retinue remained in the city for three days.

227. The text reads "her."

228. The text reads "her."

229. Text omits *nun* of *zīnat il-mulūk.*

[97] the lanterns and locked the doors and forgot God, may He be praised and exalted.

Then Joseph approached and said to her, "Let me be, and do not disobey me. I cannot bear one who hides me. What the sons of Jacob did to me is enough for me; they dressed me in the clothes of slavery and bequeathed me the clothes of humiliation, and grief and tribulation surrounded me. As for me: if I do anything such as that, may God hold me accountable. And Zulaykhā, because my father loved me and held me dearer than my brothers, they sold me and did not pity me; nor did they pity me my young age. And would that they had[230] sold me to a people who would put me to service—that would have been counted as obedience to God, may He be praised and exalted. By God, were you to[231] exchange this 'House of Victory' for the 'House of Remorse and Submission'[232] it would be more fitting for you than this house, for I fear al-ᶜAzīz whom I serve." She said to him, "O Joseph, al-ᶜAzīz whom you serve, I honor him and I adorn him with the jewels of honor and the crown of king-
[98] ship. Yet I can make for him a pitcher and a drinking vessel of silver and place poison in them that will separate his bone from his flesh. And I will bury him in the cellar of his house."[233] When Joseph heard her words, that she wanted to kill al-ᶜAzīz, he shuddered greatly and said, "God forbid that we should do such a thing, for it is not permitted by God that you kill a soul that God has created. I will not obey you and I will not heed you."

Then after this he turned his face to the corners of the house and came upon curtains.[234] And he said to her, "What is this?" She said to him, "This is my god, and I am ashamed that he see me inviting you to the Forbidden." And with that, he cried bitterly and said to her, "O Zulaykhā, you are ashamed before an idol that does not see and does not hear and does not discern and
[99] causes no harm nor benefit; a wooden painted idol without movement or benefit. O ignorant woman, O disbeliever! You and your deity deserve each other. And how should I not be ashamed before the Lord of Lords, Opener of the Gates,[235] Creator of Heaven and the Clouds and the Earth and the Sea. There is no god beside him, and no curtain or veil can obstruct His view. And He

230. JA: *wi-yareithūm.*

231. Reading *law* for *lā* (in accord with QSY[2]).

232. JA: *beit il-nadāmah w'il-khashāᶜah.*

233. See *Testament of Joseph,* 5:1. QSYTunis (31b) adds: "No one will ever find out, and I will substitute you as ruler in his place and make you sovereign of his country."

234. Literally, "concealing curtains."

235. JA: *wi-fatāḥ il-abwāb.*

knows all secrets and is capable of all things."[236] She said to him, "O Joseph, if you disobey your Lord, will He punish you?" He said to her, "Would that He punish me rather than torture me in Hell." He said to her, "Trust in God and fear Him." She said to him, "If you disobey your Lord and obey me, I have in my possession gold and silver and jewels and silk and brocade and jewelry and dresses and slave girls and male slaves and horses that I will give as alms[237] on your behalf so that He will forgive you your offense." He said to her, "My Lord will only punish me if I disobey Him, for God, may He be
00] exalted, does not accept offerings[238] save from one who is pure."[239]

She said to him, "How beautiful is your hair." He said, "With death it will decompose and fall out." She said, "How beautiful is your build." He said to her, "Praised be the One who created me." She said to him, "How beautiful are your eyes." He said to her, "After three days in my grave they will bulge out and dissolve on my cheek." She said to him, "How beautiful is your scent." He said to her, "If you took me out from my grave after three days you would flee from me." She said to him, "How beautiful is your speech." He said to her, "Praised be the One who reveals the beautiful word." She said to him, "Look at my beauty and my comeliness and my finery. I want your beauty—it is my beauty, and your comeliness is my comeliness." He said to her, "Be satisfied with al-ᶜAzīz, for he is more deserving of you than I, and more entitled to your beauty and your comeliness." She said to him, "If you obey me, I will love you and honor you and hold you dear. And if you do not obey me, I will hang
01] you by your beautiful hair." Then he said, "Never will I obey you." And once more she said to him, "Obey me," and he said to her, "I will not obey you."

And Zulaykhā was possessed of beauty and comeliness, and she had on her cheek a beauty mark. And she had eighty braids of hair, and upon her were seven woolen dresses. And she had made herself up for Joseph in all the beautiful adornments, and she wore necklaces of all manner of jewels and rubies, and she wore al-ᶜAzīz's crown. She said to Joseph, "Look at my beauty and

236. Cf. al-Thaᶜlabī, 200. See, as well, BR 87:5: "R. Abin said: She brought him in and out of rooms and from chamber to chamber until she stood him before her bed, above which was carved an idolatrous figure. And she took a sheet and covered its face. He said to her, 'You have covered its face; how much more should you be ashamed before Him of Whom it is written: *The eyes of the Lord run to and fro throughout the world* (Zechariah 4:10).'"

237. JA: *aṣdāq.*

238. JA and H: *qurbān.*

239. In QSYTunis (32a–33b) there follows at this point a lengthy prose interlude with poetic insertions in which Zulaykhā laments Joseph's rejection of her, while he, the object of her passion, seeks unsuccessfully to dissuade her.

comeliness." But Joseph lowered his head to the ground and did not consent to look at her. And when she came up close to him, she sat down beside him and said to him, "There is no doubt that you are mine, so jest with me and laugh with me," but Joseph did not consent to that. [Now] Zulaykhā was a virgin; no man had ever drawn close to her.[240] And with that, Joseph brought his hand in under his garment and began knotting seven knots in the waistband of his trousers: the first knot in the name of Abraham the Friend; the second in the name of Isaac; the third in the name of Jacob, his father; the fourth in the name
[102] of Moses the Messenger;[241] the fifth in the name of Aaron the Priest; the sixth in the name of David the Prophet; the seventh in the name of King Solomon. Then he approached her with this prayer in which there was no sin: "O my God, dress me in the gown of Your honor, and do not turn aside Your face, and do not provide Satan[242] any inroads upon me, for You are capable of all things."

Then he approached her saying, "Rely upon God and trust Him and fear Him. For I fear God that if I fall in sin, I will be erased from the Book of Prophecy and be written in the Book of Sin. And the angels will keep me from the path of Paradise and surround me with the fire of Gehenna, and I will be tormented and upon the wings of the angels poisoned,[243] upon all manner of beasts and birds and [. . .][244] deprived, and upon the leaves of the trees [. . .],[245] and upon the Gate of the Happy erased, and they will say, 'Woe unto Joseph, would that he had not been created.'"

Then after that she said to him, "O Joseph, I have spread for you the silk
[103] linens and set up for you al-ʿAzīz's divan, and I have adorned you like no one else has been adorned, for you are in the residence of hospitality in which only one of your beauty can be."

The Sages, peace upon them, said that Joseph, all the while Zulaykhā was promiscuous[246] with him, did not raise his head and did not look at her—from the day on which he arrived at her place until she put him in the prison. Then

240. QSYTunis (33a) here adds: "Al-ʿAzīz did not have any love for women, and on his wedding day Pharaoh had placed him in charge of the city and commanded him to leave that very night, and so he had not approached his wife up until that time."

241. JA: *il-rasūl.*

242. QSY² reads in Hebrew "the Tribes."

243. JA: *masmūm.* Meaning uncertain.

244. JA: *dabīr.* Meaning uncertain.

245. JA: *zāniyā.* Meaning uncertain. QSY² reads *mantūr,* "scattered."

246. JA: *ikhtalaṭat bihu.*

after that she said to him, "O Joseph, consider my anger." He said to her, "I have a purpose, and, moreover, my Lord is content with me." Then she said to him, "The more I draw close to you, the more you withdraw from me." He said to her, "Withdraw from me. Draw close to my Lord."[247] She said to him, "Why do you reject my entreaty to you?" He said to her, "All the while you entreat me, I entreat my Lord to save me from you. If I sin, then on the Day of Resurrection He will not accept me." She said to him, "For what reason do you withhold yourself from me?" He said to her, "I am ashamed before my
04] Master who is in Heaven and my other master who is upon the earth." And she said to him, "I will take to him a cup in my right hand and will give him to drink. And he will be poisoned and his flesh will rot on his bone, and I will bury him under his building. As for your Master who is in Heaven: I have possessions and blessings which I will give as alms for you, and he will forgive your sin." He said to her, "My Lord does not accept bribes. What will I say when I stand before Him at the time of judgment on a future day, and what will my answer be if I do what you command me to do?" Then she left him and entered her house, and she cried bitterly over what had befallen her with Joseph. Then she went out and said, "O Joseph, you have adorned yourself with my blood." He said to her, "God forbid! I have not adorned myself with the blood of any one of God's creatures who is without sin."

05] *The Sages, peace upon them, mentioned* a certain old Coptic woman[248] who entered that day unto Zulaykhā and said to her, "O my mistress, what is wrong with you?[249] Your body has grown thin. Perchance al-ʿAzīz hates you, or perhaps you are in love with someone?" She said to her, "All that is within me is because of this youth; I love him, and yet he does not love me." And the old woman said, "Depend on me for relief." And Zulaykhā said to her, "I will give you gold and silver and jewels that will suffice the length of your life, and it will be an incentive for you if you will drive away from me this sorrow." The old woman said, "Madam, build me a house in the middle of your palace according to what I tell you." And [Zulaykhā] did that, and she built her a house in the center of her palace and decorated it. Then she painted in its four corners an image in her likeness. And [the old woman] said to her, "Madam,

247. JA: *qūrbī ilā rabbī.*

248. JA: *aqbāṭ*. This word, *aqbāṭ,* originally from the Greek, was initially used to refer to Egyptians in general. In later parlance it came to mean specifically "the Copts," i.e., the Christian population of Egypt.

249. Scribal error. Reading of *aḥdan* instead of *abdan* is also supported in QSY^{2}.

wear your adornments and go into this house, and send after Joseph that he come to you."

Then she sent after Joseph, saying to him, "Come, I command you!"
[106] And when he approached and entered the house and looked at Zulaykhā all adorned, he raised his head upwards and saw her image; then he looked to his right and saw her image; then he looked to his left and saw her image; then he looked at the ground and he saw her image. And as soon as he saw that, he trembled violently, and Joseph became afraid of committing a sin. And God, may He be praised and exalted, cast upon Joseph at that time a lust like that of forty young men, and he desired women. And at that moment He cast upon Zulaykhā a lust like that of eighty women, and she desired men.[250] And when she saw that he was favorably disposed, she was overjoyed, and she adorned him in the most beautiful adornments.

Then she drew close to Joseph and presented herself to him, and she said, "O Joseph, are you not my mameluke and my slave and my wealth's purchase at a price which no one else can afford?" He said, "Yes, indeed, all that you
[107] say about me is true." She said to him, "I want to set you free and I will be your mameluke." He said to her, "I am your slave and your mameluke and your servant except for this that God hates." She said to him, "Obey me." He said to her, "I will not obey you." She said to him, "By the right of my deity, if you do not do what I say to you, by God, I will kill myself . . . and then al-ʿAzīz will kill you." He said to her again, "Satan is an enemy of man,[251] and know that whatever God wants will be, so do not kill yourself." She said to him, "Killing myself out of love for you is in order that you suffer." And with that he became confused, not knowing what to do. So he raised his head to Heaven and cried, and he said, "My God and my Master, You are capable of all things."

And when Joseph looked at her—and she was adorned in jewelry and dresses the like of which no one had ever seen—he became infatuated with her. When he saw her beauty and her comeliness, he relaxed and sat down beside her, and he placed his knee on hers and did not remove himself from her. When he leaned toward her, she was happy and said to him, "You are the delight of my eye. Will I not do for you whatever you want, for you are my master and I am your mameluke?" Then Joseph sat on the bed, saying, "I seek

250. In al-Thaʿlabī (199), we read the following: "Then, according to Ibn ʿAbbās, the devil rushed into the space between the [Joseph and Raʿīl], and putting one hand around Joseph and the other around the woman, he drew them together."

251. JA: *il-shayṭān l'il-insān ʿudūw.* Cf. Q 12:5: *al-shayṭān l'il-insān ʿudūwun mubīn.*

God's protection from accursed Satan!"[252] And his heart began to throb[253] and his eye to weep. Then he brought his hand into his trousers and untied the first knot, and he remembered the one in whose name he tied it. And he untied the second knot, and a hand appeared to him and inscribed on it was: "[As for] the adulteress: only[254] an adulterer or polytheist may satisfy her in that which is forbidden."[255] Then he untied the third knot, and a hand appeared to him, and written upon it was: "[As for] the adulteress and the adulterer: each one will be beaten one hundred times with a lash of fire."[256] *The Sages, peace upon them, said* when he untied the fourth knot, a herald[257] came out of Heaven
09] saying, "O Joseph, O son of Jacob, know and be aware that if a sin should fall from you, I will erase you from the Book of Prophecy."[258]

Then the angels shouted to God, may He be exalted, in sanctification and glorification and praise, and they said, "Our Lord and our Master, fortify Your prophet Joseph before there falls from him a sin." And with that, God said, "O angels, O bearers of My canopy and My might and My loftiness, I will not separate Joseph from his grandfathers and his fathers: Abraham the Friend, and Isaac the Trustworthy,[259] and Jacob the Prophet."[260] And he commanded the angel Gabriel and said to him, "Descend to my servant Joseph

252. JA: *aʿūz b'i-llāh min il-shayṭān il-ragīm.* This oath is invoked numerous times in the Qurʾān. QSYTunis (36b) adds to Joseph's prayer to God: "You who saved my forefather Isaac from the sacrifice when the knife was upon his altar (*madhbaḥhu*). According to this version, Satan plays an active role, both in stimulating Joseph's and Zulaykhā's lust for each other at this point, and also when Joseph begins untying the knots in his pants.

253. QSYTunis (ibid.) adds: "like the heart of a dove."

254. Scribal error. I have read the letters *ʾl* preceding *mushrik* as *ʾilla* ("only"), instead of as the Arabic definite article.

255. JA: *il-zāniya mā mūrḍihā illā zānī wi-mushrik fī il-ḥarām.* Cf. Q 24:3: "As for the adulteress: none but an adulterer or an idolater may marry her. True believers are forbidden such [marriages]" (*w'al-zāniya lā yankiḥuhā illā zānin aw mushrik waḥurima dhālika ʿalā al-muʾminīn*). QSYTunis (36b) has inscribed upon the hand: "And the adulterer and the adulteress will be pelted with stones, and they will remain eternally in Gehenna."

256. JA: *il-zāniya w'il-zānī yuḍrabū kull wāḥid minhum mīt ḍarba biṣōt minil-nār.* Reading *sōṭ* ("lash") for *ṣōṭ*. Compare Q 24:2: "As for the adulterer and the adulteress: give each one of them a hundred lashes" (*al-zāniyatu w'al-zānī f'ajlidū kulla wāḥidin minhumā miʾata jalda-tin*). QSYTunis (ibid.) has written on this second hand: "[God's] friend Abraham stands at the entrance to Paradise to prevent the adulterer and adulteress from entering."

257. JA: *munādī.*

258. See *Jubilees* 40:10.

259. JA: *yiṣḥaq il-amīn.* Note that on page 113 of the manuscript, in a similar list of Joseph's meritorious ancestors, Isaac is referred to as "Your [i.e., God's] sacrificial victim" (*dhabīḥak*).

260. JA: *yaʿaqov il-nabī.*

and pull him from sin."[261] And then Joseph lifted his head, and he saw Gabriel in the image of his father Jacob,[262] and the angel stood, saying, "O Joseph, remember your Lord, because if a sin should befall you I will erase you from the Book of Prophecy." And he trembled violently when he heard these words
[110] from the angel,[263] but Joseph could not restrain himself from untying the fifth [knot]—and he fell unconscious upon the divan . . . until he escaped and left through the door.

[Now] Zulaykhā had locked the door upon [Joseph], but God gave him great strength in his left foot, and he kicked the door and broke it into seven pieces—corresponding to the seven knots that he had tied—and he ran out and fled.[264] So she ran after him and caught up with him, but he did not obey her at all, and she grabbed his shirt and tore it from behind. And when Joseph went out, lo and behold, his master al-ʿAzīz was before him. And when al-ʿAzīz came upon him, he saw [Joseph] running out[265] and fleeing from his wife, and his color had changed and his shirt was torn.[266] So al-ʿAzīz said to him, "O Joseph, what is it that is afflicting you?" He said to him, "My master, I have seen someone who afflicts you with a reprehensible deed"—for Joseph was afraid and was ashamed to say to al-ʿAzīz, "Your wife has afflicted me."[267] So
[111] al-ʿAzīz said to him, "Go back and do not be afraid," and then he took him by the hand and brought him into the palace. And Zulaykhā, when she saw al-ʿAzīz, she spread out her apron as was the custom, and she seated herself down. And when al-ʿAzīz approached, she immediately rose and kissed his hands and his feet, saying to him, "What is the reward of this youth of yours? Will they not torture him and jail him and place his hands and feet in irons?" And [al-ʿAzīz] said to her, "And what evil did he desire of you?" She said to him, "This slave sought to seduce me into doing that which is forbidden." When al-ʿAzīz heard her words, he turned his face to Joseph and said to him, "This is my reward from you! I bought you for a great deal of money, and I placed you in [a position of] might and honor. And you were not ashamed to terrify your mistress!" And when Joseph heard al-ʿAzīz's words, he was greatly

261. QSYTunis (37a) adds: "because Satan has overpowered him and he is confused."

262. See *Aseneth* 7:4–5; BR 87:8; BT *Soṭah* 36b.

263. QSYTunis (37b) has instead: "When he saw that and heard this come out of his father's mouth, he could not open the fifth knot."

264. For the motif of the broken door, see *Jubilees* 40:9–10.

265. Scribal error. Text should read *khārig* instead of *khāgir.*

266. QSYTunis (ibid.) adds that he ran out "naked and without clothing."

267. QSY[2] has Joseph say that he "encountered something fearful" and that his shirt had been ripped by a doornail.

embarrassed, and he said to him, "O al-ʿAzīz, she is the one who sought to seduce me." He said to him, "And how is this so, O Joseph?" He said to him, "She took me and brought me into the house, and she sought to seduce me.
12] And I did not obey her in this, and she oppressed me." And when Zulaykhā heard Joseph's words, she said, "Upon your life, O al-ʿAzīz, he is the one who sought to seduce me," and al-ʿAzīz believed her. Then he turned to Joseph and said, "O youth, behold I will torture you severely in return for what you did to your mistress." Then al-ʿAzīz took Joseph by the hand and took him off to the torturer,[268] and he said to him, "Take this youth and torture him with the harshest of tortures." Then the torturer approached and took Joseph in order to torture him, and he said to him, "O youth, you have brought grief upon yourself by seducing your mistress." So Joseph cried bitterly, and he said, "Torture me until I die, but, O jailer,[269] leave me so that I might pray to my Lord and call to my Lord for He is near at hand." And so the jailer said to him, "Do as you wish." And Joseph lined up his feet and prayed,[270] and he raised his head to Heaven and said, "My God and my Master, take pity on the tenderness of my age and the feebleness of my strength and the paltriness of my means.
13] And remember me, my Lord, by my forefather Abraham the Friend, and by Isaac Your Sacrificial Victim,[271] and by my father Jacob Your Beloved." And Joseph cried bitterly, and the angels cried with him and shouted in praise and glorification to God, may He be praised and exalted, on behalf of Joseph the Righteous, peace upon him.

The Sages, peace upon them, said that Zulaykhā had a sister from her father but not from her mother, and this sister was the mother of a three-day-old infant, and her sister lived next to Zulaykhā.

The Sages said that God, may He be exalted, inspired the angel Gabriel to go down to the newborn and tell him to speak and walk and prove that Joseph was innocent, and Gabriel accepted God's command, may He be exalted, and acceded to it. Then Gabriel descended to the child while al-ʿAzīz and his entourage were sitting in Zulaykhā's sister's house. And the infant got up and walked until he stood before al-ʿAzīz, and he said to him, "O al-ʿAzīz, O king, [why] are you torturing this youth?"[272] Al-ʿAzīz said to him, "Because

268. JA: *ṣāḥib il-ʿidhāb.*

269. JA: *saggān.*

270. JA: *fī ṣāff yūsuf qadamayh.*

271. JA: *dhabīḥak.* QSY[2] reads "the one who stretched out his neck [for slaughter]."

272. Employing the dialectical present continuous *bi*-prefixed verb, the text reads *bi-tiʿdhab hādhah il-ghulām* lacking an interrogative. I have emended according to QSY[2].

[114] he seduced his lady against her will." The child said to him, "These words are not true; rather, it was his mistress who made the demand and he did not acquiesce."[273] Al-ᶜAzīz said to him, "And how do you know of that?" The infant said to him, "Examine the youth: if his shirt is torn from the back, then he is telling the truth and she is the liar; however, if it was torn from the front, then he is the liar and she is telling the truth." And al-ᶜAzīz called for Joseph and examined him, and, indeed, his shirt was torn from behind—from his shoulders to the vertebrae of his spine—and al-ᶜAzīz was greatly embarrassed. Then al-ᶜAzīz said to Zulaykhā, "Joseph is more truthful than you."[274] And he rebuked her[275] and swore that [Joseph] would no longer come to her for forty days.

And al-ᶜAzīz departed from Zulaykhā and tarried in his kingdom. Zulaykhā went for days in which she did not see [Joseph].[276] And al-ᶜAzīz retained Joseph in his kingdom, and Joseph was overjoyed at how he had become inaccessible to Zulaykhā, but Zulaykhā was mournful and sorrowful—neither talking nor speaking. And she locked the doors of her private chamber[277] and ordered that
[115] no one should walk about in her palace. And Zulaykhā—whenever she remembered Joseph—her eyes would squeeze out tears like a flowing river, and no one could mention Joseph in her presence. When her neighbors saw her crying every day, they said to her, "Madam, what is wrong with you? Are you not well?" And she[278] said, "How should I be when I am separated from my youth, Joseph, my beloved and the delight of my eye."[279]

The Sages, peace upon them, said that Zulaykhā had no peace—neither by night nor by day—and whenever she would recall Joseph she would sigh over him, and she took no delight in food or drink. And she built a house, the name of which was "The House of Sorrow," and whenever she longed for Joseph, she would go into the house that Joseph used to occupy, and would sit in his seat, and she would lock herself within and cry until her eyes were darkened.

273. JA: *liʾannu rāwada sittū ᶜalā nafsihā.* The response of the infant is omitted in QSY[1] but is supplied in QSY[2].

274. JA: *aṣdaq.*

275. JA: *ᶜātabhā.*

276. Text reads *wi-qāmat zulaykhā ayām lam raʾat.* QSY[2] has *qaʾdeit*—"sat, remained"—instead of *qāmat* and supplies as well the missing objective pronoun suffix "him."

277. JA: *il-khalwah.* This appears below as *beit il-khalwah.*

278. The text reads "he."

279. QSYTunis (39a) adds that her neighbors advised her to be steadfast. Similarly, as part of this version's sympathetic portrayal of Zulaykhā, she is depicted here as remorseful over her previous treatment of Joseph.

Then Zulaykhā employed artful means[280] against Joseph until she brought him without al-ʿAzīz's knowledge and placed him by her side. And she said to him, "O Joseph, you have made your mistress ill and enervated her body, but
16] it is inevitable that there be peace between me and you." Joseph said to her, "O Zulaykhā, trust in God and repent."[281]

The Sages, peace upon them, said that there were in Egypt seven women who were children of kings, and although they had heard of Joseph's beauty, they had not yet seen him. And it occurred to them to go see him. And they would scold Zulaykhā. And they sent word, saying to her, "We are guests[282] of yours in love of Joseph." So she sent after them and invited them, and they came. And she refurbished the House of Honor and opened its doors, lit its lanterns and hung its curtains, poured its liquor and its honey, and spread out its rugs, and renewed its decorations. Then she gave to each of the women a gown, a robe of honor, a crown, and a golden drinking vessel containing liquor. Then she brought Joseph into the House of Solitude and veiled him in curtains, and she said to him, "O Joseph, when I tell you 'Come out,' then
17] come out to these women who are being entertained."

And she brought the hand-mill for saffron and set up the flags. And she set up a golden throne and brought the gazelles:[283] the first gazelle, liquor; and the second, milk; and the third, honey; and the fourth, rose water; and the fifth, pure river water.[284] Then she seated each [woman] on a seat. And Zulaykhā offered to each one of them adornment and dressed them in gowns. Then she went in unto Joseph and dressed him in a garment of red brocade, placed on his head a diadem of jewel and a head cloth of pearl, and girded him with a girdle in which there were three hundred and eighty stars of gold. And she put ten gold rings on his hand[s], and she placed on his head a kerchief decorated with feathers of gold. And she put into his hand a gold staff encrusted with ruby stones, and she said to him, "O Joseph, when I command you to do so,
18] come out so that the women may see your beauty and comeliness."[285] Then

280. JA: *itḥayyalat ʿalā yūsuf.* In QSYTunis (ibid.) it is the jailer Zulaykhā deludes, as according to that version, al-ʿAzīz has not brought back Joseph with him to his kingdom, but instead has returned him to prison.

281. JA: *ittaqī allāh wi'rgaʿī ileih.*

282. JA: *maʿzūmīn.*

283. Note that this list seems to complete the description of the gazelles from pages 92–93. There, however, mention is made of only four gazelles.

284. JA: *mā khalāf.* Meaning uncertain. Emended on the basis of QSYTunis (40a).

285. QSYTunis (ibid.) adds: "so that they will no longer censure me for keeping you close by."

Zulaykhā offered to each of the women a gold basin containing a citron[286] and white purified honey. And she gave them knives of molded gold and whose handles[287] had inset stones, and she said, "When my mameluke comes to you, cut from this citron and eat it." Then Zulaykhā drew open the curtains that concealed Joseph, and she said to him, "Come out, O Joseph," and he came out to them. And each one of [the women] began to cut the citrons with the knife, but instead they[288] cut their hands, so entranced were they in looking at Joseph and his beauty and his comeliness. And when they saw him, they said, "This one is not human, but one of the heavenly angels."[289] And with that, [each] one of them turned to her hands, and these were wounded and had blood flowing from them, although they had not been aware of that. And when Joseph approached
[119] Zulaykhā, she was gladdened, and she began to recite this verse:

My beloved has come near, and in his cheek there are ten species:
Blossoms,[290] and Egyptian willow, and jonquil,[291] and sweet basil,
And aloe, and [. . .],[292] and menthol, and poppy:[293]
And she breathed musk, and he said, "The *kul*[294] and the *ben*-tree."[295]

And after she recited that verse to Joseph, she said to him, "O Joseph, I have compared you to the apple tree; if the wind comes, it shakes [the tree], but if the wind doesn't come to it, a person will sit and imagine that it does. You are the apple tree and I am the wind: if I shake you, obey me and you will do my will; and if we do not shake you, a person imagines it so." Then she brought him unto the apple tree, and she commenced saying this verse:

286. JA: *turūngah.*

287. JA: *wālāyāh.* Meaning uncertain, although the context would suggest a reference to the handles of the knives.

288. Literally, "she"—connoting that each of the women did so.

289. JA: *mā hādah min banīʾadam illā min malāʾikat il-samā.* Compare with Q 12:31, which reads: "This is no mortal; this one is nothing but a noble angel" (*mā hādhā basharan ila malakun karīmun*).

290. JA: *il-zahr.*

291. JA: *il-nasrīn. Narcissus jonquilla.*

292. JA: *il-nād.* Meaning uncertain. See Dozy, s.v. "*nad*" yields "amber" and *ʿūd al-nad* "aloe."

293. JA: *nūʿmān* (from Dozy).

294. JA: *kl.* See Dozy, s.v. "*kūlh*"—a fruit from India similar to an orange.

295. JA: *il-bān;* a species of moringa possessing an aromatic fruit.

The wind blew the apple-tree and cast its leaves,
    And my heart inclines to the one it desires and longs for.
Tell Joseph, the mate of the comely woman, to loosen his morals.[296]
    This, her saliva,[297] is honey; the one who tastes it will no longer be safe.

20] Then Zulaykhā left off reciting this verse, and she said to him, "Remember when you were with al-ᶜAzīz, and you went with him in the open country of the Turks who sympathized with you like I do.[298] And I, O Joseph, am crying and lamenting, and I say, 'Who will show sympathy unto my mameluke while I am crying and in worry over you?' And I have become sleepless all night long with mourning." And she began to recite this verse:

A bird shouted in the darkness of night. He called me
    And said to me, "O Zulaykhā, where is your companion?"
        I said, "He has not come to me."
The bird cried for me in my condition and moved me to tears,
    And he said to me, "O Zulaykhā, where is your beloved?"
        I said to him, "He has not come to me."

Then Zulaykhā left off reciting this verse, and she said to him, "O Joseph, how much do I love you, and how much do I cherish you, and how much do I revere you, and how much do I adorn you, and how much do I honor you—
21] and yet you pay me no mind. Come, O Joseph, let us remain awake tonight." And Zulaykhā commenced reciting this verse:

O slumberers, sit up and watch these night-revelers.
O you have ignited within me a fire.
O to find him,
    I have fled family and nation.
Had only the one who has veiled my fate from view never existed.

Then Zulaykhā left off reciting this verse, and she filled the drinking cup for him and said to him, "Take and drink, O Joseph, this cup from my hand." And she grasped the cup in her hand, and she began to recite this verse:

296. JA: *qūl li-gōz il-melīḥah yūsuf akhlāqu.* Meaning uncertain. Emended on the basis of QSYTunis (41a).

297. QSYTunis (ibid.) has "his saliva."

298. The allusion is apparently to the period during which al-ᶜAzīz takes Joseph back to his kingdom. See above, *Joseph,* 114. QSYTunis (41a) has Zulaykhā instead compare her anguish over Joseph's imprisonment to al-ᶜAzīz's relative indifference.

The cup of love passes, O noble of leaves.
O one who in the beauty of his comeliness tempts the lovers.
And I have become by this love thin of leaves.
He said, "You have but one third what I have of desires."

[122] *The Sages, peace upon them, said* that when Zulaykhā left off saying this verse, the women said to her, "O Zulaykhā, you are entitled to do all that you do out of love for this youth." And she said to them, "I love him, but he is haughty over me." They said to him, "O Joseph, why don't you obey your mistress's will?" He said to them, "Prison is better to me than sin and that which she summons me to do."[299]

The Sages, peace upon them, said that Joseph raised his head to Heaven and said, "My Lord, prison is preferable to me than sin or what is forbidden." And God, may He be exalted, inspired Gabriel and said to him, "Go down to my servant Joseph and say to him, 'By My might and My glory, had you asked for anything other than prison I would have given it to you. However, since you asked for prison, surely I will place you in it.'" And the angel Gabriel descended and said these words to Joseph. Then Zulaykhā urged al-ʿAzīz to imprison Joseph, and he listened to her in this.

[Now] al-ʿAzīz had three prisons: a prison for torture; a prison for execu-
[123] tion; and a prison for well-being.[300] Then Zulaykhā ordered that they imprison Joseph in the Prison of Torture. The Prison of Torture was underground; in it were scorpions and snakes, and it was dark and narrow—one imprisoned in it knew neither night nor day. And if the king were angry with someone, he would imprison him in that prison, and they would lower him down into the well to the snakes and scorpions and reptiles that would bite him until he died. As for the Prison of Execution: it was dug out forty fathoms under the ground. Anyone they needed to kill they would throw from the top, and by the time he reached the bottom he would be dead. As for the Prison of Well-being and Health: it was located beside the palace gate; he whom al-ʿAzīz did not wish to destroy, they would put in this prison.

Now Zulaykhā wanted to imprison Joseph, and so she sent after the jailer and said to him, "Imprison this youth for me." And the jailer took him and brought him into the prison and the inmates surrounded him, and Joseph cried

299. See Yelamdeinu in *Yalquṭ torah; Tanḥuma,* Va-yeishev.

300. JA: *wi-sign l'il-ʿāfiyaʾ*. Apparently, the reference is to a prison whose inmates were not tortured or killed but merely incarcerated. See *Jubilees* 40:11 where Joseph is placed in the jail where the king kept prisoners—as opposed to those he sought to execute.

bitterly. At that time, the angel Gabriel descended to Joseph and said to him,
24] "Why are you crying?" And he said to him, "For a place in which I can pray." And he said to him, "O Joseph, whenever you want to pray you may pray, for the entire prison is pure upon your entering it." And Joseph stood and prayed and called to his Lord. This is what happened to Joseph: his body became emaciated and the hair of his head fell down upon his eyes.

[Now] along with Joseph there had entered into the prison two of the king's servants with whom the king had grown angry, and so he jailed them and jailed Joseph. The name of the first one was Asṭarkhūn, and the name of the other was Amṭarkhūn—the head of the cupbearers and the head of the bakers, respectively.[301] And all the inmates would gather around Joseph and cry with him during the time he was in prison. And the two servants said to each other, "Let's have fun and laugh at the expense of this youth." So they came to him and said to him, "We have seen wondrous visions in our sleep." He said
25] to them, "And what have you seen?" The cupbearer said to him, "I saw that the king took me out of jail and returned me to my former position. And I was walking in the palace and found a grapevine on the top of a date palm with the grapes intermingled with the dates. And on [the tree] were three clusters of grapes and panicles of fresh dates, and I pressed the grapes and I gave the king to drink." And Joseph said to him, "It is a pleasant dream." Then the other one—that is, the baker—approached, and wanting to diverge from his companion in his vision, he said, "O Joseph, I saw that the king released me from prison, and I had a tray of bread on my head, and black birds were pecking at that. So tell us what it is about, O Joseph." And Joseph said, "Know that in three days time the cupbearer will pour liquor for the king as he used to do before. As for the baker: in three days he will be whipped and the birds will eat from his head." And they said to him, "O Joseph, we did not see anything of that; we did not come but to taunt you." And Joseph said to them, "The matter
26] has been decreed, and that which will be will be, but that which is executed you will receive in full." Then Joseph turned to Asṭarkhūn, the cupbearer, whom he knew would be saved, and he said to him, "When you get out of this prison, do remember me unto Pharaoh." He said to him, "Certainly." And when three days passed, the king awoke in the morning, and he called for the two servants. Then the cupbearer returned to his position as before; while the baker's skin was lacerated and they crucified him on wood on which there

301. These are also the names supplied in QSYTunis (43a), where it is explained that they are of Persian origin and that they mean "royal cupbearer" and "royal baker," respectively. In al-Kisāʾī (177), their names are given as Abruha and Ghālib.

were birds, and the black birds pecked at his flesh.[302] That was confirmation[303] of the words of Joseph the Righteous.

The Sages, peace upon them, said that in the prison was a man whom al-ʿAzīz had purchased from the kings of the West.[304] And he caused trouble[305] in prison, and they were up in arms over him.[306] Then al-ʿAzīz ordered that he be bound up and carried off to imprisonment in Mesopotamia,[307] where al-ʿAzīz had a cousin. Then they led him forth, and when they arrived at the Valley of
[127] Canaan,[308] Jacob came out and stood in the middle of the road. And when they passed by him, Jacob said to them, "Where have you come from and where are you going? Is there among you one who can inform me what happened to Joseph in Egypt?" They said, "Yes indeed." [He said] to them, "Bring him to me." And the fettered one approached him, hopping in his chains. And when he approached Jacob, [the prisoner] fainted, and Master Jacob did not cease to feel sorry for the prisoner's leg, and so he burst the iron. And Jacob cried bitterly, and he said, "O prisoner, have you seen in Egypt an unbearded youth called Joseph? What has time done with him?" The westerner said, "Yes, indeed, he was with me in jail. His master grew angry with him and imprisoned him. And I believe, O Prophet Jacob, that he died in prison."

And with that, Jacob fell unconscious for three days, and they thought that he had departed this world, as he was sunken on his face. And when he awoke, he got up and prayed. And the Angel of Death came to Jacob and called to him,
[128] "Peace upon you, O Prophet of God." And Jacob said, "And upon you peace, O Angel of Death. Have you grasped the soul of my beloved Joseph?" He said to him, "O Prophet of God, Joseph is alive and prospers."

The Sages, peace upon them, said that when Zulaykhā imprisoned Joseph, she was rueful. And she left the House of Honor and she lifted its curtains, extinguished its lanterns, locked its doors, pulled out the water from its rivers, and cut down its trees. Then she sat in the House of Sorrow crying by night and by day. Her body became emaciated and her color changed, and she was

302. See Q 12:41.

303. JA: *taṣdīq;* i.e., from the same root used in the appellation given Joseph—"the Truthful."

304. JA: *mulūk il-gharb;* i.e., from North Africa, or specifically, Morocco.

305. Reading *adhiya* instead of *wādhī.*

306. JA: *wi-ḍāgū minhū.*

307. JA: *il-gazīrah.* Literally, "the island," but as a proper definite noun it refers to Northwest Mesopotamia. See EI, s.v. "*al-Jazīrah.*"

308. JA: *wādī kanāʿan.* On page 165 the location is referred to as "the mountain of Canaan."

miserable over Joseph. When her longing for Joseph intensified, she said to the warden, "Bring Joseph out by the gate so that I might see him."[309] Then they spread out for her carpets of silk from her door to the door of the prison, and they brought Joseph out for her. When Zulaykhā saw that his leg was
29] fettered and that he had on a woolen *gibba,* she fell unconscious because of him. Her slave-girls were afraid for her lest al-ᶜAzīz learn of her, and so they carried her all the way[310] back to her house and placed her on her bed in the palace. And she did not cease crying until her body wasted away. And she wanted to exhort al-ᶜAzīz that she should take Joseph out, for he had sat in prison for seven years.[311] And when the seven [years] had drawn to a close, God wanted to take him out and make known to him the promise that his Lord had made him.

The Sages, peace upon them, said that every ten years the king of Egypt would take his ministers with him and take rest and recreation[312] upon the bank of the Nile.[313] And if he wanted to appoint a minister, he would send word to all the inhabitants of his land that they should come to him, and he would feed them the finest foods, and provide drink of the purest kind, and adorn them in the most beautiful jewelry and vestments. And his divan, decorated with
30] gold and all sorts of jewels, was set upon four silver legs—its height was forty cubits and its width ten cubits, and it had twenty-four steps of jewels inlaid with all sorts of priceless stones. And they set it up on the bank of the Nile, and he had spread out for them silken rugs. Then they set up a cupola above that gathering-place, and he called it the Dome of Purple.[314] Then they set it over a divan, and it had twelve supports of sandalwood upon which was brocade and around which they suspended chains of gold and silver. Then he brought tables that were set up about it, and all the people would eat and drink.

The Sages, peace upon them, said in the meantime, the king was sitting upon his bed while the inhabitants of his kingdom surrounded him. And the king fell asleep in his minister's lap, and God, may He be exalted, showed
31] him a vision. And the king awakened in terror, and he got up and screamed. And his ministers and his soldiers said to him, "O king, what is it you have

309. In QSYTunis (44a–b) Zulaykhā is unable to find a pretext by which to bring Joseph out of prison; however, she is able to bribe the jailer with one thousand dinars.

310. Reading *ḥatā* for *ḥqʾ*.

311. QSY² reads "ten years."

312. JA: *yirūḥ ᶜalā.*

313. QSY² reads: "Every ten years a new king would be coronated" (JA: *yatawalah*).

314. JA: *qūbat il-argawānī.*

seen in your dream?" And he said to them, "I saw a wondrous thing, the likes of which no one has ever seen. So bring me wisemen and sorcerers and interpreters to sit in council so that I may inform them of what I have seen." And so the people of learning gathered around him and said to him, ["Tell us about it, O king." He said to them],[315] "I saw the Nile, which had dried up so that its land appeared to me. And there came up out of it seven fat black cows, and each one of them had four horns of gold and each one of them [had a hide] of silk and each one had a teat pouring forth milk. And they were adorned—beautiful of form, elegant of shape[316]—and they stood before me while they were eating, and the field was merry.[317] And while I was looking at them in amazement, all of a sudden, seven other cows, lean, and in which there was not any milk, ascended from the Nile. They had fangs like [. . .][318] and fiery sparks coming out of their eyes, each one had a long horn in the middle of its
[132] head. And as I looked at them, they came and stood before them, beside the beautiful cows, and they swallowed the fat ones, but nothing appeared in their bellies. Then they departed from me. And then [there were] seven fat ears, the stalks of which were of gold and purple. And [when] I reached out to take one of them it became infested with golden termites.[319] Then I turned to my left, and lo and behold, there were seven withered, lean ears. And I reached to take one of them, and I did not see anything in them. Then the lean swallowed the fat. It is as I have told you, O sages, and if you are knowledgeable about this vision tell me." Then they said to him, "We have been rendered speechless, and we are not knowledgeable about these dreams."

The Sages, peace upon them, said that then the youth who was imprisoned with Joseph came (and he was the one to whom Joseph brought good tidings and said to him, "Remember me to the king," but Satan caused him
[133] to forget.)[320] And the name of this king was Diyān,[321] and al-ʿAzīz was his

315. Missing in QSY¹, but present in QSY².

316. JA: *milāḥ il-ṣūrah ẓarīfat il-shakl.* Note similarity of beauty with that of Joseph.

317. JA: *fa-fakahat il-gheiṭ.*

318. JA: *daraghāb.* Meaning uncertain. QSY² and QSYTunis read: *anyāb khargīn,* "protruding fangs."

319. JA: *ṣār lahā arḍan dahab.* Meaning uncertain. Wehr gives *araḍ* as a collective noun meaning "termite," or "woodworm." QSYTunis (46a) has "it was as if the stalks were formed of gold."

320. Cf. Q 12:42.

321. This would appear to be a scribal corruption of the name he is given in Islamic tradition—Rayan. This is the only time where he is mentioned in the story by name; otherwise, he is referred to only as "the king" or "Pharaoh."

minister. And the king said, "O wise men and sages, interpret this dream for me; and if not, your offense will be upon your neck."[322] Then the cupbearer said, "O king, release me that I may bring you the interpretation of the words." And so, the king dismissed him. And he came and said to [Joseph], "O Joseph, peace upon you, O Veracious One."[323] And Joseph said to him, "And upon you peace and the mercy of God and His blessing."[324] Then [the cupbearer] sat down beside [Joseph] and said to him, "O Joseph, I have seen a vision." And Joseph said to him, "And what was the vision that you saw?" He said to him, "I saw seven fat, green ears, and seven dry ears ate them." And Joseph said to him, "You are lying. You did not see this vision; it is not fitting that any but a king should see this vision. And it is not proper that he see it on Friday night or Saturday night, and not at the New Moon. For my Lord has informed me of this vision; it is the vision of the king." And [the cupbearer] entreated Joseph
34] to tell him what this dream was about, but Joseph did not consent to tell him. So the cupbearer entreated him by the prophet Jacob, whereupon Joseph said to him, "For seven years you will sow and you will not be successful in sowing nor in your labors, and you will not eat and will not drink."

Then the youth went and informed the king of the dream's interpretation. And the king said to him, "It is not suitable that anyone except one who is a child of prophets should interpret this vision. Tell me who interpreted this dream for you; if not, I will cut off your head." And the youth said to him, "O king, when you first grew angry with us, with the baker and me, and you placed us in the prison, there was with us a youth called Joseph, son of the prophet, Jacob.[325] And he began saying in prison, 'O people, whoever has dreamed a dream and does not know its interpretation, come to me and I will advise him and interpret for him.' And the baker and I came to taunt him,
35] and we came to him and he interpreted for us without any difficulty, and just as he told us, you crucified[326] [the baker]. So I went to him just now, and he interpreted this utterance for me." [Now] al-ᶜAzīz was sitting by the king, and

322. In QSY^{2} the wisemen interpret the dream to mean that seven sons will be born to the king, but they will die and be replaced by seven homely [in QSYTunis (46b) they are beautiful] daughters. The king rejects this interpretation. According to this version, he had known the meaning of the dream but had forgotten it. Thus, when the cupbearer relates Joseph's interpretation, the king recognizes it as true. In QSYTunis (ibid.) the interpreters ask for and receive a reprieve of three days.

323. JA: *yā ayahū il-ṣiddīq.*

324. JA: *wi-ᶜaleik il-salām wi-raḥmat il-lāh wi-barakātū.*

325. In QSYTunis (47b) Joseph is referred to as a "Syrian Jew."

326. JA: *ṣālabathū.*

so [the king] said to al-ʿAzīz, "How is it that you jail a prophet of God?" Al-ʿAzīz said to him, "He wanted to go to prison." And the king said to him, "How can it be that he wanted to go to prison?" And al-ʿAzīz said to him, "An incident befell him with his mistress."[327] And the king said, "Such a one as this in whom is God's spirit would not do anything of the sort." And the king said, "It is not that this one lured his mistress to that which is forbidden; rather, it is abundantly clear that it was his mistress who lured him to the forbidden." And the king decreed that they bring Joseph to [him].[328] And so one of the king's servants came to Joseph in prison and said to him, "O Joseph, the king has decreed that you be let out of prison." And Joseph said to him, "I will not leave until my Lord reveals my innocence."[329]

[136] *The Sages, peace upon them, said* that when the servants returned to the king, they informed him about that which Joseph had said to them, whereupon the king said to al-ʿAzīz, "You told the truth:[330] this one wanted to go to prison." Then the king said to al-ʿAzīz, "Bring me Zulaykhā and all the women who were present with her." And al-ʿAzīz ordered that Zulaykhā and all the women be brought. And they came before the king and al-ʿAzīz, and the king said to them, "Tell us what happened to Zulaykhā with Joseph." And the women said, "Far be it that it occurred that he committed a sin."[331] Then the king turned to Zulaykhā and said to her, "What do you have to say?" But she kept silent.

The Sages, peace upon them, said Zulaykhā wanted to speak falsehood,
[137] but God, may He be exalted, made her tongue speak truth.[332] And she said, "Al-ʿAzīz, here I am before you, do with me what you will. I am the one who sought to seduce him, and he is one of the righteous."[333] And the king was overjoyed. So the king sent servants to Joseph bringing these good tidings, and they said to him, "O Joseph, know that God has made manifest your proof and your righteousness[334] before the king, and that Zulaykhā has confessed her offense."

327. JA: *garā lahū amar maʿa mawlathū.*

328. Text reads "to me" in the manner typically employed to report indirect speech.

329. JA: *ḥatā yuẓhir lī rabbī b'il-ḥaqq.*

330. JA: *inta il-ṣādiq.*

331. JA: *ḥashā an yikūn ḥūṣūl fiʿil khaṭʾ.* See Q 12:51: "They said: 'God forbid (*ḥāsha l'il-lāh*)! We know no evil of him.'"

332. JA: *inṭāq ʿalā lisanhā b'il-ṣaḥīḥ.*

333. JA: *wi-huwa min il-ṣiddiqīn.* Cf. Q 12:51: "The Potentate's wife said: 'Now the truth must has come out—it was I who attempted to seduce him against his will. He is certainly one of the truthful.'"

334. JA: *ṣāliḥātuka.*

And Joseph was overjoyed, and the angel, Gabriel, descended to Joseph and said to him, "O Joseph, your Lord extends greetings to you and says to you, 'If I had not fortified you, you would have fallen into the sea of sin.[335] You would not have triumphed on your own; I am the one who displayed your proof amongst the disbelievers.'"[336] And Joseph said, "My soul is innocent and I trust in God; He is my Lord and He is merciful."[337]

The Sages said that al-ᶜAzīz was happy at Joseph's leaving the prison; so too was Zulaykhā, and she announced Joseph's release to the women, and they were overjoyed. And with that, the king sent word to the inhabitants of
38] his kingdom that they gather to see Joseph. And the king ordered al-ᶜAzīz to decorate the royal plaza. Its length was one hundred cubits, and it was paved with marble.[338] It had balconies with columns of gold and silver and on each balcony was a green flag. It had two gates—the first gate was large and was for the king, while the small gate was for the people. And the large gate, whose height was one hundred cubits, had an inlay[339] of sandalwood and ivory and ebony with nails of silver and gold, and it was studded[340] with all manner of jewels. And each inlay had seventy rings of gold, and the width of each inlay was one hundred cubits. When they opened [the large gate] they would hear the noise to the end of the city. Above the gate was a green flag: if they unfurled it above the gate, the people would know that the king was in the plaza.[341] Draped over the king's gate was a curtain whose length was one hundred cubits, and it was shot through with pearl, and in each corner were
39] two chains of white gold on the front of the curtain, and in its middle a date palm woven in pearl and ruby. This curtain was woven long ago, in the time of the Giants;[342] then they bequeathed it until it became the king's. And the king would not hang the curtain except on days of joy and happiness; thereupon, they hung it on that day because [the king] was joyful because of Joseph, and he ordered that Joseph be brought. And when Joseph approached, the king

335. JA: *baḥr il-khataʾ*. For the identical expression, see page 87 of the manuscript.

336. JA: *il-kafirīn*.

337. The same exchange between Gabriel and Joseph appears in al-Thaᶜlabī. See also Q 12:53 where Joseph says, "It is not that I absolve myself: surely the soul is prone to evil unless my Lord shows mercy. Indeed my Lord is All-merciful, All-forgiving."

338. JA: *rukhām mrkhām lahū*. While the meaning is uncertain, Wehr lists the second form of the root *rkhm* as meaning "to tile with marble."

339. JA: *mrṣᶜn*. Meaning uncertain; however, the root meaning is "to inlay, set, stud; to adorn, decorate, ornament."

340. Text reads *mṣᶜ* for *mrṣᶜ*.

341. Scribal error. The text reads *mīrānū* for *mīdānū*.

342. JA: *gabbār*.

got up and kissed him between his eyes and seated him by his side. And he ordered the bringing of the ministerial garb, and he made him Grand Vizier.[343] Then [Joseph][344] entered the square, approached the cupola, and went into it. And the king descended from his throne, and Joseph sat down.[345] And the king said to Joseph, "There is no kinsman in the world who is as trustworthy[346] as you." And Joseph said, "Place me, O king, over the treasury of the land, for I am trustworthy, attentive, and knowledgeable."[347] The king said to him, "It
[140] is yours." Then Joseph sat in dominion and took the keys to the storehouses in his hand. Then the king said to him, "And in this land I shall be above you only in name."[348] And al-ᶜAzīz went to his residence, and Zulaykhā said to him, "What did you do with Joseph?" And al-ᶜAzīz said to her, "O Zulaykhā, don't start up![349] How could you tell lie and falsehood about Joseph when you were among the sinners? God has displayed his proof before the scholars." And she said, "You are right,[350] O al-ᶜAzīz, in what you say."

The Sages, peace upon them, said when Joseph sat and became established in his rule, the people rejoiced and delighted in Joseph. Then Joseph ordered the cultivation of the land and its intensive sowing. When the days of harvest came, he stored food for seven years, storing the food of each city that had yield. And each village had food beyond measure because the yield was great like the sand of the sea. When, after that, the rain and the Nile were
[141] shut off—the rain from the Heaven and the Nile from the Earth—and not a seed sprouted, then the people went out and gathered together, and they came to Joseph so that he would sell them food. And he sold to them that year for silver and gold until there remained no more silver or gold in the land of Egypt. And when the second year came, they said to him, "O king, sell to us in exchange for jewelry and clothing," [and so he sold to them] until there did not remain in the land of Egypt either jewelry or clothing. And when two

343. JA: *wazīr aᶜẓam.*

344. The ambiguous antecedent is clarified in QSY² and QSYTunis.

345. QSYTunis (49a) makes it clear that Joseph sat down on the king's throne.

346. JA: *amīn.*

347. Compare Q 12:55: "Set me over the land's granaries for I am a skillful custodian."

348. JA: *fī laysa dil bilād gheir il-ism faqaṭ.* Meaning uncertain. Emended on the basis of QSYTunis (49a).

349. JA: *lā taftaḥī ᶜalā nafsik.*

350. JA: *ṣaddaqta.*

years of the drought had passed, Joseph said, "Certainly my brothers, Jacob's sons, will come to take food."[351]

[Now] Egypt had twelve gates: the Gate of the King; the Gate of the Queen; the Gate of the Minister; the Gate of Prosperity; the Gate of Syria; the Gate of the West; the Gate of Iraq; the Gate of the Sea; the Gate of the Soldier; the Gate of al-Fayūm; the Gate of Victory; and the Gate of the East. And the Gate of the King was sixty cubits high and twenty cubits wide, and its [doors] were inlaid with ebony, ivory, and silver. And the Gate of the Queen was fifty
42] cubits high and twenty cubits wide, and [its doors] had inlays of ivory pierced with ivory.[352] And the Gate of the Minister was forty cubits long and twenty cubits wide—and likewise the rest of the gates were according to this description. And Joseph ordered the gatekeepers and the chamberlains to write down the name of all who entered from behind the gates. Then they would read it to Joseph at the end of the day, and that was because of his brothers.[353]

The Sages, peace upon them, said that Jacob the Prophet, peace upon him, when he saw the scarcity arising in the land and the prosperity in Egypt, he said to [his] sons, "Go to Egypt. Buy food for us." Then, ten of Joseph's brothers prepared to go. As for Benjamin: his father did not consent to send him with them because he was afraid for him. And his sons said to him, "Are you not sending our brother with us?" And he said to them, "I am fearful that what befell his brother Joseph will befall him." So they said to him, "O father,
43] the wolf is always attacking us in order to destroy one of us." And he said to them, "Since the loss of my beloved Joseph, the wolf has not continued to attack you." They said to him, "Then you suspect that the wolf did not eat him, in which case we are all liars; yet your prophethood should inform you of our lie. And God knows that we are truthful."[354] And he said to them, "For

351. QSYTunis (49b–50a) inserts here a rather remarkable narrative, in which Joseph would not consent to sell the Egyptians grain until they "purify" themselves; i.e., undergo circumcision. A delegation of notables goes to complain to the king, and when the king asks them why they hadn't save up grain as had Joseph, they respond that they had done so, but that these stores had been consumed by rats. The king, furious, responds that this was not by chance: Joseph had prayed to God that He destroy the grain; moreover, he is able to kill them should he desire. He rebukes them for coming to complain about a prophet and son of a prophet. In the end the people have no choice but to accede to Joseph's condition.

352. JA: *mufḍāḍīn b'il-ʿāg.*

353. See BR 88. In QSYTunis (50b) Joseph tells the scribes that his purpose is to track the extent of the famine and to ensure that the city's resources remain concealed.

354. JA: *ṣādiqīn.*

God's sake, do not renew upon me[355] the sorrow of Joseph, for whatever God intended, happened." Then Joseph's ten brothers set out to go down to Egypt to buy food. And Jacob said to them, "When you go down to Egypt, do not enter by one gate, because I fear the evil eye[356] for your sakes; rather, each one should enter by a separate gate and when you arrive in Egypt you should meet up again."[357]

Then they came to Egypt, and each one went in from a separate gate. And the gatekeepers wrote down their names and the name of their father; and the purpose was that Joseph would meet up with his brothers. And when the scribes came to Joseph at the end of the day, they would read to him the names. And
[144] when the scribes read beside Joseph, lo and behold, there were the names of his brothers. And Joseph cried bitterly and said, "Shall I do unto them what they did unto me? How can that be?" And he began to reckon in his mind and say, "Perhaps my brothers have come." And he said again to the scribes (who were twelve in number), "Tell me what it is you have written." And this one began to say, "Reuben, son of Jacob"; and the second one to say, "Simeon, son of Jacob"; and the third to say, "Levi, son of Jacob"; and the fourth to say, "Judah, son of Jacob"; and the fifth to say, "Issachar, son of Jacob"; and the sixth to say, "Zebulun, son of Jacob"; and the seventh to say, "Dan, son of Jacob"; and the eighth to say, "Naphtali, son of Jacob"; and the ninth to say, "Gad, son of Jacob"; and the tenth to say, "Asher, son of Jacob."[358] And Joseph said to himself, "Why did my brother Benjamin not come with them?" And whenever they would mention
[145] a name to him, he would appear to intensify in crying.

And when the day broke, Joseph's brothers girded themselves with their swords, mounted their horses, and stood before him. [Now] Joseph would only sit in council veiled. And all the soldiers and the people of state and Pharaoh's ministers would remain standing before him with folded arms, but Master Joseph was sitting, and he was called the Grand Prime Minister.[359] And

355. Text reads "him." Emended on the basis of QSYTunis (51a).

356. JA: *il-ʿayn.*

357. Compare Q 12:67: "My sons, don't enter from a single gate; rather, enter from different gates. In no way can I shield you from God; judgment is His alone. In Him I have put my trust; in Him let the faithful put their trust." In the Qurʾān, however, this counsel is given only upon the second trip of the Brothers down to Egypt.

358. The sons are listed according to their birth mothers: first, the sons of Leah; then, the sons of Rachel's concubine, Bilhah; finally, the sons of Zilpah, Leah's concubine. Within each matrilineal grouping the names are given according to order of birth as they appear in Genesis 35:23–26.

359. JA: *wazīr il-wuzarāʾ il-ʿaẓim.*

when Jacob's children stood before him, they entered blessing him from the top of the square all the way up to him. When Joseph first saw them, he said to them, "Where have you come from? And where are you from and what is your land?" They said to him, "We are your servants, sons of a single man whose name is Jacob, and our land is the land of Syria," and then he bowed down to the ground for a long time.

Then Joseph raised his head. And Joseph had before him a goblet of gold studded with all manner of jewels. And he took the goblet—that is, the cup—in his hand and said, "O sons of Jacob, my goblet informs me that you are fugitives and conspirators,[360] but you have a brother—you say ten, but you
46] have lied in your statement." And he raised the goblet before him and said to them, "You are nothing but twelve brothers and that which I have told you is the truth, that you are conspirators." They said to him, "You are correct,[361] O king, we are twelve brothers; one is with our father and the other is not present."[362] He said to them, "It is true that you are conspirators; otherwise, for what reason did each one of you enter by way of a separate gate?" They said to him, "O master, we were afraid of the evil eye." And he said to them, "You are conspirators of the land; otherwise, for what reason did you enter the prostitute market? Were you not conspirators, you would not have entered that market." And they said to him, "O master, we were pasturing our father's sheep and we, your slaves, were eleven souls; we, the ten, and another one, whose name was Joseph, was lost from us and we could not find him. And when we returned to your servant, our father, we told him and he was greatly saddened for him. So we said to each other, 'Let us go down to Egypt and search for our
47] brother Joseph. And right after we rode up and arrived, we said to each other, 'We will search for him in the marketplaces.'" And he said to them, "When you came to Egypt to search for him, why did each one enter from a separate gate?" They said to him, "O master, we were afraid of the evil eye." He said to them, "Why did you enter the prostitute-market?" And they said to him, "O master, our brother who was lost from us was beautiful of form[363]—great is God who created that form—and we said to each other, 'Perhaps he strayed, and being a stranger of this land, perhaps he entered the prostitute-market.'" He said to them, "It is as I said to you: you are conspirators of the land."[364]

360. JA: *ḥārbīn wi-dawāsīs.*

361. JA: *ṣadaqta.*

362. JA: *mā huwa ḥāḍir.*

363. JA: *melīḥ il-ṣūrah.*

364. See BR 91:6. In QSYTunis (52a–53a) there appears an expanded version of the interrogation in which Joseph seizes on other supposed inconsistencies in the Brothers' account.

And with that, Joseph ordered their imprisonment, and he ordered that food be carried to them from Joseph's fare. So they remained in jail speaking to each other, and each one rebuked his companion and said, "All this is due to our crime against Joseph our brother." And Reuben said to them, "O sons of Jacob, I told you that if you oppress your brother, Joseph, then God, may
[148] He be exalted, will see that justice is done the oppressed. O woe unto you from God on the Day of Resurrection." And they did not speak, but screamed a great scream and tore their garments. And they said, "O Reuben, you have killed us without a sword. And you were correct[365] back then, but we did not heed you. However, this one is dead, so now tell us what you counsel us in this calamity, in this matter of al-ʿAzīz, for he is punishing us." So Reuben said to them, "This is a divine matter: God wishes to recompense you for what you have done to Joseph and to Jacob, your father,[366] and what you did in exposing your brother to a gruesome deed, for it will never be forgotten." And Reuben proceeded to rebuke them, and they were remorseful and cried.

And [Joseph] was sitting in the doorway of the prison listening to their words, but with that,[367] [he] entered the Gate of Solitude and cried bitterly.
[149] Then he went out, washed his face, and adorned himself. And he sat down at his place and ordered that they bring his brothers before him, the color of whose faces had changed as a result of Reuben's rebuke. And when they came before him, they lowered their heads, and Joseph said to them, "Come forward." And Reuben came forward before him, and Joseph raised his head to them and said to them, "I do not see among you anyone else who has come forward other than this one, and my cup informs me that you are people of cunning and artifice.[368] However, I trust in God concerning you, in his clarifying for me what you are about. By the life of the king, you are devising a plot against me,[369] but send one of you to bring your brother who is with your father so that your truthfulness[370] will be clearly demonstrated to me and you will not be destroyed."

Then Joseph ordered that they be returned to the prison. Then he[371] sent them special food and choice drink from all the fruits. When night came

365. JA: *wi-la-qad kunta ʿalā il-ṣawāb.*

366. Scribal error. Text reads *mā faʿaltū bi-yūsuf wi-mā bi-yaʿaqov akhūkūm:* literally, "that which you did to Joseph and that which you did to Jacob your brother."

367. Scribal error. JA: *fī ʿand dakhal dalik,* where the last two words should be interchanged.

368. JA: *ahl makar w'il-ḥeilah.*

369. JA: *intū qalbīn lī maḥālah.*

370. JA: *ṣidqukūm.*

371. Text reads "they."

upon them, they began to rebuke each other in the matter of Joseph, and he sneaked in on them and listened to all that they said. And they were speaking
50] in Hebrew, and no one among [the Egyptians] knew what they were saying except for Manasseh. And Simeon said to them, "O brothers, if our matter with this al-ʿAzīz is settled and he lets us out, we will sally forth into Egypt and roam about so that we may pursue Joseph whether he is alive or dead." And Reuben said, "O Simeon, [all of you] renew your anxiety[372] in the deeds that you have done to Joseph, and do not try to interfere in the affairs of God, may He be exalted." And when Reuben rebuked them[373] with his words, lo and behold, Joseph's brothers screamed a great scream, and they slapped their faces and tore their garments and said, "O Reuben, we have admitted our offense." Then when Joseph heard the words of his brothers, he went into his house and cried until his garments and his eyes were awash with tears.

[Now] Joseph had two sons, Manasseh and Ephraim, and when they saw their father Joseph in this state of sadness and crying, it was unpleasant for
51] them. And this matter was troubling unto them, so they said to him, "O master, tell us what is wrong." Joseph said, "O children, these people that are in prison are my brothers, and they are the ones who sold me, and I will honor them[374] until God wills my being reunited with them." And when Manasseh and Ephraim heard their father's words they were overjoyed.

When day broke, Joseph sat on his throne; then, finished with the concerns of the people, he ordered the bringing of his brothers. And they came before him, and Joseph said to them, "What have you done in the matter of your brother who is with your father?" Judah said to him, "O master O king, we are your slaves: if you wish, release us, and if you wish, put us in prison." And Joseph said to him, "What is your name?" He said, "Your slave, your mameluke, Judah." And Joseph said to him, "It has become clear to me that you are better than your brothers and that you are truthful and trustworthy."[375] And Judah prostrated himself with his face to the ground out of gratitude for Joseph's kindness to him. And Joseph said, "O Judah, where[376] is your silver
52] which you brought to buy food with?" And Judah said, "O king, we have silver." And so he said, "Bring it before me," and they brought it. And Joseph wrote down the silver of each one according to his name, and he handed it

372. JA: *tagaddadū b'il-hamm.*
373. Text appears to read *stthūm.*
374. JA: *ukimahūm.*
375. JA: *wi-inta ṣādiq amīn.*
376. Reading *ayna* for *an.*

over to his deputy.[377] And [Joseph] said, "O Judah, set your souls at ease,[378] for I fear God regarding you. And I will give you food and sustenance for your houses, but I will take [a deposit] from you so that you will bring your brother and we may believe your statement."

Now Simeon alone among the Brothers had wanted to kill Joseph, so Joseph ordered his servants to take Simeon and imprison him.[379] And when they approached him to take him, he let forth a yell and the walls of the square fell down upon one hundred and fifty men. Of them, one hundred were injured—some of whom had their hands broken and some of whom were thrown to the ground—while fifty died. Then Manasseh got up from his throne, and he took a cane and beat Simeon and put him in prison. And Manasseh let forth a yell—the Tribes fell on their faces, even their brother Joseph fell off his
[153] throne—and the Tribes said to each other in Hebrew, "There is no doubt that this fellow is one of us." And Joseph said to them, "This one will remain under my hand until you bring your brother of whom you spoke." And he ordered that food be measured out for them, but that the silver be placed back in each brother's sack.[380] And they did as Joseph ordered. When the day broke he let them go and said to them, "Hurry on your way to your father and set his heart at rest, and bring your brother before me."[381]

When the morning broke, Joseph's brothers left Egypt and began to rebuke each other, each one saying to his companion, "You are the sole reason for the death of Joseph," and they continued in this vein until they halted at a stopping place. And when one of them, opening his sack to place fodder for his donkey, found his silver with its seal in his container, he said, "O my brothers, I have found my silver in my container." And so all of them opened their containers and each one found according to its [original] weight. And they raised
[154] an outcry and screamed and tore their garments and said, "What has God done to us? All these misfortunes are in return for what we did to Joseph." And Reuben said to them, "May this be sufficient for you,[382] but you will remain

377. JA: *wakīlū.*

378. JA: *ṭayyabū anfūskūm.*

379. QSYTunis (54b–55a) has an expanded account in which Simeon resists imprisionment. In al-Thaʿlabī (214–15) the Brothers draw lots to determine who will be kept as ransom. In al-Kisāʾī, Joseph does not require any brother be held back as ransom upon the Brothers' return to their father; however, after Benjamin is detained for the "theft" of the cup, Judah remains behind with him while the others return again to Canaan (see 180–86). Thus, the Brothers make a total of three trips to Egypt before Joseph reveals himself to them.

380. JA: *wʿātū.*

381. Text (reflecting indirect speech) reads "before him."

382. JA: *kafākūm hādah.*

[culpable] for the oppression of Joseph until the Day of Resurrection." And the sons of Jacob saw, lo and behold, their father coming out to greet them, but when he heard their clamoring and screaming, his heart was startled, and he said to himself, "A calamity has befallen them." And when they reached him, he did not see Simeon with them and he said to them, "Where is my son Simeon? Has the wolf eaten him as he ate my beloved Joseph?" And they said to him, "O father, we have encountered something harsher than being eaten by a wolf." Jacob said to them, "And what did you encounter exactly?" They said to him, "O father, al-ʿAzīz of Egypt contended with us and said to us, 'You are conspirators who have come to Egypt.' And we said to him, 'O master, we are twelve men from one father; our little brother [is no longer] and the other is with our father[383] in the land of Canaan.'[384] And he said to us, 'I will
55] not believe your words unless you bring your brother who is with your father.' And he took Simeon as ransom[385] in order that we will bring him our brother who is at home."

And when Jacob heard their words, he tore his garments and let forth a scream so great that the birds of the sky fell, and he threw himself to the ground and fainted. And when he regained consciousness, he shouted at the top of his lungs and said, "O my son, O Joseph, was what you brought me not enough for you? Was I separated from you so that I will become so from your brother Benjamin?" and he continued to scream until his children carried him to his residence. And he joined his family, and they began to cry while he was crying and screaming.

Then Judah approached him and said to him, "O father, we have been slain and you have broken our heart, but you are a prophet; do you not know that what has afflicted us is entirely from God, may He be praised and exalted? And perhaps our being without him[386] will be for a blessing, and the punishment will be for the best." And when he heard the words of Judah, Jacob knew that Judah
56] was being solicitous for him, and so he fortified himself and said, "I will rely on God, because He will recompense the patient with blessing."[387]

And Judah spoke again to his father, "O father, give us Benjamin that we may take him with us." But Jacob said to them, "He will not go with

383. This word is inserted in the margin.

384. The text here is corrupt and should most likely read in accord with Gen. 42:32: "We are twelve, brothers, sons of our father; one is no longer and the small one is today with our father in the land of Canaan." Note that in *Joseph,* 145, the land is referred to as the "Land of Syria."

385. JA: *istarhan.*

386. I.e., Joseph.

387. JA: *itakaltu ʿalā il-lāh liʾannahū yuʿwār il-ṣābirīn kheir.*

you. What happened to his brother Joseph is enough; you shall not take the other."[388] Judah said to his brothers, "Be patient until the food runs out." And when the food that they had ran out, Jacob said to them, "Go buy food for us." And Judah said to him, "O my father, the king said to us, 'Show us your faces only if your brother is with you'; so if you let our brother come with us, we will go, but if you will not let him, we will not go." And Jacob said, "Never shall my son go with you." Then Reuben got up and said to him, "O father, my two children will be a ransom[389] for Benjamin," but he said to them, "My
[157] son will not go with you." And Judah stood up before him and said, "O father, do not accept guarantee[390] for Benjamin except from my hand, for I will safeguard him; and if I do not bring him back, I will remain a sinner to you forever." And when Jacob heard Judah's words, he said to them, "Take Benjamin and take a gift for the king so that his heart will have mercy upon you and he will send Simeon and Benjamin with you." And they took Benjamin and left.

When Joseph saw them, he sat down upon his throne, and they approached offering up praise to him. And he said to them, "This is your little brother about whom you told me?" They said, "Yes indeed, our master." He spoke again and said to them, "How is your father? Did you convey to him my greetings?" They said to him, "Yes indeed; your servant, our father, extends his greetings to you: accept this gift from him." And he accepted the gift and brought Simeon out of the prison. And he went into the private chamber and called to his brother [Benjamin] that he should sit by him. And Benjamin the Righteous,[391] peace upon him, knew astrology.[392] Joseph said to Benjamin, "Grasp this divining arrow[393] in your hand and see if you recognize your
[158] brother Joseph or not." And he grasped the arrow in his hand and looked at it and said, "You are my brother Joseph." At that time, Joseph and Benjamin made a pledge not to let his brothers know. And Joseph said to Benjamin, "Would you like to stay with me a few days until I am reunited with my brothers?" He said to him, "O brother, what will you do?" He said to him, "As soon as we give you your sacks,[394] I will put this arrow in your sack and I will know

388. Compare Q 12:64: "Am I to trust you with him as I once trusted you with his brother?"

389. JA: *fidāʾ binyamīn.*

390. JA: *tʿrf.* Meaning uncertain.

391. JA: *il-ṣiddīq.*

392. JA: *yaʿraff 'il-nagm.*

393. JA: *qadaḥ.*

394. JA: *shikaratkūm.* Wehr gives *shikāra* as a word of Egyptian dialectical origin.

what to do." And he set out for them food and drink and gave to the oldest according to his older age, while to the youngest—who was Benjamin—he gave twice their measure. And he took the cup and grasped it in his hand and said, "The cup tells me that you, Reuben, are the oldest, sit here; and you, Simeon, sit here," and each one sat according to the order of his birth.[395] When they left off eating, Joseph got up and placed the arrow in Benjamin's sack,
59] and [the Brothers] departed.[396] And Joseph said to his entourage, "Go, run[397] after this people and bring them."

As soon as they came, they offered up praise to him. And he said to them, "Is this my reward from you, that you take the silver arrow from the tablecloth? Where is this arrow so that I may pronounce your judgment upon it?" And all of them said, "O our master, the king, whomever you find the arrow with shall be killed." And he said to them, "I will not kill; instead, he will be a slave unto me." And all of them said, "Whatever you judge for us is permissible." And they were searched from the oldest to the youngest, and the arrow was found in Benjamin's sack. And they proceeded to tear their garments and cry. And he said to them, "You will go to your father in peace, but the young one most certainly will be a slave unto me." And Judah stood up before him and said to him, "You, my master, let this young one go to his father and I will serve in his place." Joseph said to him, "Never. The one with whom it was found is my slave." And Judah began to shout and say, "O my master, do not take this boy; he is beautiful,[398] not for service; if it be for splitting wood, I
60] am stronger than him, and if it be for service, I am cleverer than him. Also, he is a beardless boy. My forefather, Abraham the Faithful—on account of Abimelech taking my lady Sarah for one night only (though he did not approach her), God tried [that king] with epilepsy, so how will you take this child?" And Joseph said to Judah, "I am not moved by these words." And Judah began to shout and say, "Give us our brother out of kindness." And Joseph said, "This one is my slave." And Judah said, "If you do not give us our brother, by God, we will destroy wall on top of wall." And Joseph said to them, "Show me your cleverness."

And Judah arose and shouted to Naphtali, saying to him, "Go see how many cities and how many walls there are in Egypt," and he sent off

395. See BR 92:5, 93:7; *Tanḥuma* Va-yigash 4.
396. Scribal error. Text reads *yā rāḥū*.
397. Reading *igrū* for *igdū*.
398. JA: *shayq*. The word *shāʾiq* means "beautiful, or arousing longing."

Naphtali.[399] And Naphtali returned and said to him, "Twelve cities[400] and three walls." And Judah got up and said, "I will take three cities and a wall, and each one of you a city, and then together descend upon the two walls and destroy
[161] them." And Joseph said, "Why did you not react so when you first sold Joseph your brother? And why did you, O Judah, say upon the selling of your brother, 'Throw the son of Rachel in the well'? And why did none of your brothers protest except you?" And Judah said, "O master, I have guaranteed him for his father." And Joseph said, "This one will definitely be my slave."

The Sages, peace upon them, said that when Judah's temper flared against Joseph, he drew his sword from its scabbard and said to his brothers in Hebrew, "There is no doubt that this one is from the Tribes."[401] And Judah gave a yell and the world was laid waste; and the sun was concealed; and the walls fell down; and pregnant women miscarried; and Joseph fell off his throne onto his face. [Now] Judah had two hairs on his nipples; when his temper flared, those two hairs would burgeon forth.[402] At that time, the two hairs went out
[162] and burned his garments and blood spurted. At that time, Joseph signaled[403] his son Manasseh because he felt sorry for Judah. And Manasseh got up out of sympathy for Judah and soothed his temper.

And with that, Joseph said to all the soldiers who were present, "Go outside, all of you, except for this people; leave them with me so that I may speak with them." Whereupon Joseph said to his brothers, "What would you say to one who brings you your brother Joseph?" And all of them were astonished and began to say, "O Joseph, O son of Jacob, come to me. O Joseph, O son of Jacob, come to me." And they began to look right and left. And Joseph said to them, "You need not look all about you: I am Joseph, the son of Jacob." And all of them were amazed, and they were unable to answer him. At that time, Joseph did an unwholesome deed[404] because he and his brothers were sitting alone and he knew his soul,[405] and he showed them his circumcision and so

399. Based on Jacob's blessing of him in Gen. 49:21—"Naphtali, a hind let loose," which the Rabbis interpreted as a reference to his swiftness and the reason he was delegated to act here as messenger.

400. JA: *itnashar bilād.* QSY^2 has "ten markets."

401. This same motif of recognition as a kinsman appears below (*Joseph,* 162) when Manasseh is able to soothe Judah's temper through his touch.

402. See above, *Joseph,* 81.

403. Or, "winked at." JA: *ghamaz.*

404. JA: *ʿamlah mā tanfaʿ.*

405. JA: *ʿaraf rūḥū.* Meaning uncertain. In BR 93:10, it is recorded at this point in the story that Joseph *paraʿ et ʿatzmo.* Thus, we may have here a bilingual pun on the word *paraʿ* (with the transposition of the first and third radicals).

they recognized him.[406] And at that moment they praised him three times,
63] and he gave them gifts and they were overjoyed. Then he fell upon his full-brother, Benjamin, and he cried, and all his brothers cried with him.

Then after that, Joseph arose and opened the treasury and gave to each brother a precious suit, and they sat with him in joy and happiness. And Joseph ordered that fodder be given to their donkeys, and he gave them from all the blessings of Egypt. (Seraḥ, daughter of Asher, all the while Joseph was in Egypt and Jacob was in sorrow, would say, "Manasseh and Ephraim and Joseph are alive in Egypt," and the prophet Jacob would rebuke her and say to her, "Why do you cause me pain, O daughter?" And as soon as Joseph was reunited with his father, Jacob, God arose and called her to enter the Garden of Eden alive.)

Then after that, he sent a gift to his father and said to his brothers, "Arise and travel to him and bring your father. Do not weary yourselves on the way." They set out and began to rebuke themselves, each saying to the other, "You
64] were the cause of Joseph's sale." And Reuben said,[407] "You did not heed me, but God, may He be exalted, issued His command, and He saw Joseph's broken heart and his father's sorrow." And they said to him, "O Reuben, how will we greet our father Jacob and inform him of Joseph, as that shameful deed happened because of us?" And Reuben said to them, "Do not be afraid. We will all of us gather together and send word to our sons and our daughters to come out and greet us, and we will order them to clap and cheer, and we will inform them about Joseph." And they said to him, "This is a beautiful idea."

Now when Joseph was lost, prophecy was lifted from Jacob for nineteen years. And God, may He be praised and exalted, inspired Gabriel, peace upon him, to descend to Jacob, who was sitting upon the roadways looking for Benjamin with eyes blinded from crying for Joseph. When Gabriel came up to him, he said to him, "Peace upon you, O Prophet of God." And Jacob lifted
65] his head and returned the greeting to him. And he saw before him a magnificent man,[408] and Jacob said, "And upon you peace. Have you come to deliver tidings of my beloved Joseph?" Gabriel said to him, "I did not announce it to you, so who informed you that Joseph is alive?" And he said to him, "Since my beloved Joseph departed I have been deprived of my sight and prophecy

406. H: *il-mīlah*. See BR 93:4, 10. In al-Kisāʾī (188), Joseph removes his crown from his head, revealing a mark identical to one on Jacob's head.

407. Scribal error. The text reads *qāla li-reʾūven*.

408. JA: *rūglan bahīq*. Hinds-Badawi gives *bahi* as "radiant, pleasant, full of happiness," and *bahīy* with the same meaning, but in reference to Muḥammad, it is used as an epithet for the Prophet: *bahiy al-nūr*—"Shining with light."

has been lifted from me. But when you greeted me, I lifted my head and saw your face, and I knew that you were coming to announce Joseph."[409]

Three days later, Jacob went out to meet his children, and with him were his children's children, and his wives, and his slaves, and all who were in his household. And all who heard that his sight had returned to him came to him to congratulate him. Then after that, Master Jacob arose along with all those who were with him, and no one stayed behind, not bird or beast; rather they followed Jacob with shouts and clapping until the earth shook at that time. And when Jacob's sons drew near to the mountain of Canaan[410] and they heard shouting and clapping and dancing and drumming, they said to each other, "What can this be as our father, Jacob, has not yet heard about Joseph?" And
[166] Judah said, "O brothers, perhaps some woman has given birth to a male child and this rejoicing is for him." And when they drew near, they saw Jacob in front of his sons and his daughters, and he was girdled at the waist and he was shouting and clapping and dancing and saying, "Praised be God who fortified my heart and showed me my beloved Joseph." And when they saw their father, they were overjoyed. And when they saw that his eyes were open, they said, "O prophet of God, who brought you tidings of Joseph?" And he said to them, "My fear of what will come of your evil deeds is not for my sake." And they fell down in his presence and kissed his feet and threw themselves down before him and said, "O prophet of God, we ask you by God and by the gray hair of Abraham the Faithful not to blame us for what we did." And he said to them, "It is as I have told you; He will reward the patient with good."[411] Then Jacob entered his residence, and no one remained behind, but all came there; even the beasts and the birds came to congratulate him.

[167] And when Jacob saw the carts that Joseph had sent to carry their father, he did not accept it as true[412] until he went to Joseph. And his sons carried him on the carts in joy and happiness until they reached the outskirts of Egypt. And when they came to within seven miles of Egypt, the scout came to Joseph and told him that his father was coming. And Joseph entered unto the king and

409. In the Qurʾān, 12:92–96, along with his brothers, Joseph sends to Jacob his shirt, whose scent the father is already able to perceive when they set off. Moreover, this shirt restores Jacob's sight once it is cast upon his face in accord with Joseph's directions. According to al-Kisāʾī (182), this shirt is the very same one that the Brothers had presented to Jacob spattered with blood. It has made its way to Egypt after Jacob gave it to Benjamin to wear when he departs with his brothers. Al-Kisāʾī also identifies "the bearer of good news" as being Judah (189).

410. JA: *gabal kanaʿan.*

411. JA: *la-qad yuʿāwid il-ṣabirīn kheir.* See *Joseph,* 156 and 170 for the same expression.

412. JA: *ṣaddaq.*

informed him that his father was coming. And the king sent to Jacob saying to him, "Halt where you are. Do not enter Egypt until I come to you." Then Jacob sat down and, lo and behold, the famine came to an end so that [the Egyptians] might be blessed by Jacob.[413]

And when five years of the famine had elapsed, the people of Egypt came to Joseph asking food of him. He said to them, "Bring gold and silver and I shall provide you food." And they said to him, "There does not remain in the land of Egypt neither silver or gold nor jewelry or clothing; nothing remains save ourselves and our children and our women." And Joseph said to them, "Sell yourselves and you shall be slaves unto the king." And there did not remain in Egypt neither man nor woman nor infant who did not become
68] Joseph's slaves. And when the time of sowing came, he said to them, "You shall give a fifth part to Pharaoh and the [other] four will be yours." And they said, "Yes indeed!" And Joseph recorded it in his handwriting and it served as witness for them that they and their children had become Pharaoh's slaves. That is what happened.

As for what happened with Zulaykhā: her body became emaciated and her vision was obscured. And every Thursday, Joseph would go around his kingdom, direct the affairs of the people, deliver[414] the oppressed from oppression, and treat the subjects with fairness. And God, may He be exalted, let love of him fall in their hearts. And Zulaykhā moved from her kingdom and built a hut of cane and sat in it. And Joseph would not turn toward her. And she had an idol that she worshipped. And when Joseph passed by her, she held his horse and said to him, "O Joseph, by the right of the one who raised you up and brought me down, and made you mighty and humbled me, hear a couple of words from me." And he did not raise his head to her until she [. . .][415] in
69] God, may He be praised. And she went in unto her idol and said to him, "I despise you; you have liberated from me my slave and my mameluke," and she threw it with all her bodily strength and broke it. And she said, "I am a disbeliever in you and a believer in my Lord, the Lord of Joseph." And when Joseph passed her way a second time, she grabbed the horse's reins and said, "O Joseph, I am a disbeliever in idols and a believer in your God." And when she believed in God, may He be exalted, she turned to Joseph, and Joseph

413. The text here is missing the account of Jacob's actual entrance into Egypt and his reunion with Joseph. In contrast, QSYTunis (62a–b) details the elaborate preparations made to welcome Joseph's father.

414. JA: *yunṣur.*

415. JA: *tʿtdnī.* Meaning uncertain.

said, "Carry this old woman to my residence." And when Joseph returned to his residence, he brought her before him and said to her, "O old woman, do you have a request?" She said, "Yes indeed, I have three requests: the first, that you call out to your Lord that He may restore my sight to me; the second, that He make me to be a twelve-year-old girl again; and the third, that you marry me, for I believe in God." And he said to her, "Beforehand I was not free to do to you as you deserved. But I am your mameluke, so do not be of the ignorant." At that time he struck her neck with the sword and left her and went away.[416]

The Sages, peace upon them, said that Jacob the Prophet lived in Egypt
[170] seventeen years in honor and great comfort in Joseph's kingdom. And when Jacob grew old, he called his sons and kissed Joseph between his eyes and said, "O my son, I bid you to obey God with respect to your brothers—not to punish them for what they did with you—for God requites the patient with good." And when [Joseph] heard the words of his father, he cried and said, "O my father, if I had wanted evil for them that would have been beforehand, but now I know that this was not from them, but from God, so that He might make me a king in Egypt." Then Jacob called his sons and said to them, "I charge you by God that you are Joseph's slaves under his authority." And they bowed their heads to the ground in deference to Joseph.

Then Jacob said to Joseph, "I am [. . .][417] to my people, and I desire of your kindness[418] that you will take me out of Egypt and bury me with my two forefathers, Abraham and Isaac, in the cave which [Abraham] bought for four
[171] hundred *miskal* of silver."[419] And Joseph said, "Your wish is my command, my father." And he said, "Swear it to me." So he extended his hand and made a compact with his father. Then Jacob saw Joseph's children and said, "Who are these?" He said, "My sons. Bless them, my father." And Jacob said, "I will not bless them." And so Joseph got up and brought the certificate of marriage,[420] and when Jacob saw that, he blessed them. And he bade farewell to his sons and began to say this verse:

416. QSYTunis (64a) has this as a hypothetical statement: Were it not for his fear of god he would have struck her with his sword. Contrast this, for example, with al-Kisāʾī (179–80), where Joseph restores to Zulaykhā her wealth, while God restores her beauty, and she becomes Joseph's virginal bride and the mother of Ephraim and Manasseh.

417. JA: *mnḍār.* Meaning uncertain.

418. JA: *astahī min iḥsanak.*

419. I.e., the Cave of Machpelah in Hebron. According to Hinds-Badawi the *miskal* is a unit of weight that in Egypt is equal to 4.68 grams.

420. H: *ketūbah.*

Bid me farewell, my children,
    But I do not have the heart to give you my final testament.
And you will not be my eyes, so how,
    My children, will I bring reason to you?
I will say to you only a single word;
    It will not pain you.
Gentlemen, my heart, and my soul,
    And my thoughts[421] go with you.

Then after that, Gabriel descended, and with him were seventy thousand Angels of Delight,[422] and they came to Jacob, and [Gabriel] said to him, "O prophet of God, I bring the glad tidings that God extends His greetings to you and says to you that your abode is with your forefathers." And thereupon, Jacob was taken unto God's mercy. And Joseph fell upon his father and cried; even
72] the king cried and their sorrow was great. Then Joseph directed the embalmers to embalm Jacob and place him in a box of white crystal inlaid with all manner of jewels.[423] And the king said to Joseph, "Take with you all the soldiers of Egypt and go forth and bury your father in the cave as he entrusted you." And Joseph set out, and with him went all the soldiers and merchants of Egypt. And the sorrow and crying for Jacob was great. Then Joseph did as his father had enjoined him, and Jacob was united with the Righteous Forefathers.[424]

Then when Joseph's brothers saw that their father had died, they said to each other, "Perhaps Joseph will treat us as we did him." And Judah said to them, "Do not be afraid, for Joseph is a merciful man and fearful of God. If he had wanted to destroy you, he would have done so already." And they fell down
73] before Joseph and said to him, "We are your slaves." And Joseph cried and said, "O my brothers, indeed I fear God, may He be exalted, and though you had reckoned me the most wicked cruelty,[425] God has accounted it for good."

And Seraḥ the daughter of Asher, arose and took up her instrument and began to recite a song of praise[426] about what happened to Joseph:

421. Literally, "mind."

422. Mentioned in *Joseph,* 46, in connection with the blessings brought to the land upon Joseph's entrance into Egypt.

423. This embalming is in accord with biblical account (see Gen. 50:2–3). The Rabbis were subsequently to forbid this practice.

424. JA: *il-abāʾ il-ṣāliḥīn.*

425. JA: *wiḥish awsharr.*

426. JA: *tasbīḥā.*

Joseph was beautiful in his day,
    And no one was perfect like him.
And all knowledge was in his breast,
    And the crown of prophecy, complete.
To seven forefathers of his forefathers,[427] a protégé
    Like unto perfection, he was related.
He saw in a dream, peace upon him, the interpretation of the words set up above
    the throne:
    "And to him bowed down the sons of Jacob."
He began to his brothers to boast,
    And by the design of the dream to mock—
"I have seen a dream, O my brothers
    All of us will return to the tree.
Their trees, all of them will lag behind,
    While I will bow down in comfort."
His brothers say, "He is insolent with us."
    They prepared spells for him.[428]
[174] He[429] said, "Joseph is cherished by our father."
    [Joseph] did not go out at all because of fear.
When his father said to him that day,
    "O Joseph, go to the pasture.
        See for me what is the news of this people
            And the sheep that are grazing."
[Joseph] departed from him; he was asleep,
    He did not know what he was called to do.
The angel saw him. He said to him, "We see you.
    Go back, O miserable one. They have sat you down in an oppressive
    place."
When he approached them, they said, "The dreamer has approached his
    slaughter."
They beguiled him, "And he reached us and was obtained.
    God, may He be exalted, is great.
        He has cast him down for us in the well."
And they dropped Joseph bound
    to the depths of the well, with hands tied and arms crossed.
Then they sat down to lunch.
    Every living thing is prepared for its slaughter.

427. These may very well be identical to those in whose name he tied the knots in his trousers. See *Joseph,* 101–2.

428. JA: *ʿabū lahū il-suḥūr.*

429. These lines of verse are excerpted from a longer poetic version that follows in the codex and constitute the first four stanzas (as well as the first line of the fifth) of that work.

75] And Joseph resided, he and his brothers, after the death of their father, in great comfort for seventy years. And Joseph saw his sons and the sons of his sons, and he died at the age of 110 years. And the people of Egypt mourned him until Moses, peace upon him, came, and the Israelites ascended with him out of Egypt. Then Moses came and brought them out of Egypt. And peace on all of Israel. Amen. Thus may it be Thy will. Amen Selah. And peace upon all Children of Scripture.[430]

I have finished with the help of God, may He be exalted. And this is
76] all.[431] I wrote this with my own hand, the servant, the youth, Joseph ha-Levi,
the rabbi, May he meet a good end,[432] son of the Elder and the Teacher,[433]
Abraham ha-Levi, May He Rest in Eden, son of the Rabbi the Elder and the
Teacher, Moses ha-Levi, May He Rest in Eden.[434] Amen Selah. Amen May
It Be Thy Will. Cursed is the plagiarizer of it and blessed is the reader of it.
Cursed is the eraser of my name from upon it. A[men] A[men] A[men].

Its completion was on the fourth day of the week in the order of Mishpaṭim.[435] And it is the 23rd day of the month of Shevaṭ in the year five thousand and five hundred and seven and ninety since the creation of the world. This corresponds to the Arabic month of Shuwāl in the year 1252.[436] And peace upon all of Israel. Amen. Selah.

77] [Hebrew alphabet]

Bought by me, the servant, the youth, the pleasant, the beautiful, Isaac, may his end be good, son of my father and my lord and the crown of my head, Rabbi Joseph, Head of the Community, may his end be good, son of [. . .][437] Elisha the Cantor, may he rest in Eden, who asks of his God

Up from Egypt to bring him,
And in Jerusalem to settle him,
And the Temple to show him.

430. I.e., the Karaites. The whole sentence is given here in Hebrew: *wi-shalom ʿal kol yisraʾel a[men] k[en] y[ihyeh] r[atzon] a[me]n s[elah] wi-shalōm ʿal kol bʾnei miqraʾ*. (The word *selah* is of uncertain etymology but appears seventy-one times in the Book of Psalms.) *The Story of Yusuf, Son of Jacob* ends with a corresponding Muslim formula: "May the grace of Allah be upon every Muslim man and woman, amen. And praise unto Allah, Lord of the Universe" (*Yusuf,* 227).

431. JA and H: *kamalt bi-ʿ[ezrat] allāh tʿ[ālā] wi-shalōm.*

432. H abbr.: *s*[*ofo*] *ṭ*[*ov*].

433. H abbr.: *ha-z*[*aken*] *ha-m*[*oreh*].

434. H abbr.: *n*[*ishmato*] *ʿ*[*eden*].

435. I.e., the weekly reading from the Torah.

436. Corresponding to January/February 1837 CE.

437. *ʾhy wʾhw.* Meaning uncertain.

II

THE MOST BEAUTIFUL OF STORIES

1

A Pearl in the Dust

And Jacob dwelled in the land of his father's sojournings, in the land of Canaan. This is the lineage of Jacob—Joseph, seventeen years old, was tending the flock with his brothers. . . .

Gen. 37:1–2

While *The Story of Our Master Joseph* may be viewed as primarily an adaptation of an Islamic tale, from the perspective of its Jewish Arabic-speaking audience the tale was an unquestioned part of their own cultural legacy. Moreover, on a deeper level, it exhibits an eclectic pattern of intertextual relationships with a wide range of exegetical material from different cultures (a fact that also characterizes its ostensible *Vorlage, The Story of Yusuf*). As an expanded retelling of the scriptural stories of Jacob's favorite son, *Joseph* makes use of Islamic and Jewish aggadic motifs surrounding this figure, gathering them together and weaving them into a relatively seamless whole. Both of these Abrahamic traditions have themselves been influenced by ancient Near Eastern and Hellenistic material. The catholic tendencies of the Judeo-Arabic text serve to confirm the claim set out in its preamble to comprise an exhaustive and accurate telling of the tale. The narrative demonstrates the gap-filling role midrash plays vis-à-vis the scriptural versions; it also serves as an excellent example of the relative open-endedness of the midrashic mode, and, of particular importance for our purposes, its permeability to outside traditions. Indeed, what is most fascinating about this work is the extent to which it seemingly, without hesitation, incorporates material from both Judaic and Islamic cultures, thereby blurring the boundaries between them.

Tracing the intercultural connections within the midrashic elaborations of the Joseph story has of late been the focus of several studies that explore the development of these hermeneutic traditions. This may very well constitute another manifestation of the liberal zeitgeist that has predisposed scholars to search out intersections and possible areas of "symbiosis" or synergism between religio-cultural systems otherwise viewed as mutually competitive, or even hostile, toward one another. Such an effort to seek out a palliative within the context of the contemporary history of strife and contention between Muslims and Jews no doubt adheres to the present study.[1]

Drawing on these works and the theoretical insights derived from the literary study of the Hebrew Bible and midrash, we will now examine *The Story of Our Master Joseph,* focusing on the parallel Jewish and Islamic traditions that time and again intersect in this particular text. Of special import will be the rich Islamic exegetical traditions of "The Stories of the Prophets" (*qiṣaṣ al-anbiyāʾ*). The perspective adopted will be one that views the body of extrascriptural material on those characters that appear in both the Bible and the Qurʾān as comprising a discourse transcending religious, historical, and linguistic bounds. Wherever possible, we will attempt to locate the element within the biblical or quranic narrative that serves as the trigger for a specific expansion or, to switch metaphors, the "hook" upon which the elaboration may be hung—whether it be an unexplained gap, repetition, or seemingly incongruous detail. However, the focus will most squarely fall on the pattern of integration of this diverse material within *The Story of Our Master Joseph,* and thus, in general, the often murky question of the origins of a specific motif will remain open.

We will begin by looking at the character of Joseph as presented in the scriptural versions and developed in subsequent versions of the story, focusing on his physical beauty and moral attributes and the exegetes' concern for their genetic source. Afterwards, we will trace the narrative expansions that treat the relations between Joseph and Jacob's other sons. Here the emphasis will be on the theme of sibling rivalry and the roles of the father and favored son in fomenting such familial strife. The story of Joseph and Zulaykhā will next be examined for its incorporation of midrashic and extraquranic material that treat the mistress's desperate attempts to entice her servant and his ability to resist her. Finally, the analysis will culminate in an exploration of the suggestive ways in which these two subplots are linked in the exegetical traditions, and what the selective use of these traditions may teach us about the tensions characterizing the minority culture that generated *The Story of Our Master Joseph.* We will explore the ways in which *Joseph* functions as an independent work: one that draws on *midrashīm* generated by the Bible but whose origins and ad hoc nature are now concealed in an attempt to create a continuous narrative. In addition to a general analysis of metatextual elements within the story—namely, the midrashic expansions of the biblical story contained within the various midrashic accounts—we will also be highlighting the intertextual relationship of *The Story of Our Master Joseph* to other Jewish and Islamic traditions surrounding the story. Thus, the analysis will proceed on two fronts: by exploring the ways in which gaps in the Bible motivated certain interpretations, we will be attempting to recover to the extent possible the "lost origins" of these midrashic expansions. At the same time, by considering the pattern of borrowing that ensued in Jewish and Islamic works we will hope to better understand the nature of the byways, or "the subterranean passageways," along which these narrative elaborations traveled.

"This Is the Lineage of Jacob—Joseph"

The Story of Our Master Joseph, befitting its singular focus on Joseph and its independence from a larger narrative framework (as opposed to the Joseph cycle in Genesis), makes do with a most brief introduction to Jacob and his family. In cursory fashion, it mentions only that there are twelve sons and four wives and that two of the sons were from the most beautiful and righteous of these women, Rachel; similarly, among the sons one of these was the most beautiful and righteous of all the sons. With just this barest of backgrounds, the plot commences directly with Joseph's boyhood dreams of his future ascendancy within the family hierarchy. This immediate zooming in on the single character of Joseph out of all Jacob's sons—who are at this point unnamed (as are the wives other than Rachel)—has of course its rationale in the narrative imperative of such a bildungsroman, but it also has an ancient precedent in the perplexing beginning of the story of Joseph in the Bible.

Genesis 37 seems to begin with a genealogical listing of Jacob's descendants, but then inexplicably the needle of the narrative record player, as it were, gets lodged in a groove and for the bulk of all the remaining chapters of Genesis we hear the story of one specific son—Joseph. The Joseph cycle, in its length (overwhelming by far the tales of all the other ancient Israelite ancestors), its development of characters, and its interweaving of several narrative threads, exhibits literary sophistication not yet encountered within the biblical narrative. In contrast to the preceding case of Esau, and as one might anticipate from the use of the identical introductory formula—"this is the lineage of Jacob" (*eileh toldot yaʿakov*)—there is no detailed list of generations of Jacob. Instead, the expected flow is jarringly disrupted by the words that ensue. Robert Alter's sensitive translation of the book of Genesis has preserved here the roughness of the original with the syntactic disjunction between the two phrases indicated graphically by the insertion of an em-dash between them: "This is the lineage of Jacob—Joseph, seventeen years old, was tending the flock with his brothers. . . ." (Gen. 37:2). The tenth-century Babylonian scholar, Saʿadya Gaʾon, in his Arabic commentary on this verse, supplies the emendation necessary for the verse to make any literal sense—"When Joseph was [seventeen years old] . . ."[2]—and yet the disjunction here also serves a narrative purpose. This is a braking of the anticipated rapid pace of the genealogical list or summary which in the Bible typically serves as a transition between events, or for the presentation of background material. It is also therefore a "breaking" of the convention for such lists that calls out for the audience's attention.

The character of the narrative in the previous two chapters of Genesis reinforces our anticipation that a list will ensue. At the end of chapter 35, following the birth of Benjamin, Jacob's last son, and the death of Rachel, the number of Jacob's sons is totaled and their names listed according to their birthmother: "And the sons of Jacob were twelve. The sons of Leah: Jacob's firstborn Reuben and Simeon and Levi and Judah and Issachar and Zebulon. The sons of Rachel: Joseph and Benjamin. And the sons of Bilhah, Rachel's slavegirl: Dan and Naphtali. And the sons of Zilpah, Leah's slavegirl: Gad and Asher. These are the sons of Jacob who were born to him in Paddan-aram" (Gen. 35:22–26).[3] Immediately afterwards the text records the death of Isaac. This intermediary figure of the triad of Israel's patriarchs is not nearly as developed as his father or son in Genesis, and has at this point been absent from the narrative since the middle of chapter 28. However, his death brings together his sons Jacob and Esau, who have for many years been estranged from one another. Their joining now to bury their father is the occasion for the digression relating the line of Esau, the firstborn, which takes up all of chapter 36.

In keeping with biblical convention, the passing of the father (Isaac)—his death representing at least a putative threat to the continuation of the line—motivates the lists that confirm his descendants in accordance with the divine promise. The genealogy of Esau's descendants, like that of Jacob later, is given in two forms: first, the line of immediate descent of his sons according to their respective mothers: "And this is the lineage of Esau, that is, Edom. . . ." (Gen. 36:1–5). After mentioning that Esau needed to relocate his family, as the land could not support the cattle of both brothers, the remainder of the chapter consists of the extension of the list to Esau's descendants born in the land of Seir. While this listing begins with the very similar formula and recapitulates the first generation of descent, there follows a more detailed accounting stretching over thirty-five verses that establishes the clan lines and various etiologies and the names of the tribal chieftains: "And this is the lineage of Esau, father of Edom, in the high country of Seir. These are the names of the sons of Esau: Eliphaz son of Adah. . . ." (Gen. 36:9–10ff).

The beginning of chapter 37, then, would seem to be a resumption of the narrative stream after a fairly long digession on the descendants of Esau. However, while the chapter begins with an introduction to the genealogy of Jacob—"And Jacob dwelled in the land of his father's sojournings, in the land of Canaan. This is the lineage of Jacob . . ." (37:1–2)—the reader's expectations of a list commensurate with those supplied for Esau's line are immediately undermined by the abrupt insertion of the Joseph story. This detour will stretch on for the ensuing ten chapters. Now, as the primary function of the Joseph story within the context of Genesis is to explain the descent of Israel into Egypt in accord with God's plan for His people, when the biblical narrator eventually provides the delayed list of Jacob's descendants according to birth order, it is explicitly within the context of this migration: "And these are the names of the children of Israel, who came to Egypt, Jacob and his sons: Jacob's firstborn, Reuben . . ." (Gen. 46:8).

The digressive character of the Joseph tale thematizes the tale's significance in providing the complicated sequence of events that will bring about this peregrination and so set the stage for Israelite liberation under Moses, the revelation at Sinai, the consolidation of national identity, and the conquest of Canaan—that is, the realization of Jewish peoplehood. Indeed, in this regard it is interesting that Josephus in the *Antiquities* ends Book One of the work with the death of Isaac (corresponding to the end of chapter 35 in Genesis), while Book Two begins anachronistically with a flashback to Esau's sale of his firstborn rights that leads directly into the listing of his descendants. The entire remainder of this Book is nearly equally divided between the narration of the story of Joseph and the story of the Exodus from Egypt, thereby emphasizing the link between these two pericopes.

Alter has succinctly described this technique of "slowing-down" narrative time, a disruption of the summary mode that sets off and defines a narrative "event":

> A proper narrative event occurs when the narrative tempo slows down for us to discriminate a particular scene; to have the illusion of the scene's "presence" as it unfolds; to be able to imagine the interaction of personages or sometimes personages and groups, together with the freight of motivations,

> ulterior aims, character traits, political, social, or religious constraints, moral and theological meanings, borne by their speech, gestures, and acts. . . . These are the moments when the fictional imagination . . . is in full operation.[4]

In the case of the Joseph cycle, this is not simply a "narrative event" or a focusing on a particular scene, but rather a shift into an expansive mode. The transition from the cursory listing of Esau's descendants to the fleshed-out account of Jacob and his sons was noticed by earlier "critics." The eleventh-century Provençal biblical exegete, Rashi, in his comment to this first verse of the Joseph cycle, relates that:

> After it [Scripture] has described to you the settlements of Esau and his descendants in a brief manner, since they were not distinguished and important enough, . . . it explains clearly and at length the settlements made by Jacob and his descendants and all the events which brought these about, because these are regarded by the Omnipresent as of sufficient presence to speak of them at length. Thus, too, you will find that in the case of the ten generations from Adam to Noah it states "So-and-so begat so-and-so," but when it reaches Noah it deals with him at length. Similarly, of the ten generations from Noah to Abraham it gives but a brief account, but when it comes to Abraham it speaks of him more fully. (Rashi, *Commentary on Genesis* 37:1)

Midrash Tanḥuma provides a parable that explains why the expansive story of Jacob and his sons is preceded by the brief account of Esau and his descendants:

> *This is the lineage of Jacob—Joseph* . . . What precedes this? *These are the chieftains of the sons of Esau* . . . (Gen. 36:15ff). Why did The-Holy-One-Blessed-Be-He occupy Himself first with the genealogy of the gentiles (*umot ha-ʿolam*)? This may be compared to a king who had a pearl that had been cast amongst dust and bundles. The king had to dig about in the dust and bundles in order to find the pearl. Having found it, he left the dust and bundles and occupied himself with the pearl. Thus did The-Holy-One-Blessed-Be-He occupy himself with the past generations in outline and left them, etc. When He reached Abraham, Isaac, and Jacob he began to occupy himself with them. For that reason, the section on the chieftains of the sons of Esau is juxtaposed to this one. (*Tanḥuma* [Zundel edition] Va-yeishev 1)

Reflecting the relative lack of importance of the older brother's chain of descent, Josephus actually abbreviates the listing of Esau's progeny, omitting all those named in Genesis 36:20–42.[5]

Indeed, the purpose of first providing Esau's genealogy is analogous to the justification underlying the earlier listing of Ishmael's descendants in chapter 25, after it becomes clear that Isaac will supplant him. In each case, the biblical narrator provides in summary form the limited blessings of fertility and power that each firstborn son will receive, despite their ultimately being passed over as bearers of the covenantal line. The narrative must first dispense with the seeming incongruity of the firstborn son's loss of that status—which should be his by "natural" right—before it may move on to consider those through whom the line will continue in fulfillment of the divine plan. In this case, however, despite Joseph's superior status, the other sons of Jacob are the fathers of the respective tribes and forefathers of the Jewish people and, therefore, they cannot be summarily dismissed by means of a genealogical listing. Indeed, it is at this point in Genesis that the narrative moves from vertical tales of descent from father to son, to a horizontal mode detailing the events that transpire within the family of Jacob.

In perhaps the most extreme aggrandizement of Joseph's stature within the biblical history, the Rabbis bring a variety of prooftexts to show that Joseph was the underlying motivation for events both preceding and following his life:

> *This is the lineage of Jacob—Joseph* (Gen. 37:2). These generations (*toldot*) were born only for Joseph's sake. For Jacob went to Laban for no other purpose than to marry Rachel. These generations waited until Joseph was born, as it says: *And it happened, when Rachel bore Joseph, that Jacob said to Laban, "Send me off"* (ibid., 30:25). Who brought [the Children of Israel] down to Egypt? Joseph. The [Red] Sea was divided only for Joseph's sake. Thus it is written: *The waters saw You O God* [*and were rent in two*], which is preceded by: *You have with Your arm redeemed Your people, the sons of Jacob and Joseph* (Ps. 77:16–17). R. Judan said: The Jordan too was divided only for Joseph's sake. (BR 84:5)

The Qurʾān itself refrains from providing any introduction to the tale. After an initial prologue vaunting the sublime quality of the tale, with no exposition presenting the characters (including, for that matter, their names) or the setting, the narrative launches right into Joseph's report to his father of his dream of the celestial bodies. The actual dream event is not recorded, nor is any other context provided. This interpretive vacuum is filled by the literature of the Stories of the Prophets; these, in turn, often had recourse to biblicist sources. Al-Kisāʾī, for example, like the author of *Joseph,* considers each of the mothers of Jacob's children a wife. This interpretation could very well have its origin in a literal reading of the biblical verse, which refers to these women as "[Joseph's] father's wives" (Gen. 37:2). Moreover, al-Kisāʾī, in clear contrast to the biblical account, has the other two wives, who are assigned names with no apparent connection to the biblical proxy-wives, also be daughters of Laban; Jacob marries each sister in succession following the death of the previous wife. Al-Kisāʾī also gives the names of Jacob's other sons and relates some of Joseph's earlier history. These include reference to five precious items that have been passed down to Joseph from Abraham; a dream of the Brothers' staffs; mention of Jacob's failure to provide food to a poor boy; and his ominous dreams of a wolf attack on Joseph. These all lead up to the single dream recorded in the Qurʾān that begins the story there.[6] In all these extra-biblical retellings, Jewish and Muslim, we see how the gaps or idiosyncrasies of the Genesis narrative have been exploited to offer a more "complete" account.

"He Takes After His . . ."

At various junctures over the course of *The Story of Our Master Joseph* narrative, Joseph's connection with Rachel is emphasized—as is the special status of both mother and son in the heart and mind of Jacob. This is evident from the outset when we are introduced to both characters:

> *The Sages, peace upon them, said* that there was among the prophets one whose name was Jacob, peace upon him, who had four wives. And among these wives there was one more righteous than the others. She was beautiful to behold and of elegant appearance, and he [Jacob] loved her greatly. And Jacob the Prophet had twelve righteous sons—saints of God, of whom two were from that righteous woman. And one of them was more righteous than his brothers, and his name was Joseph. And Jacob, peace upon him, loved Joseph greatly, more than his brothers, due to Jacob's love for Joseph's mother, Lady Rachel, peace upon her. And Joseph was more righteous than his brothers; moreover, he was perfect in beauty and comeliness. And there was no one like him in that generation, or in all the other generations down to this very day. (*Joseph,* 1–2)

The text here, while singling out Rachel as the preferred wife, initially fails to identify her by name; neither are the names of the other brothers mentioned (even that of Benjamin, Rachel's other son), all of which serves to point the narrative spotlight directly at Joseph. Just as Rachel is distinguished from Jacob's other wives, so too is Joseph from his brothers; she embodies in her person the ideal union of beauty and righteousness, and so does Joseph. Joseph's special status is conveyed by the depiction of the special love his father bore him as "the most righteous and beautiful" son of "the most righteous and beautiful" of Jacob's wives.

How were the Rabbis to explain the seemingly redundant pair of terms used to describe both Rachel's and Joseph's beauty in Genesis: *yefeh to'ar* and *yefeh mar'eh* (in the case of the feminine, *yifat to'ar* and *yifat mar'eh*)?[7] These terms form a *hendiadys,* a literary device commonly employed for metric weight and emphasis in biblical parlance in which a single idea is expressed through two words typically linked by the word "and." These expressions typically assume the status of fixed clichés; however, given the rabbinic hermeneutic assumption of no textual redundancy, that every word in the Bible is necessary and has meaning both in itself and within the narrative context, the exegetes were able to exploit this apparent superfluity. In effect, they are able to defamiliarize the cliché and squeeze an interpretation into the space occupied by the conjunctive *vav* separating the two terms.

Here, the Hellenistic ideal of beauty, linking together both moral and physical attributes, has influenced the Rabbis. Thus, early Jewish interpreters of this pair of terms, motivated as well by the identity of the first terms of the construction ("if these are identical, surely the distinction must reside in the nature of the second term") sought to differentiate them by positing that they refer to Joseph's physical beauty *and* his moral/spiritual virtue, respectively. In an early pseudepigraphic work (going back possibly to the first or second century BCE), we see an extension of his physical attributes to the ethical plane and the positing of an explicit connection between inward and outward beauty: "Therefore Joseph was comely in appearance and beautiful to look upon, because no wickedness dwelt in him—for the face makes manifest the troubles of the spirit" (*Testament of Simeon* 5:1).

Josephus, the first-century Jewish historian and exegete, in his magnum opus, *Judean Antiquities* (completed in 93–94 CE), sought to establish the equal stature of the Jewish heroes according to these Hellenistic norms. Thus, Joseph, along with Moses, is distinguished among the heroes of Jewish history by the extent to which he combines in his person both moral virtue and physical beauty. While Josephus does relate Jacob's love for Joseph to his birth mother, the primary reason for the father's great affection derives from his son's physical and spiritual traits: "Jacob having fathered Joseph by Rachel, loved him more than the other sons because of the handsomeness of his body, owing to the nobility of his birth and the excellence of his soul, for he was outstanding in sagacity" (*Antiquities* 2:9). This abundance of love correlates with Josephus's earlier descriptions of the affection between Jacob and Rachel in which he extends the depth of Jacob's devotion well beyond the convention for betrothal scenes involving the Patriarchs. This level of ardor continues on even after Rachel's death, and in fact perhaps intensifies the degree to which it is transferred to her son. That central kabbalistic text, the *Zohar,* records this phenomenon: "R. Simeon said: At first Jacob spent all his days in grief; but once he had Joseph with him, then whenever he looked at his son he became whole in spirit, as though he were seeing Joseph's mother again, since Joseph in his comeliness resembled his mother. Then Jacob felt as though he had never suffered at all" (*Zohar* 1, 216b). While the description of Joseph's physical beauty is characteristic of Hellenistic writing, significantly, in this case it is related directly to the genetic link to Rachel.

However, it is clear in the passage from QSY that Joseph's priviledged status within the family is not because of any superior physical and moral endowments he may enjoy but rather simply because Rachel is his mother. Indeed, his mother's name is delayed and only provided when Jacob's predilection for Joseph is described. The text, however, then proceeds to elaborate why it is that descent from Rachel was not the only reason for Jacob's preference for Joseph. In all of these interpretations, the problem that was bothering the exegetes was ostensibly the fact that if this were the sole reason, then Benjamin should have been loved as much as his older sibling. The narrator thus needs to distinguish Joseph further and account for Jacob's love for him—and the envy of the Brothers—on the basis of his physical and moral beauty: "And Joseph was more righteous than his brothers and moreover, he was perfect in beauty and comeliness" (*Joseph,* 1).

In *Joseph,* the exegetical link to the original biblical hendiadys has been effaced, leading to a maximal interpretation of Joseph's physical and ethical traits. This pair of terms comes to emphasize his physical beauty, yet at the same time it is extended to provide a scriptural prooftext for his moral excellence. Indeed, the rectitude of his character is here given precedence over his beauty, as in context the mention of the latter quality strikes one as something of an afterthought. (Of course, his great beauty will play a crucial role in the plot, captivating as it does his master's wife.) Indeed, Joseph's greater degree of righteousness vis-à-vis his brothers is repeated twice, while the word "righteousness" functions as a *Leitwort* in this passage, appearing five times.

This same problem is dealt with in a somewhat different way in *Pirqei de-rabbi eliʿezer* where the father's preference for Joseph is due to his future leadership role. In Jacob's old age, Joseph would save the family from famine. The author here turns the declarative "for" (H. *kī*) of "for he was the child of his old age" (Gen. 37: 3) into an interrogative: "*And was Joseph the child of his old age?* Was not Benjamin the child of his old age? But because Jacob saw in a prophetic vision that Joseph would rule in the future, therefore he loved him more than all his sons" (PRE, 38).

The Rabbis, in their obsessive tracing of genealogical linkages, then ask the question: From whom was Joseph's beauty actually inherited—was it passed down from his mother or from his father? The predominant midrashic tradition here is alert to the fact that in the Pentateuch it is only Rachel who is similarly described with the same pair of adjectives "shapely and beautiful," albeit in the feminine (*yifat toʾar vifat marʾeh*).[8] Moreover, in both instances, when this pair of terms is invoked it is in the context of the attraction these qualities generate in a member of the opposite sex. In the case of the mother, her great beauty, highlighted further by the contrast to her older sister, accounts for Jacob's love for her: "And Laban had two daughters. The name of the elder was Leah, and the name of the younger Rachel. And Leah's eyes were tender, but Rachel was comely in features and comely to look at (*ve-raḥel haytah yefat tóʾar vifat marʾeh*), and Jacob loved Rachel" (Gen. 29:16–17).[9] Similarly, the identical paired expression employed by the narrator to denote Joseph's physical attributes is not mentioned in the Bible until justified by the effect his looks have on Potiphar's Wife: "And Joseph was comely in features and comely to look at (*va-yehi yosef yefeh-tóʾar vifeh marʾeh*). And it happened after these things that his master's wife raised her eyes to Joseph and said, 'Lie with me'" (Gen. 39:6–7). *Bereishit raba* derives from the parallelism of these verses the genetic connection between Rachel and her first-born son, citing an Aramaic aphorism—*zerok ḥuṭra le-avira ve-ʿal ʿikareih hu qaʾim*—analogous to the English expression, "The apple doesn't fall far from the tree": "Said Rabbi Isaac: 'Toss a stick in the air and it will fall root-end first.' As it is written: *And Rachel was comely in features and comely to look at;* thus, in the same way: *And Joseph was comely in features and comely to look at*" (BR 86:6).

Islamic tradition records similar interpretations depicting the great beauty possessed by Joseph and his mother. Thus, according to al-Ṭabarī: "Jacob's son Joseph had, like his mother, more beauty than any other human being."

He also cites here a *ḥadīth* traced back to the Prophet himself: "Joseph and his mother were given half of all the beauty in the world" (*Prophets and Patriarchs,* 148). Al-Kisāʾī, citing a tradition from Kaʿb, states simply at the very beginning of his rendition of the Joseph tale that while Rachel gave birth to two sons, Joseph was distinguished from his brother by the good looks bequeathed to him by his mother: "Then Rachel conceived and bore Joseph, and after him, Benjamin; and Rachel's beauty was inherited by Joseph" (*Tales of the Prophets,* 167).

As both the Qurʾān and Torah are silent on the etiology of this beauty, this left room for the development of parallel traditions that trace Joseph's beauty through the male line. This is derived hermeneutically from the interpretation of the phrase applied in Genesis to Joseph to explain why it was that "Israel loved Joseph more than all his sons" (Gen. 37:3). As is explained in the second half of the verse, this was because Joseph was to him a "*ben zekunīm.*"[10] This problematic expression has variously been interpreted to mean that he was "a child of Jacob's old age," or, as in the Aramaic paraphrase of Onkelos,[11] that Joseph was born possessing already "the wisdom of an old man" (*bar ḥakīm*).[12] Thus, the Rabbis are able to anachronistically place Joseph as a halakhic scholar: "R. Nehemia says that all the laws (*halakhōt*) that Shem and Ever transmitted to Jacob, he [Jacob] transmitted to him [Joseph]" (BR 84:8).[13]

However, a third argument in favor of Jacob being the source of Joseph's beauty derives from the similarity of the Hebrew *ben zekunīm* to the words meaning "the splendor of his countenance" (*zīv ikonīm*), and thus the physical beauty of the father and son are related:[14] "R. Yehudah says that the splendor of his [Joseph's] countenance (*ziv ikonim*) was similar to his own" (ibid.). This is merely part of a long list of ways in which the father and son were deemed by the Rabbis to be alike, or to have shared similar experiences. The evidence for this was to be found in the jarring beginning of the Joseph story that led them to interpret the (asyntactical) juxtaposition of Jacob and Joseph in the second verse of chapter 37 as bespeaking their identical destinies:

> R. Samuel b. Naḥman said: Surely Scripture should have said, "These are the events [*tōldōt*] of Jacob: Reuben"! Why [does it instead say] *Joseph*? Because whatever happened to the one happened to the other. Jacob was born circumcised, and so was Joseph;[15] Jacob's mother was by nature barren, and so was Joseph's; the mother of each bore two children; both were firstborn; the mother of each suffered severe labor pangs; both were hated by their brothers, who desired to kill them; both were shepherds; both were

> detested; both were stolen twice;[16] both were blessed with ten blessings; both went out of the Land; both married and both became fathers outside the Land; both were escorted by angels; both attained greatness through dreams; both brought blessings to the houses of their fathers-in-law; both went down to Egypt; both brought an end to famine; both exacted oaths; both gave orders; both died in Egypt; both were embalmed; and the bones of both were carried [back to the Holy Land]. (BR 84:6)

Such a reading is justified hermeneutically by the absence of punctuation in the biblical text that would have placed a caesura between the names of father and son, while the homiletic derivation of *tōldōt* to mean "events" is based on a verse in Proverbs (27:1): *For you do not know to what the day will give birth* (*yeiled*).[17]

The Story of Our Master Joseph never explicitly commits itself either way on this question of heredity, although the parallelisms present in these initial descriptions of Rachel and Joseph would seem to indicate that his qualities derived from hers (nor is there any conflicting attribution of his beauty to Jacob, or for that matter, any mention that Jacob was similarly endowed). Moreover, Joseph's descent from Rachel and his being identified with her is a key motif throughout the story. For example, during the Brothers' interrogation of Joseph following his attempt to convince them that he never had the dream, they assert that his very descent from Rachel is sufficient to warrant his death: "And they said to Joseph, 'Joseph, are you the son of Rachel?' He said, 'Yes, my brothers.' They said to him, '[Then] your murder is inevitable'" (*Joseph,* 6). Later on, after Joseph has sat in the pit for some time, the Brothers return and Zebulun refers to him, not with the honorific by which he will come to be known—*al-ṣiddīq* ("The Truthful," or "The Righteous")—but mockingly by his matrilineal affiliation: "And when they came to the well where Joseph was, Zebulun called out and said, 'O Joseph, O son of Rachel, have you not died yet?'" (*Joseph,* 20–21). Similarly, immediately before the climax of the story, as Joseph is poised to reveal his true identity to his brothers, he rebukes Judah for his harsh words and again cites this maternal affiliation: "And why did you, O Judah, say upon the selling of your brother, 'Throw the son of Rachel in the well?'" (*Joseph,* 161).

A similar thread is found in Islamic tradition; for example, al-Thaʿlabī records a tradition from Qatādah that in the wake of the grain-measure being discovered in Benjamin's satchel, the Brothers contest their blameworthiness on the basis of matrilineal affiliation:

> Then they turned to Benjamin, "What have you done to us? You have humiliated us and blackened our faces. Because of you, sons of Rachel, we have had unending distress, and now you have taken this grain-measure." Benjamin said to them, "Nay, rather it is the sons of Rachel whom you have caused endless suffering, since you took my brother to the wilderness and killed him. He who placed the measure in my bag is the one who placed the dirhams in your bags." (Al-Thaʿlabī, 219–20)

In some Islamic versions, as it is Joseph's descent from Rachel that is given as the cause for the Brothers' hate, their enmity is depicted as extending by logical necessity to Benjamin as well. This is reflected already in the Brothers' words in the Qurʾān: "Joseph and his brother are dearer to our father than ourselves" (Q 12:8). Al-Kisāʾī conceives of the two brothers as being twins, as indicated by his situating Rachel's death at the time "when the boys were two years old"—but Joseph is here distinguished by his inheriting Rachel's beauty: "Then Rachel conceived and bore Joseph, and after him, Benjamin; and Rachel's beauty was inherited by Joseph" (*Tales of the Prophets,* 167).

In *The Story of Our Master Joseph,* Benjamin is referred to with the same epithet as Joseph, *il-ṣiddīq,* specifically in the context of mention of his astrological knowledge and his ability therefore to divine that the Egyptian "ruler" is in fact Joseph, his brother (*Joseph,* 157). In any case, solidarity between the sons of Rachel is the cause for Joseph's extreme solicitude for his younger brother throughout all traditions. Benjamin was regarded by Joseph as his charge, and will be the tool for "the test" he administers to his brothers to determine if they have changed their attitude vis-à-vis Rachel's children. This parallel among Genesis, the Joseph *sūrah,* and the exegetical traditions is further established by Jacob's hesitation in sending Benjamin with the Brothers to Egypt, and the prolonged campaign by the Brothers to convince him that they may be trusted. Nevertheless, as can be seen in the passage from *The Story of Our Master Joseph* cited above, it was the combination of Joseph's descent from Rachel with his outstanding physical and moral attributes that elevated him above his brothers, including his one full-brother, Benjamin.

While in our text Joseph's beauty is most often simply compared to the stock image of the full moon (perhaps another allusion to his beauty deriving from his mother, the putative "moon" in Joseph's second dream), or that of an angel or genie (*jinn*), al-Thaʿlabī describes in detail its multiple manifestations:

> The beauty of Joseph was like the light of day: his skin was fair, his face comely, his hair curly, eyes large; he stood upright, had strong legs, upper arms, and forearms, a flat belly with a small navel; he was hook-nosed, and

> had a dark mole on his right cheek which beautified his face, a white birthmark between his eyes resembling the Moon when it is full, and eyelashes like the fore-feathers of eagle wings. His teeth sparkled when he smiled, and light emanated from his mouth between his incisors when he spoke. No human would be able to describe Joseph, no one! It is said that he inherited his beauty from his grandfather Isaac, son of Abraham, who was the most beautiful man (Isaac means "the one who laughs" in Hebrew), who, in turn, inherited his beauty from his mother Sarah. God fashioned her in the image of the wide-eyed *houris* [nymphs in the Muslim Paradise], but did not give her the same purity. He gave Joseph an unblemished skin, and so much beauty as He had not given to any other human. When he swallowed, greens and fruits which he ate could be seen in his throat and chest until they reached his stomach. Sarah had inherited her beauty from her foremother Eve. (Al-Thaᶜlabī, 184)

Thus, here Joseph's beauty is traced through the paternal line; however, this handsomeness does not come directly from his father, Jacob, but from his grandfather, Isaac, who inherited it from his mother, Sarah, who in turn inherited it from her "grandmother," Eve. This linking of Joseph's beauty with that of Isaac may very well derive from the midrashic sensitivity to the fact that Joseph's grandfather is also referred to in Genesis as a *ben zekunim* (21:2); *viz.*, that Isaac also resembled *his* father in the "splendor of his countenance."[18]

The Qurʾān, while it does mention the *effect* Joseph's good looks have both on his master's wife and the Women of the Assembly, does not provide any direct statement of Joseph's beauty—nor of its origins. And yet, while Muḥammad saw Joseph as a forbear in overcoming strife to reach his divinely ordained position, within later Islamic tradition the two figures were connected in terms of their physical beauty. Al-Thaᶜlabī records a tradition related by ᶜAbdallāh ibn Masᶜūd, according to whom Muḥammad said:

> Gabriel descended and said, "Muḥammad! Verily God says to you, 'I have covered Joseph's beauty with the light of My Seat and I have covered your face with the light of My Throne.'" A scholar was asked, "Who is more beautiful, Joseph or Muḥammad?" He replied, "Joseph was one of the most beautiful of men, but Muḥammad was the most beautiful." This is indicated in an account of Jābir ibn ᶜAbdallāh, who said, "I saw the Messenger of Allah clad in a red garment, and then looked at the moon when it was full—and he was more beautiful in my eyes than the moon." (Al-Thaᶜlabī, 184)

That is, since Joseph's beauty is compared to that of the moon, if Muḥammad's beauty exceeds lunar magnificence, then ipso facto it also surpasses that of

Joseph. With expressive detail similar to that employed in his description of Joseph, the traditionist, Abū ʿĪsā al-Tirmidhī,[19] describes Muḥammad's physical appearance in the following way:

> Muḥammad was of middling size, his hair was neither lank nor crisp, he was not fat and had a white circular face, with wide black eyes, and long eyelashes. When he walked, he moved as though he were descending down a declivity. He had the "seal of prophecy" between his shoulder blades. . . . He was of solid build. His face shone like the full moon. He was taller than average, but not so much so as to be conspicuous. He had thick, curly hair, the plaits of which were parted and reached below his earlobe. He had a luminous complexion. Muḥammad had a wide forehead and fine, long, arched eyebrows which did not meet. Between his eyebrows there was a vein that bulged when he became angry. The upper part of his nose was hooked; he had a thick beard, smooth cheeks, a strong mouth, and evenly spaced teeth. He had thin hair on his chest. His neck was like that of an ivory statue, pure as silver. Muḥammad was well-proportioned, sturdy, with a firm physique, a flat belly and breast, broad in the chest and shoulders.[20]

Joseph the Righteous?

In postbiblical and postquranic tradition, Joseph is assigned the appellation in Hebrew, *ha-tzadīq,* and its Arabic cognate, *al-ṣiddīq,* respectively. While the two words are cognate, the distinction made in the two languages in the very meaning of this word highlights an example of linguistic tension over the claims to ownership of the text. Many of the biblical protagonists came to have epithets attached to their names, which serve to highlight their unique status as *the* claimants to that name (and thus differentiate them from any future bearers of the name) and point up some unique exegetical characteristic to be associated with them. The epithet attached to Joseph's name—in both the Judaic and Islamic traditions—exerts a stabilizing influence on his characterization in the narrative expansions surrounding him, and thus, indirectly, on the textual communities' understanding of his original portrayal in Scripture. If Joseph is *the* Righteous or *the* Veracious, he must be shown in all ways to conform to the stereotype. In this manner, such epithets function as condensed proverbs and identify the person in question as the standard against whom all others may be measured. Islam, when it absorbed these biblicist characters into its tradition, also appropriated their characteristic epithet, known in Arabic as the *laqab.*

The Hebrew term given Joseph, *ha-tzadīq,* is generally translated "the Righteous," and, as pointed out by Louis Ginzberg, this came to describe the general upstanding moral nature of Joseph and appears already several times in *Bereishit raba.*[21] But obviously many of the biblical characters were viewed as paragons of moral virtue. Indeed, we have already discussed the ambiguity in *Joseph* where the Brothers are also alluded to as righteous; this quality is also obliquely attributed to them in *Bereishit raba* when the Rabbis determine the upper limit that God will allow the righteous to be discomfited: "*And [Joseph] put them under guard for three days* (Gen. 42:17). The-Holy-One-Blessed-Be-He never leaves the righteous (*ha-tzadīqīm)* in distress for more than three days" (BR 91:7). Why then was Joseph singled out? Specifically, and this point is developed by James Kugel, his righteousness came to be associated with that feature uniquely attributed to Joseph in later tradition: his ability to withstand the advances and temptations of the biblical wife of Potiphar.[22] This is, as we have discussed earlier, the most pronounced expansion of the Genesis story in *The Story of Our Master Joseph.*

However, in *The Story of Our Master Joseph* there exists a tension between the two cognate meanings that is reflected in the overlap of their respective semantic fields. Here, Joseph's characteristic epithet is invoked in the very first line of the tale that gives the tale its title: "We shall begin now the story of Master Joseph *il-ṣiddīq.*" Although the term's meaning is ambiguous at this point, it would seem that truthfulness is established as a primary motif by the culminating line of the *tasbīḥ* (the laudatory preface in praise of God) with which the text opens: "And this is what happened, words of truth exactly" (*Joseph,* 1). Thus, the truthfulness of the narrator is inextricably bound up with the major theme of the story and the one that is defining for its protagonist. This wording significantly echoes the quranic statement with which the Joseph *sūrah* closes:

> And when at length the Messengers despaired and thought they had been repudiated, Our help came to them. We have delivered whomever We please, but Our might will not be averted from the evildoers. There is in the tales [of these Messengers] a lesson for those endowed with reason. Our story is not one that could be invented, but a *confirmation* [*tasdīq*] of what has come before it, an explanation of everything, and a right guidance and a mercy for a believing people. (Q 12:111) [my emphasis]

There are many places in *The Story of Our Master Joseph* in which the theme of veracity is emphasized. For example, there is the contrast between the ruse of the blood-stained shirt brought by the Brothers, and Jacob's "believing" (*ṣadaqa*) their claims about Joseph's demise (*Joseph,* 14). Another case is that of the testimony of Zulaykhā's infant nephew. There the parallel structure further highlights the contrast between the protagonists, specifically with regard to this quality of truthfulness: "Examine the youth: if his shirt is torn from the back, then he is telling the truth and she is the liar; however, if it is torn from the front, then he is the liar and she is telling the truth" (*Joseph,* 114). Similarly, the Qurʾān highlights the contrast between Joseph's honesty and al-ʿAzīz's wife's mendacity: "And a witness from her household testified: 'If his shirt is torn from the front, then she has spoken truly (*fa-ṣadaqat*) and he is among the liars; however, if his tunic is torn from the back, then she has lied (*fa-kadhabat*) and he is among the truthful'" (Q 12:26).

This sense of "truthfulness" is extended to apply to the "accuracy" or "truth" of Joseph's dreams, as well as to his ability to interpret those of others. The Brothers' attempt to overcome God's will (as evidenced in Joseph's dreams) by murdering Joseph highlights this truth factor: "Let us take him and kill him and we will be rid of him and his dreams and we will see what good will come of his treacherous dreams" (*Joseph,* 5). At this point, his brothers mock him by calling him "Joseph the Dreamer" (*ṣāḥib il-aḥlām; Joseph,* 5), a title that sarcastically departs from the one by which he will eventually be known: "Joseph the Truthful." Similarly, his ability to interpret dreams is attested to by the narrator after what he tells Pharaoh's cupbearer and baker comes true: "That was the confirmation (*taṣdīq*) of the words of Joseph the Truthful (*il-ṣiddīq*)" (*Joseph,* 126). Overlaying all of these examples, however, is the "truth" of Joseph's childhood visions that indeed is realized at story's end, whereas the prediction of the Brothers that he will no longer return to his father (*Joseph,* 7) is proven false.

While this is clearly one of the major themes of the work, there are significant places where the ambiguity of the two meanings of *ṣiddīq* is maintained. Such is the case in the beginning of the story where both Joseph and his brothers (!) are referred to as *ṣiddīqīn.* This would seem to imply a more general quality of righteousness, one that Joseph shares with his brothers, merely exceeding them in degree: "And one of them was *asdaq* [either 'more righteous' or 'more truthful'] than his brothers, and his name was Joseph" (*Joseph,* 2). When the proof of the infant substantiates who between Zulaykhā and Joseph was truly the sexual predator, the shame-faced al-ʿAzīz reproves his wife Zulaykhā with "Joseph is *asdaq* [again, either 'more righteous' or 'more truthful'] than you" (*Joseph,* 114). Afterwards, when Zulaykhā admits to the King her crime, she employs the same plural nominative form used in reference to the Brothers: "I am the one who sought to seduce him and he is one of the *ṣiddīqīn* ['truthful' or 'righteous']" (*Joseph,* 137). All of these examples allow for an equivocation in the reader's determining if it is Joseph's overall upright moral character that is being referred to, or either of the sub-categories of his chasteness or his truthfulness. As we have seen, this last possibility can be broken down even further to reflect the distinction between the common sense of "one who tells the truth" (the opposite of "liar") and one who is accurate in interpreting dreams—that is, one whose interpretations come true.

Given the distinction between Arabic and Hebrew in the primary meaning of the triliteral root *ṣ-d-q,* one could argue that this semantic idiosyncrasy alone might be used to determine the ultimate origin of any particular element in the Joseph story. Thus, in any given version where it is clearly his chasteness that is brought out, the source could be posited to be of Hebrew origin, while in a version where it is his quality of telling the truth—whether it be concerning his ability to read dreams, or his being contrasted to the lying Brothers or Zulaykhā—is emphasized, the origin is Arabic. As we will see below, however, the situation is somewhat more complicated than this hypothesis. Of course, another alternative is that this connotation of *ṣ-d-q* as "truthful" reflects an old Jewish etymology for the Semitic root that became lost over time, a process that would have coincided with the expansion and focus on the account of Joseph's relationship with Zulaykhā. Thus, for example, the Book of Isaiah describes God as one "who foretells reliably, who announces what is true (*dover tzédek magīd meisharīm*)" (Isaiah 45:19).

Another motivation for the move from "truth" as being the primary quality associated with Joseph is the presence of elements in the Genesis text that seem to subvert such a designation and to which the Rabbis who constructed the traditions were sensitive. Never mind Joseph's being characterized as *the* Truthteller, does he in fact always tell the truth? In terms of his ability to accurately interpret dreams, the Midrash offers several counterexamples. It cites the apparently anachronistic allusion to Joseph's mother, Rachel, in the dream where the eleven planets, the sun, and the moon bow down to Joseph (Gen. 37:9): The Rabbis ask the question, how could he have dreamt about the moon coming to bow down to him when Rachel had passed away some years before? Of course, this problem could also be solved by recourse to the rabbinic hermeneutic dictum: "there is no early or late in the Torah" (*ein mukdam o me'uḥar ba-torah*).[23] The quranic text, while making explicit the connection between the portents of Joseph's dream and its fulfillment, simply passes over the problem, and has both of Joseph's parents come to Egypt at the conclusion of the story: "And when [all of Jacob's household] went in to Joseph, he took his parents unto himself to reside and said: 'Come into Egypt in safety, if God wills!' and he elevated his parents upon the throne. And [the whole family] fell down to him in prostration, and he said: 'Father, this is the meaning of my earlier vision: my Lord has made it come true!'" (Q 12:99–100). The Stories of the Prophets literature, on the other hand, avoids this problem by assuming that Joseph is here referring to his stepmother.

The Story of Our Master Joseph provides an example that runs counter to the theme of the protagonist's truthfulness. In a last-ditch but failed attempt to save himself from the Brothers' wrath, Joseph dissimulates by asserting that his vision was "a dream of falsehood" (*manām kadhdhāb, Joseph,* 6). Joseph is apparently seeking to retract the legitimacy of his dreams in order to protect himself.[24] Of course, this transgression might be overlooked, occurring as it does in the context of Joseph's attempts at self-preservation (reflected in his obsequious addressing the Brothers as "my masters"), but, nevertheless, it should still have disturbed these exegetes who would insist on nothing less than absolute honesty in a prophet. Similarly, the Brothers' characterization of Joseph as a thief (pp. 26, 32, and 33), which we will discuss in the next chapter, represents an internal challenge to the characterization of Joseph as truthful. Thus, while there could be no denying Joseph's external beauty, the Brothers could call into question his internal qualities—his honesty and his ability to tell the truth in the larger sense of prophecy or interpretation of dreams—and thus break down the confluence of Joseph's physical and moral beauty established in the Hellenistic tradition.

Although it appears that either of these manipulations of the etymology of the Semitic root *ṣ-d-q* may be associated with one or the other of the traditions of Judaism and Islam, it is precisely these instances of ambiguity that may be adduced as further evidence for the hybrid nature of *Joseph.* In the following chapters we shall explore the oscillations between these two senses of *al-ṣiddīq* as they are reflected in the accounts, first of Joseph's interactions with his brothers, and then his confrontation with Potiphar's Wife. This division into chapters is solely for the convenience of analysis; as we shall see, the story is an integrated whole and there exist deep intratextual linkages between the two component subplots that are uncovered and enhanced by the exegetes.

2

Joseph, His Father, and His Brothers

For love is as strong as death (Song of Songs 8:6): this applies to Jacob's love for Joseph. *Jealousy is as cruel as the grave* (ibid.): that is, his brothers' jealousy of him. And what can love avail by the side of jealousy, and what brought hatred upon Joseph if not the excessive love which his father showed him.

Tanḥuma (Buber recension) Va-yeishev 19

The conventions of the romance genre provide that the hero best encounter some initial challenge preparatory to the "life-and-death" struggle that will represent the climax of the story. In the case of the first of the two subplots that make up the tale of Joseph, that of his interactions with the Brothers, our protagonist will face this threat while still a youngster. The danger that Joseph encounters, rather than being brought about by some outside hostile force, will arise from within his nuclear family, coming at the hands of these half-brothers. In a complicated and shifting pattern of interpretation, the exegetes read the biblical text as suggesting different motivations for the Brothers' enmity. The central question asked is who is responsible for this pattern of dysfunctional familial relations. Was it solely the petty jealousy of the Brothers, the unchecked favoritism of their father, Joseph's overweening vanity, or some combination of these factors that brought on this dismal state of affairs? These incipient tensions will rapidly mount and lead up to the situation of mortal peril in which the Brothers place Jacob's favorite son. Serendipitously or, according to the Midrash, providentially saved from an early death, Joseph is sold by his brethren into slavery in Egypt. After the passage of many years and upon his ascension to power in Egypt, Joseph will reencounter his brothers, and again his life will be placed in jeopardy. In the end, however, the conflict and rivalry that characterized the early family history will be resolved, and in that final stage of the romance, the anagnorisis, Joseph will indeed be exalted—his superior status recognized and accepted by all. The tale will draw to a close with the rehabilitation of the family and the fulfillment of Joseph's childhood dreams. Through this mechanism, God will achieve his plan for the Children of Israel to experience exile in Egypt. Along the way, *The Story of Our Master Joseph the Righteous* will assemble a rich blend of midrashic motifs drawn from a variety of ancient Near Eastern, Hellenistic, Persian, and Islamic traditions.

The Favorite Son

In contrast to the Genesis account, glaringly absent from the beginning of *Joseph* is any overt indication that Jacob's favoritism is the source of the Brothers' animosity toward their younger sibling. Although the text records that Jacob preferred Joseph above his brothers, the narrator never confirms that the Brothers were aware of this partiality. This editing of the story is symbolized most concretely by the absence in this Judeo-Arabic retelling of the *ketonet pasim,* that elaborate and iconic tunic that in Genesis and most other accounts serves as the marker of Joseph's privileged status in the father's eyes. Such a noteworthy elision is seemingly part of an agenda that seeks to remove any blameworthiness from Jacob. In contrast, in Genesis, it is Jacob's preference for Joseph and his blindness to the sensitivities of his other sons that lead to his fashioning for him this garment: "And Israel loved Joseph more than all his sons, for he was the child of his old age, and he made him an ornamented tunic [*ketonet pasim*]. And his brothers saw it was he their father loved more than all his brothers, and they hated him and could not speak a kind word to him" (Gen. 37:3–4). While it is unclear what made this tunic so extraordinary, it must have been of some elaborateness, as in its only other appearance in the Hebrew Bible (2 Samuel 13:18–19) it is mentioned as being the garment of princesses. Moreover, we see that the very first thing the Brothers do to Joseph once they become set upon removing him from the scene is to strip him of this garment. In the focalization of this act, the metonymic relationship between the tunic and Joseph is highlighted—his possession of it, and his wearing of it—by the repetition of both objects of the Brothers' opprobrium: "And it happened when Joseph came to his brothers that they stripped Joseph of his tunic, the ornamented tunic that was upon him" (Gen. 37:23). This association will be augmented by the Brothers' smearing the tunic with blood of a goat kid before they bring it to Jacob as evidence of Joseph's death.

The Rabbis were sensitive to and critical of this open and material display of Jacob's preference for Joseph. Typical of their interpretations is the following didactic aphorism: "Reish Laqīsh said in the name of R. Elʿazar b. ʿAzaryah that a man should not treat any of his sons differentially, because due to the *ketonet pasim* that our father Jacob made for Joseph, *they hated him*" (BR 84:8).[1] The interpretation follows on the juxtaposition of the biblical verses to form a symmetric structure in which the *kutonet* is the marker for the father's favoritism (Jacob loves Joseph → Jacob makes him *kutonet* → Brothers perceive father's preference for Joseph through *kutonet* → Brothers hate Joseph): "And Jacob loved Joseph more than all his sons, for he was the child of his old age, and he made him an ornamented tunic. And his brothers saw it was he their father loved more than all his brothers, and they hated him and could not speak a kind word to him" (Gen. 37:3–4). The Babylonian Talmud records the view that indeed it was this tunic that was the catalyst for the entire succession of events leading to the exile of Jacob's household: "Raba, son of Maḥsiya, on the authority of Rav, said: Never should a man treat one of his sons differentially, for because of two *selahs* weight of silk that Jacob gave to Joseph over his sons, the Brothers envied him and thus it transpired that our forefathers descended to Egypt" (BT *Shabat* 10b, *Megilah* 16b).

Unlike the Genesis account, in *Joseph* the sole reason for the Brothers' hatred appears to be Joseph's two dreams, whose transparent meaning the Brothers readily interpret. In the first instance, when Joseph naively relates the dream of the bowing sheaves, they understand what his dream portends in terms of their future subordination to his authority: "[When] they heard his dream, all of them treated it seriously because they understood [from it] that he would rule over all of them and it would be their destiny to bow down to him" (*Joseph,* 3). In the second dream, there is an incremental change in their reaction, in that now they not only understand what the future bodes but hate their younger brother for it: "*The Sages, peace upon them, said* that his brothers learned of the dream and interpreted it. And they drew inferences from that dream, and because of it they hated him greatly and no longer wished him peace" (*Joseph,* 4).

Adopting a psychoanalytic perspective, we may see how the development of Joseph's personality is based on the formative experiences of his childhood.[2] His ascendancy within the family hierarchy reflects a common motif in other Genesis accounts. Many of the tales in this book of origins revolve around a character's overcoming through talent or predisposition the hard-and-fast rules of priority imposed by birth order—what Alter has referred to as "the reversal of the iron-clad law of primogeniture."[3] Although Joseph was the eleventh-born son of Jacob, as the firstborn of Jacob's favored wife, Rachel, he occupied a special place in his father's heart. Moreover, as this was the wife Jacob intended to marry before Laban duped him into the union with her older sister, Leah, there is a certain justice in this reversal. Given the priorities in Israelite society for wives to produce sons, and specifically, Rachel's need to curry favor with Jacob, Joseph would also necessarily have been very precious to his mother. She, after all, had bided her time in order to marry Jacob, then waited long years for a male child, all the while tormented by the fertility of her sister and co-wife, Leah. Within what was to become the Rachelite subunit, Joseph was the firstborn of Rachel's two sons and thus was able to benefit in his early years from the undivided love of both parents. Any possible competition from Benjamin for their mother's affections was moreover rendered moot upon her death, which, not insignificantly, occurred during the birth of her second son. Indeed, the connection of the mother's death with the birth of this second son might have established Benjamin in Jacob's mind as being the cause of his beloved wife's passing and resulted in Jacob favoring Joseph.[4]

The animosity that Joseph's half-brothers felt toward him had its roots already in the complicated relationship between Jacob's primary wives—the sisters, Rachel and Leah—and their competition for the affections of the husband they shared. The significance of this legacy is expressed only indirectly in *Joseph* when the Brothers rhetorically question him as to whether he is Rachel's son; his affirmation of this fact is sufficient basis for them to reject his pleas to return to his father. In order to understand the full import of these statements we need to unpack the biblical background. That Jacob first falls in love with the younger sister is a female analogue for the undermining of "natural" birth order as the determinant of divine and matrimonial favor. It is in fact this reversal that Laban rebels against; he justifies his duplicitous "bait-and-switch" substitution of Leah for Rachel on the conjugal night by informing Jacob that "It is not done thus in our place, to give the younger girl before the firstborn" (Gen. 29:26). The Midrash, always eager to show how the biblical characters receive their just deserts, has Leah respond to Jacob's condemnation of the deceit she and her father, Laban, have practiced upon him by invoking the subterfuge by which Jacob and Rebecca wrested the birthright from Esau:

> All that night Jacob kept calling his bride Rachel, and Leah answered to that name. *And when morning came, look, she was Leah* (Gen. 29:25). Said Jacob

> to Leah, "What is this, O tricktress and daughter of a trickster [i.e., Laban]? Did I not call you Rachel all night long and you answered to that name?" She replied, "And is there a scribe who doesn't have students? Did not your father call out to you 'Esau,' and you answered him; so, too, you called me and I answered you." (BR 70:19)

This uneasiness of the sororal relationship continues after Jacob works for Laban an additional seven years in order to wed Rachel, and is expressed in the main arena of competition open to the biblical matriarchs—the production of sons. Leah, because of God's compassion for her unloved state, is triumphant early on in this competition: "And the Lord saw that Leah was despised and He opened her womb, but Rachel was barren" (Gen. 29:31). This is a motif seen as well in the case of Sarah and Hagar (Gen. 16), and Hannah and Peninah (1 Samuel 1)—the fertile co-wife posing a threat to the preferred but barren wife.[5] In the case of Laban's daughters, the distress that this causes the barren younger sister is wrenchingly manifest when, after Leah gives birth to four sons, Rachel cries out to Jacob: "Give me sons, for if you don't, I'm a dead woman!" (Gen. 30:1).[6] Although this heartfelt plea can be seen as a sign of her desperation, it is also a most pointed contraversion of the requirements of the annunciation type-scene[7] in which God or His messenger informs the chosen woman that she will conceive; here, Rachel directly confronts her husband and demands of him offspring. Jacob's angry rejoinder—"Am I instead of God, Who has denied you fruit of the womb" (Gen. 30:2)—comes to point up the theological error of her ways.

The contest is so intense that first Rachel and then Leah (after she ceases to bear children) offer Jacob their maids to function as proxy-cum-surrogate mothers.[8] It is clear then that the pattern of envy that will characterize the relationship between Joseph and his brothers had its roots in the rivalry between their mothers. In both cases, the envy is for the affection of the same man—Jacob: in the first instance, in his role as husband, while in the case of the rivalry amongst the Brothers, in his capacity as father. This is subtly suggested in the biblical text where the same verb connoting jealousy (*q-n-ʾ*), later employed to characterize the feelings of Joseph's brothers toward him (Gen. 37:11), here describes Rachel's attitude toward her sister: "And Rachel saw that she had borne no children to Jacob, and Rachel was jealous (*va-teqaneʾ*) of her sister" (Gen. 30:1). Leah's own feelings of resentment toward her younger sister would stem from her not being the wife chosen by Jacob but instead one foisted upon him through Laban's ruse. This essential insecurity is repeatedly emphasized in the naming speeches that accompany the births of her sons:

> And Leah conceived and bore a son and called his name Reuben, for she said, "Yes, the Lord has seen my suffering, for now my husband will love me." And she conceived again and bore a son, and she said, "Yes, the Lord has heard I was despised and He has given me this one, too," and she called his name Simeon. And she conceived again and bore a son, and she said, "This time at last my husband will join me, for I have born him three sons." Therefore is his name called Levi. And she conceived again and bore a son, and she said, "This time I sing praise to the Lord," therefore she called his name Judah. And she ceased bearing children. (Gen. 29:32–35)

Insight into Rachel's own perspective is provided upon the birth of her maid's son, Naphtali: "In awesome grapplings I have grappled with my sister and, yes, I have won out" (Gen. 30:8).

This tension was bequeathed to the sons of the sisters themselves and came to characterize the relationships between them. Commenting on the first verse of the Joseph narrative, the Babylonian Talmud records evidence of this strain, as it points out the back-and-forth nature of the conflict conducted through the sisters' ovaries. Here, it is commenting on chapter 37's subversion of the typical pattern of genealogical lists that we have already discussed above. While the convention dictates that all of Jacob's offspring should be enumerated in order of birth, such a cataloging is undermined by listing first the eleventh-born son, an interruption that is prolonged throughout much of the remainder of the Book of Genesis. However, as we know, Joseph was not the firstborn, and it is only through a complex series of machinations that a reversal of the pattern of primogeniture occurs: "R. Yonatan . . . said: 'The *bekhorah* [birth-right of the firstborn] was supposed to come out of Rachel, as it is written (Gen. 37:1): *This is the lineage of Jacob—Joseph,* but Leah preceded her because of [divine] mercy. However, due to Rachel's modesty the Holy One, blessed be He, returned the *bekhorah* to Rachel" (BT *Baba batra* 123a).

Even before Rachel's death, recorded in Genesis 35:16–20, the tension passed down to the sons is reflected in the episode of the mandrakes (Gen. 30:14–18). There, Reuben (Leah's firstborn son) brings back for his mother mandrakes (*dudaʾīm*—literally, "pair of lovers") whose root in the ancient Near East was regarded both as a fertility drug and an aphrodisiac.[9] Rachel asks to be given some, but Leah's resentment toward the favorite wife is clear in her response to this request: "Is it not enough that you have taken my husband, and now you would take the mandrakes of my son?" (Gen. 30:15). Rachel, in desperation over her failure to conceive, proceeds to bargain for them, agreeing in exchange to let the older sister sleep with Jacob.[10] Jacob throughout this scene is a passive actor; the silence of the biblical narrator speaks volumes, as nowhere does it record that he voiced any opposition to the deal. In this specific instance, his muteness must signal to the reader that he offers no opposition to Leah's direct and emphatic statement: "With me you will come to bed, for I have clearly hired you with the mandrakes of my son" (Gen. 30:16).

Joseph, the son of Rachel, is inextricably bound up with this conflict, as evidenced by the double-etiology given his name in Rachel's naming speech. This speech reflects the cultural imperative attached to the bearing of sons, while also foretelling the future birth of Benjamin: "And God remembered Rachel and God heard her and He opened her womb, and she conceived and bore a son, and she said, 'God has taken away (*asaf*) my shame.' And she called his name Joseph (*yosef*), which is to say, 'May the Lord add (*yosef*) me another son'" (Gen. 30:22–24).

However, perhaps the clearest example of the joining of the rivalries of the sisters with that of the sons follows immediately after Rachel's death. In what otherwise comes as a non sequitur within the narrative flow, the Genesis narrator laconically records that Reuben sleeps with Jacob's concubine: "And Rachel died and she was buried on the road to Ephrat, that is, Bethlehem. And Jacob set up a pillar on her grave; it is the pillar of Rachel's grave to this day. And Israel journeyed onward and pitched his tent on the far side of Migdal-eder. And it happened, when Israel was encamped in that land, that Reuben went and lay with Bilhah, his father's concubine, and Israel heard" (Gen. 35:19). Bilhah, as Rachel's slave-girl, presumably would have some role as foster mother to Rachel's children following her mistress's death. Thus, the incestuous "acting-out" by the eldest son, especially in its juxtaposition to the text's recording Rachel's death, reveals both Oedipal urges and sexual retribution against the father for the mistreatment of Reuben's mother. This is recorded by the Rabbis in the Talmud, who note that he sought to demand satisfaction for the insult of his mother: "[Reuben] said, 'Was it not enough that my mother's sister was a rival wife (*tzarah*); shall the handmaiden of my mother's sister also be a rival wife to my mother?' So Reuben went and 'disturbed' her bed (*bilbeil et matza*ᶜ*ah*)" (BT *Shabat* 55b).[11] Jacob's reaction to the illicit sexual act is not noted here; there is merely enigmatic mention of the fact that "Israel heard" (*va-yishma*ᶜ *yisra*ʾ*el*);[12] only later, in the final testament he delivers to each of his sons, do we learn of his outrage and the grave consequences for the firstborn son:

> Reuben, my firstborn son are you—
> my strength and first yield of my manhood,
> prevailing in rank and prevailing in might.
> Unsteady as water, you'll no more prevail!
> for you mounted the place where your father lay,
> you profaned my couch, you mounted!
>
> (Gen. 49:3–4)

Bereishit raba explicitly mentions the transfer of the rights of the firstborn from Reuben to Joseph in its comment on these verses: "Jacob said to him: You were supposed to have prevailed over your brethren in three aspects: the birthright, the priesthood, and the kingship. But when you sinned, the birthright was given to Joseph, the priesthood to Levi, and the kingship to Judah" (BR 1205).[13] The postexilic book, Chronicles, although it remarkably omits discussion of the story of Joseph, does record this transfer of the birthright to him from Reuben, while making clear that future rule would devolve upon the descendants of Judah: "Now the sons of Reuben, the firstborn of Israel (for he was the firstborn; but since he defiled his father's bed, his birthright was given to the sons of Joseph the son of Israel—but not so as to have the birthright attributed to him by genealogy. For Judah prevailed over his brothers and of him came the chief ruler; but the birthright was Joseph's)" (1 Chronicles 5:1).

When we are first introduced to Joseph in Genesis 37:2, the biblical narrator places him squarely within this rivalry of the wives, mentioning that he is shepherding in the company of Bilhah's and Zilpah's sons. However, the first tangible evidence of this tension is Joseph's bringing to Jacob an "evil report" (*dibah ra*ᶜ*ah*) about his brothers. While the narrator does not inform us whether or not the Brothers were aware of or affected by this activity, the Midrash records this as the beginning of the trials that Jacob would face through Joseph: "R. Yoḥanan said: 'Any place at which [Scripture] says "*And he settled*" (*va-yeishev*) is but a foreshadowing of grief, as it says, And *Israel settled* (*va-yeishev*) *in Shittim, and the people began to commit harlotry with the daughters of Moab* (Num. 25:1). [So here too, the verse] *And Jacob settled* (*va-yeishev*) . . . [is followed by] *And Joseph brought ill report of them to their father* (Gen. 37:20)" (BT *Sanhedrin* 106a).

The Rabbis exploit the nonspecificity of what these reports contained to detail a series of slanderous accusations for which God will ultimately requite Joseph:

> What did he say? R. Meir said: [He told his father,] "I suspect them of eating limbs torn from the living animal." R. Judah said: "They despise the sons of the bondmaids [Bilhah and Zilpah] and treat them as slaves." R. Simeon said: "They cast their eyes on the heathen women of this country." R. Yehudah b. Pazzi commented: *Honest scales and balances are the Lord's; all the weights in the bag are His work* (Proverbs 16:11). As to the first charge, the Holy One, blessed is He, said: "I will prove that they slaughter ritually and eat": *And they slaughtered*[14] *a kid and dipped the tunic in the blood* (Gen. 37:31).—"You accuse them of insulting the sons of the bondwomen and treating them as slaves": accordingly, *Joseph was sold as a slave* (Psalms 105:17).—"Do you say that they cast their eyes on the heathen women of the country? I will incite a she-bear against you": thus, *his master's wife raised her eyes to Joseph* (Gen. 39:7). (JT *Pei'ah* 1)

We see then that sibling rivalry is a key motif in the Joseph story in Genesis, and its delineation is a primary focus as well of the Judeo-Arabic retelling in *The Story of Our Master Joseph.* As such, the life of Joseph as presented in the Bible and in postbiblical literature sets him apart from the patriarchs: Abraham, Isaac, and Jacob—Joseph's great-grandfather, grandfather, and father, respectively. Although the conflicts between Isaac and Ishmael, and then Jacob and Esau, are significant as adumbrations of a divinely sanctioned overturning of the "natural law" of primogeniture, the identity struggles of Joseph's forebears revolved around a father-son nexus construed primarily in their relationship with God (from which follows their designation as "Patriarchs"). Biblical ideology reads the history of Israel as the history of those in whom God alternately places or removes his blessing. Although God is portrayed as the behind-the-scenes manipulator of events, He conspicuously lacks any overt presence in the Genesis story of Joseph; unlike the three Patriarchs, Joseph is not the recipient of a divine revelation. This coincides with the movement away from a vertical consideration of father-to-son lines of descent to the broad horizontal consideration of intra-generational conflicts. All these features make the tale one more suited to a novelistic retelling, and one in which the focus will be the protagonist's resolution of issues surrounding his status as half-brother and favored son. Joseph's exclusion from the rolls of the Patriarchs can furthermore be anchored in the historical "fact" that all twelve sons of Jacob share equivalent status (albeit with some significant deviations) as the eponyms of the federated tribes of the Israelite amphictyony. Another reason for Joseph's exclusion may be his identification as the ancestor of the northern tribes, which did not survive the Babylonian conquest (as distinct from the descendants of the southern tribes who did, and claimed the tradition as their own).[15]

Such realia connected to the details of Israelite tribal history did not of course pose a problem for the adherents of Islam and, given Joseph's prominence in the Qurʾān, it is not surprising that in Islamic tradition he is directly linked to the Patriarchs. This connection is already intimated in the quranic prologue to the Joseph story: "According to this [vision] your Lord will choose you and instruct you in the interpretation of stories, and He will fulfill His favor upon you and upon Jacob's household, as He fulfilled it beforehand upon your two forefathers, Abraham and Isaac" (Q 12:6). Similarly, later in the *sūrah,* Joseph declares to his two fellow prisoners: "And I have followed the faith of my forefathers, Abraham, Isaac, and Jacob" (Q 12:38). This grouping of Joseph with the Patriarchs is picked up in the commentaries. Thus, al-Bayḍāwī refers to the "four generations of noble ones, Joseph, son of Jacob, son of Isaac, son of Abraham" (*Commentary on Sūrah 12,* 2).

As far as the Islamic treatment of the sibling rivalry: in the Qurʾān, the only reason given for the Brothers' resentment toward their youngest siblings is the favoritism they perceive Jacob shows both Joseph and Benjamin. However, in contrast to Genesis, we do not have any "objective" affirmation of such a preference by the narrator, only the Brothers' own testimony: "It is clear Joseph and his brother are more loved by our father than we are, even though we are a sizeable bunch" (Q 12:8). Al-Thaʿlabī includes both Joseph's dreams and the father's favoritism as factors contributing to the Brothers' hostility but notes that the initial source of their enmity was Joseph's behavior concerning a miraculous tree that grew outside Jacob's house: "In fact, scholars who are knowledgeable in the tales of the prophets and accounts of past (peoples) have said (that) the beginning of the affair of Joseph and Jacob and the start of Jacob's love for him and preferring him over the rest of his children, was that God made a tree grow for Jacob in the courtyard of his house" (Al-Thaʿlabī, 185). According to this version, Joseph has two dreams that are a further source of the Brothers' jealousy and anger toward their younger sibling. The second is the celestial vision familiar from the Bible, Qurʾān, and the postscriptural accounts. However, the first dream of the bowing sheaves is replaced here by a vision of a tree in which the branches of all the Brothers are planted in the ground, but only Joseph's branch flourishes and puts forth fruit, while the others are uprooted by a wind from Heaven and blown out to sea. Al-Kisāʾī records these same two dreams, but here the Brothers apparently learn only of the second dream of the sun, moon, and stars. They attribute the grandiosity reflected in this vision to the favoritism of the father. Here, the single biblical tunic has been expanded to include five markers of Jacob's preference for the younger son: "Why shouldn't Joseph be like that, for his father has given him the Coat of Friendship, the Turban of Majesty, the Ring of Prophethood, the Girdle of Victory and Contentment, and the Staff of Light? That is why he brings us these fabricated visions" (*Tales of the Prophets,* 167).

Grandiose Visions

Throughout *Joseph,* as in the Genesis *Vorlage* and the midrashic expansions and retellings, dreams and their interpretation play a critical role in developing narrative tension as we await their fulfillment and confirmation. An examination of the specific dreams will help us understand their use as a literary device and the contours of biblical theology, but we can also learn much from them about the complicated pattern of cross-cultural borrowing exhibited in *The Story of Our Master Joseph.* Joseph's childhood visions are a significant locus for discussion of his personality in the midrashic accounts. In the Genesis version it is clear that he told his brothers both dreams; with regard to the second dream, moreover, it is emphasized that he also tells his father: "And he dreamed yet another dream and recounted it to his brothers, and he said, 'Look, I dreamed a dream again, and, look, the sun and the moon and eleven stars were bowing to me.' And he recounted it to his father and to his brothers" (Gen. 37:9–10).

In *Joseph,* he tells his brothers the first dream, but gauging their reaction, "because he knew that deceit and wickedness were in their hearts" (*Joseph,* 3), he does not relate to them the second dream. This departure from the Genesis version is perhaps based on the specific mention made in Genesis of the hatred that the first dream provoked in the Brothers: "And his brothers said to him, 'Do you mean to reign over us, do you mean to rule us?' And they hated him all the more, for his dreams and for his words" (Gen. 37:8). To have Joseph proceed to tell them a second dream would implicate Joseph in consciously compounding the Brothers' (and possibly also the father's) antagonism, so instead, in *Joseph,* he tells it only to his father. Jacob here confirms the dreams' portents, but out of fear for his son's safety cautions him against informing his brothers. The father is thus depicted as being cognizant and accepting of his son's future greatness, a greatness that will eclipse his own:

> Then after that [Joseph] dreamt a second dream in which the sun and the moon and eleven planets were bowing down to him. And he awoke but did not tell his brothers anything because he knew that deceit and wickedness were in their hearts. So he went and told his father, who looked at him and said to him, "Conceal your dream from your brothers. There is no doubt but that you will attain a high station and all of us will come and kiss your hands; but do not let them know; your brothers will rely upon this. O son, do not make me have to urge you to take care of yourself." (*Joseph,* 3)

This version of Jacob's reaction is contrary to the reproof he administers his son in the Genesis version: "And his father rebuked him and said to him, 'What is this dream that you have dreamed? Shall we really come, I and your mother and your brothers, to bow before you to the ground?'" (Gen. 37:10). However, the exegetes were anxious to provide an interpretation that would portray Jacob as gladdened by Joseph's destiny. Thus *Sefer ha-yashar* records that in response to the first dream, Jacob showers him with attention and affirmation: "Then [Joseph] told his father Jacob the same thing, and Jacob kissed Joseph when he heard those words, and Jacob blessed Joseph. When Jacob's sons saw how their father blessed Joseph, and kissed him, and loved him very much, they became jealous of him and hated him even more than before" (*Sefer ha-yashar,* 84).

The interpretation of the second dream is sensitive to the fact that Genesis notes that he told it to his father and to his brothers and that this is juxtaposed to the words "and his father rebuked him." This reading is thereby able to portray Jacob as putting on a show of chastising Joseph in the presence of his brothers because he realized they bore him a deep-seated hostility: "And his father heard what Joseph said about his dream and saw that his brothers hated him because of that. Then Jacob scolded Joseph before his brothers for what he had said" (ibid., 84–85). Such a reading accords neatly with the version in the Qurʾān. Here, however, the "rebuke" takes the form of a warning that Jacob administers Joseph, and there is no indication that Joseph informs his brothers of the contents of the dream: "He said: 'My son, don't tell your vision to your brothers lest they will come up with some plot against you, for Satan is an enemy devisive to Man'" (Q 12:5). This softening also appears in al-Kisāʾī, where Jacob apparently fails to comprehend the portents of his son's vision:

"'My son,' said Jacob, 'Not every dream has an explanation or interpretation, so do not let it frighten you'" (*Tales of the Prophets,* 168).

The significance of dream interpretation, oneiromancy, its connection to prophecy and (in the worldview of the Rabbis) its heir, rabbinic exegesis, is highlighted in the esoteric teachings of the *Zohar:*

> R. Hiyya and R. Yose were wont to study with R. Simeon: [Once] R. Hiyya asked: "We have learnt that 'a dream which is not interpreted is like a letter which is left unread' (BT *Berakhot* 55a). Does this mean that it will be fulfilled nonetheless, but [the dreamer] will know nothing of this? Or, will it not be fulfilled at all?" [R. Simeon] replied: "The dream will come true, but without his knowledge; he has not discovered [the dream's meaning], and hence will not know if it is realized or not. There is nothing in the world that is not indicated through a dream or a proclamation before it comes about. For it has been stated that before anything occurs in the world it is proclaimed in heaven, and thence does it spread abroad to inform this sphere, in accordance with the verse, '*The Lord God will do nothing but He reveals His counsel to His servants the prophets*' (Amos 3:7)—i.e., when prophets lived; when prophecy is gone, sages are more than prophets, but if they too are not extant, then are matters foretold in dreams." (*Zohar* 1, 183b)

The various nighttime visions in *Joseph,* both those dreamt by Joseph and those he is called upon to interpret, parallel those recorded in the Bible and in Islamic tradition. Again, from a psychoanalytic perspective, Joseph's childhood dreams of his future superiority may very well represent a defensive tack revealing his essential insecurity. Joseph, orphaned from his mother, must confront alone the enmity of his half-brothers and, we must assume, that of his stepmother aunt—his mother's sister and rival. Not only the content of the dreams but also Joseph's temerity in relating them (with their obvious portents) directly to his brothers bespeak either a naiveté borne of young age or an arrogance that might be a protective posturing mechanism reflecting his own vulnerability. He is, after all, first depicted in Genesis as a field hand assisting the "low-born" sons of the slave-girls (Gen. 37:2). The precarious state of the motherless Joseph leads him to attempt to curry the favor of his father through the bringing of "ill report" about his siblings. His dreams, similarly, point to a wish for aggrandizement and the exchange of his precarious subordinate position for one in which his putative superiors would in future time bow down to him.

In the Genesis story, Joseph's second childhood dream has him surrounded by eleven planets, and the sun and the moon, which stand for his brothers, his father and mother, respectively. As Rachel had already died (a fact recorded in chapter 35 and thus, according to a linear understanding of the narrative progression, occurring before Joseph's dreams), the exegetes, following on Jacob's censure of his darling son, place in the father's mouth the question as to how the deceased wife could be included in this revelation with its obvious portents for the future. According to Rashi, this is merely evidence of Jacob's obtuseness in that he didn't realize that the moon here refers to Bilhah who raised him as a mother. The second dream seems to repeat the portents of the first with an incremental extension: the information added is that the implied future ascendancy of Joseph over his brothers will apply to his parents as well. His father's reaction here seems to parallel that of the Brothers who had earlier rebuked Joseph in similar fashion.

Of course, another explanation for this incongruity is simply that the story of Joseph, as a separate vignette tracking the life of Joseph, is distinct from the overall flow of Genesis; that is, the dream occurred while Rachel was still alive and Joseph was a very young child. Such an interpretation would explain why first the Brothers and then the father must supply the interpretation of dreams that are so transparent in their meaning. While the Joseph tale in Genesis begins with mention of the fact that Joseph is seventeen years old, in *Joseph* no age is provided at this early juncture; this is deferred until the time of the protagonist's sale to al-ʿAzīz. In the Stories of the Prophets literature, however, it is assumed that the dreams of future ascendancy are visions accorded him by God and that Joseph is a young lad who naively reports their content to his family. Thus, in these traditions a specific (young) age for each dream is provided. This solves the problem of the arrogance or obtuseness that would attach to an adult Joseph relaying fairly self-evident portents of his future superior status. Al-Thaʿlabī (185–86), on the authority of Wahb, states that Joseph is seven years old when he has his first dream and twelve at the time of the second. In al-Kisāʾī (167–68), Joseph is somewhere between his fourth and tenth year when he has his first dream. These readings are made possible by the more regular chronological sequence of the quranic narrative, which places the dream at the beginning of the story (12:4).

Throughout nearly all versions of the Joseph story there exists a pattern of doubled dreams, whether it be the childhood dreams of Joseph's future ascendancy, the dreams of the king's cupbearer and baker, or the dreams of the king himself. This duplication of dreams may be seen as analogous to the parallelism of biblical poetry where the repetition in the second hemistich of the verse lends emphasis to the statement or image conveyed in the first hemistich, represents some incremental shift, or conveys some nuanced meaning.[16] Two dreams, like points in space, are enough to define a narrative line from which meaning can be derived—thus, these are not "idle" dreams but ones that reveal a pattern.

Moreover, by means of their repetition, any ambiguity of interpretation is ruled out; the reader, either with or without the help of the Brothers or Jacob, in the first instance, and Joseph's interpretation, in the others, can ascertain the dreams' meaning by isolating the common thread. Later on in the Genesis narrative, or in other versions of the story, a principle of literary economy was often adopted whereby reference was made to only one of Joseph's dreams. An example is seen in the Qurʾān where only the dream of the planets is related. In the biblical cycle's last instance of doubled dreams this quality is highlighted by the text itself—at the beginning and end of Joseph's relating their interpretation to the king (where its significance is further thematized by its own repetition!): "Pharaoh's dream is one. What God is about to do He has told Pharaoh" (Gen. 41:25). And: "And the repeating of the dream to Pharaoh two times, this means that the thing has been fixed by God and God is hastening to do it" (Gen. 41:32). Based on this interpretation, the reader thus learns retrospectively that the other instances of paired dreams are evidence of their divine provenance.

Joseph's second dream in Genesis conveyed additional meaning by its implication that in days to come he will be superior not only to his brothers, but to his parents as well. While, as we have noted, the Qurʾān contains only the dream of the stars, the dream of the sheaves is replaced in postquranic tradition by a description of a miracle. According to how this motif is recorded in al-Thaʿlabī, a tree grows near Jacob's house. At the birth of each son, it sprouts an additional branch; however, at Joseph's birth no such limb grows. Al-Thaʿlabī's version of the tale has an interesting twist in that it portrays Joseph, and not his brothers, as the initially envious one, as he alone among them did not have such a branch. Indeed, it is this envy of Joseph's that is cited as primary cause behind the rivalry with his brothers: "In fact, scholars who are knowledgeable in the tales of the prophets and accounts of the ancients have said that the beginning of the affair of Joseph and Jacob, and the start of Jacob's love for him and preferring him over the rest of his children, was that God made a tree grow for Jacob in the courtyard of his house" (Al-Thaʿlabī, 185). Upon Joseph's urging that a branch be brought for him from the Garden,

Jacob prays to God, and the angel Gabriel brings a branch of chrysolite, a green gem, directly from Paradise. In provocative fashion, and as a correlate for the *ketonet pasim* of Jewish tradition that symbolizes his elevated status, Joseph would take this branch wherever he went with his brothers. Moreover, it is the stimulus for Joseph's first dream in which all the branches are planted in the ground, but only his puts forth limbs, blooms, and yields fruit.[17] A version of this story is also contained in the sixteenth-century Aljamiado work, *The Story of Yusuf, Son of Yaʿqub*. According to this account, the Brothers initially love Joseph; it is only upon their hearing of his dream in which the tree bears fruit from which all the prophets eat (including, Jacob, Moses, Jesus, and Muḥammad) that they come to envy and hate him.[18]

Such ambiguity in Joseph's feelings toward his brothers is parallel to the mutual envy of Rachel and Leah recorded in Genesis. This accords with a corollary midrashic tendency to blame Joseph's behavior for inciting his brothers to hate him. After all, had Joseph not realized before the dreams that because of his father's preference for him the Brothers "hated him and could not speak a kind word to him" (Gen. 37:4), surely after relating to his brothers the first dream, he must now be aware of the extent of their enmity. The biblical text makes this abundantly clear through repetition of the fact of their hatred both before and after the relating of the dream: "And Joseph dreamed a dream and told it to his brothers and they hated him all the more" (Gen. 37:5). The text then reiterates Joseph's relation of the dream, at which point the Brothers realize that he means to rule over them, and the fact of their hatred for him is repeated: "And they hated him all the more, for his dreams and for his words" (Gen. 37:8). This repetition using the same language—*va-yosīfu ʿod senoʾ oto* ("And they hated him all the more"), in which the auxiliary verb *yosīfu* is itself a pun on Joseph's name—constitutes an incremental repetition, which adds the word "dreams" in the plural. Moreover, mention of "his words" makes explicit and palpable both the speech act by which Joseph communicates the dreams to them and his bringing of "evil report," thus highlighting his blithe insensitivity and self-absorption.

If midrash in the postprophetic era was to become the substitute conduit for communication between God and his chosen messengers, dreams in Genesis, in effect, represent the precursor to prophecy. They are the means by which Israel's patriarchs and heroes receive divine messages in the form of oneiric visions. The dream represents a divine distillation of the desired course of events according to God's overall plan.[19] In the Qurʾān, upon hearing of Joseph's dream, Jacob informs his favorite son that God will instruct him in the interpretation of stories (*taʾwīl al-aḥadīth*) (Q 12:6).

To return to the topic of Joseph's dreams in *The Story of Our Master Joseph:* When Joseph is in the well and the Brothers rebuke him for complaining of thirst and hunger, they refer to the second dream, even though Joseph had related to them only the first dream (5). This might reflect their glee at being able to inform "the dream master"[20] that they have obtained knowledge of the incriminating dream, and that they are now engaged in negating its validity. However, the Brothers are also quoted as saying that they sought to "be rid of him and his dreams." Here, as in Genesis, it is "dreams" in the plural, and given the avoidance of the nominative dual, this appears to be in the generic sense. Additional support for a single dream is contained in Seraḥ's song at the end of *Joseph,* where only one dream is mentioned (*Joseph,* 173–74). Alternatively, these examples from *The Story of Our Master Joseph* could be an expression of quranic influence and further evidence of the text's hybrid Judeo-Islamic nature.

If in contrast to the Genesis account it is not Joseph himself who relates the second dream to his brothers, who then is responsible for disclosing this information? The Qurʾān mentions only that Joseph told his father the single dream recorded there; there is no indication that the Brothers know of even this dream. This, too, is the version reflected in al-Ṭabarī's account (*Prophets and Patriarchs,* 139). However, this theme does appear in other *isrāʾīliyyāt* traditions. Thus al-Thaʿlabī implicates "the wife of Jacob" (Leah) as the source for the leaked report; it is she who, despite Jacob's admonitions not to do so, informs Joseph's brothers (her sons) of the second dream (186).[21] This motif is present as well in *The Story of Yusuf,* where Jacob's wife seeks to claim that she technically adheres to his demand not to divulge knowledge of the dream to the sons. Although she tells them about the dream, she does not interpret it but "merely" points out that by the sun he meant herself, by the moon their father, and by the stars the Brothers (*Yusuf,* 167). In *The Story of Our Master Joseph,* as in al-Kisāʾī (168), there is no such attempt to blame either Joseph or Leah; it is stated merely that "his brothers learned of the dream and interpreted it and drew inferences from that dream" (4). Subsequently, this knowledge will be adduced as one of the reasons for the Brothers' despising Joseph.

The elision of the first dream from the quranic account may in fact have something to do with the economy of that text, but more significantly, it is also consonant with a program of not casting Joseph in any unfavorable light. Such a sanitized conception of Joseph would preclude his portrayal as one who, out of conceit and insensitivity to his brothers' feelings, would, not once but on two separate occasions, relate to them dreams foretelling his future superior status. Nowhere in the Qurʾān is it related that Joseph even told his brothers of this dream or that they in any way knew about it. The sole basis given there for the Brothers' hatred is the preference that Jacob showed both Benjamin and him. This paternal favoritism is presumably a consequence of their descent from the favored wife, Rachel: "[The Brothers] said: 'It is clear Joseph and his brother are more loved by our father than we are even though we are a sizeable bunch: our father is deluded, so kill Joseph or cast him to some land so that your father's favor will fall to you and afterwards you will be a redressed people'" (Q 12:8–9). Although it is not explicitly stated so in the Qurʾān, as there is no indication otherwise, we can assume that Joseph follows his father's advice not to tell the Brothers of his dream. The Bible, in contrast, lodges an oblique critique of the protagonist when it has Joseph relate both dreams to the Brothers, which serves to intensify their contemptuousness. Despite its lack of any explicit critique of his behavior by the narrator, the Bible allows for interpretations critical of both Joseph and the Brothers that are closed off to the Islamic accounts that must uphold their heroes' incorrigibility as prophets.

And Jacob Kept the Thing in Mind . . .

By another, more provocative reading, Jacob might himself have harbored some feelings of ambivalence towards Joseph, his "favorite" son. Thus, the verse recording Jacob's reaction to Joseph's second dream may indicate the congruence of the Brothers' and father's sentiments, if we read (as do the Jewish Publication Society and Alter translations) the prefixed particle *vav* of the Hebrew as conveying the sense of the conjunction "while," rather than a disjunctive "but": "And his brothers were jealous of him, while his father kept the thing in mind" (Gen. 37:11). The commentators read this as reflecting, if not an outright positive response, at the very least a tacit acceptance of the vision of Joseph's future superiority. However, within the text there is a certain degree of ambiguity in Jacob's words, preceded as they are by his "rebuke" of Joseph (although even here the Rabbis interpret his speech rhetorically): "And he recounted [the second dream] to his father and to his brothers, and his father rebuked him and said to him, 'What is this dream that you have dreamed? Shall we really come, I and your mother and your brothers, to bow before you to the ground?'" (Gen. 37:10).

Seen in this way, then, the Genesis narrative manifests a reversal of the "anxiety of influence" according to which the sons must do battle with the father. Reading the enigmatic conclusion to the dreams thusly, we sense the father's disquiet at the prospect of being surpassed by the son. This would constitute, in effect, the paternal side of the Oedipal struggle whose roots might lie in the competition between the father and son for the affection of Rachel. In any relationship where there is a high degree of identification, as that of Jacob with his son Joseph, there is repressed hostility in the desired obliteration of that person. Moreover, Jacob might ironically have envied Joseph's status as the father's favorite son whereas he himself was the less favored son of Isaac. Similarly, Jacob's later role in not perpetuating Joseph's name might also reflect such tension, although it is glossed over as reflecting his preferred status. On his deathbed, Jacob promises Joseph a double inheritance, and yet, replacing Joseph's name in the tribal hierarchy with those of his sons, Ephraim and Manasseh, represents his being supplanted by them.[22]

The Midrash seems to be exploiting the ambiguity of the expression with which the episode of the dreams concludes: "And his brothers were jealous of him, while his father *shamar et ha-davar*" (Gen. 37:11). The Rabbis interpret this to mean either that Jacob kept the matter to himself or that he remembered the affair. (The anachronistic reference to Rachel in Joseph's dream does not seem to have bothered the biblical Jacob, who, in his response to Joseph, includes reference to Joseph's ostensibly deceased mother.) Rashi's commentary on the preceding verse ("shall we come . . .") explains this anomaly by suggesting that Joseph had, after telling his brothers of the dream (v. 9), then proceeded to tell his father in their company. Jacob is portrayed as denying the plausibility of the portents of the dream coming to fruition, anxious to preserve family harmony.

> And Jacob sought to thereby remove the matter from their hearts, so that they shouldn't envy [Joseph]. Thus, by his words "Shall we really come, I and your mother and your brothers, to bow before you to the ground?" he intended to remove the thing from his sons' hearts so that they would not envy [Joseph], therefore he said: "Shall we come . . ."—as it is impossible vis-à-vis your mother, so too is the rest invalid. (Rashi, *Commentary on Genesis* 37:10)

In *The Story of Our Master Joseph,* it is not Jacob who denies the validity of the dream but Joseph himself, in a failed attempt to stave off their assault: "And Joseph said to them, 'O brothers, O masters, all who have said fire, their mouths will burn, but all who have said words of truth will flourish; indeed, this is a dream of falsehood'" (*Joseph,* 6). Here as well the father is unambiguously depicted as confirming the dreams' portents and motivated to protect his favorite son. The reading seems to stem from an interpretation of *shamar et ha-davar* that seeks to withhold from Jacob any unbecoming (to a prophet) jealous thoughts; thus, Jacob "kept the dream to himself" out of concern for his envied son. Furthermore, he advises Joseph to keep the matter secret and not to divulge this dream to his brothers. Rashi, in like manner, interprets this to mean that Jacob implicitly accepted the veracity of the dream, while his "keeping it in mind" refers to his expectantly awaiting its realization. In *Joseph,* Jacob's concern to protect his son could very well reflect a literalizing exegesis that would read "the thing" (*ha-davar*) that Jacob "guarded" (*shamar)* as referring to Joseph.

A parallel thread in the exegetical discourse seeks to lay responsibility at Jacob's own door for the trials and travails that befall him. The Rabbis pick up on the words that begin the Joseph cycle—*va-yeishev,* "he settled"—and read them as bespeaking an implicit criticism of Jacob for his presuming that the divine promise of inheriting the land would not include the period of exile from it. The Rabbis end this hubristic attempt to circumvent divine destiny by having God play his trump card:

> *And Jacob settled* (Gen. 37:1). R. Elʿazar said: "What is the meaning of *And Jacob settled*? It comes to teach us that Jacob thought to himself, "The-Holy-One Blessed-Be-He already told Abraham that his children would be strangers; now I have been a stranger for twenty years in Laban's house, a servant for his flocks." And when he saw that Esau had gone to another city to live, Jacob said "Thereby is the four-hundred-year enslavement fulfilled," and his mind was put at ease. The-Holy-One-Blessed-Be-He, said "My thought is deeper than yours," as it is said, "*For My thoughts are not your thoughts*" (Isaiah 55:8), thereupon, he immediately brought upon him the tribulation of Joseph, etc. When did He bring this upon him? When he had resolved that the Egyptian enslavement had been rescinded and his mind had become settled (*nityashvah daʿato*), thus it is written, *And Jacob settled* (*va-yeishev yaʿakov*).[23] (*Yalquṭ talmud torah*)

Of all the Patriarchs, it is to Abram alone that God mentions in Genesis a period of exile that the Chosen People will be required to undergo, and this only upon the occasion of the initial nocturnal covenant He makes with him.[24] Significantly, it is Joseph's birth that is the occasion for Jacob's requesting leave from his father-in-law to return to the Land: "And it happened, when Rachel bore Joseph, that Jacob said to Laban, 'Send me off, that I may go to my place and to my land'" (Gen. 30:25). The permanence of this return would seem to follow from the language of God's following promise to Jacob at Beit-el; this includes a change of name, a command to procreate, and the information that kings will be among his descendants and that God will give the land to him and his offspring:

> "Your name Jacob—no longer shall your name be called Jacob, but Israel shall be your name." And He called his name Israel. And God said to him,
>
> "I am El Shaddai.
> Be fruitful and multiply.
> A nation, an assembly of nations shall stem from you,
> And kings shall come forth from your loins.
>
> And the land that I gave to Abraham and to Isaac, to you I will give it, and to your seed after you I will give the land."
>
> (Gen. 35:11–12)

None of these blessings gives any indication that the habitation of the land will be interrupted; the Rabbis exploit this gap to project onto Jacob an assumption that the divine decree of exile had been revoked.

Returning to a consideration of Jacob's possible Oedipal tergiversation vis-à-vis Joseph, we can see this further exemplified in his fateful decision to send Joseph in search of his brothers. In Genesis, Jacob displays no hesitation in sending Joseph; however, even though this event is introduced with a suggestion of remoteness in time ("one time, when his brothers had gone to pasture . . ."), the verse's proximity to Jacob's rebuke of Joseph establishes a connection between the two events. This association is strengthened with the narrator's recording that "his brothers were jealous of [Joseph], while his father kept the thing in mind." Strange as well to the rabbinic mind was the fact that initially no indication is given of Jacob's concern for the Brothers or the flock; he mentions to Joseph merely that his brothers are pasturing at Shechem. This seemingly innocuous observation is followed directly by his command to Joseph: "Come, let me send you to them."[25] Only after Joseph indicates his willingness to comply does Jacob make clear that he wants to know "how your brothers fare, and how the flock fares" (37:11–14).

Of course, as the Rabbis interpreted it, all this could merely serve to point up Joseph's unquestioning obedience to his father's will, even if it gives rise to personal peril. Here they are establishing a parallel with the theme of the *ʿaqeidah,* the binding of Isaac, in the Bible and midrash. A source-critical interpretation might alternatively take this episode to have been originally contiguous with the first verse of the narrative proper, that "Joseph, seventeen years old, was tending the flock with his brothers . . ." (Gen. 37:2). The anomalous presence of this statement here would then constitute the introduction to a specific narrative event—the confrontation with his brothers—that has been displaced in the text by the "digression" of verses 3–11. In the context of this interlude we are told of Jacob's excessive love for Joseph, the fashioning of the special tunic, and Joseph's two dreams. This retarding the action is not merely a device to increase suspense, for if it were, it would need to be constructed in such a way that it does not entirely fill the present. Such a putative "false start," highlighted as well by the awkward syntax of the verse, could reflect a subcurrent pointing to Joseph's utter compliance with his father's command. Simultaneously, this reading overrides any suggestion of ambiguity in his father's attitude toward him.

The Story of Our Master Joseph has the Brothers' delay in returning from pasture be the cause of Jacob's uneasiness. Despite his premonitions, he sends his beloved son off in search of the Brothers. With irony borne of our omniscient perspective, we read of his reasoning: "I fear for them; I pray that a catastrophe has not befallen them" (*Joseph,* 4). Perhaps to counter such a failing of nerve on Jacob's part, QSY^2, in contrast, has Jacob expressly caution Joseph *not* to go to visit his brothers: "Do not go to see your brothers in the pasture because I fear for you" (QSY^2 1b). The reason for Jacob's fear on behalf of the other sons is not specified in *Joseph*—neither is their exact location given—but there is a rich midrashic tradition that connects this apprehension with Jacob's reluctance to avenge the rape of Dinah (Gen. 34), as well as his fear of a Canaanite reprisal after the Brothers have executed retribution. For example, *Targum Pseudo-Jonathan* (37:13) interpolates this as the reason for his sense of dread: "I am afraid lest the Hivites come and smite them for having smitten Hamor and Shechem and the inhabitants of the city." Similarly, according to Josephus, the sons had gone to pasture their flocks without informing their father. Not knowing their whereabouts, Jacob had "conceived the gloomiest of forebodings concerning them," and so sent Joseph off to find out what had happened (*Antiquities* 2:18–19). This is the author's explanation as to why in Genesis Joseph eventually finds his brothers in Dothan and not in Shechem where their father had thought them to be, because "it was said to [the Brothers] in prophecy that the Hivites sought to engage in battle with them" (idem.). Thus, Josephus conceives of Jacob's decision as a tragic error, and one that would instill in the audience a sense of sympathy and trepidation for Joseph's fate and Jacob's sorrow. In *Joseph,* we are told that Jacob, who as a prophet might otherwise be expected to have foreknowledge of the Brothers' plot, lost his powers of clairvoyance and thus sent Joseph off unconcerned for his fate. Here, as in Josephus's account, the plotting of the Brothers is prefaced to his departure; through this vilification the audience experiences a simultaneous sense of foreboding for the unsuspecting emissary, Joseph, and the father who sent him.

Jacob's Mourning

Jacob's loss of prophetic powers is also invoked in the extrascriptural traditions to account for his credulity in accepting the Brothers' tale of Joseph's demise—and for his consequent emotional breakdown. This motif is recorded as well in *The Story of Our Master Joseph.* Perhaps due to this connection the story diverges here from the order of the biblical narrative where the scene recording Joseph's sale to the caravan precedes the Brothers' ruse of presenting Jacob with his bloodied garment; here, after the Brothers toss Joseph in the pit they come before their father to relate to him the "tragic" news:

> *The Sages, peace upon them, said* that at that time prophecy departed from Jacob, his father, peace upon him, and he believed them and he shouted at the top of his lungs, letting out a great scream. Then he fell face down upon the ground and was unconscious for three hours, so that they raised a hue and a cry thinking that he had departed this world. When he awoke from his fainting he cried bitterly and said, "O Joseph, I used to hold you close to my breast out of my fear for you, but none of that was of any benefit now that you are in the belly of the wolf. O that I were with you and what befell you had befallen me instead." (*Joseph,* 14–15)

Robert Alter has noted Jacob's role in the Bible as the "histrion of paternal sorrow."[26] In *Joseph,* this tendency borders on the melodramatic as not only is Jacob cast into a prolonged state of bereavement, he also gives up all of life's pleasures and totally isolates himself from human contact:

> Then Jacob built a house of wood and named it "The House of Mourning for Joseph," and around it the birds nested and the wild animals dwelled. In that location Jacob commenced to mourn and refrain from sleep; neither did he raise his head (which was between his knees) from the ground. And

> he abstained from food and drink, and sleep did not come upon him all the while he was mourning over Joseph. And he became weak, and his face became pale, and his body grew thin. (*Joseph,* 17–18)

Such emotional extravagance has its roots, however, in Genesis. Already in the immediate aftermath of viewing Joseph's bloodied garment, we are given insight into the depth of Jacob's mourning over his lost son: "And Jacob rent his clothes and put sackcloth round his waist and mourned for his son many days. And all his sons and all his daughters rose to console him and he refused to be consoled and he said, 'Rather I will go down to my son in Sheol mourning,' and his father bewailed him" (Gen. 37:34–35). The phrase "I will go down to my son in Sheol mourning" will become a constant refrain in connection with Jacob the father: it is invoked by Jacob when he refuses the Brothers permission to take Benjamin down with them to Egypt (42:38); again, when Judah confronts Joseph and reports Jacob's words (Gen. 44:29); and once more when Judah states to Joseph the dire consequences for his father if Benjamin were not to return with them (Gen. 44:31). *The Book of Jubilees,* dating to possibly the second century BCE, in accordance with its calendrical interests and the correlation of biblical events with specific holidays, connects Jacob's mourning over Joseph with the institution of the Day of Atonement: "Therefore, it is ordained for the children of Israel that they should be distressed on the tenth [day] of the seventh month, on the day Jacob received the news of Joseph's death. Each year on this day, the sin-offering of atonement was to be a goat kid because they [Jacob's sons] transgressed with a kid, and thereby brought sorrow upon Jacob" (*Jubilees* 34:18).[27] Another, metaphysical, reading assigns Jacob's "refusal to be consoled" to Joseph's still being alive: "A Roman matron asked R. Jose: 'It is written *Judah was strongest amongst his brethren* (1 Chronicles 5:2), and we read of him, *And Judah was consoled* (*va-yinaḥem,* Gen. 38:12); yet of this man, who was father of them all, [the text says] *and he refused to be consoled* (*lehitnaḥeim*)!' He said to her, 'One may be consoled for the dead, but one is not consoled over the living'" (BR 84:21).[28] It is only when Jacob learns of Joseph's survival that these deep feelings of bereavement are removed from him.

In some traditions, Jacob will be informed of the survival of Joseph and his sons by his granddaughter, Seraḥ, the daughter of Asher. This character, who figures broadly in the Midrash, is known in the Bible through the mention of her name in the list of Jacob's descendants who go down to Egypt, and, enigmatically, her name reappears in the list of those who leave at the time of the Exodus (Gen. 46:17; Numbers 26:46).[29] From this, the Rabbis determined that her life miraculously spanned the entire time period between the two events. Moreover, being the sole survivor of that first émigré generation, it is she who in the Midrash reveals to Moses Joseph's burial site so that he may transport his bones to the Land of Canaan in accordance with Joseph's last wishes (*Bereishit raba* 84:9).[30] The aggadists' imagination did not stop even here, and there arose traditions maintaining that Seraḥ was numbered among the very limited ranks of those privileged to enter the Garden of Eden alive (*Yalquṭ shimᶜoni* II: 367). Be that as it may, the primary reason the traditions give for her long life or immortality is her role in revealing to Jacob that Joseph was still alive in Egypt. In *Joseph* the narrator provides a parenthetic account in which Jacob refuses to believe her claims: "Seraḥ, daughter of Asher, all the while Joseph was in Egypt and Jacob was in sorrow, would say, 'Manasseh and Ephraim and Joseph are alive in Egypt,' and the prophet Jacob would rebuke her and say to her, 'Why do you cause me pain, O daughter?' And as soon as Joseph was reunited with his father, Jacob, God arose and called her to enter the Garden of Eden alive" (*Joseph,* 163). Instead, the text records that the blind and miserable Jacob, awaiting Benjamin's return at the road-crossing, will finally become aware of Joseph's survival through an encounter with the angel Gabriel:

> Now when Joseph was lost, prophecy was lifted from Jacob for nineteen years. And God, may He be praised and exalted, inspired Gabriel, peace upon him, to descend to Jacob who was sitting upon the roadways looking for Benjamin with eyes blinded from crying for Joseph. When Gabriel came up to him, he said to him, "Peace upon you, O Prophet of God." And Jacob lifted his head and returned the greeting to him. And he saw before him a magnificent man, and Jacob said, "And upon you peace. Have you come to deliver tidings of my beloved Joseph?" Gabriel said to him, "I did not announce it to you, so who informed you that Joseph is alive?" And he said to him, "Since my beloved Joseph departed I have been deprived of my sight and prophecy has been lifted from me. But when you greeted me, I lifted my head and saw your face and I knew that you were coming to announce Joseph." (*Joseph,* 164–65)

In other traditions his epiphany occurs when Joseph sends Jacob his garment, which preternaturally restores the father's vision: both literal, in that he has been blinded from a surfeit of tears over the course of Joseph's absence, and prophetic, deprived as he has been of his vaticinal powers. The symmetry of this device is clear: the garment by which he was deprived of his clairvoyance is precisely that which will return it to him after long years of tribulation. The Genizah materials actually preserve a wonderful record of the salience of this motif for Jews in a letter written by an elderly woman residing in Raqqa on the Euphrates to one of her sons in Egypt. In response to his failure to send any word with travelers during the course of the summer months, she writes: "Send me your worn shirts along with their dirt so that I may revive my spirit with them."[31] This motif of the shirt that restores sight is recorded as well in the Qurʾān:

> He said: "Let there be no blame upon you today. May God forgive you: He is the most merciful of all those who show mercy. Take this tunic of mine and throw it over my father's face—he will recover his sight—and come to me with all your family." And when the caravan departed, their father said: "I perceive Joseph's scent even though you think me senile." They said: "By God, you are deluded as before." And when the bearer of good news arrived, he threw [the tunic] over [Jacob's] face and he regained his sight. He said: "Didn't I tell you? From God I know what you do not." (Q 12:92–96)

Are We Our Brother's Keeper?

Much of the narrative tension surrounding the events involving Joseph and his brothers concerns precisely the question of fraternity—do Jacob's other sons regard Joseph as a brother, or do they categorically renounce any such relation? Early on in the narrative (*Joseph,* 17), after the establishment of the wolf's innocence, this sibling relationship is given special poignancy when Jacob turns to his sons and asks, "What have you done to Joseph, your brother?" However, the conflicting perspectives on this matter are most clearly limned when Judah seeks to convince the other siblings not to murder Joseph: "'All the more so, this is your brother, your flesh and blood, and he does not deserve that.' And they said to him, 'O Judah, he is not our [brother] but yours; you will not allow us to do to him what we want. Let's kill him and be rid of his false dreams and of him'" (*Joseph,* 25). This theme and even some of the language directly echo the text in Genesis: "And Judah said to his brothers, 'What gain is there if we kill our brother and cover up his blood? Come, let us sell him to the Ishmaelites and our hand will not be against him, for he is our brother'" (Gen. 37:26–27). Indeed, Judah is relentless on this point; in the dialogue that ensues in the Judeo-Arabic retelling, the appellation "brother" acquires the force of *Leitwort:* "I'll advise you what to do regarding your brother. Is it not enough for you that you have separated him and Jacob his father? Indeed, murdering your brother is not proper, my brothers, nor is it sound" (*Joseph,* 26). In the end, the as-yet incognito Joseph will provide a revisionist countermemory of this scene (absent from Genesis), when he points up Judah's hypocrisy in now so vehemently defending Rachel's other son: "And why did you, O Judah, say upon the selling of your brother, 'Throw the son of Rachel in the well'?" (*Joseph,* 161). Here, Joseph self-consciously refers to himself as Judah's brother, in contrast to Judah's rejection of him as the son of a different mother.

Reflecting the underdetermined nature of the scriptural versions, on the one hand, and the polysemic character of midrash, on the other, the text seems to be of two minds with regard to Joseph's brothers: are they to be considered saints or villains? We have already noted the ambiguity in the narrator's presentation of Joseph, and the words "one of them was more righteous" (*Joseph,* 1) would seem to attribute to the Brothers a degree of virtue. Such a conception is preserved in a midrash on the Book of Psalms, which establishes the Brothers' unimpeachable character by alluding to the allegorical interpretation of the Song of Songs wherein Israel is God's beloved: "Jacob was the father of twelve sons, all of them perfect [in their loyalty] to The-Holy-One-Blessed-Be-He. As it says [in Scripture]: *We are all the sons of one man. We are honest* (Gen. 42:11). As it is written: *You are thoroughly beautiful, my companion; there is no blemish within you* (Song of Songs 4:7)" (*Midrash tehilim* 118:20).

Indeed, *The Story of Yusuf, Son of Yaʿqub* contains a tradition, cited from Kaʿb, that Joseph initially enjoyed the Brothers' love and favor. Thus, when Joseph goes out to watch the herd with his siblings their affection for him is unabated: "And at that time they loved him with a strong love." The text then records Joseph's terror when he awakens from the dream of the staffs, and the doting reaction of the Brothers: "And he [Kaʿb] said: and his brothers hugged him to their breast and kissed him between his eyes and said unto him: 'O beloved, what has happened to you, and what has frightened you?'" When he proceeds to relate to them the contents of the dream, however, they understand what it augurs, and so "they envied and hated him" (*Yusuf,* 165–66).

Similarly ambiguous in the traditions is the way the Brothers treat Joseph once they seize him, and the manner of the torments to which they subject him. Although in *Joseph* some of the brothers (Simeon, Levi, and Zebulon are named explicitly) are intent on stoning him, they are ostensibly deterred through Reuben's and Judah's exertions. Any acts of physical abuse are not recorded at the time of his being placed in the pit but are only alluded to in retrospect. This occurs first in the context of Joseph's speech to the spirit of his dead mother:

> For from my father Jacob they have separated me,
> And my young age they did not pity me,
> And with all the torments they tortured me.
> They stripped his shirt from upon me,
> And into the well they threw me,
> And with rocks they stoned me,
> And after beasts they dropped me.
> And they rejoiced while they despised me,
> And peddled as a wretched slave they sold me. (*Joseph,* 37)

While at the very end of the tale, Seraḥ's poem notes the Brothers' victimization of Joseph and their indifference to his suffering:

> And they dropped Joseph bound
> to the depths of the well, with hands tied and arms crossed.
> Then they sat down to lunch.
> Every living thing is prepared for its slaughter. (*Joseph,* 174)

This elaboration of the details of the physical torment to which the Brothers exposed Joseph was triggered by a seeming redundancy in the biblical passage where they cast him into the pit: "And they took him and flung him into the pit, and the pit was empty; there was no water in it" (Gen. 37:24). Why does Scripture here record both that the pit was empty and that it contained no water? Combining this seeming superfluity with the biblical portrayal of the violence with which the Brothers fling Joseph (H: *va-yashlīkhu oto*) into the parched cistern, the Rabbis determined that the emphatic description of its dryness must signify that it was full of vermin: "R. Kahana said: R. Natan b. Minyomi lectured, quoting R. Tanḥum: Why does Scripture say *and the pit was empty; there was no water in it*? If it was empty, there was obviously no water in it. Why then is this stated? To indicate that there was indeed no water, but there were snakes and scorpions in it" (BT *Shabat* 22a; *Ḥagigah* 3a).

The Brothers' indifference to Joseph's torment is deduced by the Rabbis from the juxtaposition in Genesis of this act of violence with their diffident consumption of a meal while their brother lies helpless in the well: "And they took him and flung him into the pit . . . and they sat down to eat bread" (Gen. 37:25). In *Joseph,* Seraḥ's poem also picks up this motif:

> Then they sat down to lunch.
> Every living thing is prepared for its slaughter. (*Joseph,* 174)

There, too, the Brothers refer to Joseph as one of their own only when they concoct a plan to convince Jacob of their blamelessness in his son's "death": "What's stopping us? Let's go out and hunt down the wolf that ate *our brother*" [emphasis added] (*Joseph,* 16). Even here, however, their motives may be suspect, as presumably this is said within earshot of their father, and thus for his benefit.

The Wolf Who Cried "Boy"

Jacob's obtuseness in not keeping his son out of harm's way is noted most clearly in the Qurʾān when, upon being pressed by his sons to send him with them, he tells them that he fears that a wolf will devour Joseph:

> They said: "Father, what is with you that you do you not trust us with Joseph when we only wish him the best? Send him with us tomorrow so that he can have fun and play; we will take the best care of him." He said: "It would greatly sadden me if you were to take him, for I am afraid that the wolf will eat him when you are unaware." They said: "With us being such a sizeable bunch, for the wolf to eat him we ourselves would have to die." (Q 12:11–14)

In al-Thaᶜlabī, Jacob's hesitation is expanded into a full-blown dream in which a group of wolves attacks his favorite son:

> According to Ibn ᶜAbbās and others, what Jacob said is only because in a dream he had seen Joseph on top of a mountain being attacked by ten wolves who were about to devour him, while one wolf among them was protecting him. Then he saw the earth splitting open; and Joseph entered it and did not come out for three days. It is because of this dream that Jacob said, *'I fear lest the wolf should eat him'* (Q 12:13). (Al-Thaᶜlabī, 188)

This motif is picked up in *The Story of Yusuf,* but is absent from *Joseph.* (Later in Genesis, the Brothers *will* need to sway Jacob to send Benjamin with them down to Egypt.) In the commentaries (al-Bayḍāwī, Jalāl al-Dīn, al-Zamakhsharī, and so on), this dream is seen as a reference to the Brothers—transparent to the reader, but not deciphered by Jacob. This ambiguity of Jacob's fear is reflected in the divergence between QSY[1] and QSY[2] concerning the object of his trepidation—the Brothers, who are late in returning from pasture, or Joseph. The former option shares the ironical overtones of the biblical version (37:12–14): because of Jacob's fear for his other sons, a catastrophe befalls the most treasured of his offspring. QSY[2], on the other hand, has a fearful Jacob decline to send him off in search of his brethren.[32]

In Genesis, when the Brothers return from pasture without Joseph, Jacob does not seem to harbor suspicions concerning any role they may have played in his end. Upon being presented the evidence of his bloody "death," Jacob, in a powerful line that scans like verse, jumps to an erroneous and fateful conclusion:

> "A vicious beast has devoured him,
> Joseph's been torn to shreds!"
> (*ḥayáh raʿáh akhalát-hu,*
> *ṭaróf ṭoráf yoséf*) (Gen. 37:33)

This echoes the very words the Brothers earlier employed when they impulsively devised their plot: "Here comes that dream-master! And so now, let us kill him and fling him into one of the pits and we can say, *a vicious beast has devoured him*" (*ḥayah raʿah akhalát-hū*) [emphasis added] (Gen. 37:20). Unprompted, Jacob's utterance of these same words will be heightened by a parallel second hemistich that adds poetic and pathetic force to the cold-blooded statement of the Brothers.

Alternatively, Jacob's gullibility might reflect a darker, subconscious attitude toward the beloved son whose dream presages his future superior station relative to the father. Without going so far out on the proverbial limb, the loss of Joseph, with whom Jacob so clearly identified, constituted a partial annihilation of the self. This trauma may simply have overwhelmed Jacob's critical faculties. His credulity could also be a defensive action, as it was he who sent the youth in search of the Brothers despite being fully aware of their enmity. Seen in this light, Jacob's precipitous conclusion when presented with the false evidence reflects his anxiety about sending Joseph off in the first place. Such a need to deny any accountability is seen later in the story when the Brothers, in accord with Joseph's demand, seek their father's permission to take Benjamin with them to Egypt. Jacob initially refuses, brushing aside any responsibility for Joseph's "death" and laying it at the Brothers' feet: "Me you have bereaved. Joseph is no more and Simeon is no more, and Benjamin you would take!" (Gen. 42:36). Jacob's suppression of his suspicions regarding his sons might also be due to the discomfort this might engender for the role he played within his own family of origin. This history included the duplicity he practiced upon his own father that caused him to live for many years in dread of *his* brother, Esau. Thus, Jacob, as the father, needed to repress any thoughts of his sons' negligence, or, even worse, involvement in foul play. We have already cited the tradition wherein Leah justifies her role in tricking Jacob into consummating their marriage by invoking his deception of Isaac. In the *Zohar* the Brothers' treachery is similarly connected with Jacob's own perfidy:

> The Holy-One-Blessed-Be-He requites man measure for measure. Because Jacob deceived his father and made him say, *"Come close, pray, that I may feel you, my son, whether you are my son Esau or not"* (Gen. 27:21), the Almighty requited him, and his sons made him say, *"It is my son's tunic"* (Gen. 37:33). R. Hiyya said: "Because he made Isaac express this doubt, he was now confronted in similar terms: *"Recognize, pray, is it your son's tunic or not?"* (Gen. 37:32). R. Judah said: "Because Jacob made his father tremble, he was now made to tremble at his son's fate." (*Zohar* 1, 144b, 186a)

In contrast, the Qur'ān portrays Jacob as doubting his sons' account almost from the outset. Moreover, it would seem that the Brothers presume his disbelief:

> And they came weeping to their father in the evening. They said: "Father, we went off to compete together and left Joseph behind with our belongings, and then the wolf ate him; but you don't believe us even though we're telling the truth," and they brought forth his shirt with false (*kadhib*) blood. He said: "It isn't so! You yourselves have plotted something. But Fair Patience! In God may aid be sought against what you describe." (Q 12:16–18)

The commentators held that the blood on Joseph's tunic stands metonymically for the sons' deceit, thus, according to al-Bayḍāwī's interpretation of these verses, *kadhib* connotes "that which is possessed of lying."

The Story of Our Master Joseph combines the credulity of the biblical Jacob with the skepticism of the quranic figure. While the text initially depicts Jacob as trusting in his sons' words, upon his examination of the evidence he is convinced otherwise. The phrasing here parallels in several ways that of the

Islamic Scripture: "Then they approached him and said to him, 'O father, we went to water the flock and left Joseph behind. And a wolf came and ate him. And if you do not believe our speech and we are not trustworthy in your view, then here is his shirt upon which is the blood.' And they related to him the story of the wolf and took out for him Joseph's shirt which was stained with blood" (*Joseph,* 14). In the spirit of "the lady protests too much," the Brothers' vehement and hasty remonstrations against Jacob's disbelief suggest their culpability. After Jacob recovers from his swoon, he inspects Joseph's garment and notes that there is no sign of any marks left by the wolf's teeth. His need to inspect the bloodied garment confirms that he was unable to divine the truth about Joseph's fate because he has been relieved of his powers of prophecy. And yet Jacob was sufficiently suspicious of his sons to examine their evidence closely and to smell it.[33]

Whereas in the biblical text the Brothers merely present the evidence of the bloodied garment and leave the father to make his own errant inference, in *The Story of Our Master Joseph* they play a much more active role in misleading Jacob. Returning from pasture, they wail and cry, and tell their father the doleful tale of how when they went to water the flock a wolf came and ate Joseph. That central prop, the *ketonet pasim* of the Bible, is not specifically mentioned in *The Story of Our Master Joseph;* this is an especially glaring omission given the tale's acute sensitivity to aesthetic distinctions and its luxuriating in lengthy descriptions of elaborate detail. The absence of this item could reflect an ambiguity as to what sort of garment was meant. Moreover, not specifying any particular characteristic of this garment also served the purpose of not drawing out its distinctiveness, allowing for parallels to be easily drawn to the significant role Joseph's various gowns will play later in the narrative. Most importantly, however, by eliding this detail, which in the biblical story symbolizes the father's preference for Joseph, the narrator absolves Jacob of responsibility for fomenting the Brothers' envy.

Truthfulness in a religious or spiritual sense is understood as an ability to penetrate beneath the surface ephemera that ordinarily obscure human awareness. It is in the arena of dreams or other prophetic experiences that perception of true reality and awareness of God's plans are granted the initiated. Others besides Joseph are continually misreading reality. The Brothers fear that Jacob, through his prophetic powers, will come to know that they have sold Joseph. Jacob, however, believes them, which the text cites as evidence of his having lost the gift of prophecy. This points up the distinction between the perfect omniscience of God and the more limited knowledge possessed by His prophets. Prophecy therefore seems to indicate a degree of clairvoyance with regard to knowledge of unseen events: "*The Sages, peace upon them, said* that the fear which entered Master Jacob did not depart until he was reunited with Joseph; while the power of prophecy abandoned him from the time Joseph left his father's side" (*Joseph,* 5). Thus, from the parallel structure we learn that the presence of fear is equivalent to the absence of the power of prophecy, or, alternatively, that Jacob's ill-conceived decision to send Joseph out in search of his brothers was the cause of the departure of prophecy.

The Qurʾān, as if anticipating this claim, has Jacob voicing a premonition of Joseph's downfall: "It would greatly sadden me if you were to take him, for I am afraid that the wolf will eat him when you are unaware" (Q 12:13). Nevertheless, the father still allows Joseph to go with the Brothers after they reassure him of their vigilance. As we have seen, this element is expanded in the literature of the Stories of the Prophets and Jacob has a vision in which ten wolves attack Joseph while one of them (corresponding to the solicitous brother) seeks to protect him. As al-Thaʿlabī makes clear, Jacob is unable to display any creativity in interpreting this dream and reads it literally. It is on this basis that al-Thaʿlabī also records an aphoristic tradition from the Prophet: "Do not give people the idea for an untrue story, for they may use it—as indeed happened in the case of the sons of Jacob: they did not know that wolves eat people until their father suggested it to them, when he said, '*And I fear lest the wolf should eat him* (Q 12:13),' for then they told him, '*The wolf devoured him* (Q 12:17)'" (Al-Thaʿlabī, 188). Al-Kisaʾī records the wolf's speech, but here it is filled out with the wolf himself having similarly undergone the loss of a child:[34]

> "O prophet of God, I did not devour your child, for the flesh of the prophets is forbidden wild birds and beasts. I am but a foreign wolf who have lost my child and had come looking for him from the regions of Egypt when your creatures took me and lied before your very eyes about a crime I did not commit. By Him who caused me to speak, if you let me go, I shall bring you every wolf in the land, and they all will swear that they have not devoured your child." Therefore, Jacob set the wolf free. (*Tales of the Prophets,* 171)

The Solicitous Brother

If in the Muslim accounts of Jacob's dream of the wolves, one of the ten animals seeks to shield Joseph from the others, this represents a particular adumbration of the motif of "the Solicitous Brother." As recognized by critical scholarship, the text in Genesis surrounding the period when Joseph is in the pit reflects a certain merging of traditions. In particular, researchers have focused on the question as to whether the sympathetic sibling is Judah or Reuben and whether the caravan to whom he is sold is Ishmaelite or Midianite. Whatever may be the textual history of these "roughnesses," what is also remarkable is the way the biblical narrator has succeeded in folding them into the narrative. Initially, it is Reuben who saves Joseph from death at the hands of the Brothers by recommending they place him in the pit. His intention is to take Joseph out of the pit once it is safe to do so. Reuben's motivation for doing so is attributed to the favorable impression of him held by Joseph, despite the sin of sleeping with his father's concubine: "R. Neḥemiyah said: Reuben said, 'I am the first born and thus the stink will only hang about me!' The Rabbis said: Reuben said, 'He counts me among my brothers and I will not save him! I thought that I was cast aside because of that act and yet he counts me among my brothers . . . as it said: *And eleven stars were bowing to me* (Gen. 37:9)" (BR 84:15).

According to this tradition, Reuben is not present at the actual sale, although we are not told where he has gone. This creates a problem surrounding Joseph's purchase price as, assuming Benjamin's absence, there would only be nine brothers present to share the money. In *The Story of Our Master Joseph,* the amount cited is twenty light Egyptian pharaonic dirhams (recognized by the Brothers as a paltry amount). The number twenty is also what is recorded in Genesis, although there it is given in units of silver shekels. This accords with Mosaic law, which prescribes a valuation of twenty shekels for a male slave between the ages of five and twenty years (Lev. 27:5). An alternative Christian typological reading maintains that the purchase price was thirty pieces of silver, or the amount paid to Judas for his betrayal in the Gospel narrative (Matt. 26:15).[35] In any case, all these sums can be divided evenly by ten brothers, thereby implicating Reuben as well; and yet the words *va-yishmaʿ* ("he heard"—that is, he was not witness) and *va-yáshov Reʾuven* ("And Reuben returned") that follow this scene, contradict such a reading. It is sensitivity to these words that likely lies behind the rise of traditions that give the price as eighteen pieces of silver. Further support for Reuben not being in on the plot is his earlier behavior and his instinctive ripping of his clothes when he discovers that Joseph is no longer in the cistern (Gen. 37:30). A rabbinic tradition interprets verse 37:22—*And Reuben heard it and came to his rescue*—as being an implicit indication that he was not present and only later learned of the plot:

> Where had he been? R. Judah said: Each brother attended his father on a set day, and that day it was Reuben's turn. R. Nehemiah said: Reuben reasoned, I am the firstborn, and I alone will be held responsible for the crime. Our Rabbis said: Reuben reasoned, He includes me among my brothers—shall I not then save him? I thought that I had become an outcast on account of that affair [when I slept with Bilhah], yet he counts me among them—as it says, *and eleven stars* (Gen. 37:9); shall I then not save him? (BR, 84:15)[36]

Another tradition alluded to in *Joseph* accounts for the Brothers' silence, the absence of Reuben, and the perplexing fact that God did not disclose his designs to his prophet, Jacob: "[The brothers] said: We will establish a ban (*naḥrīm*) amongst us that no one of us should tell Jacob, our father. Judah said to them: Reuben is not here and a ban is valid only with a quorum of ten. What did they do? They included the Holy One, blessed be He, in that ban so that [Reuben] would not tell their father" (*Tanḥuma* [Zundel edition] Va-yeishev 2).[37]

Joseph, like the biblical text, has two versions of the motif of the solicitous brother; in the first instance it is Reuben, while later Judah also comes to Joseph's aid and counsels the Brothers not to murder him:

> No, by God, may He be praised and exalted, there is no god like Him nor anything worshipped but Him. Do not kill and adorn yourselves in his blood. By God, if you do not accept my advice today, I will betray you to your father and he will wash his hands of you, and I will become an enemy to you throughout my life. O brothers, if anyone did such a thing to a dog of yours, you wouldn't desist from him. All the more so, this is your brother, your flesh and blood, and he does not deserve that. (*Joseph,* 24–25)

Here we may see remnants of the midrashic tradition that had the Brothers sic dogs on Joseph, and this motif has a double origin. It is motivated by the biblical verse that mentions the Brothers plotting Joseph's demise while he is still a ways off: "And they saw him from afar before he drew near them and they plotted against him to put him to death" (Gen. 37:18). However, it is also generated by the Brothers' desire not to shed their brother's blood by their own hands (Gen. 37:27). In response to these verses, the Rabbis determined that the plot involved the setting of dogs upon Joseph: "They said: 'Come, let's set the dogs upon him!'" (BR 84:14). This motif is explicated in the commentary of the Roqeiʾaḥ on this verse (based on BT *Pesaḥīm* 118a): "Regarding whoever bears tales (*motzīʾ dibah*) it is written *you will cast* (*tashlikhūn*) *him to the dogs.*

This is juxtaposed to *You shall not bear tales in vain.* Therefore about Joseph, who bore tales, [the Brothers] said: 'Let's sic the dogs upon him!'"[38]

The midrashic work *Sekhel ṭov* elucidates verse 37:18 by noting the unusual use of the direct object marker in the phrase, *va-yitnaklu oto:* "It should have said *va-yitnaklu lo* or *va-yitnaklu bo* ('and they plotted against him'). What do we learn then from this use of *oto*? It teaches us that they did not plot to kill him with their own hands, but rather to kill him by the sheep-dogs, to sic the dogs upon him." This is posited then as part of the Brothers' tactic of deniability, by which they will be able to maintain to their father that it was not *their* hands that shed the blood.

Joseph, in addition, singles out Zebulon as one who sought to murder Joseph: "And when they came to the well where Joseph was, Zebulun called out and said, 'O Joseph, O son of Rachel, have you not died yet?'" (*Joseph,* 20–21). And yet in *The Testament of the Twelve Patriarchs,* it is precisely this brother who alone is portrayed as being solicitous about his brother's fate:

> I am not aware, my children, that I have sinned in all my days, except in my mind. Nor do I recall having committed a transgression, except what I did to Joseph in ignorance, because in a compact with my brothers I kept from telling my father what had been done, although I wept much in secret. I was afraid of my brothers because they had all agreed that, if any one disclosed the secret, he should be killed by a sword. Even when they wanted to kill him, I exhorted them with tears not to commit this lawless act . . . I had no share in the price received for Joseph, my children . . . After they had thrown him into the pit, they sat down and began to eat; as for me, I tasted nothing for two days and two nights, being moved with compassion for Joseph. (*Testament of Zebulon* 3:1)

The Qur᾿ān leaves open the question of which brother it was that was pre-occupied with Joseph's welfare by stating simply "One of [the Brothers] who spoke said" (Q 12:10). However, in postquranic tradition, the commentators attempt to posit an identity: al-Bayḍāwī's comment on this verse relates that the tradition says it was either Reuben or Judah, while al-Thaʿlabī provides evidence that it was Judah alone who acted to protect Joseph: "When [the Brothers] were about to kill him, Judah, the son of Joseph's maternal aunt and the only brother with good intentions towards him, said to them, 'Have you not made an agreement with me that you would not kill him?'" (*Commentary on Sūrah 12,* 189).

The Story of Our Master Joseph casts Reuben as the one who initially shields Joseph from those set on his murder and then brings food to sustain him while he lies in the cistern. In this version, Reuben is prevented from making any attempts to take Joseph out of the pit because of the pact that the Brothers have made (*Joseph,* 20), and yet Joseph has to advise Reuben not to take any of the purchase price in order that God not hold the eldest brother responsible on the Day of Resurrection (*Joseph,* 30–31). Following the arrival of the caravan, however, it is Judah who takes up the role as Joseph's benefactor and protector. Simeon and Levi seek to break Joseph's head with stones, but Judah castigates them for treating Joseph in a manner in which they would not permit anyone to treat a dog of theirs, much less their own brother.[39] Eventually, Judah's great temper is aroused against his brethren, and his breast hairs burst through his clothes and attack the others "like a double-edged sword." When the Brothers relent, Judah tells them that murdering their brother is improper and proposes instead another way to get rid of Joseph: "Let us go to this caravan and say to them, 'Our slave was previously stolen, and today marks three days that we have been searching for him and we haven't been able to find him. And he will confirm to you his slavery.' So sell him and conceal the affair" (*Joseph,* 26). By telling the caravan that Joseph has been stolen from them, they will allay any suspicions that Joseph is not their slave. The Brothers' initial response to Judah's intercession, that "he is not our brother but yours" (*Joseph,* 25), is further evidence of their renunciation of any fraternal connection with Joseph.

Another trend within rabbinic exegesis held Judah responsible for not doing enough to prevent Joseph's mistreatment; moreover, they were able to find within Jacob's blessing of Judah evidence for his leading role in the Brothers' plot: "*A wild beast* is none other than Judah, for the lion is *the* 'wild beast.' Therefore [Jacob] exclaimed, *Joseph's been torn to shreds*—by Judah, who was called a lion (Gen. 49:9). 'Had you not torn him to shreds,' said he [Jacob] to him, 'no creature could have done so'" (Yelamdeinu in *Yalqut talmud torah*). However, for the most part the Midrash exonerates Judah. According to this interpretation, then, Judah declined to take part in attacking his brother and, unlike Reuben, is able to convince the Brothers not to kill Joseph. *Sekhel ṭov* connects Jacob's reaction to Joseph's reported death—"Joseph's been torn to shreds [*ṭarof ṭoraf yosef*]" (Gen. 37:33)—with the father's blessing of Judah: "They agreed when [Judah] made this proposal but not when Reuben made it. Therefore his father gave *him* the 'credit,' as it says

A lion's whelp is Judah, from the prey (*ṭeref*), *O my son, you have risen up* (*ʿalīta*)" (Gen. 49:9). This is the first of two instances in which Reuben's proposals are ignored in favor of those of his younger brother, Judah. Later, Jacob will reject Reuben's guarantee of Benjamin's safe transport to Egypt, only to accept a similar proposal made by Judah. In the end, Judah will become the sole spokesman for the Brothers when they come before "the Egyptian viceroy" (Joseph), as for example, when Judah rises to Benjamin's defense: "*The old lion perishes for lack of prey* (Job 4:11): this applies to Judah, who sacrificed himself for Benjamin's sake, saying, 'Perhaps the Almighty will forgive me the sin of my saying to my father *Joseph's been torn to shreds*'" (BR 93:7 [version of *Yalqut shimʿoni* 1:150]).

Despite the general implicating of the Brothers in the plot, the interpreters also took pains to limit the number of participants directly responsible. As we have already seen, *Joseph* mentions specifically only Simeon, Levi, and Zebulon as potential murderers. Similarly, in *Tanḥuma* (Buber recension) Vayeishev 13, the phrase, *And each man said to his brother* (*va-yomru ish el aḥīv*) . . . [*let us kill him*] (Gen. 37:19), is interpreted as referring to Simeon and Levi. Indeed, it is this pair that is most commonly singled out for opprobrium in the Midrash.[40] In doing so, the Rabbis were again able to draw a link to Jacob's parting words to these two sons: "Simeon and Levi, the brothers—weapons of outrage their trade" (Gen. 49:5). In the sequence of "blessings" administered by Jacob to his sons, they are the only pair referred to explicitly as brothers. Furthermore, their fraternity is portrayed as one rooted in violent behavior, a trait that was revealed most demonstratively in the destruction of Shechem (Gen. 34). The Rabbis provide another very close intratextual reading from Jacob's blessing of Simeon and Levi to support the attribution to them of the crime against Joseph. Interpreting "at their pleasure they tore down ramparts [*shor*]" (Gen. 49:6), they note the enigmatic use of this same term *shor* in Jacob's words to Joseph: "A fruitful son is Joseph, a fruitful son by a spring, daughters strode by a rampart [*shor*]. They savaged him, shot arrows and harassed him, the archers did" (Gen. 49:22–23).

Elsewhere, the circle of those who actually sought Joseph's demise is restricted to one: "The consonantal text is in the singular, for it was only Simeon. When did [Joseph] exact retribution for him? Later, as we read: *And he took Simeon from them and placed him in fetters before their eyes* (Gen. 42:24)" (BR 84:16). This is the origin for what is recorded in *Joseph* as the reason behind Simeon's imprisonment: "Now Simeon alone among the Brothers had wanted to kill Joseph, so Joseph ordered his servants to take Simeon and imprison him" (*Joseph,* 152). In al-Thaᶜlabī (214–15), in a tradition traced to Ibn ᶜAbbas, the Brothers draw lots to determine who will remain behind in Egypt. When it falls to Simeon, so as not to implicate any of the Brothers, it is recorded there that this was because "he had been the one among them most devoted to Joseph, so they left him behind."

And the Caravan Was in Two Parts . . .

The composite nature of the Genesis text is also evident in its blending of traditions regarding the ethnic identity of the caravan as being either Midianite or Ishmaelite. After casting Joseph into the pit, but just prior to Judah's recommendation to sell Joseph, the text in Genesis notes:

> And they sat down to eat bread, and they raised their eyes and saw and, look, a caravan of Ishmaelites was coming from Gilead, their camels bearing gum and balm and ladanum on their way to take down to Egypt. And Judah said to his brothers, "What gain is there if we kill our brother and cover up his blood? Come let us sell him to the Ishmaelites and our hand will not be against him, for he is our brother, our own flesh." And Midianite merchantmen (*soḥarīm midyanīm*) passed by (*va-yaᶜavru*) and pulled Joseph up out of the pit. (Gen. 37:26–29)

And yet, soon after this verse, there appears a variation on the consonantal rendering of the name of these merchants: "But the Medanites (*medanīm*) had sold him into Egypt to Potiphar, Pharaoh's *saris,* the high chamberlain" (Gen. 37:36). Finally, after the digression of Judah's descent to the Adulamites, chapter 39 resumes the tale of Joseph by noting this time that it was the Ishmaelites who had transported Joseph to Egypt: "And Joseph was brought down to Egypt, and Potiphar, *saris* of Pharaoh, the high chamberlain, bought him from the hands of the Ishmaelites who had brought him down there" (Gen. 39:1).

The Rabbis attempt to make sense of these seemingly conflicting statements in various ways. *Tanḥuma* understands this to mean that he was sold three times: by the Brothers to the Ishmaelites, by the Ishmaelites to the Midianites, and by the Midianites to Potiphar: "It was they who sold him to Potiphar in Egypt . . . Three deeds of sale were written on his account" (*Tanḥuma* [Buber recension] Va-yeishev 13). Alternatively, *Bereishit raba* records a dispute in which the number of transactions involving Joseph is given as either four or five: "How many deeds of sale were written in respect of him? R. Judan said: Four—his brothers to the Ishmaelites, the Ishmaelites to the merchants, the merchants to the Midianites, and the Midianites to Egypt. R. Huna said: Five: [all of these, but in addition] the Midianites sold him to the public trustee (*demusia de-medianah*), from whom Potiphar bought him" (BR 84:22).

After Judah makes his proposal to the Brothers, the next verse begins: "And Midianite merchantmen passed by (*va-yaᶜavru*)." The Rabbis interpreted this last word to mean that Midianites "overtook" the Ishmaelites (or, alternatively, the Brothers themselves), and reaching the cistern first, drew Joseph out. Even though the subject of the subsequent verbs is ambiguous, that the Midianites were the subject of the first verb in the verse provided a strong rationale for having them also be the subject of the following verbs.[41]

In Islamic tradition this confusion persists and the various interpretations would seem to reflect the double tradition of Midianites and Ishmaelites. Thus, al-Bayḍāwī interprets the quranic verse that "they concealed him as goods" (Q 12:19) to mean that they hid him from the rest of the caravan. He also offers an alternative explanation: this first group of traders told the other members of the caravan that Joseph's owners had transferred him to them so that the merchants would sell him on their behalf once they reached Egypt.[42] In al-Kisāʾī, there is no mention of any other group of traders; Malik brings Joseph directly to Egypt, where he is put up for auction. In *The Story of Our Master Joseph* the editorial comment that the caravan was in two parts (*Joseph,* 26) would seem to be a vestige of these dual traditions.

The Story of Our Master Joseph avoids any of the confusion of the Genesis text by not providing multiple identities for these traders; however, in accord with rabbinic interpreters (such as Saᶜadya) who held the biblical reference to Ishmaelites as being synonymous with Arabs, the leader is identified as one Malik ibn Rāʾiᶜ al-Khuzāᶜī (*Joseph,* 23; 31; 53). Al-Khuzāᶜī is an ancient Arabian tribal name whose origins are shrouded in obscurity. In time, descendants of the tribe came to rule Mecca and they were considered meritorious in their relations with the Prophet Muḥammad. In al-Bayḍāwī his name is Mālik b. Dhuᶜr al-Khuzāᶜī. In al-Ṭabarī (*Prophets and Patriarchs,* 153), Malik's lineage is given as Malik b. Daᶜar b. Yawbūb ᶜAfqān b. Madyān b. Abraham the Friend (of God); thus, he is a Midianite as in the Bible and a direct descendant of Abraham. In al-Thaᶜlabī (194ff.), he is called Mālik ibn Duᶜar, where the patronymic means "traitor" in Arabic.

The identity of this character in *Joseph* is also confused: Is he simply a trader by the name of Malik, or is he the son of the king, or even a king in his own right—or perhaps some combination of these possibilities? QSY[1] at various junctures seems to offer different answers. Thus, we read, "And the owner of this caravan was a king who went by the name of Ibn Rāʿi al-Khuzāʿī" (*Joseph,* 22–23). QSY² at this juncture also refers to him as such, but the underlying ambiguity is reflected in its calling him "a king who was called son of King al-Khūzʿī." While throughout the negotiations over Joseph's sale, the purchaser is identified as "the merchant," within the contract that is drawn up, he is referred to as "the son of King al-Khuzāʾī" (*Joseph,* 31). After the arrival of the caravan in Egypt, the local merchants as well as the narrator likewise refer to the trader as the king's son. And yet during the course of the dialogue between Malik and the merchants who have come to see what wares he has brought from Syria, the former is addressed as "the king" (*Joseph,* 49). Likewise, in the remainder of the references to this character, while there is some possible ambiguity as to whether *malik* is a job description or a proper name, it seems that in fact he is addressed as king.

"Stolen" or "Stealing"

Perhaps the most damning but also most opaque of the accusations made against the protagonist in *The Story of Our Master Joseph* is his brothers' referring to him as a thief. And yet according to Judah's intitial plan (*Joseph,* 26), the Brothers are to inform the caravan that Joseph was previously stolen (*sābiq sūrāq*)—the purpose being their title to him as their slave. This might also reflect the confusion in the sources over the identity of the merchant caravan. In addition, in the Genesis narrative it is unclear who extracted Joseph from the well. Some exegetes therefore argue—seeking to explain the confusion between Midianites and Ishmaelites—that this was done not by the Brothers but surreptitiously by the Midianite traders, who, as it were, "stole" Joseph. This interpretation is also supported by the vocalization of the verbal form *sūrāq* with a *waw* (corresponding to the stem vowel *ḍammah*), signifying an internal passive form, thus, "stolen."

However, a tension exists in the text between this motif—previously stolen—and a contradictory interpretation whereby Joseph himself is a thief. The latter alternative is suggested by the words with which the Brothers caution the head of the caravan before they go their separate ways: "*The Sages, peace upon them, said* when the merchant sought to take leave, Jacob's children said to him, 'O merchant, do not depart until we clarify a flaw for you.' And the merchant said to them, 'Tell me, O sons of Jacob, what is his flaw.' They said to him, 'We have sold our slave because he once stole; he is not trustworthy. So be wary of him and do not convey him unless he is bound by his hands and his feet'" (*Joseph,* 33).

Joseph being considered a thief is a widespread tradition that seeks to explain the Brothers' reaction after the cup planted by Joseph is found in Benjamin's saddle pack. In the Qurʾān, the Brothers protest that this is a Rachelite character trait: "If he has stolen, a brother of his [i.e., Joseph] has stolen beforehand" (Q 12:77). This motif seems to bear the influence of a midrashic tradition that held thievery to be another quality Rachel had bequeathed to her sons. This character flaw is evident when, leaving behind her native land for Canaan, she stole her father's household gods—the *terafim:*[43] "And Rachel had taken the household gods and put them in the camel cushion and sat on them. And Laban rummaged through the whole tent and found nothing. And she said to her father, 'Let not my lord be incensed that I am unable to rise before you, for the way of women is upon me'" (Gen. 31:34–35).

Al-Ṭabarī presents a variation on this same theme, but one in which responsibility is assigned to Joseph, who is incited to steal the gods by "Jacob's wife" (apparently Leah, but in any case, according to this version, not their mother, Rachel, who had already died). This account has Benjamin present in the room when Joseph commits the theft—thereby suggesting that his own "thievery" of the goblet was a behavior learned from his elder brother. Al-Kisāʾī records a tradition that the Brothers' remark that Benjamin's brother had stolen before comes from Joseph's habit of taking crumbs from the table to give to the poor.[44] Al-Bayḍāwī claims that when the Qurʾān relates the Brothers' saying of Benjamin that a brother of his stole before, the reference is to Joseph, For this, the exegete gives three possible derivations:

> They mean Joseph. For it is said that his aunt inherited from her father Abraham's girdle; and she used to nurse Joseph and love him, and when he grew up to be a youth, Jacob wished to withdraw him from her influence, so she tied the girdle round his waist and then proclaimed that it had been lost; so a search was made for it, and it was found tied round Joseph, and thereby [she was] the most entitled to him according to their law. Another story is that Joseph's mother's father had an idol which Joseph stole, broke, and threw among the carrion. Another, that there was in the house a young she-kid (or, a hen) which he gave away to a beggar. (*Commentary on Sūrah 12,* 40)

The first of these motifs became the predominant explanation because of its resonance with the theme of the search for the stolen cup, including the legal principle invoked that the one upon whom the stolen item was found would become the property of the aggrieved party. Moreover, it also accords with the theme of "the wiles of women" which we will presently discuss. In other words, Zulaykhā's attempts to possess Joseph through guile had a precedent in his early childhood with his paternal aunt. Such a direct attribution of thievery to Joseph—no matter how minor or justified—seems to be suppressed in *The Story of Our Master Joseph* as there is no support given the Brothers' statement. Moreover, the quranic statement ascribing this fraternal trait is absent from *The Story of Our Master Joseph.* This would also serve to reinforce the interpretation of Joseph being a stolen rather than stealing slave.

Repressed Memories

What exactly did the Brothers do to Joseph when they met out in the pasture? Their original plan—recorded in Genesis and retained in the midrashic accounts—was to murder him. Yet Reuben, in an attempt to save Joseph, offers the alternative strategy of throwing him alive into the pit. He explains this change to his siblings as a subterfuge that they will use to avoid direct responsibility for bringing about Joseph's death, ostensibly from thirst and starvation, in the pit. But there is no immediate confirmation from the Brothers that they consent to this change in plan; we as readers are left in suspense as to what course the Brothers will take until their actions reveal it. The version of the Brothers' plot recorded in Genesis is that they will kill Joseph, cast him into a pit, and then tell their father that a wild animal has consumed him: "And so now, let us kill him and fling him into one of the pits and we can say, a vicious beast has devoured him" (Gen. 37:20). The fact that these three separate acts are linked together in one coherent plan and that the final two components are explicitly carried out in the ensuing action further associates the Brothers with the actual killing of Joseph. Another element suggestive of violence is the Brothers' slaughter of the innocent goat whose blood is used to soak Joseph's garment. This goat's function as a stand-in for Joseph is supported by the narrator's note that it was chosen because its blood most closely resembles that of humans (*Joseph,* 13–14), so that the slaying of the goat kid in Joseph's stead metaphorically implies Joseph's own death. Al-Thaʿlabī records that the Brothers actually roasted and ate the lamb (191–92), which, while symbolizing the Brothers' indifference to Joseph's plight, even suggests a cathartic cannibalism vis-à-vis their brother. Moreover, Joseph's descent into the pit, a well-established biblical metaphor for death, figures several times in *The Story of Our Master Joseph* in descriptions of Jacob's state of mourning (*Joseph,* 6), as it does in the Genesis version (37:35).

Joseph's "murder" is furthermore implied by the parallels with the biblical archetype for sibling rivalry, the story of Cain and Abel (Gen. 4). There as well a major theme is the displacement of the elder son from his favored position: Cain, the firstborn, is envious of the preference he perceives God has extended to the more substantial offering of his younger brother. Here the father-son nexus revolves around God as Father, who for enigmatic reasons paid heed to Abel's offering and ignored Cain's. The confrontation that follows the actual murder is between God and Cain; remarkably the reactions of the parents are nowhere recorded. Another motif not included in the biblical text, but present in ancient versions, is Cain's enticement of his brother to come into the field. This would be analogous to both the quranic and midrashic expansions of the Joseph story where the Brothers are obliged to tempt Joseph to join them in the pasture.

The exegetical expansions of the tale of Cain and Abel in several ways parallel the progression of the plot of Joseph and his brothers as developed in the Midrash and in *The Story of Our Master Joseph:* the envy of the elder brother for the fatherly affections enjoyed by the younger; the murder plot; the concealing of the corpse in the field; the dissimulation of the perpetrator; the credulity of the father. Josephus thus records the murder event and the ensuing interrogation of Cain by the all-knowing God:

> Consequently Cain, provoked that Abel had been valued more highly by God, killed his brother, and rendering his corpse unseen, supposed that he would escape notice. But God, being aware of the deed, came to Cain, inquiring about his brother, whither he had gone, since He had not seen him for many days, whereas at all other times he had beheld him in His company. Cain, being at a loss and not having anything to reply to God, kept answering at first that he too was perplexed at not seeing his brother, but angered by God's persistent pressuring and detailed examination, he said that he was not the guardian and custodian of him and his deeds. God thereupon now accused Cain of being his brother's murderer and said, "I am amazed that you are unable to say what has happened to a man whom you yourself have destroyed." (*Antiquities,* 20)

In addition, God's words to Cain, "the soil that gaped with its mouth to take your brother's blood from your hand" (Gen. 4:11), resonate with the well that has swallowed up Joseph who has been tossed there by his Brothers' hands. In any case, the casting of Joseph into the pit, and his resulting occlusion, is itself a metaphor for real or suppressed acts of violence.

In *The Story of Our Master Joseph,* after the Brothers' arrival in Egypt they are convinced that Joseph is no longer alive, even though, to the best of their knowledge, the merchant who purchased him had carried him down to Egypt. In an archly ironic passage they refer to Joseph as dead and refer to their persecutor, who is in fact Joseph, as al-ʿAzīz: "However, this one is dead, so now tell us what you counsel us in this calamity, in this matter of al-ʿAzīz, for he is punishing us" (*Joseph,* 148). Of course, the actual killing of Joseph is an impossibility given the narrative exigency of keeping the hero alive. This conforms to the overall Genesis framework of maintaining the hereditary line (and here the Brothers' innocence of a capital crime is pointed up by the contrast between the dead-end line of Cain and that of the Brothers, the eponymous ancestors of the Tribes of Israel). However, even the intimation of the possibility of such a deed gives rise to suspense in the narrative. In perhaps an exaggerated formulation of this notion, the entire story of Joseph can be seen, if not as the repressed memory of the actual killing of Joseph by his brethren, then as the subconscious working out of such a desire.

The Test

Even though the Brothers' plot to kill Joseph was not realized, nevertheless, the sheer heinousness of their proposed crime requires a cathartic cleansing. For this to have full effect, however, the initiative for any reconciliation necessarily had to come from the Brothers' side.[45] Therefore, once they arrive in Egypt, Joseph employs a strategy designed to get the Brothers to recognize the error of their past treatment of him. Joseph is able to test the ultimate sincerity of this change of heart through their treatment of his full-brother, Benjamin, Rachel's only other son. After all, despite Joseph's claim to the contrary, the mere bringing of Benjamin would not in itself prove them to be truthful in their account. Neither, for that matter, would Benjamin's arrival in Egypt refute Joseph's accusing the Brothers of being spies. Indeed, Joseph's entire proposal in Genesis is nothing more than a ruse. He himself makes it clear that the Brothers are being subjected to a test via Benjamin: "That's just what I told you, you are spies. In this shall you be tested (*be-zot tibaḥeinu*) by Pharaoh! You shall not leave this place unless your younger brother comes here. Send one of you to bring your brother, and as for the rest of you, you will be detained, and your words will be tested (*ve-yibaḥanū divreikhém*) as to whether the truth is with you, and if not, by Pharaoh, you must be spies!" (Gen. 42:14–16). Immediately afterwards, Joseph confines his brothers for three days in prison: a period neatly corresponding to the length of time Joseph was in the pit back in Canaan. The succession of "descents" that Joseph undergoes—the pit, Egypt, prison—seems to have caused him to shed some of the brazen arrogance of his youth; similarly for the Brothers, the period they spend in prison has a reforming influence on them and causes them to recognize Joseph as a full-fledged sibling. In Genesis, Joseph sets up a situation parallel to his own where Benjamin is shown favor by him as he was by Jacob: "And now I assign to you one portion more than to your brothers" (Gen. 43:44). This is all part of Joseph's examination of his brothers, to see if they will envy Benjamin and respond in like fashion to the blatant display of favoritism. The congruency between Joseph and Benjamin is drawn out in *The Story of Our Master Joseph,* where the younger brother is also referred to as "the Truthful" (*il-ṣiddīq*) in the context of his ability to read signs and his success in identifying Joseph as his brother. The opposition of the two fraternal groups is further symbolized by the pact that Joseph enters into with Benjamin to hide the secret of Joseph's identity until the proper moment (*Joseph,* 157–58). This pact is analogous to the one concluded between the Brothers during their conspiracy to sell Joseph (*Joseph,* 20).

While the Brothers are his captive "guests," Joseph is able to observe them undergo a transformation in their acceptance of responsibility for the deed they did to him. In *The Story of Our Master Joseph,* in an expanded version of events depicted in Genesis, Joseph directly observes this remorse of the Brothers and the extreme lengths to which they are willing to go in order to return Benjamin safely to his father. Following this display, Joseph rebukes them for not similarly standing up for him, but then relents and reveals his true identity. Whereas beforehand the Brothers had seen Joseph as "the son of Rachel," at the end of the narrative the Brothers come to see him as a "son of Jacob" and their own brother: "Whereupon Joseph said to his brothers, 'What would you say to one who brings you your brother Joseph?' And all of them were astonished and began to say, 'O Joseph, O son of Jacob, come to me. O Joseph, O son of Jacob, come to me.' And they began to look right and left. And Joseph said to them, 'You need not look all about you: I am Joseph, the son of Jacob'" (*Joseph,* 162).

In the final denouement of Joseph's revelation of his true identity, he literally exposes himself, displaying for them his circumcised penis as proof (ibid.). This episode perhaps reflects the fact that in the relevant passage in Genesis, Joseph insists on privacy and excuses all his Egyptian attendants; moreover, the biblical verse is vague here as to the particular manner in which Joseph "made himself known": "And no man stood with him when Joseph made himself known to his brothers" (Gen. 45:1). It is this ambiguity that allows for a euphemistic interpretation of the biblical expression. Such an act is of obvious symbolic significance in a tale where sexual restraint plays such a large role. On a broader scale, it would also reverberate with the theme of sexual boundaries as a metaphor for cultural separation and distinctiveness. Circumcision of the male sexual organ functions as a sign of the covenant that physically marks off the Jews from others. In al-Kisāʾī's version, it is the deed of Joseph's original sale (demanded of and given by Joseph's brothers to the merchant and then by the merchant to Joseph for him to keep) that is whipped out by Joseph as confirmation of his identity. The reappearance of this document at the story's end explains its otherwise seemingly anomalous presence in *The Story of Our Master Joseph.*

The Story of Our Master Joseph consistently depicts Jacob and Joseph as steadfast in their submission to God's will and in their belief that His justice will ultimately triumph. There are numerous statements to this effect spread out over the course of the tale. While this is an inherently Muslim theme, it is also part and parcel of the story's heavy didacticism, and in turn, reflective of its role in popular religion and culture. The point of the story is to show that God's plan is always in effect, but that the actual path destiny will take is understood only by Him. The omniscient narrator is privy to this information, but passes only occasional clues to the reader for whom, in any case, the ultimate outcome is already known. However, part of the pleasure we derive as readers is suspending this knowledge and tracing the progression of the plot and the characters' growing awareness of its direction. Oftentimes, such knowledge is even withheld from God's benighted prophets who must rely on their steadfast trust in Him throughout their trials. God's role here in manipulating characters and events recalls other instances in the Bible (such as His "hardening" Pharaoh's heart, or His testing of Abraham and Job) that have provoked much commentary on the seeming callous unfairness of this procedure; however, God in such instances may be seen as pursuing some larger divine purpose or raising the odds against which the biblical heroes must struggle and thus magnifying their achievement. Such a pronounced deistic intrusion into the story is used to assert God's control over all creation and the wisdom of His ultimate design. And yet, human free will and agency are upheld, and the testing of prophets highlights their steadfastness as models of forbearance under the most difficult circumstances. This is a test in which Joseph will ultimately succeed; in so doing he resolves his rivalry with his brothers while gaining their acknowledgment of his superiority. In the coming chapter we will explore the other major test Joseph had to face, this time at the hands of the temptress, Zulaykhā, his master's wife.

3

Joseph and Zulaykhā

"Never trust what is read from a page; nor put a woman in the trust of a young man. . . ."

Al-Thaʿlabī, *Lives of the Prophets*

In *The Story of Our Master Joseph,* our protagonist is still sequestered in the pit when God informs him that better times lie in store: "I will take you out of this well after a period of three days and judge you over your brothers. And [you shall] rule Egypt, and your brothers will fall conquered into your hand" (*Joseph,* 12). Although God assures Joseph a reversal of his fortunes in the future, what He neglects to mention here is the time lag between Joseph's removal from the well and the promised ascendancy over his brothers. Further, there is no mention of the ultimate challenge Joseph will undergo at the hands of Zulaykhā, the wife of his Egyptian master. These tribulations are at the center of much of this Judeo-Arabic version of the story—and of the body of Muslim and Jewish exegesis, in general. Saved from death, Joseph is sold into slavery and transported down to Egypt, but this will become the venue for the second set of challenges the hero of this romance will need to overcome. Joseph's confrontation with his mistress, which in the Bible takes up a mere fourteen verses (Gen. 39:7–20), has undergone a most remarkable expansion whose contours will be the focus of this chapter. The predominance of this episode in *The Story of Our Master Joseph* is reflected both in its narrative richness and in its length; the events that take place between Joseph and Zulaykhā extend over two-thirds of the manuscript (pages 53–169, out of a total of 177). Even when the narrative proceeds to relate the story of Joseph's rise to power and his reunification with his family, the story is not allowed to come to a close without tying together the ends of the affair and relating Zulaykhā's ultimate fate.[1]

Joseph's Descent into Egypt and His Sale

In Genesis, after the Brothers' sale of Joseph, the narrative breaks off for the story of Judah and Tamar, resuming in chapter 39 with Joseph already in Egypt. *The Story of Our Master Joseph,* on the other hand, concentrating as it does on the single character of Joseph, allows for no such digression. Instead, it provides an account, "missing" both from Genesis and the twelfth *sūrah,* of Joseph's descent and arrival into Egypt, and his subsequent public sale there to al-ʿAzīz (corresponding to the biblical Potiphar). In this, it mirrors other Jewish and Islamic retellings of the story, such as the rendering in *Sefer ha-yashar* and al-Kisāʾī; however, in much of its content *Joseph* bears the closest resemblance to the Aljamiado version recorded in *The Story of Yusuf.* This additional material, interposed between the two transactions involving Joseph, is an excellent example of the way in which midrash can fill a perceived narrative gap in the *Vorlage* as well as link together disparate sections of the original story cycle. It also illustrates the ways in which Jewish and Islamic motifs may be integrated within a single text.

Thus, after Joseph is sold to the merchant, al-Khuzāʿī, he asks permission of his new master to go after his brothers so that he may entreat them to take care of his "bereaved, orphaned brother"; that is, Benjamin (*Joseph,* 33). This is in accord with the portrayal of Joseph as resigned to divine destiny and unconcerned with his own fate but preoccupied with that of Benjamin and Jacob. Out of pity, the merchant loosens his bonds; however, when Joseph sets out running after the Brothers, they continue to distance themselves from him until, stumbling, he falls to the ground. Reuben, turning around and seeing the prostrate Joseph, implores the others to stop, but they respond that they are only too happy to finally be free of Joseph and his dreams. Reuben chastises them for this lack of remorse for their deed and promises them that they will in the future need to "pay [Joseph's] weight in gold and silver" (*Joseph,* 34–35) in order to see him. At this they halt—it is not clear whether it is because of contrition, or anxiety over the financial loss they will one day incur—but in any case, Reuben's words here are a clear foreshadowing that the Brothers and Joseph indeed will all meet up again, albeit on completely different terms. Once they stop, Joseph is able to catch up to them, and when he does, he begs the oldest brother to look after Benjamin. Expressing dismay that Jacob will no longer have any happiness, he affirms once again his steadfast faith in God's salvation.

Joseph is placed bareback upon a camel, and the caravan sets off for Egypt. As they pass by the tomb of Rachel, her distraught son falls off his camel.

In another manifestation of Joseph's strong identification with his mother, he addresses Rachel, describes for her the torments to which he has been subjected (*Joseph,* 36–38), and prays that he will soon be united with her in the Afterlife. In response, Joseph hears a heavenly voice encouraging him not to despair. In the meantime, the caravan has moved on. When the merchant notices Joseph's disappearance, it confirms for him the truth of the Brothers' warning that the slave was not to be trusted. When al-Khuzāʿī finds Joseph, he strikes the youth on his face; there ensues a series of natural calamities in divine retribution for this assault upon one of God's prophets. The merchant, after getting the advice of his comrades (who recognize Joseph's prophethood), beseeches Joseph to pray to his god for cessation of the punishment; moreover, he invites Joseph to return the blow to him. However, in a further demonstration of his forgiving nature, Joseph forbears, and instead humbly implores his Lord to lift the torment, which God immediately does. This is merely the first instance of the blessings that Joseph's presence bestows on his masters.

As the caravan continues onward, al-Khuzāʿī overhears the angels that greet Joseph by night and day, and observes as well a white cloud that floats above his slave's head. Upon their arrival at the Nile River, Joseph performs his devotions, preceded by the ritual ablution required prior to Muslim prayer, and bathes in the river. Restored now to his natural beauty, Joseph puts on the garment that Gabriel had provided him in the well, and the merchant, overjoyed with his purchase, places him upon his best riding-camel. Thus adorned, they proceed into the City of Egypt. The ethereal glow, the nimbus that surrounds Joseph, astounds the population: "And Egypt became like unto the beauty of Joseph, and from between his eyes a light that resembled Heaven shone upon the women in their houses and upon the men in their shops. And the world glowed in Joseph's light to the point that the people of Egypt were amazed and said, 'This is the light of the sun and not the light of the moon for [even] the clouds are revealed'" (*Joseph,* 44).

People begin to gather from all over the country in order to view the source of this light, but when they arrive at al-Khuzāʿī's palace, the merchant draws curtains over Joseph so that none may see him. Joseph's mere presence in the land, however, brings about a series of positive transformations in the country's fortunes. Egypt, which had previously been in a state of decline, now begins to flourish: the Nile rises, trees bear fruit, despotic rulers are replaced, and so forth. God has effected these changes through the "Angels of Delight" in order to endear Joseph to the people. Although al-Khuzāʿī has placed Joseph in isolation, a group of Egyptian merchants comes to view the products he has brought back from Syria. After some hesitation, Joseph's master discloses to them that he has acquired from Jacob's sons a youth so beautiful that his "face is like the moon on the fourteenth night." While he declines to show him to the merchants just then, he gives them a date upon which he will be selling the boy.

When that day arrives, al-Khuzāī makes lavish preparations for Joseph's sale, adorning the youth and positioning him so as to best show off his beauty. From all corners of Egypt the people come; among them are al-ʿAzīz and his wife Zulaykhā, who arrive at the head of a grand procession. When all those assembled view Joseph, they are completely overcome by the light that radiates from him, and they fall down in a swoon. The public auction ensues, the callers announcing Joseph's asking price to be the value of all the opulent jewelry and clothing he wears. In fairy-tale manner, there come two failed attempts to purchase the lad before the successful, third offer. First to approach are a group of seven fabulously rich, Ethiopian steward-merchants who offer ten loads of gold each; they are followed by al-Qurʿa—a queen in her own right and female relative of Joseph's master. She is of the aristocratic Quraysh clan from Mecca, and has a distinguished pedigree, traced back to pre-Islamic history. Among her prestigious forebears is her great-grandfather al-Shaddād, the builder of Ramzat al-ʿImār—a corruption of the quranic *ʿIram dhāt al-ʿimād* ("ʿIram of the many columns," Q 89:7). Islamic tradition indeed records that this Arabian city was built by the legendary al-Shaddad.[2] Also extraordinarily wealthy, al-Qurʿa offers many riches in exchange for Joseph, including a priceless necklace, a family heirloom passed down to her by the same al-Shaddād. At the last moment, with the merchant poised to grab hold of the necklace and consummate Joseph's sale, Zulaykhā sends word to her husband, commanding him to buy Joseph for her. Complying with her wishes, al-ʿAzīz offers one hundred times what al-Qurʿa had bid and purchases Joseph. One small complication follows as the seller asks to be compensated for the crown still upon Joseph's head. His new master agrees to pay the extra sum, and in a further sign of Joseph's great value, he magnanimously allows the merchant to keep the crown as well. However, when al-Khuzāʿī tries to remove the crown, his hand becomes glued to it and cannot be removed; only upon Joseph's praying to God on behalf of his former master is the limb freed.

Al-ʿAzīz and Zulaykhā

In the Bible, Joseph's Egyptian master is a high-ranking officer of Pharaoh named Potiphar. In the Qurʾān, he is not named but is referred to merely by the title "al-ʿAzīz"; however, even this identification is only indirect. Both times the title appears it is within the context of the speech of the Ladies of the Assembly (verses 30 and 51), who employ it not to specify Joseph's master but the master's spouse, who is described as "the wife of al-ʿAzīz" (*imraʾat al-ʿAzīz*). According to al-Bayḍāwī's Qurʾān commentary, this title, whose literal meaning in Arabic is "mighty" or "cherished," means "king" amongst the Bedouin; although he notes that it usually occurs in construct, as in "the mighty one of Egypt" (*ʿAzīz Miṣr*). With regard to this specific term he notes as well that it seems to connote the office of chief minister under the Egyptian pharaoh, as it is applied to Joseph in the Qurʾān once he assumes his position of authority (Q 12:78).[3] In later Islamic traditions Joseph's master is called by the personal name Qiṭfīr, perhaps based on a faulty transmission of his biblical appellation; this in turn evolved into Iṭfīr, as he is generally referred to in al-Ṭabarī, al-Thaʿlabī, al-Zamakhsharī, and al-Bayḍāwī. Other variants include Qiṭfīn, Qiṭʿīn, and Qiṭṭīn, with al-Kisāʾī calling him Quṭifār, closest to the biblical name. He is also known by a patronymic—ibn Ruhayb (or ibn Ruḥayb and ibn Rūḥīt in manuscripts).[4] *The Story of Our Master Joseph* employs none of these variants and instead, like the Qurʾān, refers to Joseph's second master solely by his title as if it were a personal name.

This movement toward greater anonymity of one of the story's protagonists is reversed with regard to Joseph's mistress. While in the Bible, Qurʾān, and older aggadic works she is identified only as the wife of Joseph's master, here in this Judeo-Arabic manuscript she is known by the proper name of Zulaykhā. Originally, Islamic exegetical tradition gives her name as Raʿīl, perhaps representing some confusion (or implied connection) with Joseph's mother, Rachel, whose name in Arabic, Raḥīl, is identical, save for the transposition of the two laryngeal letters, *ʿayn* and *ḥāʾ*, a shift well attested in Arabic phonology. The name Zulaykhā is apparently of Persian origin and was picked up in the Arabic traditions. Both Firdawsī and al-Kisāʾī call the story's female protagonist by this name, while al-Bayḍāwi gives both Zulaykhā and Rāʿīl.[5] Among Jewish works, the name Zulaykhā is found first in *Sefer ha-yashar,* which dates from probably no earlier than the thirteenth century and has absorbed many Islamic motifs. In *The Story of Our Master Joseph* the female protagonist is introduced at first as the wife of al-ʿAzīz (as in the Qurʾān), and only then is her name given in apposition: "As for the wife of al-ʿAzīz (who was Zulaykhā): she had already drawn near, along with all of her women, in order to see Joseph" (*Joseph,* 54). This naming sequence echoes the dependent nature of her relationship to her husband; however, the subordination of her personal name to her conjugal affiliation also suggests that it has been interpolated to remove her anonymity in the biblical and quranic accounts. Given the expansion of the story of Joseph and Zulaykhā related here and in other retellings, she can no longer be merely the wife of Potiphar but, as the female lead in the drama, must assume an identity and a name of her own, while conversely, her spouse is relegated to relative anonymity.

Joseph and the Potiphars—The Genesis Version

As we have noted, before the tale in Genesis proceeds to recount the events that befall Joseph in Egypt, it relates the story of Judah and his daughter-in-law Tamar. This interlude, which takes up all of chapter 38, is another case of female intrigue and illicit sex involving one of Jacob's sons. Moreover, it too is a tale in which the identification of personal belongings brought before one of the protagonists will play a major role: as Joseph's tunic is presented to Jacob as evidence of his beloved son's demise, so also will Judah's seal-and-cord and staff be produced by Tamar to prove her identity as the woman with whom Judah has consorted. It is probable that this digression in the *Vorlage* influenced the expansion of the scene between Joseph and Zulaykhā in the Midrash. Such an intratextual linkage is signaled by Judah's remarks that bring to a dramatic close the events of the episode: "And Judah recognized [his belongings] and he said, 'She is more in the right than I. . . .' And he knew her again no more (*va-yaker yehudah va-yómer tzadkah miméni . . . ve-lo-yasaf ʿod ledaʿatah*) (Gen. 38:26). This verse utilizes the *Leitwort* common to both these stories—*va-yaker.* The Rabbis saw the connection this establishes between the two tales: "R. Yoḥanan said: The-Holy-One-Blessed-Be-He said to Judah, 'You said to your father, "Recognize, pray (*haker na*) [is it your son's tunic or not]?" By your life, Tamar will say to you "Recognize, pray (*haker na*)"'"[6] (BR 84:19). In each case, the one compelled to view the artifacts will be importuned with the same word: *haker*—the imperative form of the Hebrew verb "to know or recognize," preceded here in both cases by the particle of importuning, *na.* And yet the difference in these identifications of the item of personal property is significant; in the case of the Brothers' ruse, Joseph's tunic is an integral part of the deceit, whereas with Tamar, it comes as the means by which the subterfuge practiced upon Judah is disclosed. Moreover, the juxtaposition of the two cases points to the relative legitimacy of Tamar's claim to justice vis-à-vis the Brothers' plot against Joseph. The intertextual artistry of the verse cited above is evident in its conclusion, where the root of Joseph's name is linked with Judah's ceasing to "know" (in the "biblical" or carnal sense) his daughter-in-law Tamar (*ve-lo-yasaf ʿod ledaʿatah*). These few words constitute an allusion to the theme of sexual restraint that will characterize the relationship between Joseph and his master's wife. Moreover, in the middle of the verse appears a word—*tzadkah*—of the same consonantal root as that epithet ubiquitous in traditions about Joseph—*ha-tzadīq*.

Following, then, what was understood by the Rabbis to be a motivated digression, the Genesis narrative picks up the tale of Joseph in chapter 39 at precisely the point where it left off. This resumption of the narrative flow is accomplished by repeating the information with which chapter 37 ended; namely, that the Ishmaelites sold Joseph in Egypt to Potiphar, an officer in Pharaoh's court. The narrator immediately proceeds to an account of Joseph's stay in his new master's house. For the purpose of our discussion, let us cite in its entirety this wonderful example of the workings of the biblical narrative art:

> And Joseph was brought down to Egypt, and Potiphar, courtier of Pharaoh, the high chamberlain, an Egyptian man, bought him from the hands of the Ishmaelites who had brought him down there. And the Lord was with Joseph and he was a successful man, and he was in the house of his Egyptian master. And his master saw that the Lord was with him, and all that he did the Lord made succeed in his hand, and Joseph found favor in his eyes and he ministered to him, and he put him in charge of his house, and all that he had he placed in his hands. And it happened from the time he put him in charge of his house that the Lord blessed the Egyptian's house for Joseph's sake and the Lord's blessing was on all that he had in house and field. And he left all that he had in Joseph's hands, and he gave no thought to anything with him there save the bread he ate. And Joseph was comely in features and comely to look at. And it happened after these things that his master's wife raised her eyes to Joseph and said, "Lie with me." And he refused. And he said to his master's wife, "Look, my master has given no thought with me here to what is in the house, and all that he has he has placed in my hands. He is not greater in this house than I, and he has held back nothing from me except yourself, as you are his wife, and how could I do this great evil and give offense to God?" And so she spoke to Joseph day after day, and he would not listen to her, to lie by her, to be with her. And it happened, on one such day, that he came into the house to perform his task, and there was no man of the men of the house there in the house. And she seized him by his garment, saying, "Lie with me!" And he left his garment in her hand and he fled and went out. And so, when she saw that he had left his garment in her hand and fled outside, she called out to the people of the house and said to them, "See, he has brought us a Hebrew man to dally with us. He came into me to lie with me and I called out in a loud voice, and so, when he heard me raise my voice

> and call out, he left his garment by me and fled and went out." And she laid out his garment by her until his master returned to his house. And she spoke to him things of this sort, saying, "The Hebrew slave came into me, whom you brought us, to dally with me. And so, when I raised my voice and called out, he left his garment by me and fled outside." And it happened, when his master heard his wife's words which she spoke to him, saying, "Things of this sort your slave has done to me," he became incensed. And Joseph's master took him and placed him in the prison-house, the place where the king's prisoners were held. (Gen. 39:1–20)

The beginning of this section relates the success that Joseph enjoys in all of his endeavors and how he causes Potiphar's household to prosper. This, of course, pleases Joseph's master to no end and causes him to regard his servant most favorably. Indeed, the success of Joseph under a series of father figures—from Jacob, to Potiphar, to the keeper of the prison, to Pharaoh, and ultimately, back to Jacob—will be a recurrent theme throughout the Genesis cycle. (To these figures *The Story of Our Master Joseph* and other retellings add the merchant who purchased Joseph from his brothers.) However, it is primarily the episode involving his master's wife that is the focus of our attention here. The shift in emphasis in postbiblical elaborations of the Joseph story onto the biblical episode of Mrs. Potiphar is evident even in early works such as *The Book of Jubilees.* This work, a retelling of the book of Genesis and part of Exodus incorporating ancient extrabiblical traditions, may date as far back as the second century BCE. Here, while much of the rest of Joseph's story is collapsed, the incident with Potiphar's Wife is retained and even expanded:

> And Joseph was good-looking and very handsome. And the wife of his master lifted up her eyes and desired him. And she begged him to lie with her. And he did not surrender himself but remembered the Lord and the words Jacob, his father, used to read, which were from the words of Abraham, that there is no man who [may] fornicate with a woman who has a husband [and] that there is a judgment of death which is decreed for him in heaven before the Lord Most High. And the sin is written [on high] concerning him in the eternal books always before the Lord. And Joseph remembered these words and he did not consent to lie with her. And she begged him [for] one year. And he turned away and refused to listen to her.[7] (*Jubilees* 39:5–8)

Going back to the Genesis passage, the repeated emphasis there upon Potiphar's entrusting into Joseph's hand all that he had in his house cried out to the exegetes for a nuanced reading, and the Midrash was quick to provide several alternative explanations for this seeming redundancy. One of the readings given has Potiphar himself implicated in the "affair" that takes place between his wife and Joseph: as he did not explicitly specify her in the list of objects prohibited Joseph, she too would be included in the things over which Joseph would have mastery. Many commentators read a suggestive element into the statement that Potiphar "gave no thought to anything with him there save the food he ate" (*ve-lo yadaᶜ ito meʾúmah ki im ha-léḥem;* Gen. 39:6), viewing this reference to food as a euphemism for his wife, while perceiving the activity of eating to be an allusion to sexual intercourse.[8] This innuendo is intratextually supported in the Bible by the strikingly parallel structure and wording Joseph subsequently employs when he rejects Mrs. Potiphar's entreaties. At this juncture, Joseph notes that her husband "has held back nothing from me except yourself" (*velo ḥasakh miméni meʾúmah ki im otakh,* Gen. 39:9)—here, the objective pronoun referring to Mrs. Potiphar maps precisely onto the place of "food" in the previous statement. Such an insinuation is echoed once more, later, by the reappearance of the key word *meʾúmah* when Joseph seeks justification before the Pharaoh's servants in prison. At that time, he maintains that in addition to his being blameless in being stolen away from his native land, he is also innocent of any attempt to lie with his master's wife that could justify his imprisonment: "And here, too, I have done nothing (*meʾúmah*) that I should have been put in the pit" (Gen. 40:15).

Al-ᶜAzīz—The (Un?)Witting Cuckold

An even more provocative reading of this expression, that "he gave no thought to anything save the bread he ate," points to Potiphar's complete disinterest in conjugal relations. This midrashic motif is elaborated on by an interpretation of the phrase *lo yadaᶜ*, that "he gave no thought"; that is, that he did not "know" women, or, for that matter, even care to. Yet the clearest scriptural basis for the characterization of Potiphar as indifferent toward his wife, or more precisely, that he is unable to satisfy her—that he is something less than a "man"—is his twice being referred to as *serīs parᶜoh* (Gen. 37:36, 39:1). In context, this expression apparently connotes a member of Pharaoh's court; as it does when the word reappears later in the plural in reference to the sovereign's cupbearer and baker:[9] "And Pharaoh was furious with his two courtiers (*sarisav*)" (Gen. 40:2).

However, the word *saris,* elsewhere in the Bible and throughout rabbinic literature signifies "eunuch."[10] Such ambiguities in Potiphar's description and behavior in the Genesis narrative are the basis for the portrayal of al-ʿAzīz in *The Story of Our Master Joseph.* Here he is depicted both as impotent and as voyeuristic, as negligent in exercising control over his wife and as guilty of somehow facilitating her attempt at seduction—or at the very least, as being an exceedingly gullible bystander. Furthermore, Potiphar's failure to take resolute action—against Joseph, in the wake of his wife's allegations (which ostensibly, he believed), and later against his wife, following the revealing of her falsehood—is a sign of domestic and political weakness, an incapacity for which castration would serve as an appropriate marker.[11]

The Rabbis were able to uncover a further scriptural basis in Genesis for the depiction of Potiphar as a hapless "schlemiel" of a husband. Three times following Joseph's escape from Mrs. Potiphar's grasp, she charges him with sexual assault: first to her male servants and twice more to her husband.[12] With regard to the final recounting of "the heinous act" before her husband, Robert Alter has drawn attention to the ambiguity of the relevant verse: *ba elay ha-ʿéved ha-ʿivri asher-heivéita lánu letzaḥeiq bánu* (Gen. 39:17). Given the flexibility of Hebrew word order, it is possible to read this verse in two ways—as expressing either muted or, alternatively, blatant criticism of Potiphar by his wife; either "the slave came to me—the one you brought us—to dally with me," or, "the slave came to me, the one you brought us in order to dally with me."[13] By this latter reading, Mrs. Potiphar herself suggests a certain perverse voyeuristic complicity on the part of her husband. By the third time the liaison between Joseph and Mrs. Potiphar is recounted (39:19), the act has been boiled down to its most suggestive and odious essentials: "Things of this sort your slave has done to me."[14] Here, too, the Midrash adds a piquant detail, reading the ambiguous expression—"things of this sort" (*ka-devarim ha-eileh*)—as evidence that Mrs. Potiphar's disclosure took place while the Egyptian couple was engaged in the very act of sex; that is, "your servant did to me just as you are now doing."[15]

If we turn to the Islamic characterizations of Joseph's Egyptian master, al-Ṭabarī, in a remarkable acknowledgment of cross-cultural borrowing, explicitly attributes a Jewish origin to the quranic passage in which al-ʿAzīz directs his wife to take solicitous care of their new charge: "[The people of the Torah] also say that when Potiphar bought Joseph and brought him to his house, he said to his wife, (whose name, according to Ibn Humayd—Salamah—Ibn Isḥāq, was Rāʿīl): *'Be kind to him. He may prove useful to us, or we may adopt him as our son'* (Q 12:21)" (*Prophets and Patriarchs,* 154). On the most basic level, these words positing Joseph's possible future utility to his mistress and master simply allude to his promising acumen that will make him successful in managing the affairs of the household. The following quranic verse—"And when he grew to adulthood, We bestowed upon him wisdom and knowledge" (Q 12:22)—would seem to support such an interpretation. The exegetes also noted that it is possible to read this verse as implying Joseph's reaching of sexual maturity; accordingly, his ability to "help us in some of our affairs" could prefigure an adulterous role for Joseph. This interpretive undercurrent is in turn buttressed by the very next verse: "And the woman in whose house he was sought to seduce him against his will" (Q 12:23). The juxtaposition in the text of a premonition of Joseph's developing carnal knowledge with the illicit proposition of his mistress would serve to connect the two events in the mind of the audience, much as in the Bible, the mention of Joseph's beauty immediately prior to his being noticed by Mrs. Potiphar would establish a linkage between these narrative elements.[16]

Such a portrayal of Joseph's master as something of a cuckolded buffoon is evident in *The Story of Our Master Joseph.* At the very beginning of the couple's interactions over Joseph, al-ᶜAzīz rushes to fulfill his wife's order to buy the lad, paying al-Khuzāᶜī an exorbitant price. Subsequently, as al-ᶜAzīz is bringing Joseph to Zulaykhā's home, he manages to lose his way and must ask for help—an unambiguous indication not just of his incompetence but also of his profound estrangement from his wife. While giving him directions, the townspeople mock him for not knowing the location of his wife's palace; however, as if symptomatic of his ineffectiveness, even with this guidance he still winds up astray and finally breaks down in tears. When he and Joseph at long last arrive at Zulaykhā's palace, he winks at the youth and instructs him to kiss his mistress's hands. In accord with the quranic account, *Joseph* records here that he told his wife to "honor this youth for me out of respect for me. He might prove useful to me; we will treat him like our children." *The Story of Our Master Joseph,* however, is more definitive in maintaining that the reason for al-ᶜAzīz's love for his servant was related to his disinterest in members of the opposite sex: "[Now] al-ᶜAzīz did not love women at all, and because of that he loved Joseph and took him as a child in place of his child, and he loved him dearly" (*Joseph,* 67–68). Although we need to be cautious about reading all homosocial relationships as homosexual, nevertheless, such illicit designs upon Joseph constitute here a definite narrative undercurrent.[17] At the very least this would imply a lack of any prospect of progeny, a deficiency for which Joseph could compensate. A similar interpretation is cited by al-Thaᶜlabī: "Ibn Isḥāq said that Potiphar [Qifṭīr] did not lie with women, and that his wife Raᶜīl was beautiful and lived in comfort and luxury" (Al-Thaᶜlabī, 197). *Joseph* reifies the alienation existing between the Egyptian husband and wife by having al-ᶜAzīz, subsequent to delivering the boy into Zulaykhā's care, depart for his own city, some seven days' journey away. The text leaves unanswered the question of why al-ᶜAzīz would leave his beautiful (and sexually unsatisfied!) spouse with an exceedingly attractive, seventeen-year-old male youth. For the Rabbis, this becomes the paradigmatic example of why one should not place even the most chaste of individuals in a situation of sexual temptation: "From this it is said that one does not appoint as a guardian against unchastity (*apotrópos ᶜal ha-ᶜarayot*) even one such as Joseph the Righteous"[18] (*Midrash ha-gadol*). The situation is less subtle in *Joseph* in that after al-ᶜAzīz's return to his own residence, he sends a letter back to his wife telling her that Joseph is a prophet and thus should not be given work; moreover, he informs her that Joseph is "our child and our beloved" (*Joseph,* 69). Whereas in the Genesis narrative it is Joseph who is entrusted with all that is in his master's house—which, as previously mentioned, one interpretive stream held as indicating Potiphar's somehow promoting a liaison between his servant and his wife[19]—here it is Zulaykhā who is given charge by her husband of Joseph. Thus, her husband's directive—"honor Joseph as you honor me"—may bespeak an implicit encouragement of his wife's seduction of the servant.

There are many other examples of al-ᶜAzīz's "unmanliness," including the ease with which Zulaykhā is able to convince him to underwrite the costs of constructing the very houses with which she hopes to overcome Joseph's resistance (*Joseph,* 90–91). Following her failure at accomplishing this, al-ᶜAzīz will believe Zulaykhā when she charges Joseph with attempting to take her by force. But even here he fails to take resolute action and kill Joseph, instead merely imprisoning him—and this only at his wife's insistence. After Joseph is jailed, al-ᶜAzīz does not monitor his wife's behavior, and thus she is able, without her husband's knowledge, to bring Joseph to herself (*Joseph,* 115). Ultimately, following her admission of guilt in Pharaoh's court and the proof of Joseph's innocence, al-ᶜAzīz does not mete out a "fitting" punishment of death for his wayward wife; that is left to Joseph. All this contributes to an ironic depiction of Joseph's master as anything but "the mighty one" and suggests his obtuseness—if not his outright complicity in the affair.

This motif of the master's sexual ambivalence can also be seen within Jewish tradition in the attempts to account for the similarity of the biblical appellations for Joseph's master and his future father-in-law, Potiphar and

Potiphera, respectively. In the pseudepigraphic literature and several rabbinic texts the near identity of these names is understood to mean that they refer to one and the same person.[20] In the Talmud, the Sages provide such a harmonizing interpretation, explaining that both names apply to a single person who had purchased Joseph to fulfill his sexual desires: "Rabbi said that he [Potiphar] bought him [Joseph] for himself. But Gabriel came and 'interfered' (*p-r-ᶜ.*). Initially, his name is written 'Potiphar,' but in the end, 'Potiphera' (*potiféraᶜ*)" (BT *Soṭah* 13). Here we are provided an etiological basis for the otherwise inexplicable suffixing of the consonant *ᶜayn* to the second version of the name. The midrash reads this homiletically as implying that Potiphar's illicit intent had been divinely "interfered" with in some way. Similarly, another midrash explains the linkage in Genesis 37:36 of the name Potiphar with the title *seris parᶜoh*—understood as "Pharaoh's eunuch"—as connoting Potiphar's intention to molest Joseph. This plot is only foiled by the angel Gabriel's emasculation of Joseph's master.[21]

If al-ᶜAzīz in *The Story of Our Master Joseph* is not "mighty," he is also most assuredly not "cherished"—the other literal meaning of his Arabic name. His own servant, Joseph, will come to supplant him, both as minister to Pharaoh and as the "beloved" of Zulaykhā. In this way, the change in Joseph's relationship to his master mirrors his ascendancy over his brothers, both in terms of temporal power (as leader over his siblings), and in the preference Jacob shows him. In this latter regard, the conjugal usurpation of al-ᶜAzīz is symbolized by Zulaykhā's actions: she dresses Joseph in al-ᶜAzīz's clothes, places a crown on his head, spreads for him al-ᶜAzīz's bed, gives him to drink from his cup, and tells him that she will gladly marry Joseph and poison her husband. Al-ᶜAzīz's ultimate displacement is symbolized by her plan to bury his corpse under his former house.

While the text is clear as to where Zulaykhā's devotion lies, it is silent regarding al-ᶜAzīz's political demise. However, this displacement is suggested by the disgrace he falls into in Pharaoh's eyes for having imprisoned a prophet (*Joseph,* 135). His unseating is further implied by Joseph's own appointment to the viziership. In any case, from the point of Joseph's release from prison we hear no more of the former master. In al-Thaᶜlabī, this double usurpation is made explicit: "[Joseph] remained close to the king who entrusted him with the rule over Egypt, discharging Potiphar from his duties and appointing Joseph in his place. Shortly thereafter Potiphar died and the king married Joseph to Rāᶜīl, the wife of Potiphar" (Al-Thaᶜlabī, 212). This outcome is in accord with other Islamic versions of the tale that have Joseph eventually marrying the penitent Zulaykhā following al-ʿAzīz's death, they themselves borrowing from the Hellenistic romance of *Joseph and Aseneth.* In *The Story of Our Master Joseph,* of course, no such reconciliation is allowed, and the unforgiving Joseph strikes Zulaykhā dead with a sword (*Joseph,* 169).

The "Affair" of Joseph and Mrs. Potiphar

What actually transpired between Joseph and his master's wife? The Genesis story moves rapidly from a long-winded description of Joseph's elevation within Potiphar's household to the comparatively breathless account of the encounter between the would-be seductress and her servant. Immediately following Potiphar entrusting Joseph with everything "save the bread he ate," the scene is set by the otherwise anomalous description of Joseph's physical beauty: A*nd Joseph was comely in features and comely to look at* (Gen. 39:6). Whereas in *Joseph* the protagonist's attractiveness is noted from the narrative's outset—where it seemingly more naturally belongs—in Genesis this is the first mention made of Joseph's good looks. Here we should bear in mind that as a matter of general principle, the biblical narrator is not given to gratuitous descriptions of physical attributes of characters, such that when they do appear, they typically pertain to some significant turn of the plot. Indeed, mention of such a becoming outward appearance would be a danger sign to the alert reader, as in other cases in the Bible where beauty is mentioned it typically precipitates a dangerous situation—for example, the seizing of Sarah and Rebecca by the foreign ruler (Gen. 12:10–20; 20:1–18; 27:7–11). Postbiblical accounts highlight the passion that each of these Hebrew figures elicits in the male. In any case, the description of Joseph's good looks is followed immediately by the mention of Mrs. Potiphar "casting her eyes" upon her servant. The rapid pace and terse wording that the narrative assumes at this point stand in stark contrast to the preceding convoluted prose and culminate in Mrs. Potiphar's peremptory command to Joseph: "Lie with me!" (*shekhav ʿimi*) (Gen. 39:7).

The Rabbis condemn the directness of the proposition as an indication of Mrs. Potiphar's vulgarity, particularly when contrasted with another biblical example of a female initiating sexual contact with a male—that of Ruth with Boaz: "R. Shmuʾel bar Naḥman said, 'Cursed are the evildoers!' In what follows [we read about Ruth's words to Boaz]: '*Spread your wing over your maidservant* (Ruth 3:9), but this one [acted] like a beast (*ke-veheimah*): [*And she said,*] '*Lie with me!*'" (BR 87:4). The rabbinic sages additionally react to the brusque nature of her solicitation by questioning its plausibility: It would seem most unlikely that (as the biblical text seems to imply) the mere act of Mrs. Potiphar "lifting her eyes" to Joseph should have triggered on her part such a rash and dangerous command. Surely, she would have noticed Joseph's beauty beforehand? The Rabbis find support for positing an alternative pattern of events in the adverbial phrase that precedes Mrs. Potiphar taking notice of Joseph: "And it happened after these things" (*va-yehi aḥarei ha-devarim ha-eileh*). Exploiting the ambiguity of the phrase *ha-devarim ha-eileh* as referring to "these words" and/or "these things," they argue that her direct frontal assault on Joseph followed on a protracted series of both verbal and physical importuning and inducements. Further support for this interpretation is found in this very same biblical passage: "And so she spoke to Joseph *day after day,* and he would not listen to her request to lie by her, to be with her" (Gen. 39:10; my emphasis). These few words—numbering only six in the Hebrew text—are by this reading a syntactical reification of the contraction of extensive narrative time. They will become the catalyst for rich and detailed descriptions in the exegetical literature of the various enticements his master's wife employs in the attempt to seduce him. Two verses later Mrs. Potiphar again utilizes the identical terse proposition, "Lie with me," to demand of Joseph sexual favors. The use of the identical language here may also lie behind the interpretation that even her initial proposition had come after an extended period during which Mrs. Potiphar had proceeded by less confrontational means.

In *The Story of Our Master Joseph,* Zulaykhā's directness is initially most in evidence not in her propositioning Joseph but in her ordering al-ᶜAzīz to purchase Joseph for her. When she does turn her attentions to her slave, she employs a great variety of blandishments in her attempts to seduce Joseph. She may be brazen, but she is not the coarse woman of Genesis. If we are merely to list the techniques she employs:

She sets him up in al-ᶜAzīz's house, dresses him in his clothes, and gives him drink from his cup.
She proposes that he marry her.
She tells him that she is his master and he her mameluke.
She seeks to entice him by bringing him into the Garden and having him entertained by her servants to put him in a more receptive mood.
She sends him gifts.
She brings him into a series of houses.
She makes suggestive remarks.

She flatters him by praising his beauty, his eloquence, and so forth.
She threatens him with punishment or with her suicide, which would result in his death as well.
She offers to poison her husband and bribe Joseph's God.
She accepts belief in God in a final (though futile) attempt to win Joseph.

Such a list may be productively compared with the abbreviated catalog of methods Potiphar's Wife utilizes in *The Testament of Joseph.* The author there describes twelve episodes in which Mrs. Potiphar harasses her servant:

She repeatedly punishes and threatens Joseph (3.1–6).
In order to legitimate her proximity and allay his concerns, she pretends to regard Joseph as a son (3.7).
She draws him openly into impurity (3.8).
She flatters Joseph (4.1–3).
She pretends to want to convert to his religion (4.4–5).
She offers to kill her husband to marry Joseph (5.1–4).
She sends Joseph food that is enchanted to make her irresistible to him (6.1).
She falls ill and threatens suicide (7.1–5).
She tries to force Joseph into a sexual act (8.2–5).
She accuses him of attempted rape, and he is sent to prison.
She offers to have him released if he will satisfy her (9.1–4).

Finally, although her physical condition continues to deteriorate, she manages to visit Joseph in prison.

"Overkill"

In *The Story of Our Master Joseph* the hero is twice chased by the temptress and is twice delivered over for punishment after he eludes her. At first glance, this doubling would seem to represent an instance of faulty editing on the part of a copyist/author striving to incorporate disparate traditions; however, just as with many instances of apparent redundancy in the Bible, it behooves us (as it did the rabbinic interpreters) to seek out the distinctive nuance. The first chase scene (74–81) is set up after Zulaykhā lodges Joseph in the garden. She provides him entertainment, hoping to set a romantic mood; failing thus to entice Joseph, she then approaches him and tells him that she plans to spend the night with him. She prepares the scene for a lovers' tryst by setting up lanterns, spreading carpets, and grinding fragrant spices. She further seeks to ingratiate herself to him by offering him milk and honey. Then, speaking sweetly to Joseph, she begs him to look at her face, which by her own account is like the full moon in its beauty. Joseph turns his face away and leaves her, but Zulaykhā runs after him. Then, in an allusion to the element that characterizes this episode as the first "Garment Scene," she "grasps him by his gown." In doing so, she scratches Joseph's chest, and he lets out a scream that reaches the angels on High. (Contrast this with the Genesis account [39:14–15 and 39:19], where Mrs. Potiphar claims that it is her screaming that scared off Joseph.) Joseph's anger is so great that when he shouts, blood spurts from his nipples—a trait that the narrator mentions he shared with Judah, who later in the narrative will exhibit a similar sanguinary display. Finally, Joseph, in freeing himself from her clutches, gives Zulaykhā a disfiguring kick that leaves her crumpled on the ground with a huge hump—"like that of a camel"—upon her back.

The second, much more expansive version of the chase scene (105–14) follows on the lengthy account of the series of splendidly constructed and lavishly decorated houses and other enticements by which Zulaykhā sought to seduce her servant. These enticements include the building of a Sufi retreat or cloister, the *zāwiyah.*[22] In the lead-up to this scene, after untying five of the knots that he had tied to secure his pants, Joseph falls unconscious. Upon awakening, he escapes out the locked gate after breaking it into pieces with his foot. Zulaykhā, in hot pursuit, catches up to him, but he remains adamant in his refusal to obey her wishes. Then follows mention of the torn-garment motif: "She grabbed his shirt and tore it from behind" (*Joseph,* 110).

Similarly, *The Story of Our Master Joseph* records two punishments that Joseph suffers for the one mentioned in Genesis. The first of these follows the second chase scene, when Joseph is hauled off by al-ᶜAzīz to be tortured. He is freed following the examination of his torn garment, but is directly taken away by his master to al-ᶜAzīz's own land. Zulaykhā is somehow able to bring Joseph back surreptitiously to her town, so that he is present when the seven princesses of the Assembly of Ladies come to see him. After Zulaykhā has succeeded in convincing the Ladies that her infatuation with him is justified, they turn to Joseph and ask him why he refuses to obey his mistress's will. To this he responds that he would prefer prison to that which she is asking him to do. In other words, according to this version, Joseph is seeking to isolate himself from the temptress. The text notes that God, hearing these words, tells his archangel Gabriel to descend and tell Joseph that He would have given him anything he asked for, but since he asked for prison, this, as it were, leaves His hands tied. The problem of theodicy—why would God allow one of His chosen prophets to languish for years in jail—is thus eliminated. This is then the pretext for Joseph ending up back in prison and serves to realign the narrative with the Genesis account, including the ensuing encounter with the king's cupbearer and baker, Joseph's correct interpretation of their visions, and his eventual emancipation after successfully interpreting pharaoh's dreams. Zulaykhā—ostensibly to punish the recalcitrant object of her desire—urges al-ʿAzīz to imprison Joseph in "The Prison of Torture," one of three prisons belonging to the king.

The exegetes have also put forward other explanations of the rationale for Joseph's imprisonment, all perhaps stemming from the perception that al-ʿAzīz would surely have simply had Joseph executed for attempting to rape his wife. (Of course, this ignores the narrative impossibility of the storyteller killing off the hero of this romance before the appropriate time.) This "weakness"—of the plot and of the male supporting actor—is the origin of a wealth of interpretations seeking to explain the leniency of the punishment. Al-Ṭabari, for example, explains the quranic verse—"Then it occurred to them, after they had seen the signs, to imprison him for a period of time" (Q 12:35)—as suggesting that even though al-ʿAzīz had abundant evidence of Joseph's innocence, the affair was a matter of public disgrace for the aristocratic couple, and Joseph had therefore to be isolated:

> At length the ruler—even though he had seen Joseph's shirt torn from behind, and the scratches on his face, and the women cutting their hands, and even though he knew Joseph was innocent—grew disgusted with himself for having let Joseph go free. It is said that the reason for this was that which was related by Ibn Wakīʿ—ʿAmr b. Muḥammad—Asbāṭ—al-Suddī: . . . The woman said to her husband, "This Hebrew slave has disgraced me among the people, claiming by way of excuse that I asked an evil act of him. I cannot give any excuse"—that is, because he had restricted her to the house by way of punishment—"so either give me leave to go out and give my excuse, or imprison him as you have imprisoned me." That is the meaning of God's statement, *Yet, for all the evidence they had seen, they thought it right to imprison him for a time.* (*Prophets and Patriarchs,* 160)

Alternative explanations have Zulaykhā convincing her husband to imprison Joseph so that she may punish him for his rejection of her (as in *Joseph*), or so that she will get over her desire for him, or to keep him from the covetous eyes of her competitors (such as the Ladies of the Assembly).

The recurrence of the motif of Zulaykhā's "frontal" attempts to seduce Joseph may very well be generated by an interpretation of Genesis 39:10: "And so she spoke to Joseph *day after day*" [my emphasis]. Alternatively, it is possible that these two variations on the chase scene might have their origin in the very repetition (described above) of Mrs. Potiphar's original two-word command to Joseph in Genesis—"Lie with me" (39:7, 12). We see such an exegetical trend reflected in Josephus's record of the events that transpired between the two protagonists: "The fact that she did not expect Joseph to oppose her increased her passion still more; and being terribly besieged by her wickedness she again by a second attempt strove to achieve her goal" (*Antiquities* 2:44). These traditions are examples of the tension that may arise out of the attempt by the author of *The Story of Our Master Joseph* to incorporate parallel traditions surrounding the same core biblical event, all the while constrained by the exigencies of the biblical plot. This illustrates the open-endedness of the Midrash in allowing for multiple interpretations and also the manner in which it diverges from postmodernist notions of indeterminacy in that rabbinic exegesis is still bound by a fidelity to the central text. Joseph had already been accused by Zulaykhā once before; al-ʿAzīz had believed her and had had Joseph punished. The evidence of the "shirt-torn-from-behind" had already established Joseph's innocence; however, the narrator needs to imprison Joseph once again so that—as per the Genesis narrative—he may gain his freedom through the successful interpretation of Pharaoh's dreams. It is this discontinuity from the biblical narrative that the exegetes are at pains to explicate, and they do so through the interpolation of an additional incarceration.

Zulaykhā's Edifice Complex

Both these examples of narrative repetition—that of the chase scene as well as that of the imprisonment—reflect a process whereby the desideratum of preserving parallel but divergent expansions simultaneously creates a search for new *pre*texts in the *Vorlage* that justify the additional narrative events. This is most likely to occur when these additions can be attached to certain irregularities or repetitions within the source text itself. The process may be observed as well in the extensive descriptions of five magnificent houses by which Zulaykhā seeks to impress the impassive servant. The number of houses here might be a thematization of the five-fold mention of both "house" (*bayit*) and "all" (*kol*) in the passage from Genesis 39:1–20 (cited above) that records Joseph's being entrusted with all the belongings in the Potiphar household. Zulaykhā leads Joseph from house to house, from the House of Gold to those of Silver, Glass, Tin, and Ivory. He enters each house in turn and is provided various dainties and luxuries. We may surmise the latent sexual implications of such "entering" as a metaphor for an adulterous relationship in Joseph's rebuke of Zulaykhā: "Trust in God and know that your bringing me into the houses of al-ʿAzīz will not be permitted you by God, for no one but he may enter his house" (*Joseph,* 88). Moreover, the Arabic verbal root *d-kh-l* ("to enter") has also the connotation of male penetration of the female (much like *lavo*ʾ, "to come," in biblical Hebrew). That "being in the house" is a euphemism for sexual relations is suggested as well by Zulaykhā's sexual innuendos both here and at the earlier rendezvous in her garden (emphasis added): "You are with me in the residence of al-ʿAzīz, *with me and more*. . . ." (*Joseph,* 88); "Tonight I will stay beside you *and all this*. . . ." (*Joseph,* 79).

In similar fashion to the way in which the biblical narrator juxtaposes mention of Joseph's beauty with Mrs. Potiphar's casting her eyes upon him, so, too, in *The Story of Our Master Joseph,* Joseph's nearly succumbing to Zulaykhā's entreaties follows immediately upon the first mention of Zulaykhā's own considerable physical charms, as well as the beauty of her clothing and "accessories": "And Zulaykhā was possessed of beauty and comeliness, and she had on her cheek a beauty mark. And she had eighty braids of hair, and upon her were seven woolen dresses. And she had made herself up for Joseph in all the beautiful adornments, and she wore necklaces in which were all manner of jewels and rubies and she wore al-ʿAzīz's crown. She said to Joseph, 'Look at my beauty and comeliness'" (*Joseph,* 101).

Even at this point, Joseph is still able to turn his head from her beautiful visage. However, upon mention of her virginal state, his resistance weakens and he feels compelled to tie seven knots in the waistband of his pants (in the name of seven biblical heroes Abraham, Isaac, Jacob, Moses, Aaron, David, and Solomon).[23] Thus fortified, he approaches Zulaykhā with a prayer that God will "dress him [dare we say, keep him dressed!] in the gown of Your honor" and keep Satan away from him. At this point, an old Coptic woman comes to call upon Zulaykhā and, noticing her downcast state, inquires as to its cause. Zulaykhā confesses to her that she loves Joseph but that he does not return her affections. Following the old woman's advice, Zulaykhā constructs a special house in which she strategically places pictures of herself so that wherever Joseph looks he will come upon her image. Now, with literally nowhere to turn, Joseph "became afraid of committing a sin" (*Joseph,* 106).

To make matters worse, God, who we sense may be anxious to achieve His end in this tiresome charade, casts in both "lovers" a lusting for the opposite sex. In Joseph's case, this desire is said to equal that of forty men, while with Zulaykhā it is that of eighty women. Zulaykhā, sensing that Joseph is now favorably disposed, draws closer to him. She tells him that although he is her slave, she would like to set him free and in turn become his mameluke. She orders him again to obey her, but he refuses. Then, resorting to blackmail, she threatens to kill herself so that al-ʿAzīz will then kill him. In other retellings, Zulaykhā's threat of suicide is a sympathetic demonstration by the narrator of the depth of her passion and her despair; here, however, it serves to intensify the negative portrayal of Zulaykhā and her vindictive nature.

Joseph the Righteous—Does He or Doesn't He?

The primary connotation of *ṣadīq* in Hebrew as "righteous" led to the foregrounding of a unique aspect of Joseph's upstanding character—namely, his chasteness. And yet, we could also raise questions regarding this aspect of Joseph's behavior. The Rabbis interpreted the biblical narrator's use of the word *naʿar* to describe Joseph at the story's outset as defamatory.[24] According to this midrashic motif, the trial he will face at the hands of Potiphar's Wife serves as a punishment for his vanity and his primping: "*His master's wife raised her eyes to Joseph [and said, 'Lie with me.']* (Gen. 39:7). This is preceded by the statement: *Joseph was comely in features and comely to look at* (39:6). [Such may be compared] to a valiant man [H: *gibor*) who stood in the marketplace, penciling his eyes, walking mincingly, and curling his hair. They said to him, 'If you are such a man, here is a female bear (*duba*)—master it'" (BR 87:3).[25]

In a manner akin to the way the Rabbis interpret the first word of the Joseph cycle—*va-yeishev,* "and he settled"—to indicate a degree of complacency on the part of Jacob, so too they criticize Joseph for his self-satisfaction, especially given his father's suffering. Thus, they take the word "after" (*aḥar*) in the phrase "after these things" (Gen. 39:7)—with which the episode with Mrs. Potiphar commences—and, given the ambiguity of "things" and the absence of any intervening events or spoken words, connect it alliteratively with Joseph's internal thoughts or meditations (*hirhurim*): "These consisted of meditations. Who meditated? Joseph meditated. He said, 'Back in my father's household, when dad would see a nice portion there he would give it to me and my brothers would give me the evil eye. Now that I am here I am grateful to You that I am at ease.' The Holy-One-Blessed-Be-He said, 'Smug one! By your life I will incite the bear against you!'" (BR 87:4).

Although the majority of interpretations hold that Joseph went into Potiphar's house on that fateful day in order to arrange the accounts, there are also early opinions that he in fact entered with illicit intent:

> R. Yoḥanan said: This teaches that the two of them had planned to sin together. He *came into the house to perform his task* (Gen. 39:11). Rab and Samuel: the former said that it really means to do his work, while the latter, that it means "to satisfy his desires." (BT *Soṭah* 36b)

> R. Samuel b. Naḥman said [*He came into the house*] *to perform his task* (Gen. 39:11) . . . certainly (*vaday*)![26] However, *and there was not a man* (*ve-ein ish;* ibid.): he checked and did not find himself to be "a man," as R. Samuel said: His bow was tensed, but then returned [to its relaxed state], as it is written: *va-teishev be-eitan kashto* (Gen. 49:24). R. Isaac said: His seed was scattered and exited via his fingernails [according to the continuation of the verse]: *va-yafozu zeroᶜei yadav* (ibid.). (*Bereishit raba* 87:7)

Here the opinions of R. Samuel and R. Issac are based on homiletical readings of the verse in Jacob's blessing of Joseph. In the former case, the connection between "his bow" and the hardness of Joseph's penis appears as well in *Bereishit raba* (98), where the rabbis state that *kashto* ("his bow") means *kashyato* ("his hardness"). Similarly, R. Issac's interpretation is derived from a homiletical reading of the consonantal text, this time at the continuation of the verse *va-yafozu zeroᶜei yadav,* by which the root *z-r-ᶜ* yields "seed" instead of "arms" and the verb *yafozu,* whose meaning is probably something to do with "moving about quickly," is applied to the scattering of semen.

It is this ambivalent portrayal of Joseph that engages Islamic commentators. In the same way that the Jewish exegetes are concerned with showing Joseph to be something less than completely truthful or accurate in his dream interpretation, so the Qurʾān (and Islamic commentators, following suit) is able to offer evidence of Joseph being something less than the model of sexual restraint. The second half of the quranic verse, " And she desired him, and he would have desired her" (Q 12:24), being in the subjunctive mood, indicates a much more compromised state than that of the biblical account (where there is no sense that Joseph was even tempted), and is the springboard for a surprisingly vivid commentary. In al-Ṭabarī's comment on the verse, for example, we read:

> *She desired him and he would have desired her* and they entered the house and she locked the doors and he went to loosen his trousers, when suddenly

> the figure of Jacob appeared to him, standing in the house and biting his fingers, saying, "O Joseph, do not have intercourse with her. If you do not have intercourse with her, you are like the bird in the sky that is not caught. If you have intercourse with her, you are like the bird when it dies and falls to the ground, unable to defend itself. If you do not have intercourse with her, you are like a difficult ox upon which no work can be done, whereas if you have intercourse with her, you are like that ox when he dies and ants come in at the base of his horns and he cannot defend himself."[27] (*Prophets and Patriarchs,* 155–56)

In *The Story of Our Master Joseph,* even Gabriel appearing in the image of Jacob is not able to rein in Joseph's lust; the young servant proceeds to undo the fifth of the seven knots securing his pants before he is saved from sin by falling unconscious:

> *The Sages, peace upon them, said* when he untied the fourth knot, a herald came out of Heaven saying, "O Joseph, O son of Jacob, know and be aware that if a sin should fall from you, I will erase you from the Book of Prophecy."
>
> Then the angels shouted to God, may He be exalted, in sanctification and glorification and praise, and said, "O our Lord, O our Master, fortify Your prophet Joseph before there falls from him a sin." And with that God said, "O angels, O bearers of My canopy and My might and My loftiness, I will not separate Joseph from his grandfathers and his fathers: Abraham the Friend and Isaac the Trustworthy and Jacob the Prophet." And he commanded the angel Gabriel and said to him, "Descend to my servant Joseph and pull him from sin." And then Joseph lifted his head and he saw Gabriel in the image of his father Jacob, and the angel stood, saying, "O Joseph, remember your Lord because if a sin should befall you, I will erase you from the Book of Prophecy." And he trembled violently when he heard these words from the angel, but Joseph could not restrain himself from untying the fifth [knot]—and he fell unconscious upon the divan . . . until he escaped and left through the door. (*Joseph,* 108–10)

Al-Ṭabarī, in the context of Zulaykhā's self-justification before the Ladies of the Assembly, also records a tradition according to which Joseph disrobed: "She said, 'This is the one on whose account you blamed me. I asked of him an evil act, but he proved continent' (Q 12:32)—*after he had loosened his trousers* (my emphasis)" (*Prophets and Patriarchs,* 159). A parallel tradition adds Zulaykhā's bewilderment as to what kind of apparition might have caused him at the last moment to abstain from sexual intercourse:

According to Ibn Wakīʿ—ʿAmr b. Muḥammad—Asbaṭ—al-Suddī: She said, "*This is the one on whose account you blamed me. I asked of him an evil act, but he proved continent*" (Q 12:32). She said, "After he had loosened his trousers, he remained continent. I do not know what appeared to him." Then Gabriel said to him, "Did you not desire her even for one day?" And Joseph said, "*I do not excuse myself. The soul does indeed drive us to evil* (Q 12:53)." (Ibid., 159–60)

Those midrashic expansions, Jewish or Islamic, that depict Joseph as indeed sorely enticed emphasize the severity of the struggle. After all, if he had not been tempted, what would be the enormity of his achievement in not yielding? The exegetes might also be giving expression to their skepticism regarding Joseph's steadfastness. As none other than Mark Twain noted, Joseph "got into trouble with Potiphar's wife at last, and both gave in their version of the affair, but the lady's was plausible and Joseph's was most outrageously shaky."[28]

A counterexample that admits of no wavering by Joseph is the passage from al-Jawzī cited above:

ʿUmar b. al-Khaṭṭāb once told some excerpts from the Torah to the Prophet whereupon the latter responded: "Rid yourself of them, ʿUmar, especially in view of the ridiculous things that are known in Judaism such as their teachings that David sent Uriah out in order that he might be killed and then married his wife and that Joseph unloosed his garments in the presence of Zulaikha! Now the Prophets are above preposterous acts such as these. When the ignorant person hears such things breaking [God's law] becomes a trivial matter, and he says to himself: 'After all my sin is really nothing new!'"[29]

This is an example of the tendency of Islam to categorize "objectionable" traditions as being of "Israelite" origin. The rejection of this motif shows how the range of interpretation may be limited by ideology. It also highlights the ultimate didactic purposes of the Islamic text and the essential commitment to the infallibility of the prophets, their *ʿisma,* especially with regard to sexual mores. Al-Bayḍāwī offers a more nuanced interpretation of the problematic verse, arguing against too literal an interpretation:

She desired to have intercourse with him and he desired it with her. Hama bi- means "to aim at and resolve on" a thing. From it comes *humām* ["hero"], one who, when he plans a thing, carries it out. What is meant by Joseph's desiring her is natural propensity and the struggling of carnal feelings, not a rationally chosen purpose. Such feelings do not fall within the sphere of

> moral responsibility. But the person who truly deserves praise and the heavenly reward is the one who restrains himself from acting when this sort of impulse arises or is about to arise; as when you say "I was on the verge of killing him, had I not feared God." (*Commentary on Sūrah 12,* 97)

In this distinction between what we might call nonrational "instinct" and self-control, the concern here is to avoid directly incriminating one of God's chosen prophets. Similarly, in *The Story of Our Master Joseph,* Gabriel reminds Joseph that the strength for resisting Zulaykhā's temptations came from God; Joseph himself, left to his own devices, would have "drowned in the sea of sin" (*Joseph,* 137).

Although one of these interpretations—Joseph as the Truthteller, or, alternatively, Joseph as the Righteous—may predominate in a given text, neither of these characterizations of Joseph necessarily contradicts the other. On the contrary, while each of these readings seeks to exploit to its own advantage elements of different stages in the Joseph story, these hermeneutical tendencies may in fact reinforce one another. Thus, given the eclectic basis of *The Story of Our Master Joseph* and its drawing from Jewish and Muslim sources, it should not be totally surprising that we find within it reflections of both interpretations. Such a conflation of the two associated meanings of *ṣ-d-q* is present also in the Islamic tradition. For example, one contemporary scholar of Islam states that *ṣiddīq* means "very truthful" but adds that it "is really a compact word for a man who is virtuous in every sense."[30] This draws on a traditional interpretation of the quranic verse where the cupbearer requests that Joseph interpret the king's dreams. As al-Thaʿlabī notes: "'*O man of truth* (*ṣiddīq,* Q 12:46)'—meaning, regarding what you have interpreted about our dreams. A *ṣiddīq* is one who is very truthful" (Al-Thaʿlabī, 208). The predominant message of the Joseph-and-his-brothers subplot is Joseph's accuracy in dream interpretation, while with Zulaykhā, although Joseph's veracity is contrasted with his mistress's calumnies, it is his righteousness in controlling his sexual appetite that is highlighted. *The Story of Our Master Joseph* thus combines the two, offering a portrait of Joseph as a paragon of both truthtelling and righteousness.

The Assembly of Ladies

One of the most famous expansions of the Joseph story involves his being brought by his mistress before a group of Egyptian women. In the version presented in *The Story of Our Master Joseph,* Zulaykhā, mourning her enforced separation from her beloved after the second chase scene, is observed crying by her neighbors. They ask if she is suffering from some malady, and she tells them that her distress is due to her separation from Joseph. She continues to mourn for him until she is cunningly able to bring him back, but still he resists her advances. In the meantime (in a female analogue of the scene in which the seven merchants demand of Joseph's first owner that they be allowed to see him), seven Egyptian princesses, having heard about Joseph, scold Zulaykhā for not having invited them to see him. In order to justify herself in the face of this backbiting, she sends for the women to come to her palace, decorates the reception hall, and provides raiment and liquor to each of her guests. Still keeping Joseph under wraps, she adorns him and instructs him not to come out before the women until she tells him to. She then gives each woman a gold basin filled with honey, citrons, and a knife, and tells them to eat of the citrons when Joseph appears. When she signals Joseph to approach, the women are so distracted by his beauty that they slice their hands instead of the fruit. When Joseph draws near to Zulaykhā, she proceeds to recite a series of Arabic verses of the wine-and-garden genre, lamenting his coolness towards her. The women are convinced by this demonstration: "O Zulaykhā, you are entitled to do all that you do out of love for this youth" (*Joseph,* 122).

James Kugel has analyzed this particular motif of the Assembly of Ladies from a diachronic perspective.[31] The motif itself is of relatively late origin. It does not appear in any of the early postbiblical sources, Hellenistic writings, or Tannaitic material, existing only in a variety of later sources written in Hebrew, Aramaic, Arabic, and other languages. Thus, "The Assembly" is absent from the Bible; indeed, the Genesis account depicts Mrs. Potiphar as having a secret obsession and exercising a certain amount of discretion in waiting until there is no one in the house before seizing Joseph. Her concern over possible disclosure is evidenced by her preemptive lies to her attendants and her husband, constructed to avoid a public and domestic scandal. The episode of the Assembly of Ladies seemingly contradicts this impression of Potiphar's Wife. The Qurʾān, on the other hand, contains a rather full account that in many ways parallels the version in *The Story of Our Master Joseph:* The Ladies disparage the nobleman's wife for trying to seduce her slave ("We see her to be clearly in the wrong"). She hears of their gossip, sends for them, prepares a feast, and gives them knives. When Joseph comes out before them, they praise him and cut their hands, exclaiming that he is not a mortal but an angel. Joseph's mistress responds, in her first words to the ladies (up to this point she has let her demonstration speak on her behalf), that they have wrongly blamed her. Having succeeded in her self-justification, she now freely admits her attempts to seduce him and threatens to imprison him if he does not yield:

> Some women in the city said: "The wife of the potentate has sought to seduce her servant; he has pierced her heart with love. Indeed, we see her to be clearly in the wrong." And when she heard of their slander, she sent to them, and prepared for them a banquet, and she gave to each of them a knife, and said [to Joseph]: "Come out before them!" And when they saw him, they so admired him that they cut up their hands, and they said: "God save us! This is no mortal; this one is nothing but a noble angel." She said: "There before you is the one about whom you blamed me; indeed, I did attempt to seduce him against his will, yet he abstained. If he will not do what I command him, he shall be imprisoned and be one of the humbled." He said: "My Lord, prison is more to my liking than that to which they invite me; yet if You do not turn me from their cunning I will become attracted to them and thereby become one of the ignorant." And so his Lord answered him and He warded off from him their cunning, Lo! He is the Knowing Listening One. Then it occurred to them, after they had seen the signs to imprison him for a period of time. (Q 12:30–35)

In addition to these women, *The Story of Our Master Joseph* has Zulaykhā's servants and the neighbor women aware of her infatuation. Her suffering is so readily apparent that the narrator is obliged to have her husband reside in a distant town. This same tale naturally appears in the elaborations of Muslim poets and exegetes for whom the tale was part of revealed Scripture. Thus, because the tale is included in the Qur᾽ān, it is often assumed to be of Islamic provenance.

The tale is also found in later Jewish writings in very similar forms. *The Chronicles of Yeraḥmi᾽el,* a midrashic anthology from the late thirteenth or early fourteenth centuries, has the same tale but with apples as the fruit involved.[32] *Sefer ha-yashar,* a retelling of the biblical narrative in pseudobiblical style from Italy and dating from no earlier than the thirteenth century, adds that Zulaykhā is ill and that the ladies have come to pay a get-well call.[33] In *The Story of Our Master Joseph* these two elements are split, and perhaps these complaints of illness might be how word spread to the Ladies. Kugel also brings an Aramaic poem, best known from the eleventh-century *Maḥazor Vitry,* that is recited in celebration of Joseph's virtuousness in observing the seventh law of the Decalogue (the prohibition against adultery). Here the women's distraction is given concrete expression by their forgetting to drink the wine given to them. Kugel thus speaks of two variant motifs of liquor and food.[34] *The Story of Our Master Joseph* has the women served both liquor and citrons, but it is the bodily injury the women suffer in their failed attempts to cut the citrons that epitomizes the degree of their distraction (*Joseph,* 118).

Determining the ultimate source for this motif is an endeavor that has preoccupied many students of the intersection of Judaic and Islamic culture. Because of its inclusion and prominence in Muslim scripture and later tradition, the relation between the quranic story of Joseph and the Jewish biblical and exegetical sources has long interested these scholars. While it is true that the Qurʾān contains a number of early Jewish exegetical motifs (the identification of which has until recently constituted a major and apologetic trend within the scholarship), it is also apparent that the Qurʾān influenced later *Jewish* retellings or expansions of the Joseph story. A conspicuous example of this tendency to seek a Jewish source for an Islamic motif surrounds this "Assembly of Ladies" scene. Thus, Abraham Geiger, the founder of *Wissenschaft des Judentums* and student of "what Muḥammad has taken from Judaism,"[35] claimed that the quranic account of the Assembly of Ladies based itself on *Sefer ha-yashar,* which he mistakenly believed to predate the Qurʾān. In opposition, Max Grünbaum argued for an Islamic origin. Louis Ginzberg maintained that the Jewish nature of the episode was "beyond dispute," citing the introductory formula in *Tanḥuma*—"the Rabbis of blessed memory said"—as a sign of its antiquity. As Kugel points out, this argument can be turned on its head; that is, such a general reference may instead be "an attempt to cover origins which are either unknown or best left undisclosed.[36] In turn, Ginzberg's contention was countered by Bernard Heller, who maintained that the motif was of Islamic provenance—an opinion with which both Haim Schwarzbaum and S. D. Goitein concurred.[37]

In fact, Kugel has rather convincingly demonstrated that the Assembly of Ladies motif has its origins in an idiosyncrasy within the biblical text: the self-justification of Potiphar's Wife before the members of her household that takes place following her failed seduction attempt and Joseph's subsequent escape (Gen. 39:13–14). The rabbinic exegetes, wont as they were to account for the repetition of a motif, derived this whole episode by interpolating a reason for this first accounting that Mrs. Potiphar gives to her servants of "The Garment Scene." A further motivation for an expansion of this encounter is Mrs. Potiphar's reference to the object of Joseph's supposed effrontery in the first-person plural: "He had to bring us a Hebrew to dally with *us*" (39:14, my emphasis). The royal plural being rare in the Bible, the Rabbis were at pains to provide an explanation for its occurrence here. In doing so, they were able to take advantage of the semantic range of the Hebrew verb in the phrase *letzaḥeiq banu* as connoting both "to mock us" and "to dally with us." Mrs. Potiphar, in calling upon her servants for support, is by her word choice thus better able to inflame the indignation of the assembled by combining the two connotations in a single rhetorical flourish. The sexual overtone is in itself able to generate the "feminization" of Mrs. Potiphar's audience (whereas in Genesis it is simply the "neutral" masculine plural: *anshei beitah,* "the people of her house").

An additional gap noticed by the Rabbis in Potiphar's Wife's address to her servants is her saying "See!" without any following object to indicate exactly what it is they are supposed to look at. Though it could ostensibly be the shirt Joseph has left behind or, more simply, a figurative interjection equivalent to English usage, it came to be explained as referring to Joseph himself. According to this interpretation, following the attempted seduction, Joseph has been brought before the ladies as "Exhibit A." It is this interpretation that generates the need for a visual demonstration, which is precisely what the scene of the Assembly of the Ladies consists of—a carefully scripted dramatization, complete with stage directions and props.[38] A motivation for having this scene separate from that of "The Chase" is the fact that while earlier it is stated that Mrs. Potiphar took advantage of the house being vacant to press herself upon her servant, the women's proximity is implied in Genesis by "the people at her house" being able to respond immediately when she calls out to them.

While the Joseph story in the Qurʾān derives largely from biblical and midrashic accounts, it is also true that the Islamic Scripture, no matter what the origins of its material, has a separate existence that spawned the elaboration of distinct traditions.[39] For example, the presence of knives in the scene may be seen as merely a rhetorical and piquant flourish, and one that could not be easily dispensed with once included in the story. Islamic tradition, however, provides an account in which the knives are indeed of thematic significance. Thus, in addition to the knives' utility in cutting the thick-skinned fruit, they also constitute the means by which Zulaykhā will simultaneously silence the women's gossip and punish them for "their slander" (*makrihina,* Q 12:31).[40] As recorded in a Swahili version of the tale, the consequences were even fatal in some cases:

> And all the ladies who were peeling their oranges cut themselves with the knives *which Zulaykhā had whetted for the purpose.* Much blood flowed; some of the ladies cut their thumbs off and died. The reason for this upheaval was that they were so completely dazzled by Yusuf's beauty that as soon as he appeared, they could not keep their eyes off him and so forgot what they were doing. Zulaykhā had foreseen this, *and so her plan worked both ways: She took revenge for the gossiping and at the same time silenced it.* She said: "The man who you suspected I had an affair with, is the one you have just cut yourselves for." They all asked her to forgive them. [my emphasis][41]

An alternative interpretation of the ladies' criticism of Zulaykhā in the Qur'ān is that it concerns rather her failure to seduce the youth; their demand to be invited to see Joseph is thus a boast that they would fare better than she in enticing him.[42] The use here of the second form of the Arabic verb (often connoting repetition or frequency) for the cutting of the hands is evidence of the degree of the women's distraction; they are so enamored of Joseph's beauty that they fail to notice even the pain from the multiple wounds they have inflicted upon themselves.[43] Similarly, while Joseph's categorization in verses 33–34 of the Ladies' actions as *kayd*—"a scheme, intrigue or stratagem"—might simply refer to the attempt by the women to get him to assent to a sexual liaison with Zulaykhā, it also may be evidence of their own intention of seducing him.[44] This view is supported in the Qur'ān by the king's use of the second-person plural when he later confronts the ladies: "What was it you wanted when you attempted to seduce Joseph against his will?" (*mā khaṭbukuna idh rāwadtuna yūsuf ʿan nafsih*) (Q 12:51). The plural possessive pronoun here (*khaṭbukuna*) might indeed derive from the plural that Mrs. Potiphar employs in Genesis that we have seen is the likely origin for the "Ladies of the Assembly" motif. By this reading, the Ladies' comparison of Joseph to an angel after he has met their challenge is evidence of their being convinced that he is beyond temptation. There exists a certain ambiguity in this episode: either Zulaykhā is demonstrating Joseph's irresistible beauty, or, alternatively, she is seeking to prove his chasteness in the face of even the most severe temptation. In fact, neither interpretation explicitly contradicts the other. Both possibilities are alluded to in al-Bayḍāwī's comment on the knives in verse 12:31: "The first and more commonly cited interpretation is that they would be so overcome by Joseph's beauty that they would become distracted and cut their hands. However, a second interpretation is that 'Joseph would be alarmed at their guile when he came out alone before forty women with knives in their hands.'"[45]

The Story of Our Master Joseph, in its account of the "Ladies of the Assembly," also seems to reflect this tension over whether the scene showcases Joseph's beauty and irresistibility, or rather the degree of his continence. The Ladies' scolding of Zulaykhā would seem to suggest that the Ladies lust after Joseph: "We are guests (*maʿzūmīn*) of yours in the love of Joseph" (*Joseph,* 116). Wordlessly, Zulaykhā helps them prepare so that they may be their most alluring: she provides them with gowns, robes and crowns, and sets up elaborate decorations to contribute to the overall ambiance as if challenging them to try their charms out on Joseph. Similarly, she prepares Joseph to be his most attractive, adorning him in a royal diadem, head cloth, golden girdle, and staff. Then, in order to create the greatest dramatic effect, she conceals Joseph, giving him the stage direction that he is not to come out until the most opportune moment. Ultimately, however, the text supports Joseph's beauty as the cause of the Ladies' distraction. There is no hint in *Joseph* that the women are cutting their hands in attempted suicide; rather, they misdirect the strokes of their knives because they are distracted by Joseph's beauty: "And with that, [each] one of them turned to her hands, which were wounded and had blood flowing from them. And they had not been aware of that" (*Joseph,* 118).

This motif dramatizes the women being so captivated by Joseph's beauty that they are completely unaware of the great bodily harm they do themselves. Even more suggestively, the sexual imagery of knives piercing not the fruit but the actual bodies of women lost in the heat of passion generated interpretations reflecting perhaps a certain sadomasochistic titillation of the exegetes and their audience. In a remarkable misapprehension of female physiology and sexuality, al-Kisāʾī has the Ladies so stimulated by Joseph's beauty that it triggers their menstrual flow: "When the women saw him, they lauded him and sullied themselves [i.e., menstruated] on the spot out of passion for him and cut their hands as they were slicing the citrons, saying 'O Zulaykhā! No one has ever seen the likes of this boy. He is a temptation to all who see him!'" (*Tales of the Prophets,* 176). Al-Bayḍawi derives this same interpretation from the quranic word *akbarnahu* "they thought him marvelous"; that is, they menstruated because of the violence of their lust. In support, he cites the famed ʿAbbasid poet, al-Mutanabbī: "Fear God and cover that beauty with a veil, for if you appear plainly the maidens in their chambers will menstruate."[46] These interpretations may very well have suggested themselves to the commentators due to the flow of blood from the wounded hands of the women. In any case, the effect of this motif is to emphasize Joseph's beauty and Zulaykhā's (justifiable?) helplessness before it. In *The Story of Our Master Joseph,* Zulaykhā further depicts her despair in a sequence of erotic garden verse describing the beloved, the effect he has upon her, and his aloofness. In conclusion, the Ladies, themselves overcome by Joseph's beauty and impressed by his steadfastness, inform Zulaykhā that she is "entitled to do all that [she does] out of her love for this youth" (*Joseph,* 122).

The Wiles of Women

Although the "Assembly of Ladies" motif apparently has its origins in Genesis, in Mrs. Potiphar's speech to her attendants, it subsequently took on a life of its own within Islamic tradition. The Muslim exegetes deal expansively with the theme, treating such questions as: Are the Ladies merely urging Joseph to accede to Zulaykhā's seduction? Are they themselves seeking to entice him by means of their dress, incense, their behavior toward him, and, ultimately by their suicide? Does the quranic plural of "your cunning" represent a generalization of the deceit of all women? The intertextual relationships within this tradition have been traced by Fedwa Malti-Douglass in a line that leads from the twelfth chapter of the Qurʾān down to contemporary Arabic literature. Thus, the expression *inna kaydakuna ʿaẓīm*—"indeed your guile is great" (Q 12:28)—served as a set phrase during the medieval period to connote the cunning of that class of humans known as women. According to this reading of the Qurʾān, the ruler censures not just his lustful wife and her companions for their uncontrollable sexuality but *all* of womankind.[47] The very same quranic refrain is repeated by the royal duo Shāhriyār and Shāhzamān in *The Thousand and One Nights* to describe the deceptiveness of women. This notion and its shorthand derivatives—"the wiliness of women" (*kayd al-nisāʾ*), or "the wiles of women" (*makāyid al-nisāʾ*) that more concisely associate this quality with women through the grammatical construct state—came to encode an irredeemably negative conception of female sexuality. Deriving its sanction from the Holy Book, this perspective is developed throughout the medieval period to become the dominant one. The conniving lasciviousness of Zulaykhā is extended to the Ladies of the Assembly and from them to women in general. Al-Bayḍāwī's comment on the quranic use of the ending affixed to the word *kayd*—"The plural pronoun is addressed to her and those like her, or to women as a whole"—highlights this misogynistic tendency.[48]

Al-Bayḍawī expands on this in his account of the insidiousness of women's cunning and the source of its "greatness" (Q 12:28): "Because the craftiness of women is subtler, more insinuating and with greater effect on the mind, and because by it they outface men, and by it Satan whispers stealthily" (*Commentary on Sūrah 12,* 17). Similar misogynistic tendencies are also present in early Jewish tradition. Thus, in the *Testament of Reuben* we have the following description:

> The angel of the Lord told me and instructed me that women are more easily overcome by the spirit of promiscuity than are men. They contrive in their hearts against men, then by decking themselves out they lead men's minds astray. For women are evil, my children, and by reason of their lacking authority or power over man, they scheme treacherously how they might entice him to themselves by means of their looks. And whomever they cannot enchant by their appearance they conquer by a stratagem.[49] (*Testament of Reuben* 5:1–3)

Although the Arabic term *kayd* does not appear in *The Story of Our Master Joseph,* the theme of feminine guile *does* predominate, although here it is restricted to the temptress herself. Even imprisonment was not enough to keep Joseph safe from his mistress's designs: "Then Zulaykhā employed artful means against Joseph until she brought him without al-ʿAzīz's knowledge and placed him by her side" (*Joseph,* 115). The Ladies of the Assembly are not blameworthy in *The Story of Our Master Joseph;* that all guilt lies instead with Zulaykhā is reflected in Joseph's statement to the women that "Prison is better to me than sin and that which *she* summons me to do" (122, my emphasis). This is in contrast to the version in the Qurʾān that, as we have seen, employs the plural feminine pronoun at this juncture, as well as in the statements of Joseph and the ruler regarding the wiles of women.[50]

The obverse of these gynophobic tendencies is concern over the threat "Woman" poses to bonding between or amongst males. Such a pattern of "male bonding" is evident in Joseph's relationship with his own father, and following their separation, with a succession of father figures. Joseph is continually able to win their trust, establish his authority, and gain access to power.[51] Zulaykhā, in this scheme, threatens the performance of this bonding by seeking to initiate an adulterous relationship with Joseph and thereby insert herself between the two males—master and trusted servant. Joseph's killing of Zulaykhā in *The Story of Our Master Joseph* attests to the seriousness of this threat posed by the seduction of the holy man. In another elaboration, the bond becomes that between Man and God, with Woman symbolizing distance from the divine. The Joseph story is by this reading a homily for the relationship between God and His people. Moreover, the adulterous advances of Mrs. Potiphar threaten the fidelity of Man's (in the gender-specific sense) relationship with God. For those (predominantly Muslim) accounts that have her rehabilitated as Joseph's legal wife there exists the contrary possibility of reading the entire tale of Joseph and Zulaykhā as an allegory depicting the love affair between God and His believers, and this becomes the source for the Sufi fascination with the tale of Joseph and Zulaykhā.[52] In *The Story of Our Master Joseph,* of course, no such possibility of redemption exists; instead, Godliness and the Feminine are diametrically opposed to each other, and safety for the hero lies in keeping his distance from Zulaykhā and, when he is able, to peremptorily and permanently dispose of her.

Zulaykhā Redeemed or Reviled, Virgin or Vixen

In line with its didactic purpose, *The Story of Our Master Joseph* seems bent on a dualist portrayal of Good and Evil and the ultimate and just reward of each. Thus, the flip side of the whitewash performed here vis-à-vis Joseph's behavior is the depiction of Zulaykhā as the embodiment of an iniquity that is irredeemable and must be eradicated. Zulaykhā, therefore, appears in *The Story of Our Master Joseph* as much less than a well-rounded character. She symbolizes Joseph's "evil inclination" (*yeitzer ha-ráᶜ*), and his slaying of her is thereby emblematic of Joseph's internal subjugation of this impulse. In tension with this allegorical level, however, there is a sympathetic undercurrent in the depiction of the emotional distress and physical suffering that Zulaykhā undergoes at being separated from her beloved Joseph. Indeed, in quite a few ways her torment at this involuntary estrangement strikingly parallels Jacob's distress over the loss of his beloved son. Compare the two descriptions of the depths of their mourning:

> Then Jacob built a house of wood and named it 'The House of Mourning for Joseph,' and around it the birds nested and the wild animals dwelled. In that location Jacob commenced to mourn and refrain from sleep; neither did he raise his head (which was between his knees) from the ground. And he abstained from food and drink, and sleep did not come upon him all the while he was mourning over Joseph. And he became weak, and his face became pale, and his body grew thin. (*Joseph,* 17–18)

> *The Sages, peace upon them, said* that when Zulaykhā imprisoned Joseph, she was rueful. And she left the House of Honor and lifted its curtains, extin-

> guished its lanterns, locked its doors, pulled out the water from its rivers, and cut down its trees. Then she sat in the House of Sorrow crying by night and by day. Her body became emaciated and her color changed, and she was miserable over Joseph. (*Joseph,* 128)

Similarly, in the final denouement of the relationship between Joseph and Zulaykhā, the cruelty of her relentless torment is made evident. In another parallel with Jacob, she has lost her eyesight from an overabundance of crying for her beloved: "As for what happened with Zulaykhā: her body became emaciated and her vision was obscured" (*Joseph,* 168). And yet in the final analysis, Joseph's attitude toward Zulaykhā is hostile, spiteful, and violent. Following the first chase scene, she is portrayed deformed and animalized after Joseph delivers her a kick that causes a "hump like that of a camel" to form on her back. In the end, not even Zulaykhā's penitence and willingness to accept belief in God will suffice to save her from an implacable Joseph.

By contrast, the Hellenistic romance of *Aseneth* and the Islamic variants of the tale end blissfully with the now permissible union of Joseph and Zulaykhā. The Egyptian woman's virginity is a sine qua non for the consummation of the marriage; it is Zulaykhā's virtuous, unsullied nature that renders her fit for rehabilitation. The unlikelihood of her never having had sexual intercourse though a married woman is made more credible because of al-ʿAzīz's express lack of interest in her. Moreover, her resultant sexual frustration could be a further cause for sympathy toward her and legitimates her inflamed passion for Joseph. Indeed, in these versions, her very perseverance in pursuing her beloved constitutes a major positive attribute, and in the end she is rewarded with the attainment of her goal. In *The Story of Our Master Joseph,* on the other hand, reading backward from her treatment at Joseph's hands, her obsessive pursuit of him must be read only as relentless persecution. According to this counterreading, even her virginal state offers no possibility of redemption; her virginity merely stimulates Joseph further and is thus construed as part of the arsenal of sexual weaponry that she turns upon him.

We see then that there are extreme divergences in the portrayal of Joseph's master's wife. The source of these conflicting depictions of the female protagonist stretches back to early in the history of the postbiblical tale of Joseph. From very early on, the Genesis story had been subject to modifications stemming from contact with Greek culture, and this encounter had an indelible effect on its future permutations. The similarity of the stories of Hippolytus and Phaedra, as well as other figures, to the Genesis tale of Joseph allowed their recombination and fusion, especially amongst the Hellenized Jews of the Classical world. Josephus's retelling of the Joseph story (dating from the first century CE) has absorbed many of the elements of the Greek tale, but such features appear several centuries earlier in the pseudepigraphic work, *The Testament of Joseph.* Already in this text, Potiphar's Wife is given a much more prolonged treatment than in the Bible, and her stratagems mirror in remarkable ways those detailed in *The Story of Our Master Joseph.* In the course of the narrative, she suggests poisoning her husband, sends Joseph aphrodisiac foodstuffs, bares her legs and breasts, and even threatens suicide—all in an attempt to entice her beloved. As Martin Braun has argued, the author of this work was seemingly torn between the original ethical/didactic purpose of the Hebrew narrative and the Greek concept of Eros. While the overall ethical-didactic bias remains clear, there is a "humanizing" of the heroine that resulted in a more complicated depiction of the temptress. Moreover, Eros's power also serves to magnify Joseph's achievement in resisting severe temptation. As we have seen, such a possibility for the redemption of Potiphar's Wife might very well have been suggested by the ambiguity in Genesis surrounding the identity of Joseph's wife, Asenath, whom the text records was the daughter of Potiphera, priest of On. The similarity between this name and that of Joseph's master was not lost on those exegetes who, by glossing over the distinction between one woman being the daughter of Potiphera and the other being Potiphar's wife, were able to equate the two figures.[53]

Such a sentimental depiction of Mrs. Potiphar was canonized and thus frozen within the Islamic tradition by its inclusion in the Qurʾān.[54] There, in line with Hellenistic romance and associated Jewish midrashic expansions of the tale, Joseph is depicted as most sorely tempted by his master's wife's allures. This softening in attitude is also reflected in the fifteenth-century *adab* collection on the "wiles of women" compiled by Ibn al-Baṭanūnī: *Kitāb al-ʿunwān fī makāyid al-niswān.* Here, all three of Zulaykhā's wishes—that she have her sight restored, that she be made a twelve-year-old girl, and that Joseph marry her—are granted. However, this time it is Zulaykhā who must rebuff Joseph's advances. This snub merely serves to increase his desire: he grabs her by the shirt, and as she pulls away from him the shirt is torn. Then the angel Gabriel appears to tell Joseph, "A tearing of a shirt for a tearing of a shirt and an escape for an escape." Following their marriage, the couple lives happily ever after.

Although these sympathetic portrayals of Zulaykhā may very well be the result of Hellenistic influence, Thomas Mann adopted a critical view of these

Islamic traditions in his magnum opus (itself, in effect, a modern retelling of the Joseph tale):

> The people, and to please them the poets, an all too easy-going breed, have spun out in a variety of ways this tale of Joseph and Potiphar's wife, which was only an episode, if an important one, in the life of Jacob's son. Any possibility of more to follow was, of course, completely excluded by the final catastrophe. But they have written sentimental continuations and given it a predominant place within the Joseph story. In their hands it becomes a sugary romance with a proper happy ending. According to these poetasters, the temptress—who goes by the name of Zuleika, a fact at which we can only shrug our shoulders—after she had got Joseph into prison, withdrew full of remorse into a "hut" and there lived only for the expiation of her sins. Meanwhile through the death of her husband she became a widow. But when Yussuf (meaning Joseph) was about to be freed out of the prison, he had refused to have his "chains" removed until the female aristocracy of the country had come before Pharaoh's throne and borne witness to his innocence. Accordingly the entire nobility of the sex had come before the King and with one voice the whole lovely bevy had announced that Joseph was the prince and pattern of purity, the very freshest ornament in her crown. After which Zuleika took the floor and made public confession that she alone had been the offender, and he an angel. The shameful crime was hers, she frankly avowed it; but now she was purified and gladly bore the shame and disgrace. Even after Joseph's elevation she continued to do penance, growing old and grey in the process. Only on the festal day when Father Jacob made his alleged triumphal entry into Egypt—and thus at a time when Joseph was actually the father of two sons—did the pair meet again. Joseph had forgiven the old woman, and as a reward heaven had restored all her former seductive beauty; whereupon Joseph had most romantically married her, and thus, after all these tribulations, her old wish came true, and they "put their heads and feet together."

"All that," Mann adds in this postscript, "is just Persian musk and attar of roses. It has nothing whatever to do with the facts."[55] Mann might perhaps have appreciated the fate meted out to Zulaykhā in *The Story of Our Master Joseph,* for it is anything but "Persian musk and attar of roses." The swipe of Joseph's sword makes it abundantly clear that Zulaykhā was not destined to be his mate.

An additional problem facing the biblical exegetes was Asenath's very foreignness, not to mention her parentage as the daughter of a pagan priest. To counter this discomfiting anomaly there thus arose a midrashic tradition that records that Joseph's wife is of good stock, the daughter of the union between Dinah and Shechem and thus Joseph's niece, who has also been transported to Egypt and adopted by Potiphera.[56] *The Story of Our Master Joseph* finesses the whole problem of the identity of Joseph's wife by never mentioning her, even though Joseph was able to produce for Jacob a marriage contract and thus document the legitimacy of his two sons, Ephraim and Manasseh. This lacuna could be attributed to the exegetical conundrum posed by the similarity of the names Potiphar and Potiphera in the Bible and the repugnance of identifying this wife with his former mistress—as in the Hellenist and Muslim versions. Instead, there is no hope for Zulaykhā's redemption in *The Story of Our Master Joseph;* here she is an unrelenting, wily temptress who pulls out all the stops in her attempts to seduce the chaste Joseph. That *The Story of Our Master Joseph* specifically records the same three wishes Zulaykhā asks Joseph to request of his God (*Joseph,* 169) would seem to be a clear indication that his refusal to grant them—and her violent death—at his hands are a reaction to and categorical rejection of the "fairy-tale" ending of the Romance and *adab* works. In its claim to relate the story of our Master Joseph the Righteous and, moreover, to do so "in all completeness and perfection," it will allow for no such moral ambiguity on the part of its protagonist. Here, Zulaykhā represented both the allure and the threat of female wiles, both literally and as a metonym for the dangers confronting Jews living in exile. Thus, her eradication was deemed necessary for Jewish solidarity, a communal cohesion affirmed metaphorically by the reunion of Joseph with his brothers.

4

Between the Pit and Mrs. Potiphar

They took him and cast him into the pit (Gen. 37:24) . . . foreshadowing that they would eventually cast him amid the Egyptians, into a place where the principle of faith was nowhere to be found.
Zohar 1, 185a

Very deep is the well of the past. Should we not call it bottomless?
Thomas Mann, *Joseph and His Brothers*

Up till now, we have been considering in isolation the two main subplots of the Joseph cycle: our hero's interactions with his family, on the one hand, and "the affair" with Zulaykhā, on the other. Indeed, we have seen how the tension between these two components is reified by the two alternative interpretations of *al-ṣiddīq* as meaning either "The Truthful" or "The Righteous." However, there also exist significant synergies between this pair of seemingly discrete accounts. In this regard, the tale follows earlier biblical exegetes who were attuned to both the overt and latent intratextual linkages within the scriptural *Vorlage* and were able to connect up these sections. By doing so, by reading the Bible as a coherent and interrelated whole, the rabbinic scholars achieved a maximal activation of allusions that forever transformed the community's understanding of both passages. Moreover, they were able to make the biblical narrative relevant to the contemporary situation and bring it to bear on issues facing the Jewish people. Such activity served to establish the interconnectedness of Scripture at the same time that it expanded the discourse surrounding it.

The Rabbis left few stones unturned in their attempts to join together the two story lines and posit cause-and-effect relationships between them. Thus, according to Rashi, Joseph included information in his "ill report" (*dibah raʿah,* Gen. 37:2) on the Brothers' engaging in prohibited sexual behavior

(H: *ʿarayot*). Rashi maintains that in accord with the rabbinic notions of quid pro quo it was because of this tale-bearing that Potiphar's Wife "lifted her eyes to him" with lust in mind. We can surmise an additional connection between Joseph's "crime" and his punishment: this *dibah raʿah* resonates alliteratively with the *ḥayah raʿah,* the "vicious beast" alluded to by both the Brothers and Jacob as being responsible for Joseph's death (Gen. 37:20 and 33). According to the narrated events, of course, no wild animal ever threatened Joseph; throughout the midrashic tradition, Jacob himself establishes this when he fails to observe any tear in his son's bloodied garment. In these extrabiblical traditions it is rather Potiphar's Wife, functioning metaphorically as the *ḥayah raʿah,* who attacks him and tears the garment of her recalcitrant slave. The Midrash makes this connection explicit through a prophetic premonition of Jacob: "R. Huna said: The spirit of prophecy glimmered in [Jacob], and he said: *'A vicious beast has devoured him'* (Gen. 37:33). This is Potiphar's Wife" (BR 84:19).

If, then, according to this interpretation, Potiphar's Wife is an animal that menaces Joseph, as what sort of beast does the tradition cast her? The Midrash, following on this connection made between the *dibah raʿah* and the *ḥayah raʿah,* speaks of her as a bear (*dov*) that will in the future attack Joseph in punishment for his indifference to his father's mourning (demonstrated by his failure to contact him all the while he is in Egypt). In Hebrew a female bear is a *dubah,* which in typically unvocalized Hebrew texts would be identical in form to *dibáh.* According to this reading, the verse, *va-yehi yosef yefeh tóʾar,* which leads up to Joseph's encounter with Potiphar's Wife, when combined with the earlier reference to him as *náʿar,* contains an implicit criticism of Joseph's self-absorption: "He would curl his hair and God said to him, 'Your father is mourning and you curl your hair! I will incite (*megareh*) the bear (*ha-dubah*) upon you'" (ibid., 87:3). In this interpretation, then, we see the activation of three separate narrative elements to form a network of associations.

In line with its sanitized version of the events, the hero of *Joseph* is not condemned for any such display of vanity; rather, he is the passive object of Zulaykhā's obsession, an infatuation that at least in part is owing to her own narcissistic concern that he surpasses her in beauty: "Then [Zulaykhā] said, 'Bring us Joseph so that we may see if his face is like mine.' So they brought Joseph to her and when she saw him, she turned her eyes away from his face, and she was jealous of him. And she took a mirror and brought his face close to hers, and when she saw his face in the mirror, it was like the moon on the fourteenth night" (*Joseph,* 69–70). Moreover, in this Judeo-Arabic retelling, the animal that the Brothers assert preyed upon Joseph is that stereotypical villain of folk literature: the Wolf. In blaming the Wolf, *Joseph* is consistent with Islamic tradition from the Qurʾān on down: "[The Brothers] said: 'We went off to compete together, and left Joseph with our packs. The Wolf devoured him'" (Q 12:17). Perhaps it was the similarity of the Hebrew word for "bear," *dov,* unknown in Middle Eastern climes, with the Arabic for "wolf," *dhiʾb* (the grapheme *dhal* in Arabic having an underlying form identical to the letter *dal*), that gave rise to the Muslim tradition associating the vicious beast of Genesis with this predator. A possible biblical support for this identification comes in Jacob's final testament to Benjamin, where the dying father employs the phrase: *Binyamin zeʾev yiṭraf* . . . (Gen. 49:27). Instead of reading this as a nominative sentence—"Benjamin is a devouring wolf," the Rabbis exploit the syntactical flexibility of biblical Hebrew to reverse subject and object and offer a counterreading: "A wolf will devour Benjamin." In any case, by associating Mrs. Potiphar with the animal that "devoured" Joseph, a link is established between the punishment Joseph will endure at the hands of the Brothers and the trials he is subjected to by the temptress in Egypt.

This exegetical trend wherein Potiphar's Wife is a predatory female who attacks Joseph correlates with a gynophobic thread in the rabbinic discourse that extends back to Lilith, who, according to Talmudic legend, was Adam's first wife before Eve and the mother of demons born from this union. In the ninth-century narrative cycle, *Pseudo-Ben Sira* (or *The Alphabet of Ben Sira*), she is depicted as created like Adam from the earth, but when she demands equality with him (the issue being who will lie beneath whom during intercourse), Adam refuses, prompting her to run away and unite with "the great demon."[1] While in Jewish folklore she is primarily feared as the harmer of babies, she also began to appear as the temptress of pious individuals, coming to them while they sleep. Eve herself was the object of rabbinic opprobrium. Thus, in some sense, the "wild animal" (*ḥayah raʿah*) that devours Joseph evokes the primordial female, *Ḥavah* (Eve), or, as her etiology is given in Genesis 3:20, "The Mother of All Life" (*em kol ḥay*). This rubric is, in turn, a vestige of the Creatrix of Babylonian cosmogony who was vanquished in the primeval struggle for power.

Within Arabo-Islamic tradition such "fear of the feminine" is connected with the Arabic traditions surrounding one Hubā from Medina. This Hubā was a character-type that flourished in the *adab* literature of the seventh century, and she became the standard for female lasciviousness, as expressed in the

Arabic proverb: "More lewd than Hubā." Moreover, according to tradition, the women of Medina called her "Eve, the Mother of Mankind" because she taught them the various positions for sexual intercourse to which she assigned names.[2]

There is yet another way in which Zulaykhā is metaphorically connected with the subplot of Joseph's relations with his brothers. *The Story of Our Master Joseph* displays much affinity with a genre of Arabic literary works that treats the theme "relief after adversity" (*al-faraj baᶜda al-shiddah*), and the cistern or well into which the Brothers cast Joseph symbolizes the constriction of his desperate situation as a youth. This "tightness" will later contrast with the wealth and expansive power that are his reward at tale's end. The putative root of the Hebrew word for Egypt (*mitzráyim*), *tz-r,* although unrelated in a formal lexical sense, connotes in the biblical idiom both "narrowness" as well as a figurative meaning of "adversity" (as evidenced by the oft-repeated call to God in the Bible to take the supplicant out from the narrow places to the wide, from constriction to expanse). When the biblical narrator has Joseph employ the word *bor* ("pit") for the dungeon where he is being kept, this is an explicit marker of the intratextual relationship between the two pits: "For in truth, I was kidnapped from the land of the Hebrews; nor have I done anything here that they should have put me in the dungeon" (Gen. 40:15). Egypt and Joseph's trials there at the hands of Mrs. Potiphar are thus an extension of the pit and the torments to which his brothers had earlier subjected him.

"The Scene at the Well" is also significant for what *doesn't* transpire there. Borrowing from scholarship on the Greek epic, Robert Alter has applied to biblical literature the analytical category of *type-scenes.* The Bible contains various examples of certain set motifs that appear more than once in the course of its narratives. Turning the obsessive "excavative" or "atomistic" nature of Source Criticism on its head, what these repetitions point to in this view is not necessarily, or mainly, a corruption or splicing together of multiple sources; rather, they represent the artistic conventions that are the background against which the biblical narrator could demonstrate his virtuosity.

The episode of "Joseph and the Well" represents a flaunting of one particular convention, that of the "Betrothal at the Well," which serves as its backdrop. According to the pattern, the young man (or his emissary) must travel to a foreign land where he will encounter a beautiful and kindly maiden who will become his wife. Noting that in arid climes the well is an absolute necessity for the sustenance of life and symbolizes fertility, Alter also points out that in Freudian terms it represents the Female herself. Reading the Bible against itself, then, the seemingly redundant reference to the dried-up state of the well—that it was "empty and had no water" (Gen. 37:24)—emphasizes the themes of impotence and infertility. Joseph will come upon no nubile, young maidens drawing water as a prelude to a marital match; instead, he will be roughly cast down to its bottom by brothers intent on his murder, only to be hauled up by travel-hardened, profiteering, caravan drivers.

In chapter 2 we explored Joseph's descent into the pit as a metaphor for death and his suppressed "murder" at the hands of his brothers. To pursue this psychoanalytic vein a bit farther, the pit in the Joseph story also represents the female genital passageway, a place of narrowness or constriction that "swallows" the male. As such, the pit can be seen to stand in metonymic relation to Woman and her wiles. In a figurative sense then, Joseph, by being cast into the pit by his brothers, is thrown directly into Zulaykhā's vagina. Moreover, this Egyptian woman is no favored and fertile mate for Joseph as is required by the conventions of the biblical type-scene, one from whom his descendants will spring and the Israelite line will continue, but rather a lascivious female, bent on an illicit sexual escapade.[3] The Qurʾān itself (bearing in mind the connection we've drawn between "The Well" and "The Female") suggests the sex-death nexus in its recording of the Brothers' scheme to do away with Joseph: "So kill Joseph or cast him to some land so that your father's favor will fall to you and afterwards you will be a redressed people" (Q 12:9).

Seen in this light, then, *The Story of Our Master Joseph* juxtaposes and conflates two primal anxieties when facing creatures perceived as possessing insatiable appetites: the rapacious beast of prey and the human female. Moreover, the two metaphorical interpretations offered here of Zulaykhā—as (dry!) well and as devouring animal—correlate both with the nonprocreative (and hence, according to normative tradition, the illegitimate) desire for sex and with the male's anxiety at being swallowed by the vagina of the female. Such castration anxiety might also be reflected in the tradition that interpreted the reference to Potiphar as *serīs parʿoh* to mean that he was a eunuch, one who is both sexually and otherwise impotent; that is, that he has been literally emasculated by his temptress wife.

Torn Garments and Israel in Exile

In the previous chapter, we discussed how Joseph's harsh treatment of his mistress seems greatly overdetermined. Much of the narrative appears to be building to a resolution in which Zulaykhā will come to be a legitimate mate, and there is much in her depiction that would militate to a sympathetic appraisal of her character. Moreover, even if she was guilty of calling Joseph on multiple occasions to sin with her, we need to bear in mind his merciful attitude to his brothers who it could be said wronged him far more grievously. Something else must be going on.

In a larger sense, the ambivalence toward women displayed in the Joseph narrative serves as a trope for Jewish communal angst vis-à-vis its exilic condition. Robert Alter astutely points out this possibility when he states "the foreign land is chiefly a geographical correlative for the sheer female otherness of the prospective wife"[4]; but conversely, "Woman" may stand for the allure and temptations of the dominant culture that threaten to overwhelm the mores of the minority and undermine its ancient tribal cohesion. According to the version of events in Genesis, Joseph, chased by Potiphar's Wife, merely leaves his garment behind. Mrs. Potiphar subsequently uses the abandoned piece of clothing as evidence when she makes her accusation against Joseph. In the Midrash, this motif of "The Abandoned Garment" has evolved into a full-blown chase scene, in the course of which Joseph's tunic is torn by the master's wife. This fulfills a need to present Joseph physically resisting the forceful attempts of Mrs. Potiphar (the Rabbis here are obviously curious that Joseph in Genesis makes no such attempt to defend himself); the element of "the torn shirt" has the additional advantage of providing tangible proof of Joseph's innocence and the falsity of the testimony of Potiphar's Wife.

However, on a figurative level, this tearing of Joseph's garment functions as a metaphor according to which violation of the body or its boundaries represents Israelite cultural anxiety over life in exile. Mary Douglas has shown that concern over the integrity of the body is symbolic of this diasporic disquietude:

> When rituals express anxiety about the body's orifices the sociological counterpart of this anxiety is a care to protect the political and cultural unity of a minority group. The Israelites were always in their history a hard-pressed minority. In their beliefs all the bodily issues were polluting, blood, pus, excreta, semen, etc. The threatened boundaries of their body politic would be well mirrored in their care for the integrity, unity and purity of their physical body.[5]

In *The Story of Our Master Joseph* the threat is depicted even more vividly in the first chase scene: as Zulaykhā desperately lunges after her escaping servant boy, her fingernails pierce the skin of his chest and blood spurts forth (80–81). Extending this metaphor, the tearing of Joseph's garment and the scratching of his flesh are a shredding of the "tissue" of the Text, the biblical narrative, and a threat to the continuity of Israel's sacred history and the chosen status of its lead character at this juncture.

In the biblical account, Potiphar's Wife is symbolic of the threat to Jewish identity and continuity as a minority population in the Diaspora. This conforms to anxiety voiced throughout the biblical text over Israelite men marrying foreign wives, a theme that begins with Abraham's concern that a wife for his son Isaac be taken from Aram-Naharayim; that is, from within his ancestral tribe (Gen. 24:1–10).[6] The seizing of the beautiful Sarah and Rebecca by foreign rulers (Gen. 12:10–20; 20:1–18; 27:7–11) mirrors—with a flipping of the gender roles—the illicit seduction of the handsome Hebrew slave by the powerful foreigner. A similar concern over the violation of sexual and national boundaries may also be seen in the case of the rape of Dinah (Gen. 34) and the liaison between the Midianite woman and the Israelite man (Numbers 25). To take just the former instance, the Brothers' outrage and the terrible vengeance they exact upon the Shechemites seem predicated not so much on concern over a violent act perpetrated against a sibling as on the desecration of tribal or national honor. Her sexual violation is thus seen in communal terms as "a scurrilous thing in Israel" (Gen. 34:7). This conception of "Woman" as the repository of national or familial pride is merely the obverse of a conception of "Woman" as being wily and lascivious. With regard to the Joseph story, such identity angst would be heightened at the beginning of the period of sojourning in Egypt that it recounts, a period of exile from the Land that would come to serve as the archetype for all dispersions of the Jewish people.

At the beginning of this book, I discussed the significance of the Joseph story as paradigm for Israel in exile, an allegory for the need to maintain cultural boundaries. There, I mentioned the absence of a rehabilitation of the Joseph of the Genesis narrative in postexilic biblical material—most significantly, its absence from the recapitulation of Israelite history in the canonical book of Chronicles. In the wake of the Return from Babylonia, this glaring omission acquires further poignancy due to the continued anomalous existence in Mesopotamia of the vast majority of the nation. However, given the great literary merit of the Joseph tale and its weight within the Genesis narrative, it is not altogether surprising that we should find the themes recycled in a story of exile more directly related to the experience of the Jews of the Babylonian Diaspora. Thus it is that the book of Esther has appropriated and absorbed many elements from the story of Joseph in Genesis.[7] Perhaps the most direct allusion is the adjectival phrase employed there to describe Esther's beauty, only slightly modified from the form in which it appears when applied to Joseph and his mother: "And Mordechai brought up Hadassah, that is, Esther, his uncle's daughter for she had neither father nor mother, and the girl was fair and beautiful (*yefat tóʾar ve-tovat marʾeh*) and when her father and mother were dead, Mordechai took her as his own daughter" (Esther 2:7).

It is highly significant that the theme of sexual taboos surrounding Joseph's relationship with his master's wife received the most attention in the midrashic interpretations of the story of Joseph. The very existence in exile was deemed defiling, and the midrash stressed this theme through application of the metaphor of prohibited exogamous relationships. As Douglas has shown, that which is considered by the culture to be outside the system, that which is deemed repugnant or regarded with revulsion, paradoxically serves to define the system and help preserve it from such threats. Thus, Israelite food practices paralleled their intermarriage taboo; both were means of guarding the individual and national/corporate body from contamination, assimilation, or apostasy. Such a perspective may be profitably applied to the rabbinic ambivalence at Esther's indulging in forbidden food and illicit sex in the palace even in the cause of saving her people. With Joseph, the taboo acts would be his implication in the affair with his mistress, and his later marriage to an Egyptian priest's daughter. These transgressions and commissions of taboo acts constitute a theme largely suppressed in the text but were fertile ground for iconoclastic rabbinic readings of the tradition.[8]

The continued existence of thriving Jewish communities in the Diaspora gave rise to a need to reconcile the existential state of exile with the tradition or, as Levenson argues, a new theology:

> So long as salvation was equated with return and Diaspora existence was seen as a curse, the continued existence of Israelite communities outside the Land was a theological absurdity. . . . It was within the tension of this contradiction that . . . the theology of Esther was conceived.
>
> The new theology allows for limited redemption even in exile. The Jews are exposed and vulnerable; there is potential for calamity in every event. But God intervened—through human actors—to transform them from a weak, vulnerable band into a powerful community, with one of their own as prime minister.[9]

Thus, despite the ubiquity of Jewish suffering as a weak minority population living in exile, partial (albeit temporary) redemption was still possible for

Diaspora Jews, and hope for such became a portable haven wherever Jews resided. This motif has its origin in the Joseph story, where the protagonist rises from the depths of servitude to become second in power to the Pharaoh. While this would seem to represent the height of security and autonomy, before Jacob and Joseph pass away they each sound a note of premonition in their insistence that their bones be brought out of Egypt. Indeed, within the biblical narrative framework the danger is not long in coming and, when it does, is introduced with an explicit allusion to Joseph: "And a new king arose over Egypt who knew not Joseph" (Exodus 1:8).

The sense of the inherent precariousness of exile felt by the Egyptian Jewish community may be reflected in the widespread popularity of both *The Tale of Joseph* and *The Tale of Moses* (judging from the numbers of extant copies of manuscripts). Also, Egyptian Jews, like many other communities the world over, celebrated a "Minor Purim," in this case commemorating their salvation from a despotic sixteenth-century pasha.[10] In this regard, the character of Joseph represents a political model of leadership based on accommodation or assimilation, which in the Bible is explicitly contrasted with—and superseded by—that embodied by "Moses the Lawgiver."[11] Thus, it is not insignificant that their stories are joined together in the Bible, both physically and narratively. According to this view, Jews, even when they ascend to the uppermost positions in gentile society, remain dependent upon their overlords and subject to their whims; no matter how high Joseph climbs, even when he is made Pharaoh's minister, ultimately he is denied total control. As is explicitly recorded in Genesis, Pharaoh remains superior to him with regard to the throne, and in time all of Israel will be subject to the tyranny of the new pharaoh. The model of assimilation that Joseph represents is abrogated by the Exodus: Israel must leave Egypt in order to receive God's revelation directly, coalesce into a nation, and come into the inheritance of its land. In line with the explicit statements of the biblical text itself, Joseph represents an essential stage in the evolution of Jewish peoplehood—the experience of exile and redemption, the experience recorded in the words of the Passover Haggadah of moving "from slavery to freedom."

The necessity of this process—or, in terms of biblical theology, the divine imperative—is reflected in Joseph's words following the reunion with his brothers:

> And now, do not be pained and do not be incensed with yourselves that you sold me down here, because for sustenance God has sent me before you.

> Two years now there has been famine in the heart of the land, and there are yet five years without plowing and harvest. And God has sent me before you to make you a remnant on earth and to preserve life, for you to be a great surviving group. And so, it is not you who sent me here, but God, and He has made me father to Pharaoh and lord to all his house and ruler over all the land of Egypt. (Gen. 45:5–8)

The inevitability of this step in the process is signaled already in God's promise to Jacob's grandfather, Abraham. At the Covenant of the Pieces, God assures Abraham that the Land will be the inheritance of his people. He stipulates, however, that first Abraham's descendants will need to undergo a period of exile.

> Know well that your seed shall be strangers in a land not theirs and they shall be enslaved and afflicted four hundred years. But upon the nation for whom they slave I will bring judgment, and afterward they shall come forth with great substance. As for you, you shall go to your fathers in peace; you shall be buried in ripe old age. And in the fourth generation they shall return here, for the iniquity of the Amorites is not yet full. (Gen. 15:13–16)

This is paralleled in God's words to Jacob, reassuring him before he leaves Canaan for exile in Egypt: "Fear not to go down to Egypt, for a great nation I will make you there. I Myself will go down with you to Egypt and I Myself will surely bring you back up as well, and Joseph shall lay his hand on your eyes" (Gen. 46:3–4).

By specifying Israel's destiny, God Himself is thus depicted as establishing the narrative tension in His Torah, a tension that must now be resolved by an account of the specific manner in which Israel descended to Egypt. Thomas Mann states this most cogently:

> In other words, God had destined these populations [the present inhabitants of the Land] to defeat and subjection in the interest of the man from Ur and his seed. But all this must be accepted with caution, or at least with understanding. We are dealing with later interpolations deliberately calculated to confirm as the earliest intentions of the divine political situations which had first been established by force. (*Joseph and His Brothers,* 6)

In homiletic explanation of the unusual use of the passive voice when, following the interlude of the tale of Judah and Tamar, Genesis resumes the story in chapter 39—*and Joseph was brought down* (*ve-yosef hurad mitz-*

ráyim)—the Rabbis in the Talmud provided an alternative homiletic reading of the consonantal text and render it in the active voice: "He [Joseph] brought down: don't read 'he was brought down' (*hurad*), rather 'he brought down' (*horid*)" (BT Soṭah 13b). Extending this reading in the midrash, they provided an analogy drawn from their quotidian reality:

> *And Joseph was brought down to Egypt:* Scripture states elsewhere that *Come and see the works of God; He acts circuitously in His dealings with the children of man* (Psalms 66:5) . . . hence, *And Joseph was brought down to Egypt.* Don't read *hurad* (he was brought down), but *horid* (he brought down) his father and the Tribes to Egypt. R. Tanḥuma said to what may this be compared? To a cow on whose neck they are seeking to place a yoke, but she refuses to comply. What did they do? They took her son from behind her, and while the calf would low, pulled her to the place wherein they sought to plow. The cow heard her son and went against her best interests for the sake of her son. So The-Holy-One-Blessed-Be-He sought to fulfill the decree of *Know well* [*that your seed shall be strangers in a land not theirs and they shall be enslaved and afflicted four hundred years. But upon the nation for whom they slave I will bring judgment, and afterward they shall come forth with great substance*] (Genesis 15:13) and brought about all these things in a roundabout manner, and they went down to Egypt and redeemed the bill of debt. As it is said: *And Joseph was brought down to Egypt* (Genesis 39:1). Hence, *He acts circuitously in His doing toward the children of man* (Psalms 66:5).[12] (*Tanḥuma* [Zundel edition] Va-yeishev 4)

This in turn may be compared to a scene depicted in Egyptian Old Kingdom (2650–2150 BCE) tombs of the technique employed for leading a herd of cattle across a canal. One example, from the tomb of a high Sixth Dynasty official named Ni-ankh-nesut and on view at the Detroit Institute of Arts, depicts a group of cattle lined up in a straight row except for a cow at the front separated from the rest. Her head stretches forward to touch tongues with her calf, borne on the herder's shoulders, but with its head and eyes turned longingly toward its mother.

This touching image of filial and maternal love and of "crossings" seems a fitting place to end our discussion of the Jewish and Muslim tales of Joseph. We have seen how midrash and "the exegetical imagination" are the primary means of making the central texts of Jews and Muslims relevant for successive generations living under highly divergent conditions. Both the alluding and the evoked texts are given greater saliency by their mutual reference to one another, and the resultant new associations that are generated for the reader expand the discourse surrounding scriptural events and characters. Retellings of biblical and quranic stories by folk writers take this process a step further by stitching together discrete exegetical and homiletic motifs to form a continuous narrative. *The Story of Our Master Joseph,* through its long line of antecedent intertexts, has made this leap of assimilating what originally were often discrete midrashic interpretations, providing a rereading of the Joseph tale within its own narrative framework. While this story, largely an adaptation of a Muslim tale, is remarkable for its absorption of material from diverse sources, there are limits to this eclecticism. In addition to or in tandem with the ties that bind the exegetes to the core text of their tradition, allegiance to a moral system constitutes another factor limiting the exegetical polysemy. *The Story of Our Master Joseph* maintains an overriding didactic concern, focusing on the story as one that can inspire readers to emulate the protagonist both in his stoicism in the face of suffering and in his restraint in the face of temptation. And yet we have seen how it has radically departed from its model in order to highlight the hazards of exile that are a perennial concern for the Jewish people in Diaspora.

The Story of Our Master Joseph is an intricately woven tale exhibiting the rough artistry of integration that one might associate with a popular work that drew, directly or indirectly, consciously or unconsciously, on a multitude of sources from an enormous range of time periods and cultures. What we have here is a remarkable example of the migration of cultural artifacts: a Jewish text has taken its form from an Islamic prototype, which itself is largely based on midrashic works, Hellenistic literature, ancient Near Eastern material, and so on and so forth, back all the way into the mists of the earliest human stories of parental favoritism, sibling rivalry, separation from loved ones, sexual mores, and the struggles for continued communal existence outside of the homeland. Midrash and the Legends of the Prophets coalesce in this specific text to provide a window into the cross-cultural flow of ideas, motifs, and traditions between Jews and Muslims at their points of contact.

Within less than one hundred years, we have witnessed the virtual demise of age-old Jewish communal life in the Arab world. The history of Jews in Arab lands (or of Jews and Islam) has special cogency as we grapple for a way out of the current political impasse in the Middle East and struggle to overcome the mutual lack of understanding between the West and the Arab-Muslim world. During brighter times and over the course of centuries, there was a great sharing of creative and scientific knowledge across religious lines.

Stories about biblical and quaranic figures are but one result of this relationship and reflect an environment in which not only a literary genre and modes of interpretation but particular motifs could be utilized by both religious traditions. *The Story of Our Master Joseph* epitomizes this historical interdependence of the Hebraic and Arabic literary traditions. Such a text tells us much about the common experiences and concerns of Muslims and Jews and the shared pool of tradition from which both were able to imbibe. While itself an instantiation of cross-cultural exchange, its selective use of this material can also illuminate collective constructions of "the other"—and consequently, and ultimately, of "the self."

As I finish writing these words here in the city holy to all three Abrahamic or Biblicist faiths, I offer a prayer to "the most Merciful Compassionate One" that dreams of fraternal concord will become reality and that Jerusalem will "speedily and in our day" indeed become for all *ʿīr ha-shalōm* and *madīnat al-salām*: the City of Peace. How good and how pleasant it would be for Brothers to live together in harmony. Amen.

Yerūshalayim/Jerusalem/Al-Quds
5764 AM/2005 AD/1424 AH

Appendix: The *Sūrah* of Joseph

In the name of God, the Merciful Compassionate One.

, 2] *'Alif lām rā'*.[1] These are the verses of the Elucidating Book. We have sent it
down to you people as an Arabic Recitation so that you may grow in under-
[3] standing. We relate unto you [Muḥammad] the finest of tales in revealing to
you this Recitation, while beforehand you were among the unaware.

[4] When Joseph said to his father: "Father, I saw eleven stars, and the sun
[5] and the moon; I saw them prostrating to me," [Jacob] said: "My son, don't
tell your vision to your brothers lest they will come up with some plot against
[6] you, for Satan is an enemy divisive to Man. According to this [vision] your
Lord will choose you and instruct you in the interpretation of stories, and He
will fulfill His favor upon you and upon Jacob's household as He fulfilled it
beforehand upon your two forefathers, Abraham and Isaac; surely your Lord
is All-wise, All-knowing."

[7] In Joseph and his brothers were signs for those who inquire.

[8] When [the Brothers] said: "It is clear Joseph and his brother are more
loved by our father than we are even though we are a sizeable bunch: our
[9] father is deluded, so kill Joseph or cast him to some land so that your father's
10] favor will fall to you and afterwards you will be a redressed people," one of
[the Brothers] who spoke said: "Don't kill Joseph, but if you do anything,
throw him into the bottom of the well so that some company of travelers will
take him up."

11] They said: "Father, what is with you that you do you not trust us with
12] Joseph when we only wish him the best? Send him with us tomorrow so that
13] he can have fun and play; we will take the best care of him." He said: "It
would greatly sadden me if you were to take him, for I am afraid that the wolf

1. Such mysterious groupings of Arabic letters are found at the beginning of several quaranic chapters and have been variously interpreted by traditional commentators as comprising abbreviations of names for the Divine, or simply as a means to arouse the listener's curiosity.

[14] will eat him when you are unaware." They said: "With us being such a sizeable bunch, for the wolf to eat him we ourselves would have to perish."
[15] So when [the Brothers] went with [Joseph] and combined to put him in
the bottom of the well, We then revealed to him: "You shall inform them of
this matter of theirs when they are unaware."
[16, 17] And they came weeping to their father in the evening. They said: "Father,
we went off to compete together and left Joseph behind with our belongings,
and then the wolf ate him; but you don't believe us even though we're telling
[18] the truth," and they brought forth his shirt with false blood. He said: "It isn't
so! You yourselves have plotted something. But Fair Patience! In God may aid
be sought against what you describe."
[19] And a company of travelers came, and they sent forth their water-drawer
who lowered down his pail [into the well]. He said: "What good news this lad
[20] is!" And they[2] concealed him as goods, but God knew what they did. And they[3]
sold him for a trivial price, for a few dirhams, and they cared little for him.
[21] And the one who bought him, an Egyptian, said to his wife: "Provide him
with worthy accommodations; he may be of use to us, or we may adopt him
as our son." Thus We established Joseph in the land so that We might teach
him the interpretation of stories. And God is ascendant over His affairs though
[22] most men do not know. And when he grew to adulthood, We bestowed upon
him wisdom and knowledge, for that is how We reward the virtuous.
[23] And the woman in whose house he was sought to seduce him against his
will, and she locked the doors and said: "Come, you!" He said: "God be my
refuge! My lord has provided me pleasant accommodations. Surely wrongdo-
[24] ers will not prosper!" And she desired him, and he would have desired her had
he not seen his Lord's proof. We did this in order to turn him from evil and
licentiousness; he is surely one of Our faithful servants.
[25] And they both raced to the door, and she tore his tunic from behind, and
at the door they both met her master. She said: "What is the reward of one
who sought to harm your family other than that he should be imprisoned, or
[26] painful torture?" He said: "It was she who attempted to seduce me against my
will." And a witness from her household testified: "If his shirt is torn from the
[27] front, then she has spoken truly and he is among the liars; however, if his tunic
[28] is torn from the back, then she has lied and he is among the truthful." And
when [the Potentate] saw that his tunic was torn from behind, he said: "This

2. Either the Brothers or the travelers.
3. Again, either the Brothers or the merchants.

29] is clearly of the cunning of you women; indeed your cunning is great! Joseph,
turn away from this; and you, woman, ask forgiveness for your crime: you are
clearly among the sinners!"
30] Some women in the city said: "The wife of the potentate has sought to
seduce her servant; he has pierced her heart with love. Indeed, we see her to be
31] clearly in the wrong." And when she heard of their slander, she sent to them,
and prepared for them a banquet, and she gave to each of them a knife, and
said [to Joseph]: "Come out before them!" And when they saw him, they so
admired him that they cut up their hands, and they said: "God save us! This is
32] no mortal; this one is nothing but a noble angel." She said: "There before you
is the one about whom you blamed me; indeed, I did attempt to seduce him
against his will, yet he abstained. If he will not do what I command him, he
33] shall be imprisoned and be one of the humbled." He said: "My Lord, prison is
more to my liking than that to which they invite me; yet if You do not turn me
from their cunning I will become attracted to them and thereby become one
34] of the ignorant." And so his Lord answered him and He warded off from him
their cunning, Lo! He is the Knowing Listening One.
35] Then it occurred to them,[4] after they had seen the signs, to imprison him
36] for a period of time. And two servants entered the prison with him. One of the
two said, "I see myself in a dream pressing wine," and the other said, "I see
myself in a dream carrying upon my head bread which the birds are eating.
Inform us of its interpretation; we can certainly see that you are among those
37] who are skillful." He said, "No food by which you will be sustained shall reach
you before I inform you of its interpretation. This is knowledge my Lord has
taught me. I have left the faith of a people who do not believe in God—they,
38] the Hereafter they deny— and I have followed the faith of my forefathers,
Abraham, Isaac, and Jacob. It was not for us to associate anything with God;
such is God's largesse to us and to the people, but most men are ungrateful."
39] "My two fellow prisoners! Are various gods better or the One Subduing
40] God? That which you serve besides Him is nothing but names invented by
you—by you and your fathers—for which God has sent down no authority.
Judgment belongs only to God; He has commanded that you not serve any but
Him. That is the true faith; but most people do not know."
41] "My two fellow prisoners, one of you shall pour wine for his lord; as for
the other, he shall be crucified and the birds will eat of his head. Thus has the

4. The plural object would seem to imply that this was the initiative of al-ʿAzīz and his wife and/or the Egyptian courtiers.

[42] matter of which you seek interpretation already been decreed." And he said
to the one of them he thought would be released: "Mention me in your lord's
presence," but Satan caused him to forget to mention him to his lord, and so
[Joseph] lingered in prison several years.
[43] And the king said: "I see seven fat cows which seven lean ones are eating,
and seven green ears of corn and seven others withered. O trusted counselors,
[44] expound for me this vision if you are capable of interpreting visions." They
said: "[Such] a hodgepodge of dreams. And we are not among those knowl-
[45] edgeable in dream interpretation." And of those two [former prisoners], the
one who had been released, remembering after this passage of time, said: "I
myself shall inform you of its interpretation: so send me forth."
[46] [The cupbearer said:] "Joseph, O man of truth, explain for us the seven fat
cows that seven lean ones were eating, and the seven green ears of corn and
the others withered so that I may go back to the people in order that they will
[47] understand." [Joseph] said: "You shall sow seven years as usual, but what you
[48] have harvested leave in the ear, except a little which you may eat. Then there
shall follow seven ones of hardship which will consume what you have laid
[49] up for them, all but a little of what you keep in store. Then shall come a year
in which the people will be saved[5] and will press [grapes]."
[50] And the king said: "Bring him to me!" but when the messenger came to
him, [Joseph] said: "Go back to your lord and ask him what is the opinion of
the women who cut up their hands, for certainly my Lord is aware of their
[51] cunning." [The king] said [to the women]: "What was it you wanted when
you attempted to seduce Joseph against his will?" They said: "God forbid!
We know no evil of him." The Potentate's wife said: "Now the truth has come
out—it was I who attempted to seduce him against his will. He is certainly one
[52] of the truthful." [Joseph said:] "This is so he may know that I did not betray
[53] him in secret, and that God does not guide the cunning of the traitors. It is not
that I absolve myself: surely the soul is prone to evil unless my Lord shows
mercy. Indeed my Lord is All-merciful, All-forgiving."
[54] The king said: "Bring him before me so that I may appoint him exclusively for my service." And when [the king] had spoken with [Joseph], he
[55] said: "As of today you are with us securely established." [Joseph] said: "Set
[56] me over the land's granaries for I am a skillful custodian." Thus did We establish Joseph in the land to dwell there wherever he pleased. We bestow Our
mercy on whomever We please, and shall not deny the righteous their reward;

5. Alternatively, "the people shall have rain."

57] and yet the reward of the Hereafter is better for those who have believed and
have been pious.
58] And Joseph's brothers arrived and presented themselves before him, and
59] he recognized them, but they did not know him. And when he had given them
their provisions, he said: "Bring me a brother of yours from your father. Don't
60] you see that I give full measure and provide the best of lodgings? But if you
refuse to bring him, you will have no measure from me, nor will you come
61] near." They said: "We will try to coax him from his father; this we will do."
62] And he said to his servants: "Put their goods into their saddlebags so that they
may notice it when they return to their people and then will come back."
63] And when they returned to their father, they said: "Father, [any further]
allotment of grain has been denied us, so send our brother with us so we can
64] obtain our allotment and we will take good care of him." He said: "Am I to
trust you with him as I once trusted you with his brother? But God is the
best of guardians, and of all those that show mercy He is the most merciful."
65] And when they opened their packs, they discovered that their goods had been
returned to them. They said: "Father, what more could we wish for? Here are
our goods returned to us: we will provide for our family and will take good
care of our brother, and we will receive in addition an extra camel-load: that
66] should be an easy measure."[6] He said: "I will never send him with you until
you give me a pledge in God's name to bring him back to me unless you are
beset on all sides." And when they had given him their pledge, he said: "God
is witness to what we say."
67] And [Jacob] said: "My sons, don't enter from a single gate; rather, enter
from different gates. In no way can I shield you from God; judgment is His
alone. In Him I have put my trust; in Him let all the faithful put their trust."
68] And when they entered as their father bid them, he could in no way shield
them from God, but this soothed an apprehension in Jacob's soul. He was
possessed of knowledge that We had taught him, but most men have no [such]
knowledge.
69] And when they went in unto Joseph, he embraced his brother [Benjamin]
70] and said: "I am your brother; do not be saddened over what they did." And
when he had given them their provisions, he hid a drinking-cup in his brother's
pack. Then a herald called out after them: "Travelers, you are surely thieves!"

6. I.e., they will have no trouble in attaining the additional allotment of grain. Alternatively, in using the demonstrative pronoun the Brothers may be referring here to the lightness of the shipment they have just brought in comparison to what they will bring next time.

[71] And as [the Egyptians] caught up to them, [the Brothers] said: “What have
[72] you lost?” They said: “We’re missing the king’s drinking cup.” “Whoever
[73] brings it will have a camel-load of corn: I pledge my word for it.” They said:
“In God’s name, you know we did not come to this land to cause trouble; we
[74] are no thieves.” They said: “What will be the punishment of the one who stole
[75] it if it turns out you are lying?” They said: “The one in whose pack the cup is
found will become your slave: that shall be his punishment. This is how we
punish those who despoil others.”
[76] [Joseph] searched the bags, beginning with theirs before he searched his
brother’s, and then he pulled out [the king’s drinking cup] from his brother’s
bag. Thus We contrived for Joseph. According to royal law he had no right
to seize his brother, but God willed otherwise. We elevate by stages whomever We will, but above any possessor of knowledge there is One who is
All-knowing.
[77] [The Brothers] said: “If he has stolen, a brother of his has stolen beforehand.” And Joseph kept the secret to himself and did not reveal it to them; he
[78] said: “You are in a bad situation. God knows best what you describe.” They
said: “O Potentate, this boy has a very old father, so take one of us instead of
[79] him; we can see you are among the virtuous.” He said: “God forbid that we
should take any but the one with whom our property was found, otherwise we
would certainly be unjust.”
[80] And when [the Brothers] despaired of [Joseph], they went aside to confer
in private. The eldest of them said: “Don’t you know that your father took
from you a pledge in God’s name, and that beforehand you wronged Joseph? I
will not leave this land until my father gives me permission or God rules in my
[81] favor: He is the best of judges. Return to your father and say to him: ‘Father,
your son stole. We testify only to what we know; we could not guard against
[82] the unforeseen. Ask the city where we were and the caravan with which we
traveled. We are speaking the truth.’”
[83] [Jacob] said: “It isn’t so! You yourselves have contrived something: but
Fair Patience! Perhaps God will bring all [of my sons] to me. He alone is the
[84] Wise Knowing One.” And he turned away from them and said: “O my grief
for Joseph!” And keeping silent, his eyes went white with grief from sadness.
[85] They said: “By God, won’t you stop thinking about Joseph before you waste
[86] away or die?” He said: “I complain to God about my sorrow and sadness.
[87] God has made known to me things that you don’t know. My sons, go and seek
news of Joseph and his brother and do not despair of God’s consolation; none
but the unbelieving people despair of God’s consolation.”

88] And when [the Brothers] went in unto [Joseph], they said: "O Potentate,
misfortune has befallen our family and us, and we have brought only meager
goods, so give us full measure and be charitable to us: God surely rewards the
89] charitable." He said: "Do you know what you did to Joseph and his brother
90] when you were unknowing?" They said: "Can you really be Joseph?" He said,
"I am Joseph and this is my brother. God has been gracious to us. Those who
are pious and endure with patience, God will not deny the reward of the virtu-
91] ous." They said: "By God, He has preferred you above us and we have been
92] sinners." He said: "Let there be no blame upon you today. May God forgive
93] you: He is the most merciful of all those who show mercy. Take this tunic of
mine and throw it over my father's face—he will recover his sight—and come
to me with all your family."

94] And when the caravan departed, their father said: "I perceive Joseph's
95] scent even though you think me senile." They said: "By God, you are deluded
96] as before." And when the bearer of good news arrived, he threw [the tunic]
over [Jacob's] face and he regained his sight. He said: "Didn't I tell you? From
97] God I know what you do not." They said: "Father, beg forgiveness for our
98] sins; we have indeed done wrong." He said: "I shall beg my Lord to forgive
you: He is the Merciful Forgiving One."

99] And when [all of Jacob's household] went in to Joseph, he took his parents unto himself to reside and said: "Come into Egypt in safety, if God wills!"
00] and he elevated his parents upon the throne. And [the whole family] fell down
to him in prostration, and he said: "Father, this is the meaning of my earlier
vision: my Lord has made it come true! He was good to me when He released
me from prison and brought you all from the desert after Satan had stirred up
trouble between my brothers and me. Indeed my Lord is kind to whomever
01] He wishes; He alone is the Wise Knowing One. My Lord, You have given
me authority and taught me about the interpretation of stories. Creator of the
heavens and the earth, You are my Guardian in this world and in the world to
come! Allow me to die in submission and unite me with the righteous."

02] This is of the hidden tidings that We reveal to you [Muḥammad]. You
03] were not with them when they cunningly agreed on their affair. But most men,
04] though you strive, will not believe. You ask them no recompense for this, as it
05] is a remembrance for all humankind. How many are the signs of the heavens
06] and the earth that they pass by while turning away. Most of them believe in
07] God only if they can associate partners unto Him. Do they consider themselves safe from God's Universal Punishment or the Hour that will overtake
08] them suddenly unawares? Say: "This is my path. With certain knowledge I—I

and those that follow me—have called you to God. Glory be to God! I am
[109] no idolater." We have not sent prior to you any but mortals from among their
townspeople whom We have inspired. Have [the disbelievers] not traveled the
land and seen what was the end of those before them? And is not the abode
of the Hereafter best for those who were pious? Can you [disbelievers] not
[110] understand? And when at length the Messengers despaired and thought they
had been repudiated, Our help came to them. We have delivered whomever
We please, but Our might will not be averted from the evildoers. There is in
[111] the tales [of these Messengers] a lesson for those endowed with reason. Our
story is not one that could be invented, but a confirmation of what has come
before it, an explanation of everything, and a right guidance and a mercy for
a believing people.

Notes

Preface

1. Rita Kohl has commented that, rather than prism, "hall of mirrors" might constitute an optic metaphor that better captures the vagaries and complexities of the incongruities between reality and literature. Personal communication.

2. Daniel Boyarin, *Intertextuality and the Reading of Midrash* (Bloomington: Indiana University Press, 1990). For a description of the notion of polysystem, see Itamar Even-Zohar, "Polysystem Theory," *Poetics Today* 1, no. 1–2 (1979): 287–310.

3. Little is known of this figure; however, most modern scholars—as well as early Muslim sources—distinguish between his followers, the ʿAnanites, and the later Karaite movement. See Leon Nemoy, "ʿAnan ben David: A Reappraisal of the Historical Data," in *Karaite Studies,* ed. Philip Birnbaum (New York: Hermon, 1971), 309–18.

4. Robert Alter, *The Five Books of Moses: A Translation with Commentary* (New York: Norton, 2004); *JPS Hebrew–English Tanakh: The Traditional Hebrew Text and the New JPS Translation,* second edition (Philadelphia: Jewish Publication Society, 1999).

Introduction

1. The collocation, "literary artifacts," is employed by Jacob Lassner in his insightful study of the Solomon and Queen of Sheba legends in Jewish and Islamic traditions: Jacob Lassner, *Demonizing the Queen of Sheba: Boundaries of Gender and Culture in Postbiblical Judaism and Medieval Islam* (Chicago: University of Chicago Press, 1993).

2. The prophets Jonah (Ṣūrah 10), Abraham (Ṣūrah 14), and Noah (Ṣūrah 71) comprise the other instances in which a quranic *sūrah* bears the name of a figure from the Hebrew Bible.

3. A term coined by James L. Kugel to refer to the exegetical amplification of biblical material inserted in a later retelling of the text or in a commentary. This augmenting of the text often seizes upon some anomaly within the biblical text, which serves as a trigger for the expansion. Kugel utilizes this locution in his seminal studies of early interpretations of the Hebrew Bible: *Traditions of the Bible: A Guide to the Bible as It Was at the Start of the Common Era* (Cambridge, Mass.: Harvard University Press, 1998). See as well his earlier, more limited study that focused primarily on the story of Joseph and his Egyptian master's wife: Kugel, *In Potiphar's House: The Interpretive Life of Biblical Texts* (San Francisco: Harper, 1990).

4. Abū Jaʿfar Muḥammad ibn Jarīr al-Ṭábarī (839–923 CE) was a Muslim scholar whose major works are his Qurʾān commentary and a universal history titled *The History of Prophets*

and Kings (*Tāʾrīkh al-rusul w'al-mulūk*. He condensed and consolidated a vast wealth of historiographical and exegetical material that would constitute the foundation for Islamic historical and quranic scholarship. Here, his primary contributions consisted in the editing and reorganization of material. In the *Commentary* he follows the quranic text word by word, juxtaposing a variety of juridical, lexical, and historical explanations from the *Ḥadīth* literature. *The History* commences with Creation, followed by accounts of the pre-Islamic patriarchs and prophets and the Persian Sassanian dynasty, the career of Muḥammad, and then terminates with events in the year 915.

5. ʿAbdallāh ibn ʿUmar al-Bayḍāwī: Descended from a family of jurists in Persia, he is the author of highly celebrated commentary on the Qurʾān, *Anwār al-tanzīl wa-asrār al-taʾwīl* (based on al-Zamakhsharī's *al-Kashshāf*), which occasioned the composition of numerous supercommentaries. In addition, he wrote on juridical topics, grammar, and philosophy, and also composed a universal history in Persian.

6. Abū Isḥāq Aḥmad b. Muḥammad al-Nīsabūrī al-Shāfiʿī al-Tháʿlabī (died 427 AH/1035 or 1036 CE): Renowned anthologist of prophetic legends and quranic commentator, he is best known for his collection of Stories of the Prophets, *Kitāb ʿarāʾis al-majālis fī qiṣaṣ al-anbiyāʾ*, or "The Book of the Brides of Sessions on the Stories of the Prophets" ("brides" here apparently connotes "the most beautiful," while "session" refers to each individual pericope). As distinct from al-Kisāʾī, his collection utilizes the traditional Muslim scholarly apparatus, citing Qurʾān and Ḥadīth in the majority of the tales, and the stories themselves are typically given in more detail but in less fanciful fashion.

7. Muḥammad b. ʿAbdallāh al-Kisāʾī (ca. twelfth century?). No definitive identification is possible for this putative author of a classical collection of Stories of the Prophets entitled *Kitāb badʾ (khalq) al-dunyā wa-qiṣaṣ al-anbiyāʾ*. In comparison to that of al-Thaʿlabī, modern scholars view this work as reflecting folk traditions perhaps orally transmitted by popular preachers (the *quṣṣāṣ*). The latter were often condemned by the *ʿulemāʾ*.

8. See EI, s.v. "*Qiṣaṣ al-anbiyāʾ*. " For al-Thaʿlabī's work, see William M. Brinner's translation and annotated edition, *Lives of the Prophets* (Leiden: Brill, 2002). For al-Kisāʾī, see *The Tales of the Prophets of al-Kisāʾī,* trans. Wheeler M. Thackston (Boston: Twayne, 1978) (Originally published in Arabic as "Qiṣaṣ Al-Anbiyāʾ," in *Vita Prophetarum,* ed. Isaac Eisenberg [Lugduni-Batavorum: Brill, 1922]). For Abū Jaʿfar Muḥammad b. Jarīr al-Ṭabarī, see *Prophets and Patriarchs,* trans. William M. Brinner (Albany: State University of New York Press, 1987) (Originally published in Arabic as *Taʾrīkh al-rusul wal-mulūk* [*Annales*], ed. M. J. De Goeje [Leiden: Brill, 1964]). For his Qurʾān commentary, see al-Ṭabarī, *Tafsīr al-Ṭabarī: Jāmiʿ al-bayān ʿan taʾwīl al-Qurʾān* (Cairo: Dār al-Maʿārif, 1955). For an overall introduction to the work and a translation of the commentary on the first quranic *sūrahs,* see al-Ṭabarī, *The Commentary on the Qurʾān, Being an Abridged Translation of Jami'al-bayān ʿan taʾwīl al-Qurʾān with Introduction and Notes by J. Cooper* (Oxford: Oxford University Press, 1987). (While this project was to encompass the entire commentary, no further volumes have been issued.) For Abd Allāh ibn ʿUmar al-Bayḍāwī's commentary on the Joseph *sūrah,* see al-Bayḍāwī, *Baiḍāwī's Commentary on Sūrah 12 of the Qurʾān,* trans. A. F. L. Beeston (Oxford: Clarendon, 1963).

An example of Sufi interpretations of the Stories of the Prophets is the eighteenth-century treatise by Shāh Walī Allāh of Delhi, "An Explanation of Significant Events Referred to in the Prophetic Tales," trans. and ed. J. M. S. Baljon, *A Mystical Interpretation of Prophetic Tales by an Indian Muslim: Shah Walī Allāh's* Ta'wīl al-aḥādīth (Leiden: Brill, 1973). For a translation and study of a Sufi account of Joseph and Zulaykhā that exhibits many similarities to QSY (held in the collection of the University of Michigan library), see: Hirsch Hootkins, "The Story of Joseph and Zalikha (Qiṣṣat Yūsuf Wa-Zalīkhā): A Comprehensive Study of a Hitherto Unpublished Arabic Ṣūfī Manuscript" (PhD diss., University of Michigan, 1934).

9. See Gordon Darnell Newby, *A History of the Jews of Arabia: From Ancient Times to Their Eclipse under Islam* (Columbia: University of South Carolina Press, 1988), 78. For the Christian community in Arabia, see: J. Spencer Trimingham, *Christianity among the Arabs in Pre-Islamic Times* (London; New York: Longman, 1979).

10. Yathrib was apparently a neighborhood in the urban center of al-Madīnah (literally "the city"). This latter was the town to which Muḥammad migrated in the year 622 CE in the face of increasing enmity from the Meccans and attempts made on his life. The *hijrah*—literally, the "separation," or "leaving"—was the pivotal event in the foundation of Islam and formally marks the beginning of the Muslim era.

11. Its distribution is attested to by the relative abundance of extant manuscripts dating from the eighteenth to the early twentieth centuries. See Yitzḥaq Avishur, ed., *Ha-sipur ha-ʿamami shel yehudei ʿiraq,* 2 vols. (Haifa: Haifa University, 1992), 28n. 12.

12. Eli Yassif develops this notion in the introduction to his edition of the tales of Yehudah Yudl Rosenberg: *The Golem of Prague and Other Tales of Wonder* [Hebrew] (Jerusalem: Mosad Bialik, 1991), 7–72.

13. See Lawrence M. Wills, *The Jewish Novel in the Ancient World* (Ithaca: Cornell University Press, 1995). See as well: Joseph Dan, *The Hebrew Story in the Middle Ages* (Jerusalem: Keter, 1974), and the introduction to his edition of *Sefer ha-yashar:* Joseph Dan, ed., *Sefer ha-yashar* (Jerusalem: Bialik Institute, 1986).

14. Reuven Firestone, *Journeys in Holy Lands: The Evolution of the Abraham-Ishmael Legends in Islamic Exegesis* (Albany: State University of New York Press, 1990).

15. For a critical analysis of such perspectives, see Marilyn Robinson Waldman, "New Approaches to 'Biblical' Materials in the Qur'ān," in *Studies in Islamic and Judaic Traditions,* ed. William M. Brinner and Stephen D. Ricks (Atlanta: Scholars Press, 1986), 47–64.

16. Q 5:13 is among the quranic verses that were the basis for this view: "On account of [the Children of Israel] breaking their covenant, We have cursed them and made hard their hearts. They distort (*yuḥarrifūnā*) the meanings of words and have forgotten the good fortune of that by which they were admonished." See as well Q 2:75, 3.78, 4:46; and EI, s.v. "*Taḥrīf.*"

17. Typical of this trend is the classic work, *Jews and Arabs,* by S. D. Goitein, the doyen of Genizah studies. He writes there: "Never has Judaism encountered such a close and fructuous symbiosis as that with the medieval civilization of Arab Islam." This phenomenon has been acutely analyzed by Steven Wasserstrom, who in 1995 provocatively asked: "Is fin de siècle religious studies finally ready to reexamine 'creative symbiosis,' this article of faith, this humanism-as-theory so entrenched in 'our own' civilization?" Steven M. Wasserstrom, *Between Muslim and Jew: The Problem of Symbiosis under Early Islam* (Princeton: Princeton University Press, 1995), 225.

18. See EI, s.v. "Ahl al-kitāb" and "Dhimma."

19. Bernard Lewis has been at the forefront of attempts to correct both extreme versions of the history of the life of Jews under Islam. See the most influential statement of this in Bernard

Lewis, *The Jews of Islam* (Princeton: Princeton University Press, 1984). Also, see Wasserstrom, *Between Muslim and Jew: The Problem of Symbiosis under Early Islam.*

20. For an English translation of the text of the Pact, see Norman Stillman, *The Jews of Arab Lands: A History and Source Book* (Philadelphia: Jewish Publication Society, 1979), 157–58.

21. M. J. Kister, "Ḥaddithū ʿan banī isrāʾīla wa-lā ḥaraja: A Study of an Early Tradition," *Israel Oriental Studies* 2 (1972): 215–39. The quotation is from page 221.

22. C. E. Bosworth, "The Concept of *Dhimma* in Early Islam," in *Christians and Jews in the Ottoman Empire,* ed. B. Braude and B. Lewis (New York: 1982), 8. Cited in Wasserstrom, *Between Muslim and Jew: The Problem of Symbiosis under Early Islam,* 172–73.

23. The Umayyads were the first major Islamic dynasty, with family origins in the Quraysh tribe of Mecca. In the first Muslim civil war (the *fitnah;* 656–61 CE)—the struggle for the caliphate following the murder of ʿUthmān, the third caliph—Muʿāwiyah, then governor of Syria, emerged victorious over ʿAlī, Muḥammad's son-in-law and fourth caliph, and established himself as the first Umayyad caliph. Muʿāwiyah centralized caliphal authority in Damascus, and the Syrian army became the basis of Umayyad strength, enabling the creation of a united empire through greater control of the conquered provinces and the suppression of Arab tribal rivalries. The dynasty reached its peak under the rule of ʿAbd al-Malik (reigned 685–705), when the caliphal armies overran most of Spain in the West and conquered provinces in India and Central Asia. Arabic became the official state language and a series of financial, numismatic, and postal reforms were instituted. Decline set in with the defeat of the army in 717 by the Byzantine Leo III, the Isaurian; financial crisis and the renewal of feuds between northern and southern Arab tribes led to a further weakening of the state. The last Umayyad, Marwān II (reigned 744–50), was defeated at the Battle of the Great Zab River (750). Members of the Umayyad house were hunted down and killed, but one of the survivors, ʿAbd al-Raḥmān, escaped and established himself as a Muslim ruler in Spain, founding the dynasty of the Umayyads of Córdoba in 756.

In the East, the Umayyads were succeeded by the ʿAbbasid caliphal dynasty, whose rulers traced their descent to Muḥammad's uncle, al-ʿAbbās ibn ʿAbd al-Muṭṭālib. Claiming that only a direct descendant of the Prophet's house (through the male line) could be the legitimate caliph, they overthrew the Umayyads in 750 and reigned, if in some periods only nominally, until the Mongol sack of Baghdad in 1258. Under the ʿAbbasids, the focus of the Empire shifted further to the East, and the capital was moved to the new city of Baghdad. In addition, the base for influence in the empire became international, emphasizing membership in the community of believers rather than Arab nationality. The ʿAbbasids encouraged translation from pre-Islamic languages, particularly Middle Persian, Greek, and Syriac, and this activity provided a channel through which older thought could enter and be reoriented by Islamicate societies. In order to garner support, ʿAbbasid rulers at times catered to pietistic elements by purifying Islam of what were deemed to be foreign elements; however, this "purification" ironically coincided with some of the most significant absorption of pre-Islamic monotheistic lore.

24. Here, Harold Bloom's notion of the "anxiety of influence" may be apposite. See Harold Bloom, *The Anxiety of Influence: A Theory of Poetry,* 2nd ed. (New York: Oxford University Press, 1997).

25. ʿAbdallāh (died 43 AH/663–4 CE) was a Jew of Madīnah belonging to the Banū Qaynuqā tribe, one of the three main Jewish tribes of the town. His name was originally al-Ḥusayn, but Muḥammad gave him the name of ʿAbdallāh upon his conversion to Islam. In Muslim tradition

he became the archetype of a learned Jewish scribe who recognized Muḥammad as the Prophet, whose coming was foreordained in the Torah. In many traditions ʿAbdallāh is portrayed as posing questions to Muḥammad, whose ability to answer them serves as evidence of his prophethood. For the most part, these traditions—along with the Ḥadīth material ascribed to him—have their origins in Jewish sources. While some of his contemporaries held him in reproach for his Jewish origins, subsequently traditions were circulated in which Muḥammad assures him entry into Paradise. Al-Ṭabarī incorporated much biblicist material attributed to ʿAbdallāh in his *History.*

Kaʿb (died ca. 32–35/652–655) was a Yemenite Jew who converted to Islam ca. 638 and is considered the earliest authority on Judaic traditions. Little is known of him, but posterity sought to add luster to his name and greater validity to his chain of transmission by crediting him with a wide variety of traditions, including the legend of Joseph. In his recording of these traditions surrounding Joseph, al-Kisāʾī cites Kaʿb, as does Firdawsī in his *Yūsuf u-Zalīkhā.*

The third figure, Wahb (654/5–728 or 732 CE), born in Persia, was also of Yemenite origin, and is renowned as a narrator and transmitter of biblicist and ancient Arabian material. His historical writings also treated the pre-Islamic history of Yemen, the Islamic history of the Prophet, and the history of the caliphate. Stories that he converted to Islam in 10 AH are apparently unreliable and relate to his father. The question of his Jewish identity is unsettled, as the oldest sources do not mention it, but if his father converted long before, it is probable that he was born a Muslim. He acted as a judge in Ṣanʿā, and spent time in prison, most likely for his belief (perhaps later rejected) in the doctrine of free will and his contact with People of the Book. He died as a result of a flogging ordered by the governor of Yemen. He was a great authority in the field of biblicist traditions, perhaps the leading intellectual heir of a group of scholars who drew from the reservoir of Jewish and Christian scholarship in Yemen and the Ḥijāz. The contents of the books attributed to him were transmitted orally, taught, and they were recorded partly in his lifetime and later by members of his family. A large number of quotations concerning his fame are found in the works of al-Ṭabarī, al-Masʿūdī, and al-Thaʿlabī. The first book attributed to him was called by later tradition *Kitāb al-mubtadaʾ wa-qiṣaṣ al-anbiyāʾ,* which covers history from the time of the creation, and the prophets from Adam to the arrival of the Prophet of Islam. Ancient texts in which Wahb is cited as a primary source bear witness to the distribution of this material. Later authors often attached traditions to his name.

26. As Steven Wasserstrom has pointed out: "It would be absurd to suggest that early Muslims were not themselves conscious of their utilization of the old, in religion as in anything else." Wasserstrom, *Between Muslim and Jew: The Problem of Symbiosis under Early Islam,* 173.

27. On the Karaite sect in general, see *Karaite Judaism: A Guide to Its History and Literary Sources,* ed. Meira Polliack (Leiden: Brill, 2003). On the Egyptian Karaites, see the article by William M. Brinner in which he analyzes a list of community members found in another text from the Magnes collection: W. M. Brinner, "The Egyptian Karaite Community in the Late Nineteenth Century," in *Studies in Judaica, Karaitica and Islamica,* ed. Sheldon Brunswick (Ramat-Gan, Israel: Bar Ilan University Press, 1982).

For a recent, provocative discussion of this community and its disintegration in the post-Israel era, see Joel Beinin, *The Dispersion of Egyptian Jewry: Culture, Politics, and the Formation of a Modern Diaspora* (Berkeley: University of California Press, 1998). See also Yoram Meital, *Jewish Sites in Egypt* [Hebrew] (Jerusalem: Ben-Zvi Institute, 1995).

28. See Paul Fenton, *Reshimat kitvei-yad be-ʿaravit-yehudit be-leningrad* (Jerusalem: Ben-Zvi Institute, 1991).

29. In this way, *The Story of Our Master Joseph* seems to mirror the quranic claims for the superiority and authenticity of its version of the Joseph story: "We relate unto you the finest of tales (*aḥsan al-qaṣaṣ*)" (Q 12:3).

30. This is parallel to the name of a whole genre of Arabic literature, *al-faraj baʿda al-shiddah,* whose literary artifice revolved around showing that misfortune (*al-dīq* or *al-shiddah*) is not necessarily everlasting, and that relief (*al-faraj*) can in the end always be expected. The vehicle for such material was the anecdote (*nādirah*: literally "rare thing, rarity") drawn from all kinds of more or less authentic stories. Such anecdotes offered the narrator an opportunity to display his wit and cultural sophistication in social gatherings—whether intimate or official—while entertaining in the process. Anthologies of such material were compiled and probably served the *raconteur* as source material. The creator of this genre was said to be al-Madāʾinī (135–228/752–843) whose collection was entitled *Al-Faraj bayna al-shiddah wal-dīq*; others to follow him were Ibn Abī al-Dunyā and Abū al-Ḥusayn ʿUmar b. Abī ʿAmr. The acknowledged master of the genre, however, was al-Tanūkhī (d. 384/994) who incorporated many of the tales of his predecessors. These collections preserved anecdotes that would subsequently fall back into the oral domain. For a general overview of this genre, see Alfred Weiner, "Die Farag baʿda aŝ-Ŝidda Literatur" *Der Islam* IV (1913), 270–98, 387–420. For an example of a Judeo-Arabic text of this type, see Nissim ben Jacob ibn Shāhīn, *An Elegant Composition Concerning Relief after Adversity: An Eleventh Century Book of Comfort,* translated from the Arabic with introduction and notes by William M. Brinner (Northvale, NJ: Jason Aronson, 1996 [Reprint of 1977 edition]).

31. Ginzberg cites this formula as evidence of quotation from an older midrashic source. See Louis Ginzberg, *Legends of the Jews,* trans. Henrietta Szold, 7 vols. (Philadelphia: Jewish Publication Society, 1968), 5:339n. 118. On the unreliability of attributions to specific sages, see Jacob Neusner, *In Search of Talmudic Biography: The Problem of the Attributed Saying* (Chico, Calif.: Scholars Press, 1984).

32. Note that to this day, Muslims typically do not regard *translation* of their Scripture as possible and refer to such renderings into other languages as being "interpretations." On Jewish knowledge of the Qurʾān, see the appendix to the late Hava Lazarus-Yafeh's volume: *Intertwined Worlds: Medieval Islam and Bible Criticism* (Princeton: Princeton University Press, 1992), 143–60. On the sanctity and inimitability of the quranic text, see EI, s.v. "Iʿjāz al-Qurʾān."

33. See EI, s.v. "Khuzāʿa."

34. Such a phenomenon would seem to mirror what scholars assume is the insertion into the prose narrative of more ancient poetic pieces.

35. There are several Judeo-Arabic versions of the tale that in fact begin with the *basmallah.* Lazarus-Yafeh cites a Hebrew rendering of the Qurʾān that employs the *basmallah.* Lazarus-Yafeh, *Intertwined Worlds,* 154–60.

QSY[1] itself commences with a call to God in Hebrew ("In the name of the Lord, the everlasting God, may we be successful in what we do"), ostensibly an analogue for the *basmallah.*

36. In Michael D. McGaha, *Coat of Many Cultures: The Story of Joseph in Spanish Literature, 1200–1492* (Philadelphia: Jewish Publication Society, 1997), 154–227. McGaha bases his translation on the transcription and edition by Ursula Kenk, *La Leyenda De Yusuf: Ein Aljamiad-*

otext (Tübingen: Max Nermeyer Verlag, 1972). The first page of this manuscript, which would ostensibly have contained the name of the work, is missing, and thus McGaha's title is merely a provisional one. While the author of this text is unknown, McGaha notes that of the Arabic *qiṣaṣ* versions, the one that most closely parallels this Aljamiado text is that of al-Kisāʾī; however, it displays even more in common with *Joseph.*

37. A clear desideratum would be incorporation into the discussion of the many Persian and Turkish medieval works classified under the general title "Yūsuf and Zulaykhā," however such a comparison lies outside the scope of this study and beyond the competence of the present writer. With regard to Persian literature, an overview of the relevant texts and their history is found in the EI article "Yūsuf and Zulaykhā" within the relevant section written by J. T. P. de Bruijn. The oldest extant text is a *mathnawī* (the name given to Persian poems of varying length and genre composed in rhyming couplets) that exists in at least two versions. This work has long been attributed to the renowned Persian poet, one of the greatest writers of epic, and author of the *Shāh-nāma,* al-Firdawsī (d. 1020 CE), but this attribution has been thrown into question by recent scholarship. The work was translated into German by Ottokar Schlechta-Wsseherd (1899) and published in editions by (Carl) Hermann Ethé (1908, reissued 1970) and Ḥusayn Muḥammad-zāda Ṣiddīq (1990). A Judeo-Persian work that displays much in common with this is the section on Joseph from Mowlānā Shāhīn-i Shīrāzī's *Bereshit-nāmah* (composed 1358 CE). At the beginning of the twentieth century Shīmʿon Ḥakam compiled an edition of this work, which he entitled *Sharḥ-i Shāhīn ʿal ha-torah* [Hebrew characters], and Amnon Netzer transcribed the text into Arabic script in *Munatakhabi-i ashʿār-i fāarsī az āthaār-i yahūdiyyān-i* (Tehran, 1973). A section of this poem, involving the interchange between Jacob and the Wolf, has been translated by Vera Basch Moreen within her collection, *In Esther's Garden: An Anthology of Judeo-Persian Literature* (New Haven: Yale University Press, 2000, 38–55. The most famous and widespread version of the tale within Persian popular tradition is the poem by Mullā ʿAbd al-Raḥmān Jāmī, written in 1483 CE, which focuses on love relationship and contains mystical elements. An edition and German translation was published by Vinzenz Edlem von Rosenzweig in 1824; another edition was published in Tehran by Murtaḍā Mudarris-i Gīlānī in *Mathnawīyi Haft awrang* (1958). This work was translated into English by Ralph T. H. Griffith (*Yúsuf and Zulaikha: A Poem.* London: Trübner, 1882), and in an abridged form by David Pendlebury (*Yusuf and Zulaikha: An Allegorical Romance* London: Octagon, 1980). There are also Turkish versions of the tale, and these are surveyed by Barbara Flemming in the relevant section of the aforementioned EI article. For a Turkish exemplum of the Stories of the Prophets, written by Nosiruddin Burhonuddin al-Rabghūzī in 1310 CE, see: *The Stories of the Prophets: Qiṣaṣ al-anbiyāʾ: An Eastern Turkish Version,* critically edited by H. E. Boeschoten, M. Vandamme, and S. Tezcan, with the assistance of H. Braam and B. Radtke, 2 vols (Leiden: Brill, 1995). Volume 2 contains a translation into English by H. E. Boeschoten, J. O'Kane, and M. Vandamme.

38. McGaha, *Coat of Many Cultures,* 162–64.

39. See the following works by Ziva Ben-Porat: "Intertextuality [Hebrew]," 34, no. 2 (1985): 170–78; "The Poetics of Literary Allusion," *PTL* 1, no. 1 (1976): 105–28.

40. In a forthcoming study, I will be examining another Judeo-Arabic retelling of the story of a biblical figure—Moses. There I will demonstrate the ways in which *The Story of Our Master Moses* radically departs from the model of *Joseph* in that it is almost entirely a translation

and conjoining of two extant Hebrew *midrashim: Divrei ha-yamim shel mosheh rabeinu* (*The Chronicles of Our Master Moses*) and *Gedulat mosheh* (The Greatness of Moses; also known as *Ke-ta puʾaḥ beʿatzei ha-yaʿar, Like an Apple in the Trees of the Forest*). The two tales can thus be seen as comprising the two ends of a spectrum of such intertextual relations.

41. Robert Alter, *The Art of Biblical Narrative* (New York: Basic Books, 1981).

42. For this argument, see Donald B. Redford, *A Study of the Biblical Story of Joseph* (Leiden: Brill, 1970) (cited in Kugel, *In Potiphar's House,* 14, 26n. 1).

43. The translations from Genesis in this work are taken from Robert Alter's highly evocative rendering into English of the original Hebrew: Robert Alter, *Genesis* (New York: Norton, 1996).

44. Kugel, *In Potiphar's House,* 17–18. For his discussion of Samaritan exegetical traditions surrounding Joseph, see 27n. 7.

45. This theory, developed by Michael Thompson and applied originally to material objects, has been extended by Jonathan Culler to the realm of text and ideas. See Jonathan D. Culler, *Framing the Sign: Criticism and Its Institutions,* 1st ed. (Norman: University of Oklahoma Press, 1988), 168–82.

46. See al-Thaʿlabī, *Lives of the Prophets,* 3–5.

47. Joseph Horovitz, the leading scholar of Jewish-Islamic literary interactions from a previous generation, emphasized the didactic role of Muḥammad's legends and the biblicist material incorporated into the Qurʾān. Haim Schwarzbaum, however, refers as well to "the Arab time-honored penchant" for picturesque legends and folktales, giving as a specific example the twelfth sūrah: Haim Schwarzbaum, *Biblical and Extra-Biblical Legends in Islamic Folk Literature* (Walldorf-Hessen: Verlag für Orientkunde Dr. H. Vorndran, 1982), 10–11. Horovitz notes that Muḥammad's appreciation for the tale's worth is supported by the fact that the founder of Islam does not otherwise universally identify with the biblicist characters.

48. See Mustansir Mir, "The Qurʾānic Story of Joseph: Plot, Themes, and Characters," *Muslim World* 76, no. 1 (1986): 1–15.

49. John Renard, "Reprise: Joseph of the Seven Doors," in *Seven Doors to Islam: Spirituality and the Religious Life of Muslims* (Berkeley: University of California Press, 1996), 259–72.

50. Al-Kisāʾī, *The Tales of the Prophets,* 192.

51. Al-Thaʿlabī, *Lives of the Prophets,* 186–87.

52. Ibid.; al-Baiḍāwī, *Commentary on Sūrah 12,* 3.

53. Merlin L. Swartz, *Ibn al-Jawzi's* Kitab al-qussas wa'l-mudhakkirin (Beirut: Dār al-Mashriq, 1971), 96–97.

54. See: al-Baiḍāwī, *Commentary on Sūrah 12,* 2. For a discussion of the onomastics of Muslim names for biblical figures, see Josef Horovitz, *Jewish Proper Names and Derivatives in the Koran* (Hildesheim: G. Olms Verlagsbuchhandlung, 1964), 8–9. See also William M. Brinner, "Some Problems in the Arabic Transmission of Biblical Names," in *Solving Riddles and Untying Knots: Biblical, Epigraphic, and Semitic Studies in Honor of Jonas C. Greenfield,* ed. Seymour Gitin, Ziony Zevit, and Michael Sokoloff (Winona Lake, Ind.: Eisenbrauns, 1995), 19–27.

55. Daniel Boyarin, *Intertextuality and the Reading of Midrash* (Bloomington: Indiana University Press, 1990).

56. See Kugel, "Two Introductions to Midrash," 84.

57. There are other ways in which efforts were made to graft biblical order onto a recalcitrant present. These include the archaic Hebrew utilized in the book of Esther, the anthologizing Hebrew style of the Qumran *hodayot,* archaizing features of postbiblical literature, and the

halakhic reading of Scripture, especially the laws of purity that originally applied only to the priesthood. See ibid., 87.

58. Continuity with biblical notions of prophecy can also be seen in the tendency of modern Hebrew writers and poets to claim such a societal role for themselves—a claim that was based on an appreciation for the power and efficacy of the speech-act as crystallized in poetic diction. In particular, poets of the *Teḥiyyah* ("Revival"), such as Tchernichovsky and Bialik, viewed themselves as heirs to the role of social critic endowed with a perspicacious power to see the past and future.

59. For an example of such a text, see Hirsch Hootkins, "The Story of Joseph and Zalikha.

Part I

Translator's Foreword

1. The collection has yet to be systematically catalogued, but the Joseph text is contained within a codex assigned the temporary number KC8 and stored in Box 16. Mourad el-Kodsi, in his discussion of the literary production of the Ḥākhām Abraham Kohen, gives some background on the shady provenance of this particular collection: "In the middle of the 1970s, when most members of the community had left, an unscrupulous member of the community was able to sell many of the priceless community treasures. Many opportunists came to Egypt, paid the price and returned with the booty. In 1979 I went to San Francisco [*sic*], where I visited the Magnes Museum and found a handwritten book by Ḥākhām Abrāhām Kohen" (*The Karaite Jews of Egypt, 1882–1986* [Lyons, N.Y.: Wilprint, 1987], 218).

2. Apparently, Joseph belonged to a well-known family of Karaite ḥakhamim and scribes. On this family, and in particular, Moses ben Abraham (1810–1905), known as Ḥakham Moshe al-Qudsi the Second, see el-Kodsi, *The Karaite Jews of Egypt,* 267–68; Haggai Ben-Shammai, "Qirqisānī on the Oneness of God," *Jewish Quarterly Review* 73 (1985), 105–111; and Paul Fenton, "Karaites and Sufis—The Traces of Sufism in Karaite Manuscripts," *Peʿamim* 90 (Winter 2002): 5–19. Moses ben Abraham al-Qudsi was born in Jerusalem, where his father was head (*ḥākhām akbar*) of the small community. After the death of the father, his older brother David served in that role. Moses served as leader of the Cairene community from 1856–72, returning to Jerusalem after David's death, where he was the last head of the Karaite community there. El-Kodsi gives his chain of descent as Moses son of Abraham son of Moses son of Samuel son of Abraham son of Eliyahu ha-Levi al Dimashqī, which would seem to indicate that the scribe who recorded QSY^1, Joseph ben Abraham, may have been a brother. Moses copied many valuable manuscripts found in Cairene genizahs. Zeev Elkin and Menahem Ben-Sasson give a fascinating account of the role the brothers David and Moses played in escorting Abraham Firkovich and translating for him during his visit to Cairo in 1864. It was during this visit that Firkovich removed a horde of manuscripts from the Rabbi Simḥah Synagogue, apparently in exchange for underwriting renovation costs. See Zeev Elkin and Menahem Ben Sasson, "Abraham Firkovich and the Cairo Genizahs in the Light of His Personal Archives" [Hebrew], *Peʿamim* 90 (Winter 2002): 51–95.

3. All of these manuscripts have much in common with the famous treasure trove of material "discovered" at the end of the nineteenth century in the Cairo Genizah and, in some cases, may represent items that had their origins in that very cache. As Paul Fenton notes: "I can positively state that the paper, scripts, and paleographic features of the bulk of the materials

I examined, are not only of an identical character to those of other Genizah collections, but I also recognized in Leningrad pages and parts of manuscripts which are preserved in these collections."

4. *Qiṣṣat yūsuf al-ṣiddīq* (Baghdad: Maṭbaʿat al-Waṭaniyyah al-Isrāʾīliyyah, 1914) and *Qiṣṣat yōsef ha-tzadīq* (Tunis: Sion Uzan, 1910). For the former, I was able to access a copy held at the library of the University of California at Berkeley, while a copy of the latter is housed at the Hebrew University and National Library in Jerusalem.

5. Blau writes that this might very well have originated in the Jewish writers' inability to master the Classical. See Joshua Blau, *The Emergence and Linguistic Background of Judaeo-Arabic: A Study of the Origins of Neo-Arabic and Middle Arabic,* 3rd ed. (Jerusalem: Ben-Zvi Institute, 1999).

6. For a brief overview of the major accomplishments in this literature, see the G. Vajda's entry in EI: "Judeo-Arabic literature."

7. Blanc already in 1967 pointed out this shortcoming in his review of Blau's original edition of *Emergence and Linguistic Background of Judaeo-Arabic* in *Tarbiz* 36, no. 4: 406–11 [Hebrew; English abstract v–vi]. This critique has been further refined by Benjamin H. Hary in *Multiglossia in Judeo-Arabic (with an Edition, Translation, and Grammatical Study of the Cairene Purim Scroll)* (Leiden: Brill, 1992), 51–58.

8. While the term was used already at the turn of the century in a discussion of Arabic and Greek phenomena, Charles Ferguson was the pioneer in its further articulation and application. See his now classic article: "Diglossia." *Word* 15 (1959): 325–40.

9. See Hary, *Multiglossia in Judeo-Arabic,* 3ff.

10. Jews used Arabic script as well, though it would seem to a much smaller extent. Our perception of the prevalence of Hebrew script might also be skewed by documents preserved in the Genizah, intended for documents written in sacred Hebrew script.

11. See Hary, *Multiglossia in Judeo-Arabic,* 82–103. See also Haim Blanc, "The Nekteb-Nektebu Imperfect in a Variety of Cairene Arabic," *Israel Oriental Studies* 4 (1974): 202–26.

12. Blau, *Emergence and Linguistic Background,* 58. Utilizing the text of the Cairene Purim Scroll, Hary offers a preliminary grammar of Later Judeo-Arabic and outlines features of the orthographic tradition of later Egyptian Judeo-Arabic that are relevant for our study. Hary, *Multiglossia in Judeo-Arabic,* 241–325. See also two works by Geoffrey Khan: "Notes on the Grammar of a Late Judaeo-Arabic Text," *Jerusalem Studies in Arabic and Islam* 15 (1992): 220–39; and "A Study of the Judaeo-Arabic of Late Genizah Documents and Its Comparison with Classical Judaeo-Arabic" [Hebrew], *Sefunot* 20 (1991): 223–34.

13. Such is the characterization offered by Goitein. S. D. Goitein, *Jews and Arabs: Their Contacts through the Ages,* rev. ed. (New York: Schocken, 1974), 127ff.

14. Blau, *Emergence and Linguistic Background,* 35.

Part II

Chapter 1

1. James L. Kugel provides a fascinating examination of specific midrashic elaborations, or "narrative expansions," surrounding the Joseph story in Genesis: Kugel, *In Potiphar's House,*

11–155. His analysis is both penetrating and convincing; he makes use, moreover, of some Islamic material in his discussion of the "Assembly of Ladies" motif. However, he limits his discussion to several specific expansions within the story of Joseph and *Potiphar's* Wife. Shalom Goldman's work explores somewhat more widely the Islamic material surrounding Joseph: Shalom Goldman, *The Wiles of Women/the Wiles of Men: Joseph and Potiphar's Wife in Ancient Near Eastern, Jewish, and Islamic Folklore* (Albany: State University of New York Press, 1995). Michael McGaha has gathered together a fascinating collection of extrascriptural material of Andalusian origin in his anthology, *Coat of Many Cultures: The Story of Joseph in Spanish Literature, 1200–1492* (Philadelphia: Jewish Publication Society, 1997). Included in this collection (155–227) is the Aljamiado parallel to *Joseph* that McGaha entitles *The Story of Yusuf.* In addition, McGaha has published a volume containing dramatic works from the "Golden Age" treating the story: Michael D. McGaha, *The Story of Joseph in Spanish Golden Age Drama* (Lewisburg, Penn.; London: Bucknell University Press, 1998). Maren Niehoff has compared the three earliest complete treatments of the Joseph tale in Philo, Josephus, and *Bereishit* (Genesis) *raba:* Maren Niehoff, *The Figure of Joseph in Post-Biblical Jewish Literature* (Leiden; New York: Brill, 1992). These works follow in a long tradition of studies that seek to point out the cross-cultural interplay of tales surrounding this leading biblical figure. Two relatively recent works reexamine the late antique tale of *Aseneth:* Ross Shepard Kraemer, *When Aseneth Met Joseph: A Late Antique Tale of the Biblical Patriarch and His Egyptian Wife, Reconsidered* (New York: Oxford University Press, 1998), and Gideon Bohak, *Joseph and Aseneth and the Jewish Temple in Heliopolis* (Atlanta: Scholars Press, 1996). Other works that are of great relevance to this study have focused specifically on the interactions and dynamic of exchange between Judaism and Islam. We have already mentioned Reuven Firestone and Jacob Lassner. Firestone's *Journeys in Holy Lands* examines the Abraham cycle, a case study of textual transfer; Lassner, in *Demonizing the Queen of Sheba,* has undertaken a similar effort in regard to Jewish and Islamic cultural exchange surrounding the tale of King Solomon and the Queen of Sheba. John Renard has looked at the Joseph story as a window into the spiritual life of Muslims in his "Reprise: Joseph of the Seven Doors"; his analysis of the tale "reprises" the themes he explores throughout his study of spirituality and Muslim religious life.

2. *Torat ḥayim,* at Gen. 37:2.

3. In fact, Scripture seemingly contradicts itself at this point, including Benjamin among all the other Mesopotamian-born children; this just after explicitly recording the birth of Benjamin and the death of Rachel in the Land of Canaan on the road between Beit-el and Ephrat (Gen. 35:16–20).

4. Robert Alter, *The Art of Biblical Narrative* (New York: Basic Books, 1981), 63.

5. Flavius Josephus, *Judean Antiquities* (Leiden; Boston: Brill, 2000), 2:4–6.

6. Al-Kisāʾī, *The Tales of the Prophets,* 165, 167–69.

7. On the resonance of this emphasis on Joseph's handsomeness with Greek notions of the hero, see the discussion by Louis Feldman: Josephus, *Judean Antiquities,* 131–32n. 49.

8. A similar combination also appears in the biblical description of Esther.

9. The depiction of Leah as having "soft eyes" was understood in two ways by the interpreters: either Leah had some ocular defect, or indeed her eyes were "tender" or "pleasant"; but, even according to this latter interpretation, the fact that this was the only feature that could be commented on reflected how she paled in comparison to the perfect beauty of her younger sister.

See Kugel, *Traditions of the Bible: A Guide to the Bible As It Was at the Start of the Common Era* (Cambridge, Mass.: Harvard University Press, 1998), 381–82.

10. See the discussion in Kugel, *In Potiphar's House,* 69–71.

11. *Onkelos* is one of the works belonging to the ancient genre of the *targūmīm. Targūm* [Aramaic: "translation"] is a general name for a translation of the Hebrew Bible, or parts thereof, into Aramaic, a Semitic language related to Hebrew and spoken widely in the ancient Near East beginning in the eighth century BCE. Following the Babylonian exile, Aramaic became the language commonly spoken by Jews in the Land of Israel as well as in Babylonia, and therefore it became necessary to translate the biblical portions read in the synagogue into the vernacular. Following the reading of each verse in the original Hebrew, the *meturgeman* ("translator") would translate it out loud, often interpreting in accordance with rabbinic exegetical understanding. See Nehemiah 8:8; BT *Megilah* 3a. Eventually these renderings were committed to writing. *Targum Onkelos* (O), dating from the first or second century BCE, is the best known and most widely printed; *Targum Pseudo-Jonathan* (PJ) (so called because in relatively recent times it was erroneously ascribed to Jonathan ben Uzziel, author of a *targūm* to the prophetic books of the Bible), is a highly discursive *targūm* of the Pentateuch which, although containing much ancient material, did not achieve its final form until the Middle Ages; *Targum Neophyti* (N), is a *targūm* of the Pentateuch discovered in the Vatican library. *Onkelos* is, relatively speaking, a rather close rendition of the Hebrew *Vorlage*, but often diverges in order to avoid anthropomorphisms or for other doctrinal reasons; *Neophyti* and, to an even greater extent, *Pseudo-Jonathan* are far from literal translations: they often insert phrases or whole sentences in order to explain the meaning of the text, or simply to pass along some bit of Jewish exegesis.

12. This itself is based on the Talmudic statement that the word *zakein* ("old") is an acronym representing the phrase *zeh kanah ḥokhmah,* "this one has acquired wisdom" (BT *Qidushin* 32b). This homiletic technique of reading words as representing a shorthand form of longer expressions is called by the Rabbis *noṭarikon* (from Hellenized Latin).

13. *Yelamdeinu* reads the plural of *zekunim* as referring to Joseph's father and grandfather, inferring from this that Joseph studied at the two academies of Jacob and Isaac. Cited in Menahem M. Kasher, *Encyclopedia of Biblical Interpretation: Torah Shelemah (A Millennial Anthology),* abridged English translation of *Ḥumash torah sheleimah* edited by Harry Freedman, vol. 6 (New York: American Biblical Encyclopedia Society, 1948), 1397, para. 42 and note.

14. It is not insignificant that this interpretation is based on the combination of a Hebrew word in conjunction with a Greek loan word.

15. So recorded in *Avot de-rabi natan* 2, 2; *Midrash Tehilim* (also known as *Shoḥer ṭov*) 9, 84; *Tanḥuma* (Buber edition) Noah 6; *Tanḥuma* (Zundel edition), Noah 5. The other men with this distinguishing characteristic are Adam, Seth, Enoch, Noah, Shem, Teraḥ, Moses, Balaam, Samuel, David, Isaiah, Jeremiah, and Zerubbabel. As Ginzberg points out, however, PRE 24 speaks of the circumcision performed by Isaac on Jacob. See *Legends of the Jews,* 5:273–74n. 26.

16. *Numbers raba* 14, 5 establishes this link by connecting Jacob's protest to Laban over the expropriation of his livestock with Joseph's grievance at his treatment in Canaan and Egypt:

> "Stolen" is written twice in connection with each. Jacob said to him, "[What was torn up by beasts I've not brought you, I bore the loss,] from my hand you could seek it—what was stolen by day and stolen by night (*genuvti yom u-genuvti laylah;* Gen. 31:39)"; Joseph said,

"For indeed I was stolen (*kī-gunav gunavti;* literally, 'for a stealing I was stolen') from the land of the Hebrews, and here, too, I have done nothing that I should have been put in the pit" (Gen. 40:15)

The Rabbis interpreted this repetition as referring to the deception practiced by Laban by night (with the switching of Leah for Rachel) and by day (the attempt to require him to make up losses of sheep). Alter points out in his comment to 31:39 (*Genesis,* 173) the injustice of Laban's act within its historical context: both biblical and other ancient Near Eastern codes held that a shepherd was not held responsible for those losses caused by predators or thieves. In the case of Joseph, the repetition (actually, a cognate accusative form used in Semitic languages for emphasis) is interpreted to mean that he was stolen twice—from his homeland and from the pit.

17. The interpretation "Joseph resembled his father in all ways" is also found in the *Testament of Joseph* 18.4 and in *Tanḥuma* (Buber recension) Va-yeishev 5.

18. Josephus, in interpreting this expression as it applies to Isaac (Gen. 21:2: *va-táhar va-téled sarah le-avraham ben li-zekunav*), renders it as "on the threshold of old age." Thackeray, in his commentary to Josephus, maintains that this reflects a Homeric expression. See Flavius Josephus, *Josephus,* trans. H. St. J. Thackeray and Ralph Marcus (London: Heinemann; Cambridge, Mass.: Harvard University Press, 1950), 109 and note n.

19. Died 892 CE. He compiled the first book of *Shamā'il al-muṣṭafā* ("the excellent qualities of the Chosen One")—literary expositions of the Prophet's lofty qualities and outward beauty.

20. Leo Zolondek, *Book XX of Ghazzālī's* Iḥyā' ʿulūm al-dīn (Leiden: Brill, 1963), 74–76. Cited in Annemarie Schimmel, *And Muhammad Is His Messenger* (Chapel Hill: University of North Carolina Press, 1985), 34. I have here revised the translation somewhat.

21. For example in 88:1, 88:2, 93:7, 93:11, 95:4.

22. Kugel, *In Potiphar's House,* 21–26.

23. See *Sifrei* be-haʿalotkha 64; BT *Pesaḥim* 6b.

24. While the Arabic text of *Joseph* is difficult at this point, such a reading is confirmed by the continuation of his interrogation by the Brothers, where they assert that his descent from Rachel is sufficient to warrant his death. Support for this reading is also found in al-Ṭabarī's *Tā'rīkh* (*Prophets and Patriarchs,* 150), where Joseph, in the process of being lowered down into the pit, denies having dreamt the dream of the stars, the sun, and the moon.

Chapter 2

1. See as well BT *Shabat* 10b.

2. Dorothy Zeligs has laid out such an analysis in Dorothy F. Zeligs, "The Personality of Joseph," in *Psychoanalysis and the Bible: A Study in Depth of Seven Leaders* (New York: Bloch, 1974), 59–90.

3. Robert Alter, *The Art of Biblical Narrative*, 6.

4. See as well, p. 148, for our discussion of the implications of the term *ben zekunim.*

5. For an analysis of the phenomenon of barrenness amongst biblical women, see Judith Reesa Baskin, *Midrashic Women: Formations of the Feminine in Rabbinic Literature* (Hannover, N.H.: University Press of New England, 2002), 119–40.

6. Indeed, this verse serves as the rabbinic prooftext for the need to bear children: "Samuel said that four people are considered as dead: a blind man; a leper; one who has no children; and one who has lost all his wealth. We learn this vis-à-vis a person who has no children from

Rachel" (BR 71:6). See as well BR 16:2, where the same theme and proof text will be brought to bear on the infertility of Sarah.

7. For a discussion of this category (derived from Homeric studies), see Robert Alter, "Biblical Type-Scenes and the Uses of Convention," in *The Art of Biblical Narrative*. See p. 268 n.3 (notes to chapter 4) for another example of this overturning of the conventions for the type-scene.

8. Nahum Sarna has discussed the ancient Near Eastern parallels for this practice in *Understanding Genesis: The World of the Bible in the Light of History* (New York: Schocken, 1966), 127–29, 96.

9. The root resembles a human figure, which led to its association with fertility rites. The mandrake is also mentioned for its aphrodisiac qualities in the Song of Songs 7:13.

10. Her desperation at this juncture reminds us of Esau's famished state when he sells his birthright to Jacob for a bowl of lentil soup.

11. Note here the alliteration of the verb with the name of Bilhah. This is apparently deduced from Jacob's blessing, where Reuben is described as mounting his father's couch (*yetzuʿi ʿalah*) and the word for couch is derived from the same root. This is all part of a program to read out of the text the heinousness of Reuben's sin. Thus, according to the Talmudic passage that immediately precedes this one, Rabbi Yoḥanan said, "Anyone who says that Reuben sinned is in error." The Rabbis bring in support of this the fact that Jacob's words to him in Genesis 49 do not specifically mention that Reuben lay with Bilhah. Similarly, the Talmud (and subsequently Rashi) notes that the *meturgeman,* who was charged with repeating the verses of the Torah in their Aramaic translation at the public reading of the Torah portion in synagogue, would not read the translation of these words (BT *Megilah* 25b).

Note here as well the use of the word *tzarah*—derived from the word for "calamity" or "distress"—to refer to Leah's competitor wife.

12. The Septuagint completes the verse by supplying the additional words: "and it was evil in his eyes."

Apparently, as part of his agenda to portray the biblical forefathers as heroic figures, Josephus leaves out the account of this act of incest. The Rabbis were also sensitive to this impropriety; the Talmud (BT *Megilah* 25a) records that this is one of a limited number of passages in the Bible that are read out loud in synagogue but not translated.

13. See as well *Onkelos*, *Pseudo-Jonathan* ad loc.; and *Tanḥuma* Va-yeḥi 9.

14. The word *va-yisḥaṭu* would later in rabbinic parlance come to refer specifically to ritual slaughtering.

15. This also accounts for the reverence in which Joseph is held by the Samaritans, who saw themselves as his descendants.

16. For literary appreciations of parallelism of biblical poetry, see: Kugel, *The Idea of Biblical Poetry: Parallelism and Its History* (New Haven: Yale University Press, 1981). Also, Robert Alter, *The Art of Biblical Poetry* (New York: Basic Books, 1985).

17. Al-Thaʿlabī, 185. This tradition is also found in a Swahili text brought by Jan Knappert. See his *Islamic Legends: Histories of the Heroes, Saints and Prophets of Islam,* vol. 1 (Leiden: Brill, 1985), 85–104.

18. *The Story of Yusuf, Son of Yaʾqub,* trans. Michael McGaha, 165–66

19. The eighteenth-century Indian Muslim mystic, Sheikh Walī Allāh, has described this process accordingly:

> One of the root ideas is that God wants to direct worshippers onto a prudent way (*tadbīr*) by means of inspirations, transformations . . . and recommendations. . . . Accordingly, He selects out of the course of events the one which at that very moment furthers the object of pursuit in the best way. . . . The event which then appears represents the "outward shape" and the dream as such, while God's prudent management represents the root idea and the purport of the dream.

When it comes to Joseph, Sheikh Walī describes what his dreams reveal of God's purposes: "In a dream the favors were revealed to him which God eventually would bestow on him: people would have to obey him, his parents and brothers would pay him great homage. Jacob explained this dream and expounded the purposes of God. And by his perspicacity in respect of God's secret intentions he understood that Joseph was prepared for the knowledge of *ta'wīl al-aḥadīth* ('the interpretation of dreams and significative events')." Translated by J. M. S. Baljon, ed. *A Mystical Interpretation of Prophetic Tales by an Indian Muslim: Shah Walī Allāh's* Ta'wīl al-aḥādīth (Leiden: Brill, 1973), 2, 23.

20. JA: *ṣāḥib al-ahlām,* a loan translation of the corresponding *baʿal ha-ḥalomot* of Gen. 37:19.

21. With regard to the first dream, al-Thaʿlabī says—with marked ambiguity—that after Joseph told his father of his vision, "it reached his brothers" (185).

22. See Zeligs, "The Personality of Joseph," 89, 72.

23. This tradition expands upon a motif recorded in BT Sanhedrin 106a (cited earlier in this chapter), which notes the paradoxical connection between Jacob's "settling" and the ensuing "unsettled" relationship between Joseph and the Brothers. The text here is from a manuscript held in the Sassoon Library in London and is cited in Kasher, *Encyclopedia of Biblical Interpretation*, 6:1385n. 1.

This brings to mind the Yiddish aphorism: *Der mentsh trakht und got lakht*—literally, "Man thinks, and God laughs," or in the English vernacular: "Man proposes and God disposes."

24. Gen. 15:13 reads: "Know well that your seed shall be strangers in a land not theirs and they shall be enslaved and afflicted four hundred years." Upon God's initial revelation to Abram, He relates the initial blessing and promise, but there no mention is made of any interlude: "And the Lord said to Abram, 'Go forth from your land and your birthplace and your father's house to the land I will show you. And I will make you a great nation and I will bless you and make your name great, and you shall be a blessing. And I will bless those who bless you, and those who damn you I will curse, and all the clans of the earth through you shall be blessed'" (Gen. 12:1–3).

Such is the case in the other three instances (at Gen. 13:14–16; 17:7–8; 22:16–18; and 24:7) where God delivers his blessing to Abraham and Isaac. Jacob, on the other hand, after stealing his father's blessing from Esau, is forced to flee into exile and sojourn in Laban's house for many years. Eventually, God intervenes to instruct Jacob to return. The word choice employed is evocative of the original divine command to his grandfather to set out from Mesopotamia: "And the Lord said to Jacob: 'Return to the land of your fathers and to your birthplace and I will be with you' (*shuv el-éretz avotékha u-le-moladetékha ve-ehyeh ʿimakh*)" (Gen. 31:3).

25. The fact that the place name Shechem is mentioned three times—first in the narrator's description, then in Jacob's directions to Joseph, and finally in the narrator's recording of Joseph's arrival at the location—would elicit in the sensitive reader foreboding associations of that place with acts of violence. Shechem is in fact a place known for its violence, specifically that of the Brothers: it is where the Brothers visited their revenge on the town's inhabitants following the

rape of Dinah (Gen. 34). Within the context of the tale of Jacob and his sons, the mentioning of Shechem points to the fear Jacob expressed of "the land's inhabitants" in the wake of this vengeance (Gen. 34:30). Later, following the settlement of the land, Shechem will also be associated with the breakup of the tribal confederations. That the reference to Shechem is anything but gratuitous is pointed up by the fact that it turns out that it is not where the Brothers are actually pasturing, or where the encounter between Joseph and the Brothers takes place.

26. *Genesis,* 254, note on 43:14.

27. See as well the comment of Maimonides in *The Guide of the Perplexed:* "The Sages have explained why atonement for the community [of Israel] is accomplished through [the sacrifice of] goat kids: the sin of the entire Congregation of Israel is symbolized by a kid, because of its relationship to the sale of Joseph the Righteous (*al-ṣiddīq*)" (*Guide,* 3:46). For this reference I am grateful to an anonymous prepublication reader.

28. The linkage between Jacob's and Judah's states of mourning would also have suggested itself owing to the lexical similarity of the time frame stipulated in each verse: *yamim rabim* and *va-yirbu ha-yamim.*

29. See also 1 Chronicles 7:30. For an overview of the midrashic elaborations, see Joseph Heinemann, *Aggadah and Its Development* [Hebrew] (Jerusalem: Keter, 1974), 49–63.

30. This tale about an old woman who reveals to Moses the whereabouts of Joseph's grave is also recorded in Islamic texts. In al-Thaʿlabī, this character is anonymous, but she is portrayed as negotiating with Moses for entrance into Paradise in exchange for revealing Joseph's burial place. Al-Thaʿlabī also brings another version that conflates these demands with those the fallen and enfeebled Zulaykhā makes of Joseph:

> Another tradition has it that this old woman who was crippled and blind offered to tell Moses the place of Joseph's grave and he agreed. So she said to him, "But I will reveal it only if you perform four good deeds for me: free my legs, give me back my eyesight and my youth, and let me dwell with you in Paradise." This seemed too difficult to Moses, but God inspired him, "Grant her what she asked for, because you give only through Me," and he did that. (Al-Thaʿlabī, 234–35)

31. See S. D. Goitein, *A Mediterranean Society: The Jewish Communities of the Arab World as Portrayed in the Documents of the Cairo Geniza* (Berkeley: 1967–93), 3:227. According to Goitein, this is an Islamic *topos,* and one significant in mystic circles (ibid., 474n. 24).

32. This may merely be the result of a scribal error, as Jacob will soon after instruct Joseph to go see his brothers (QSY², 1b–2a).

33. As this was indeed Joseph's shirt, it is strange that he would not have detected his scent. Perhaps this latter element reflects the confluence and linking of the parallel stories of mistaken identity in which earlier it was Jacob who deceived his father Isaac into believing he was the elder Esau and thus received the blessing of the firstborn (Gen. 27:15–29). There it is distinctly related that Isaac smelled the garment in which Rebecca had clothed Jacob (which belonged to Esau) and was thus confirmed in his mistake.

34. The late and much lamented Hebrew poet, Yehuda Amichai, has a wonderful poem that ironically treats the commonalities between an Arab shepherd and Jewish father:

> An Arab shepherd is searching for his goat-kid on Mount Zion
> And on the opposite hill I am searching for my little son.

An Arab shepherd and a Jewish father
In their temporary failure.
The voices of the two of us meet above
The Sultan's Pool in the valley in between.
The two of us want the son and the goat-kid
Not to get caught in the progression
Of the terrible machine of *Ḥad Gadya.*.
Afterward we found them among the bushes,
And our voices came back to us and cried and laughed within.
Searching for a goat-kid or a son
Has always been
The beginning of a new religion in these mountains.
(*Shalvah g'dolah: sh'eilot u-t'shuvot,* 14)

35. For example, see Alfonso X the Learned, "General History," in *Coat of Many Cultures: The Story of Joseph in Spanish Literature, 1200–1492,* ed. Michael McGaha (Philadelphia: Jewish Publication Society, 1997), 337.

36. *Midrash ha-gadol* (as well as Rashi) assumes that the initial question and the following interpretations are connected to v. 29—*And Reuben came back to the pit.* As Menahem Kasher points out, the question would seem to fit better in that context, while the rabbinic answers are more suited to an explanation of Reuben's motivation in saving Joseph. Kasher, *Encyclopedia of Biblical Interpretation,* 5:23.

37. Josephus (*Antiquities* 2:12) mentions that the Brothers "made vows that nothing of what they suspected should come to fruition for him."

38. This is already incorporated in the Talmud. Cf. BT *Pesaḥim* 118a.

39. BR 98:5 calls Simeon and Levi "brothers of Dinah, but not of Joseph" because while they had not hesitated to avenge the sexual violation of their sister (Gen. 34:25–31), yet they were willing to conspire against Joseph. This reading is based on the presence of a strange qualifier in the biblical account of the earlier incident: "And two of Jacob's sons, Simeon and Levi, *Dinah's brothers*" (Gen. 34:25, my emphasis). This prima facie superfluous remark was the occasion for the interpretation that distinguished their fraternal relationship with Joseph from that with Dinah. In Josephus's retelling (*Judean Antiquities,* 123), he points out a consanguineous aspect to the two brothers' vengeance: While the other brothers initially chose to hold their peace in the wake of the rape, Simeon and Levi, "the girl's brothers, born of the same mother," agreed to take resolute action.

40. In *The Testament of Zebulon* the culpable pair is given as Simeon and Gad. Ostensibly, this is done to avoid staining the reputation of the Levite tribe from which Moses, Aaron, and the priests would descend.

41. The commentators added many other interpretations—for example, that the Ishmaelites were the employees of the Midianites and took possession of Joseph on their behalf; that the merchantmen (*soḥarim*) were middlemen in the transaction; that from a distance the caravan appeared to be made up of Ishmaelites alone, but as it drew nearer, the Brothers recognized that the actual traders were the Midianites and that the Ishmaelites had been merely hired to transport the goods on their camels; that there were two separate caravans; and that it was one and the same caravan, made up of Ishmaelites, Midianites, and Medanites, their names being

interchangeable as they were all descendants of Abraham's concubines. See "Commentary" in Kasher, *Encyclopedia of Biblical Interpretation,* 5:29–34.

42. Al-Baiḍāwī, *Commentary on Sūrah 12,* 11.

43. See Q 12: 77; Gen. 31:19 ff.

44. Al-Ṭabarī, *Prophets and Patriarchs,* 139; al-Kisāʾī, *The Tales of the Prophets,* 85.

45. See Zeligs, "The Personality of Joseph," 86.

Chapter 3

1. James L. Kugel, in his acute analysis of the Joseph story, deals with the central place this interaction between Joseph and Potiphar's Wife assumes in the midrashic development of the tale: Kugel, *In Potiphar's House.* Kugel has lucidly highlighted some of the reasons underlying this expansion. Here, I hope to expand on his work, focusing more specifically on the Muslim expansions of the motif, while highlighting their absorption in *The Story of Our Master Joseph the Righteous.*

2. *ʿIram dhāt al-ʿimād* has been identified with the city of ʿUbar. It was the center of the frankincense trade but disappeared after a natural disaster—apparently the collapse of a cavern upon which it was built. (That famed English adventurer, Lawrence, referred to it as the "Atlantis of the Desert.") See al-Thaʿlabī, 18.

3. See the commentary of al-Bayḍāwi on v. 30: *Commentary on Sūrah 12,* 17. It is interesting that the term had a quranic afterlife. Some of the classical Arabic dictionaries (e.g., Lane) give it as the title of the ruler of Cairo and Alexandria. In Ottoman texts the epithet is applied to the Mameluke sultans of Egypt. During the negotiations between the Viceroy of Egypt, Ismāʿīl Pasha, and ʿAbd al-ʿAzīz, the former proposed having the title conferred upon him in order to distinguish himself above all the other pashas of the Ottoman Empire. In the end, he was given the title of khedive in 1867. According to contemporary testimony, at least part of the reason behind the denial of Ismāʿīl's request was the title's coinciding with the sultan's own name. See EI, s.v. "ʿAzīz Miṣr."

4. The shift of the initial letter from Hebrew *peh* to Arabic *qaf* could alternatively be attributed to the absence of the hard "p" sound in the phonology of the latter. Moreover, in Arabic the base graphemes of the letters *faʾ* and *qaf* are identical, distinguished only by superlinear dots. The dropping of the first consonant altogether may reflect the shift of *qaf* to *hamza,* the glottal stop, typical of many neo-Arabic dialects.

5. Al-Bayḍāwī on Q 12:21. See *Commentary on Sūrah 12,* 13.

6. See as well BT *Soṭah* 10b.

7. O. S. Wintermute translation. Cited in Kugel, *In Potiphar's House,* 22–23.

8. *Bereishit raba* 86:6. This is also explicitly stated in *Midrash ha-gadol* and *Zohar* 1, 246a. The words *velo yadaʿ* in the biblical text also serve to introduce the sexual overtones of biblical "knowledge."

9. Although there exist interpretations that held the use of this term to be an indication that these courtiers were eunuchs as well; thus, Ramban (ad loc.), even though he cites the Aramaic paraphrases of *Onkelos* and *Pseudo-Jonathan* as supporting a meaning of high-ranking ministers: "Both of these courtiers were eunuchs because the chief cupbearer and the chief baker were also present in the king's women's quarters, and so the kings would castrate them."

10. See Hayim Tadmor, "Was the Biblical *Sarîs* a Eunuch?," in *Solving Riddles and Untying Knots: Biblical, Epigraphic, and Semitic Studies in Honor of Jonas C. Greenfield,* ed. Seymour Gition Ziony Zevit, Michael Sokoloff (Winona Lake, Ind.: Eisenbrauns, 1995), 317–25. His discussion of Potiphar is on p. 321. See as well: Kugel, *In Potiphar's House,* 75–76.

11. Compare this to the silence of David after Amnon's rape of Tamar (2 Samuel 13:21–22).

12. The scene with the male servants is entirely missing from *Joseph,* as it is from Josephus; neither in Philo nor *Jubilees* do these male servants appear. Similarly, within Islamic tradition, both in the Qurʾān and postquranic exegesis, this scene has been omitted. The servants may have been excised from these accounts so as not to distract from the struggle between the main characters. See Alice Bach, "Breaking Free of the Biblical Frame-Up: Uncovering the Woman in Genesis 39," in *A Feminist Companion to Genesis,* ed. Athalya Brenner (Sheffield, England: Sheffield Academic Press, 1993), 333–34.

13. Rashi (ad loc.), finding this latter reading too scandalous, feels compelled to rearrange the wording of the biblical text so as to take away this precious ambiguity.

14. See Robert Alter, *The Art of Biblical Narrative,* 110.

15. In BR 87:9 it is recorded on the authority of Rabbi Abahu: "She told it to him during conjugal relations (*tashmīsh mīṭah*)."

16. This concatenation brings to mind the biblical juxtaposition of Joseph's beauty and Mrs. Potiphar lifting up her eyes. See also Jubilees 39:5, where the connection between Potiphar's wife raising her eyes and her lust is made explicit: "And Joseph was good-looking and very handsome. And the wife of his master lifted up her eyes and desired him."

17. See Fedwa Malti-Douglas, *Woman's Body, Woman's Word: Gender and Discourse in Arabo-Islamic Writing* (Princeton, N.J.: Princeton University Press, 1991), 15.

18. Based on JT *Ketubot* 1:8: "Even the most pious individual one does not appoint as a guardian against unchastity."

19. The text leaves unanswered the question of why al-ʿAzīz leaves his beautiful wife with an exceedingly attractive seventeen-year-old male.

20. See *Jubilees* 40:10; *Testament of Joseph,* 18:3; BT *Soṭah* 13b; BR 86:3. Josephus, while not making this identification explicit, gives both figures the identical name. See *Judean Antiquities*, 142, 159.

21. This motif is found in the manuscript *Yalquṭ or ha-afelah* and in *Leqaḥ ṭov* 40:2. Cited in Kasher, *Encyclopedia of Biblical Interpretation,* vol. 6, 1442.

22. *Zāwiyah* (pl. *zawāyā;* literally, "corner") refers to a portion of a building set aside for instruction by the Sufi master, the *shaykh,* and his disciples. Its predecessor was the *ribāṭ,* which was originally a frontier outpost designed to house Muslims engaged in proselytizing in the newly conquered Muslim territory, but by 800 CE it came to refer to the institution used to house those engaged in the internal *jihād;* i.e., those combating their own unholy tendencies. The term was also used in reference to the residence of the shaykh and his family and often included space for meetings. At his death, the master was sometimes buried in situ, thus expanding the zāwiyah's function as a place of religious visitation. Zawāyā were spread by disciples to other locations and were often endowed by members of the elites. Unlike the ribaṭ, they were typically associated with a particular shaykh and *ṭarīqah* (a particular Sufi "path" or order). A related institution was the *khanqah;* however, these differed in that access was more controlled, they

were not typically commissioned in the name of a specific shaykh, and membership was not limited to adherents of a particular school. See EI, s.v. "Zāwiyah" and Renard, "Reprise: Joseph of the Seven Doors," in *Seven Doors to Islam* (Berkeley: University of California Press, 1996), 171–72.

23. The same motif appears in *Yusuf* (193), but there, in accord with the Muslim "pantheon" of saints, the knots are tied in the names of Abraham, Ishmael, Jacob, Moses, Jesus, and Muḥammad. Curiously, in this account the fourth knot and its corresponding saint have been omitted.

24. Josephus, in line with his agenda of placing Joseph in the most dignified light, omits entirely any of the terms that were considered degrading of Joseph, such as *naʿar, ha-yeled, ʿeved.* See Feldman's note to *Antiquities* 2:26.

25. See also Yelamdeinu in *Yalquṭ Talmud torah,* cited in *Torah Sheleimah,* 1490: "When Joseph saw how well off he was, he began to eat and drink and curl his hair. The Holy-One-Blessed-Be-He said, 'Your father is mourning for you and you eat and drink and curl you hair! Your mistress will soon seek to copulate with you (*mizdaveget lekha*) and persecute you.' There and then *his master's wife raised her eyes to Joseph* (Gen. 39:7)."

26. As pointed out by Albeck in the notes to his critical edition of the text, the formulation here is problematic, as *vaday* ("certainly") read without ironic intent would seem to indicate that R. Samuel b. Naḥman is advocating the literalist interpretation of the verse: i.e., that Joseph came into the house to work. Two plausible solutions come to mind: that Joseph was "certainly" set on committing the sin, or (as I have chosen to translate) that R. Samuel b. Naḥman's remark should be read sardonically.

27. A nearly identical passage, cited in the name of al-Suddī, appears in al-Thaʿlabī, *Lives of the Prophets,* 199.

28. *Traveling with the Innocents Abroad: Mark Twain's Original Reports from Europe and the Holy Land,* ed. Daniel Morley McKeithan (Norman: University of Oklahoma Press, 1958), 222.

29. Merlin L. Swartz, *Ibn Al-Jawzi's* Kitab al-qussas wa'l-mudhakkirin (Beirut: Dār al-Mashriq, 1971), 96–97.

30. Mir, "The Qurʾānic Story of Joseph," 12. Mir here is basing himself on Iṣḥāq, Mawḍūḍī, and Zamakhsharī.

31. Kugel, *In Potiphar's House,* 28–65.

32. *Sefer ha-zikhronot: huʾ divrei ha-yamim li-yeraḥmiʾel,* ed. Eli Yassif (Ramat Aviv, Israel: Tel Aviv University, 2001), 147.

33. *Sefer ha-yashar,* ed. Joseph Dan (Jerusalem: Bialik Institute, 1986), 96.

34. Kugel, *In Potiphar's House,* 35–40, 45.

35. The literal translation of his 1833 work about rabbinic influences on Islamic Scripture: Abraham Geiger, *Was hat Mohammed aus dem Judenthume Aufgenommen* (Bonn: F. Baaden, 1833).

36. Kugel, *In Potiphar's House,* 55–56. The Ladies of the Assembly scene is portrayed in *Tanḥuma* (Zundel edition) Va-yeishev 5. (Note that not only this scene but the entire episode between Joseph and Potiphar's Wife has been elided from the Buber recension of *Tanḥuma.*)

37. A discussion and bibliography are contained in Haim Schwarzbaum's prolegomenon to *The Chronicles of Jerahmeel,* ed. M. Gaster (New York: Ktav, 1971), 14–15, 50–51.

38. For an analysis of the dramatic elements in the quranic version of the story, see James Morris, "Dramatizing the Sura of Joseph: An Introduction to the Islamic Humanities," *Journal of Turkish Studies: Annemarie Schimmel Festschrift* 18 (1994): 201–24.

39. Waldman, "New Approaches to 'Biblical' Materials." This is in line with the argument we have made above for the narrative independence of *The Story of Our Master Joseph.*

40. Kugel argues that the knives are merely a dramatic prop with no thematic import: *In Potiphar's House,* 55–56.

41. Knappert, *Islamic Legends,* 94.

42. This is the interpretation supported by Mustansir Mir, citing the view advanced by Amīn Aḥsan Iṣlāḥī in his Qurʾān commentary. Mir, "The Qurʾānic Story of Joseph," 1–2n. 3.

43. An even more radical possibility is that the repeated or intensive cutting suggested by the verb connotes the Ladies' threatening of suicide, made in an attempt either to lure Joseph or display their willingness to suffer pain for his sake. In this view, Zulaykhā supplies the knives precisely for this purpose. Such an interpretation would reflect the assimilation of the midrashic motif of the suicide threats that Zulaykhā makes to Joseph in *The Story of Our Master Joseph* (*Joseph,* 104).

44. Ibid.

45. Al-Baiḍāwī, *Commentary on Sūrah 12,* 18.

46. Ibid., 19. The verse cited is from a panegyric on Ḥusayn b. Isḥāq al-Tanūkhī, which begins: *huwas al-baynu ḥattā mā taʾannā al-ḥazāʾiqu.* In the printed editions of al-Mutanabbi's works, the offending word is replaced with *dhābat,* "to melt." See Beeston's comment on p. 64n. 77.

47. See Malti-Douglas, *Woman's Body, Woman's Word,* 53.

48. Al-Baiḍāwī, *Commentary on Sūrah 12,* 17.

49. For a discussion of misogyny in the *Testaments*—and specifically, *The Testament of Reuben*—see Ishay Rosen-Zvi, "Bilhah the Temptress: *The Testament of Reuben* and 'The Birth of Sexuality.'" *Jewish Quarterly Review* 96, no. 1 (2006), 65–94.

50. Q 12:33 reads: "[Joseph] said, 'My Lord, prison is more to my liking than that to which they invite me; yet if you do not turn me from their cunning I will become attracted to them and thereby become one of the ignorant.'" Later, in vv. 50–51, when the king sends for Joseph, he insists on clearing his name before he will consent to come: "But when the messenger came to him, [Joseph] said: 'Go back to your lord and ask him what is the opinion of the women who cut up their hands, for certainly my Lord is aware of their cunning.' [The king] said [to the women]: 'What was it you [plural] wanted when you seduced Joseph against his will?'"

51. On such homosocial relationships, see Malti-Douglas, *Woman's Body, Woman's Word,* 54, 56.

52. Much like the role The Song of Songs assumes in Jewish tradition, which also employs garden-of-love imagery.

53. See *Jubilees* 40:10; *Testament of Joseph* 18:3; BT *Soṭah* 13b; BR 86:3. The Rabbis explained the apparent implausibility of a eunuch being the father of Asenath by explaining that either she was the offspring of the union between Dinah and Schechem and was later adopted by Potiphar or that she had been conceived before Gabriel had made him a eunuch in punishment for his purchasing Joseph with immoral intent.

54. Thackston laconically points up this change in the depiction of the master's wife by noting that in al-Kisāʾī "the roles of both Asenath and of the wife of Potiphar have been combined in the figure of Zulaykhā." Al-Kisāʾī, *The Tales of the Prophets,* 351.

55. Thomas Mann, *Joseph and His Brothers,* translated from the German by H. T. Lowe-Porter (Hammondsworth, Middlesex, England: Penguin, 1978), 987.

56. See V. Aptowitzer, "Asenath, the Wife of Joseph: A Haggadic Literary-Historical Study," *Hebrew Union College Annual* 1 (1924): 239–306.

Chapter 4

1. On the rabbinic predilection for the male superior position during intercourse, see Judith Romney Wegner, "The Image and Status of Women in Classical Rabbinic Judaism," in *Jewish Women in Historical Perspective,* ed. Judith Reesa Baskin (Detroit: Wayne State University Press, 1998), 78. The locus classicus for the female subordination to the male is found in BT *Nidah* 31b, which amongst its catalog of markers of female "otherness" includes the following: "Why does the man face downwards [during intercourse] and the woman face towards the man? He [faces the elements] from which he was created and she [faces the man] from whom she was created." Judith Baskin discusses the limited mutalistic nature of the rabbinic conception of marriage where the balance of power tilts emphatically toward the male. See Judith Reesa Baskin, *Midrashic Women: Formations of the Feminine in Rabbinic Literature* (Hannover, N.H.: University Press of New England, 2002), 105–09.

2. For a discussion of the traditions surrounding this character, see Malti-Douglas, *Woman's Body, Woman's Word,* 45–48.

3. For an analysis of a parodic treatment of the type-scene at the well within the canon of modern Hebrew literature, see my study of the story by Devorah Baron: Marc S. Bernstein, "Midrash and Marginality: The 'Agunot' of Devorah Baron and S. Y. Agnon," *Hebrew Studies* 42 (2001): 7–58.

4. Robert Alter, *The Art of Biblical Narrative*, 52.

5. Mary Douglas, *Purity and Danger: An Analysis of Concepts of Pollution and Taboo* (London: Routledge and K. Paul, 1966), 124.

6. Here, however, the connection with the Promised Land is made clear: Abraham instructs his servant Eliezer that under no conditions is Isaac to return to his father's native land.

7. For the intertextual connections between the Book of Esther and the Joseph story in Genesis, see Moshe Gan, "The Book of Esther in the Light of the Story of Joseph in Egypt" [Hebrew], *Tarbiz* 31 (1961–62): 144–49; and for a discussion of the intertextual relations both with Esther and the Book of Daniel, see Ludwig A. Rosenthal, "Die Josephsgeschichte, mit den Büchern Ester und Daniel vergleichen," *Zeitschrift für die alttestamentliche Wissenschaft* 15 (1895): 278–90. In addition to the use of identical expressions to describe the beauty of the two lead protagonists, we can cite several other parallels that point to the contrapuntal relationship between the two stories: Esther's winning of "the beauty pageant" and Joseph's sale at the auction block; Esther replacing Ahashuerus's wife, Queen Vashti, and Joseph supplanting Zulaykhā's husband; Mordechai adopting the orphaned Esther, and al-ʿAzīz's adoption of Joseph; Ahashuerus reentering his chamber to find Haman and Esther in a compromising situation, and al-ʿAzīz coming upon Joseph and Zulaykhā as he seeks to escape her advances; Mordechai's uncovering a palace plot against Ahashuerus, and the baker and cupbearer's roles in plotting against Pharaoh; the resulting rewarding and public celebration of Mordechai by the king, and of Joseph's elevation by Pharaoh for interpreting his dreams, Mordechai replacing Haman as vizier, and Joseph usurping al-ʿAzīz; etc.

8. Citing Douglas 1995. David Resnick, "Esther's Bulimia: Diet, Didactics, and Purim Paideia" (unpublished).

9. Jon Levenson, "The Scroll of Esther in Ecumenical Perspective," *Journal of Ecumenical Studies* 13, no. 3 (1976): 440–51.

10. The events surrounding this are recounted in the *Megilat mitzrayim,* a text that imitates the form and language of the Purim scroll. See Benjamin H. Hary's study of a manuscript also contained at the Magnes Museum: *Multiglossia in Judeo-Arabic (with an Edition, Translation, and Grammatical Study of the Cairene Purim Scroll)* (Leiden: Brill, 1992). In chapter 5 (115–29) of this work he discusses the historical and cultural context of this narrative.

11. See Aaron B. Wildavsky, *Assimilation Versus Separation: Joseph the Administrator and the Politics of Religion in Biblical Israel* (New Brunswick, N.J.: Transaction, 1993). Wildavsky claims that the abject status to which the Israelites are relegated following Joseph's death is foreshadowed by Joseph's own harsh treatment of the Egyptian subjects.

12. See as well the version in *Bereishit raba* 86:2 and *Tanḥuma* (Buber recension) Va-yei-shev 15 where the same strategem is employed, but where the herders are seeking to lead the mother cow to the slaughterhouse.

Bibliography

Adang, Camilla. *Muslim Writers on Judaism and the Hebrew Bible: From Ibn Rabban to Ibn Hazm.* Leiden: Brill, 1996.

Alfonso X the Learned. "General History." In *Coat of Many Cultures: The Story of Joseph in Spanish Literature, 1200–1492.* Ed. Michael McGaha, 330–417. Philadelphia: Jewish Publication Society, 1997.

Alter, Robert. *The Art of Biblical Narrative.* New York: Basic Books, 1981.

———. *The Art of Biblical Poetry.* New York: Basic Books, 1985.

———. *The Five Books of Moses: A Translation with Commentary.* New York: Norton, 2004.

———. *Genesis: Translation and Commentary.* New York: Norton, 1996.

Alter, Robert, and Frank Kermode, eds. *The Literary Guide to the Bible.* Cambridge, Mass.: Harvard University Press, 1987.

Amichai, Yehuda. *Shalvah g'dolah she͗eilot u-t'shuvot.* Jerusalem: Schocken, 1980.

Antoun, Richard T. *Muslim Preacher in the Modern World: A Jordanian Case Study in Comparative Perspective.* Princeton: Princeton University Press, 1989.

Aptowitzer, V. "Asenath, the Wife of Joseph: A Haggadic Literary-Historical Study." *Hebrew Union College Annual* 1 (1924): 239–306.

Arberry, A. J., ed. *Religion in the Middle East.* Cambridge: Cambridge University Press, 1969.

Ashtor, Eliyahu. "The Number of Jews in Mediaeval Egypt" *Journal of Jewish Studies* 18 (1967; 1968): 9–42; 1–22.

———. "Some Features of the Jewish Communities in Medieval Egypt" [Hebrew]. *Zion* 30, nos. 3–4 (1965): 128–57.

Avishur, Yitzḥaq, ed. *Ha-sipur ha-ʿamami shel yehudei ʿiraq.* 2 vols. Haifa: Haifa University Press, 1992.

Avot de-rabi natan (Version A). Ed. Anthony J. Saldarini. Leiden: Brill, 1975.

Avot de-rabi natan (Version B). Ed. S. Schechter and Menahem Kister. New York: Jewish Theological Seminary, 1997.

Awsī al-Anṣārī, Abū ʿAlī ʿUmar ibn Ibrāhīm al-. *Selected Poems from the* Kitāb zahr al-kimām fī qiṣṣat yūsuf. Ed. Leon Nemoy. New Haven: Privately printed, 1930.

Bach, Alice. "Breaking Free of the Biblical Frame-Up: Uncovering the Woman in Genesis 39." In *A Feminist Companion to Genesis,* ed. Athalya Brenner, 318–42. Sheffield, England: Sheffield Academic Press, 1993.

Bahjat, Ahmad. *Anbiyāʾ allāh.* Cairo: Dār al-Shurūq, 1973.

Bal, Mieke. "Myth à La Lettre: Freud, Mann, Genesis and Rembrandt, and the Story of the Son." In *A Feminist Companion to Genesis,* ed. Athalya Brenner, 343–78. Sheffield, England: Sheffield Academic Press, 1993.

Baneth, D. Z. H. "What Did Muḥammed Mean When He Called His Religion Islam? The Original Meaning of *Aslama* and Its Derivatives." In *The Qur'an: Style and Contents,* ed. Andrew Rippin, 85–92. Aldershot, Hampshire: Ashgate, 2001. Originally appeared in *Israel Oriental Studies* 1 (Tel Aviv, 1971), 183–90.

Baqarī, Aḥmad Māhir. *Yūsuf fī al-Qur'ān.* Alexandria: Mu'assasat al-Thaqāfah al-Jāmiʿiyyah, 1971.

Bar-Asher, Moshe. *Mesorot u-leshonot shel yehudei tzfon-afriqah* [Hebrew]. Jerusalem: Hebrew University, 1998.

Barth, J. "Midraschische Elemente in der muslimischen Tradition." In *Birkat Avraham: Festschrift zum siebzigsten Geburtstage A. Berliner's,* 33–40. 1903; Jerusalem: Makor, 1969.

Baskin, Judith Reesa. *Jewish Women in Historical Perspective.* 2nd ed. Detroit: Wayne State University Press, 1998.

———. *Midrashic Women: Formations of the Feminine in Rabbinic Literature.* Brandeis Series on Jewish Women. Hanover, N.H.: University Press of New England, 2002.

Bayḍāwī, ʿAbd Allāh ibn ʿUmar al-. *Baiḍāwī's Commentary on Sūrah 12 of the Qur'ān,* trans. A. F. L. Beeston. Oxford: Clarendon, 1963.

———. *"The Light of Inspiration and Secret of Interpretation": Being a Translation of the Chapter of Joseph (Sūrat Yūsuf) with the Commentary of Nasir al-Dīn al-Baiḍāwī.* Trans. Eric F. F. Bishop. Glasgow: Jackson, 1957.

Beaumont, Daniel E. *Slave of Desire: Sex, Love, and Death in the 1001 Nights.* Madison, N.J.: Fairleigh Dickinson University Press, 2002.

Behnstedt, Peter, and Manfred Woidich. *Die ägyptisch-arabischen Dialekte.* 5 volumes. Wiesbaden: Verlag, 1985–99.

Beinin, Joel. *The Dispersion of Egyptian Jewry: Culture, Politics, and the Formation of a Modern Diaspora.* Berkeley: University of California Press, 1998.

Ben-Porat, Ziva. "Intertextuality" [Hebrew]. *Ha-sifrut* 34, no. 2 (1985): 170–78.

———. "The Poetics of Literary Allusion." *PTL: A Journal for Descriptive Poetics and Theory of Literature* 1, no. 1 (1976): 105–28.

Ben-Shammai, Haggai. "Qirqisānī on the Oneness of God." *Jewish Quarterly Review* 73 (1985): 105–111.

Bernstein, Marc S. "Contested Cultural Space: The Story of Joseph in Judaism and Islam." *Journal of the Central Conference of American Rabbis* (Fall 2000): 41–49.

———. "Midrash and Marginality: The 'Agunot' of Devorah Baron and S. Y. Agnon." *Hebrew Studies* 42 (2001): 7–58.

———. "The Stories of the Prophets: Intertextuality in Judaism and Islam." *Journal of the Association of Graduate Students in Near Eastern Studies* (1990): 27–35.

Bialik, Hayyim Nahman, and Yehoshua Hana Rawnitzki. *The Book of Legends.* Trans. William G. Braude. New York: Schocken, 1992.

Blanc, Haim. "The Nekteb-Nektebu Imperfect in a Variety of Cairene Arabic." *Israel Oriental Studies* 4 (1974): 202–26.

———. Review of *Emergence and Linguistic Background of Judaeo-Arabic* by Joshua Blau [Hebrew]. *Tarbiz* 36, no. 4 (1967): 406–11 (English abstract, v–vi).

Blau, Joshua. *The Emergence and Linguistic Background of Judaeo-Arabic: A Study of the Origins of Neo-Arabic and Middle Arabic.* 3rd ed. Jerusalem: Ben-Zvi Institute, 1999.

———. *A Grammar of Mediaeval Judaeo-Arabic* [Hebrew]. 2nd ed. Jerusalem: Magnes, 1995.

———, ed. *Judaeo-Arabic Literature: Selected Texts.* Jerusalem: Magnes, 1980.

Bloom, Harold. *The Anxiety of Influence: A Theory of Poetry.* 2nd ed. New York: Oxford University Press, 1997.

Bohak, Gideon. *Joseph and Aseneth and the Jewish Temple in Heliopolis.* Atlanta: Scholars Press, 1996.

Bosworth, C. E. "The Concept of *Dhimma* in Early Islam." In *Christians and Jews in the Ottoman Empire,* ed. B. Braude and B. Lewis, 1:37–55. New York: Holmes and Meier, 1982.

Bouhdiba, Abdelwahab. *Sexuality in Islam.* London: Routledge and K. Paul, 1985.

Boyarin, Daniel. *Intertextuality and the Reading of Midrash.* Bloomington: Indiana University Press, 1990.

Braun, Martin. *History and Romance in Graeco-Oriental Literature.* Oxford: Blackwell, 1938.

Brichto, Herbert Chanan. *Toward a Grammar of Biblical Poetics: Tales of the Prophets.* Oxford: Oxford University Press, 1992.

Brinner, William M. "The Egyptian Karaite Community in the Late Nineteenth Century." In *Studies in Judaica, Karaitica and Islamica,* ed. Sheldon Brunswick, 127–44. Ramat-Gan: Bar Ilan University Press, 1982.

———. "An Islamic Decalogue." In *Studies in Islamic and Judaic Traditions,* ed. William M. Brinner and Stephen D. Ricks, 67–84. Atlanta: Scholars Press, 1986.

———. "Popular Literature in Medieval Jewish Arabic." In *Judaeo-Arabic Studies,* ed. Norman Golb, 59–71. Amsterdam: Harwood Academic Publishers, 1997.

———. "Prophets and Prophecy in the Islamic and Jewish Traditions." In *Studies in Islamic and Judaic Traditions II,* ed. William M. Brinner and Stephen D. Ricks, 63–82. Atlanta: Scholars Press, 1989.

———. "Some Problems in the Arabic Transmission of Biblical Names." In *Solving Riddles and Untying Knots: Biblical, Epigraphic, and Semitic Studies in Honor of Jonas C. Greenfield,* ed. Seymour Gitin, Ziony Zevit, and Michael Sokoloff, 19–27. Winona Lake, Ind.: Eisenbrauns, 1995.

Bronner, Leila Leah. "Serah Bat Asher: The Transformative Power of Aggadic Invention." In *From Eve to Esther: Rabbinic Reconstructions of Biblical Women,* 42–60. Louisville: Westminster John Knox, 1994.

Bruijn, J.T.P. de, and Barbara Flemming. "Yūsuf and Zulaykhā" (in Persian and Turkish literature). In *Encyclopaedia of Islam,* vol. 11. Leiden: Brill, 2002.

Budd, Louis J. "Mark Twain on Joseph the Patriarch," *American Quarterly* 16, no. 4 (1964): 577–86.

Bukhārī, Muḥammad ibn Ismāʿīl al-. *Al-Jāmiʿ al-ṣaḥīḥ.* Vols. 1–3 ed. M. Ludolf Krehl; Vol. 4 ed. Th. W. Juynboll. Leiden: Brill, 1862.

Burchard, Christoph, trans. "Joseph and Aseneth." In *The Old Testament Pseudepigrapha,* ed. James H. Charlesworth, 177–247. New York: Doubleday, 1985.

Burns, R. J. *Christians and Jews in the Crusader Kingdom of Valencia: Societies in Symbiosis.* Cambridge: Cambridge University Press, 1984.

Burton, John. *The Collection of the Qurʾān.* Cambridge: Cambridge University Press, 1977.

———. *The Sources of Islamic Law: Islamic Theories of Abrogation.* Edinburgh: Edinburgh University Press, 1990.

Cachia, Pierre. "The Prophet's Shirt: Three Versions of an Egyptian Narrative Ballad." *Journal of Semitic Studies* 26, no. 1 (1981): 79–106.

Chapira, B. "Legendes Bibliques Attribuées a Kaʿab el-Ahbar." *Revue des Études Juives* (1919): 86–101.

The Chronicles of Jerahmeel. Ed. and trans. M. Gaster (reprinted with a prolegomenen by Haim Schwarzbaum). New York: Ktav, 1971.

Cohen, Mark R. "Islam and the Jews: Myth, Counter-Myth, History." *Jerusalem Quarterly* 38 (1986): 125–37.

———. "The Jews under Islam: From the Rise of Islam to Sabbatai Zevi." In *Bibliographical Essays in Jewish Medieval Studies,* 169–229. New York: Anti-defamation League of B'nai B'rith, 1976.

———. "Prophets and Prophecy in the Islamic and Jewish Traditions." In *Studies in Islamic and Judaic Traditions II,* ed. William M. Brinner and Stephen D. Ricks, 63–82. Atlanta: Scholars Press, 1989.

———. *Under Crescent and Cross: The Jews in the Middle Ages.* Princeton: Princeton University Press, 1994.

Cohen, Mark R., and Abraham L. Udovitch. *Jews among Arabs: Contacts and Boundaries.* Princeton: Darwin, 1989.

Cohen, Naomi G. *Philo Judaeus: His Universe of Discourse.* Frankfurt am Main: Peter Lang, 1995.

Crone, Patricia, and Michael Cook. *Hagarism: The Making of the Islamic World.* Cambridge: Cambridge University Press, 1977.

Culler, Jonathan D. *Framing the Sign: Criticism and Its Institutions.* Norman: University of Oklahoma Press, 1988.

Dajani, Zahia Ragheb. *Yūsuf fī al-Qurʾān al-karīm w'al-tawrāh.* Beirut: Dār al-Taqrīb Bayna al-Madhāhib al-Islāmiyyah, 1994.

Dan, Joseph, ed. *ʿAlilot aleksander mokdon.* Jerusalem: Mosad Bialik, 1969.

———. *The Hebrew Story in the Middle Ages* [Hebrew]. Jerusalem: Keter, 1974.

David, Avraham, ed. *Mi-ginzei ha-makhon le-tatzlumei kitvei ha-yad ha-ʿivriyim.* Jerusalem: Jewish National and University Library, 1995.

Davies, Humphrey Taman. "Seventeenth-Century Egyptian Arabic: A Profile of the Colloquial Material in Yusuf al-Sirbini's *Hazz al-quhuf fi sarh qasid abi saduf.*" Unpublished Ph.D. thesis, University of California, Berkeley, 1981.

Dihlawī, Walī Allāh al-. *A Mystical Interpretation of Prophetic Tales by an Indian Muslim: Shah Walī Allāh's* Taʾwīl al-aḥadīth. Trans. J. M. S. Baljon. Leiden: Brill, 1973.

Douglas, Mary. *Implicit Meanings: Essays in Anthropology.* London: Routledge and K. Paul, 1975.

———. *Purity and Danger: An Analysis of Concepts of Pollution and Taboo.* London: Routledge and K. Paul, 1966.

Dozy, Reinhart Pieter Anne. *Supplément aux Dictionnaries Arabes.* 2nd ed. Leiden: Brill, 1927.

Drory, Rina. *The Emergence of Jewish-Arabic Literary Contacts at the Beginning of the Tenth Century* [Hebrew]. Tel Aviv: Porter Institute for Poetics and Semiotics, 1986.

———. "'Words Beautifully Put': Hebrew Versus Arabic in Tenth-Century Jewish Literature." In *Genizah Research after Ninety Years: The Case of Judaeo-Arabic,* ed. Joshua Blau and Stefan C. Reif, 53–66. Cambridge: Cambridge University Press, 1992.

Elkin, Zeev, and Menahem Ben Sasson. "Abraham Firkovich and the Cairo Genizahs in the Light of His Personal Archives" [Hebrew]. *Peʿamim* 90 (Winter 2002): 51–95.

Encyclopaedia of Islam, 2nd edition. Ed. P. J. Bearman, T. H. Blanquis, C. E. Bosworth, E. van Donzel, and W. P. Heinrichs. 13 vols. Leiden: Brill, 1960–2004.

Encyclopedia Judaica. 16 vols. Jerusalem: Keter; New York: Macmillan, 1971–72.

Encyclopedia Judaica Yearbook. Ed. Cecil Roth and Geoffrey Wigoder. 10 vols. Jerusalem: Keter, 1972–94.

Encyclopedia of the Qur'ān, ed. Jane Dammen McAuliffe. 5 vols. Leiden: Brill, 2003–5.

Ethé, (Carl) Hermann, ed. *Yusuf and Zalikha by Firdausi of Tus.* Reprint of 1908 Oxford edition. Amsterdam: Philo, 1970.

Even-Zohar, Itamar. "Polysystem Theory." *Poetics Today* 1, no. 1–2 (1979): 287–310.

Fagnan, E. "Arabo-Judaica." *Revue des Études Juives* 59 (1910): 225–30.

The Fathers According to Rabbi Nathan (*Avot de-rabi natan*). Trans. Judah Goldin. New Haven: Yale University Press, 1955.

Fattal, Antoine. *Le Statut Legal des Non-Musulmans en Pays d'Islam.* Beirut, 1958.

Feldman, Louis H. *Jew and Gentile in the Ancient World: Attitudes and Interactions from Alexander to Justinian.* Princeton: Princeton University Press, 1993.

———. "Joseph." In *Josephus's Interpretation of the Bible,* 335–73. Berkeley: University of California Press, 1998.

Fenton, Paul. "Karaites and Sufis—The Traces of Sufism in Karaite Manuscripts" [Hebrew]. *Peʿamim* 90 (Winter 2002): 5–19.

———. *Reshimat kitvei-yad be-ʿaravit-yehudit be-leningrad.* Jerusalem: Ben-Zvi Institute, 1991.

Firestone, Reuven. "Abraham's Son as the Intended Sacrifice (*Al-dhabīḥ,* Qurʾān 37:99–113): Issues in Qurʾānic Exegesis." *Journal of Semitic Studies* 34, no. 1 (Spring 1989): 95–131.

———. *Journeys in Holy Lands: The Evolution of the Abraham-Ishmael Legends in Islamic Exegesis.* Albany: State University of New York Press, 1990.

———. "Yūsuf." In *Encyclopaedia of Islam.* Leiden: Brill, 2002.

Fischel, Walter J. *Jews in the Economic and Political Life of Medieval Islam.* 1937; New York: Ktav, 1969.

Fischer, Wolfdietrich, and Otto Jastrow. *Handbook for the Study of the Arabic Dialects.* Hebrew translation from original German by Rafi Talmon. Jerusalem: Magnes, 2000.

Fishbane, Michael. *The Garments of Torah: Essays on Biblical Hermeneutics.* Bloomington: Indiana University Press, 1989.

Fletcher, Richard. *The Quest for El Cid.* New York: Alfred A. Knopf, 1990.

Friedberg, Hayim Dov. *Bet Eked Sepharim Bibliographic Lexicon.* 2nd ed. 4 vols. Tel Aviv: Bar Yuda, 1951–1956.

Frye, Northrop. *Anatomy of Criticism.* Princeton: Princeton University Press, 1973.

Frymer-Kensky, Tikva Simone. *Reading the Women of the Bible.* New York: Schocken, 2002.

———. "The Strange Case of the Suspected *Sotah.*" *Vetus Testamentum* 34 (1984): 11–31.

Galford, Hugh S. "Sayyid Qutb and the Qur'anic Story of Joseph: A Commentary for Today." In *Muslim-Jewish Encounters: Intellectual Traditions and Modern Politics,* ed. Ronald L. Nettler and Suha Taji-Farouki, 39–64. Netherlands: Harwood Academic Publishers, 1998.

Gan, Moshe. "The Book of Esther in the Light of the Story of Joseph in Egypt" [Hebrew]. *Tarbiz* 31 (1961–62): 144–49.

Gaster, Theodor H., and James George Fraser. *Myth, Legend, and Custom in the Old Testament.* New York: Harper and Row, 1969.

Gätje, Helmut. *The Qur'an and Its Exegesis.* Trans. Alford T. Welch. Berkeley: University of California, 1976.

Geiger, Abraham. *Judaism and Islam.* Trans. F. M. Young. 1878; New York: Ktav, 1970.

Ginzberg, Louis. *Legends of the Jews.* Trans. Henrietta Szold. 7 vols. Philadelphia: Jewish Publication Society, 1968.

Goitein, S. D. "Isrā'īliyyāt" [Hebrew]. *Tarbiz* 6 (1934–35): 89–101.

———. *Jews and Arabs: Their Contacts through the Ages.* 3rd ed. New York: Schocken, 1974.

———. *A Mediterranean Society: The Jewish Communities of the Arab World as Portrayed in the Documents of the Cairo Geniza.* 6 vols. Berkeley: University of California Press, 1967–93.

———. "'Meeting in Jerusalem': Messianic Expectations in the Letters of the Cairo Geniza." *Association for Jewish Studies Review* 4 (1979): 43–57.

Goldin, Judah. "The Freedom and Restraint of Haggadah." In *Midrash and Literature,* ed. Geoffrey H. Hartman and Sanford Budick, 57–76. New Haven: Yale University Press, 1986.

Goldman, Shalom. *The Wiles of Women/the Wiles of Men: Joseph and Potiphar's Wife in Ancient Near Eastern, Jewish, and Islamic Folklore.* Albany: State University of New York Press, 1995.

Goldziher, Ignaz. "Mélanges Judeo-Arabes IX: Isra'iliyyat." *Revue des Études Juives* 44 (1902): 63–66.

———. *Muslim Studies.* Trans. C. R. Barber and S. M. Stern. 2 vols. London: George Allen and Unwin, 1967, 1971.

Greenstein, Edward. "An Equivocal Reading of the Sale of Joseph." In *Literary Interpretations of Biblical Narratives,* vol. 2, ed. Kenneth R. R. Gros Louis, James Stokes Ackerman, and Thayer S. Warshaw, 114–25. Nashville: Abingdon, 1982.

Grünbaum, Max. *Neue Beiträge zur semitischen Sagenkunde.* Leiden: Brill, 1892.

———. "Zu 'Jussuf und Suleicha.'" In *Gesammelte Aufsätze sur Sprach- und Sagenkunde.* Berlin: S. Calvary, 1901.

Guillaume, A. *The Life of Muhammad (A Translation of Ibn Ishaq's* Sirat Rasul Allah*).* Oxford: Oxford University Press, 1955.

Haleem, M. A. S. Adel. "The Story of Joseph in the Qur'ān and the Old Testament." *Islam and Christian-Muslim Relations* 1, no. 2 (1990): 171–91.

Halkin, A. S. "The Judeo-Islamic Age." In *Great Ages and Ideas of the Jewish People,* ed. Leo W. Schwarz and Salo Wittmayer Baron, 213–63. New York: Random House, 1956.

Hartman, Geoffrey H., and Sanford Budick, eds. *Midrash and Literature.* New Haven: Yale University Press, 1986.

Hary, Benyamin H. *Multiglossia in Judeo-Arabic (with an Edition, Translation, and Grammatical Study of the Cairene Purim Scroll).* Leiden: Brill, 1992.

Hasan-Rokem, Galit. "Proverbs in Israeli Folk Narratives: A Structural Semantic Analysis." Helsinki: Suomalainen Tiedea Katemia, 1982.

Heinemann, Isaak. *Darkhei ha-agadah.* 3rd ed. Jerusalem: Magnes, 1970.

Heinemann, Joseph. *Aggadah and Its Development* [Hebrew]. Jerusalem: Keter, 1974.

———. "The Messiah of Ephraim and the Premature Exodus of the Tribe of Ephraim." *Harvard Theological Review* 68 (1975): 1–16.

———. "The Nature of Aggadah." In *Midrash and Literature,* ed. Geoffrey H. Hartman and Sanford Budick, 41–55. New Haven: Yale University Press, 1986.

Heller, Bernard. "Ginzberg's *Legends of the Jews:* V. Relation of the Aggada to Islamic Legends." *Jewish Quarterly Review* 24 (1934): 393–404.

Hilgert, Earle. "The Dual Image of Joseph in Hebrew and Early Jewish Literature." *Biblical Research* 30 (1985).

Hinds, Martin, and el-Said M. Badawi. *A Dictionary of Egyptian Arabic: Arabic-English.* Beirut: Librarie du Liban, 1986.

Hoffmeir, James K. "Joseph in Egypt." In *Israel in Egypt: The Evidence for the Authenticity of the Exodus Tradition,* 77–106. Oxford: Oxford University Press, 1997.

Hollander, Harm W., and Marinus de Jonge. *The Testaments of the Twelve Patriarchs: A Commentary.* Leiden: E.J. Brill, 1985.

Hootkins, Hirsch. "The Story of Joseph and Zalikha (*Qiṣṣat Yūsuf Wa-Zalīkhā*): A Comprehensive Study of a Hitherto Unpublished Arabic Ṣūfī Manuscript." Unpublished doctoral dissertation, University of Michigan, 1934.

Horowitz, Josef. "Das Koranische Paradies." In *Der Koran,* ed. Rudi Paret, 53–73. Darmstadt: Wissenschaftliche Buchgesellschaft, 1975.

———. *Jewish Proper Names and Derivatives in the Koran.* Hildesheim: G. Olms Verlagsbuchhandlung, 1964.

———. *Koranische Untersuchungen.* Berlin: W. de Gruyter, 1926.

Humphreys, W. Lee. *Joseph and His Family: A Literary Study, Studies on Personalities of the Old Testament.* Columbia: University of South Carolina Press, 1988.

Hyman, Naomi M. *Biblical Women in the Midrash: A Sourcebook.* Northvale, N.J.: Jason Aronson, 1997.

Ibn Ḥazm, ʿAlī ibn Aḥmad. *Al-Faṣl fī al-milal wa'l-ahwāʾ wa'l-niḥal.* 5 vols. Cairo: Muḥammad ʿAlī Ṣubayḥ, 1964.

Ibn Kathīr, Abū al-Fidāʾī Ismāʿīl. "The Account of the Amazing Events That Transpired in the Life of Israel, Including: The Story of Joseph, Son of Rachel." In *Qiṣaṣ al-anbiyāʾ.* Ed. with commentary by Yūsuf ʿAlī Bidīwī, 243–79. Damascus: Dār Ibn Kathīr, 1992.

———. *Tafsīr al-qurʾān al-ʿaẓīm.* Vol. 4. Beirut: Dār al-Fikr, 1966.

Ibn Ṣaṣrā, Muḥammad ibn Muḥammad. *A Chronicle of Damascus, 1389–1397.* Trans. William M. Brinner. Berkeley: University of California Press, 1963.

Ibn Shāhīn, Nissim ben Jacob. *An Elegant Composition Concerning Relief after Adversity: An Eleventh Century Book of Comfort.* Trans. from the Arabic with introduction and notes by William M. Brinner. 1977; Northvale, N.J.: Jason Aronson, 1996.

Ibn Ṭāhir al-Baghdādā, ʿAbd al-Qāhir. *Moslem Schisms and Sects (al-Farq bain al-firaq), Being the History of the Various Philosophic Systems Developed in Islam, Part II.* Trans. Abraham S. Halkin. Tel Aviv: Palestine, 1935.

Ilan, Tal. *Jewish Women in Greco-Roman Palestine.* Peabody, Mass.: Hendrickson, 1996.

Jami, Hakim Nuruddin Abdurrahman. *Yusuf and Zulaikha: An Allegorical Romance.* Abridged and trans. David Pendlebury. London: Octagon, 1980.

Jerusalmi, Isaac. *Sūrat yūsuf ʿalayhi al-salām = the Story of Joseph in the Qurʾān: A Philological Commentary.* Cincinnati: Hebrew Union College-Jewish Institute of Religion, 1966.

Johns, Anthony H. "Joseph in the Qurʾān: Dramatic Dialogue, Human Emotion, and Prophetic Wisdom." *Islamochristiana* 7 (1981): 29–51.

Josephus, Flavius. *Judean Antiquities.* Trans. and notes by Louis H. Feldman. Leiden: Brill, 2000.

JPS Hebrew–English Tanakh: The Traditional Hebrew Text and the New JPS Translation. 2nd ed. Philadelphia: Jewish Publication Society, 1999.

"Jubilees." Trans. O. S. Wintermute. In *The Old Testament Pseudepigrapha,* ed. J. Charlesworth, 35–142. New York: Doubleday, 1985.

Juynboll, G. H. A. *Muslim Tradition: Studies in Chronology, Provenance and Authorship of Early Ḥadīth.* Cambridge: Cambridge University Press, 1983.

Kāmil, ʿAbd al-ʿAzīz. *Durūs min sūrat yūsuf.* Kuwait: Dhat al-Salasil, 1985.

Kasher, Menahem M. *Encyclopedia of Biblical Interpretation: Torah Shelemah (A Millennial Anthology).* Abridged English translation of *Ḥumash torah sheleimah,* ed. Harry Freedman. Vols. 5 and 6. New York: American Biblical Encyclopedia Society, 1948 and 1953–79.

———. *Ḥumash torah sheleimah.* Jerusalem: Beit Torah Sheleimah, 1931.

Kassis, Hanna E. *A Concordance of the Qurʾān.* Berkeley: University of California Press, 1983.

Katsh, Abraham I. *Judaism in Islam: Biblical and Talmudic Backgrounds of the Koran and Its Commentaries.* 3rd ed. New York: Sepher-Hermon, 1980.

Khalil El Houssary, Mahmoud. *A Recital from the Holy Quran: Surat Yusuf.* Brooklyn: Orient, 1990.

Khan, Geoffrey. "Notes on the Grammar of a Late Egyptian Judaeo-Arabic Text." *Jerusalem Studies in Arabic and Islam* 15 (1992): 220–39.

———. "A Study of the Judeao-Arabic of Late Genizah Documents and Its Comparison with Classical Judaeo-Arabic" [Hebrew]. *Sefunot* 20 (1991): 223–34.

Kharshaf, Idris. *Al-Tafsīr al-ʿilmī li-fātihat sūrat yūsuf.* Rabat: Manshurat al-ʿUkaz, 1988.

Khaṭīb, ʿAbd al-Karīm. *Qiṣṣatā ādam wa-yūsuf ʿalayhimā al-salām.* Cairo: Dār al-Fikr al-ʿArabī, 1974.

Kisāʾī, Muḥammad ibn ʿAbd Allāh al-. *The Tales of the Prophets of al-Kisāʾī.* Trans. Wheeler M. Thackston. Boston: Twayne, 1978. Originally published in Arabic as "Qiṣaṣ al-anbiyāʾ," in *Vita Prophetarum,* ed. Isaac Eisenberg, 2 vols (Lugduni-Batavorum [Leiden]: Brill, 1922).

Kister, M. J. "Ḥaddithū ʿan banī isrāʾīl wa-la haraja." *Israel Oriental Studies* 2 (1972): 215–39.

Knappert, Jan. *Islamic Legends: Histories of the Heroes, Saints and Prophets of Islam.* Vol. 1. Leiden: Brill, 1985.

Kraemer, Ross Shepard. *When Aseneth Met Joseph: A Late Antique Tale of the Biblical Patriarch and His Egyptian Wife, Reconsidered.* New York: Oxford University Press, 1998.

Kodsi, Mourad el-. *Just for the Record in the History of the Karaite Jews of Egypt in Modern Times.* Lyons, N.Y.: Wilprint, 2002.

———. *The Karaite Jews of Egypt, 1882–1986.* Lyons, N.Y.: Wilprint, 1987.

Kugel, James L. *The Idea of Biblical Poetry: Parallelism and Its History.* New Haven: Yale University Press, 1981.

———. *In Potiphar's House: The Interpretive Life of Biblical Texts.* San Francisco: Harper, 1990.

———. *Shem in the Tents of Japhet: Essays on the Encounter of Judaism and Hellenism.* Leiden: Brill, 2002.

———. *Traditions of the Bible: A Guide to the Bible as It Was at the Start of the Common Era.* Cambridge, Mass.: Harvard University Press, 1998.

———. "Two Introductions to Midrash." In *Midrash and Literature,* ed. Geoffrey H. Hartman and Sanford Budick, 77–103. New Haven: Yale University Press, 1986.

La Leyenda de Yusuf: Ein Aljamiadotext. Ed. Ursula Kenk. Tübingen: Max Nermeyer Verlag, 1972.

Landau, Jacob M., ed. *Jews in Nineteenth-Century Egypt.* New York: New York University Press, 1969.

———, ed. *The Jews in Ottoman Egypt* [Hebrew]. Jerusalem: Misgav Yerushalayim, 1988.

Lane, E. W. *An Account of the Manners and Customs of the Modern Egyptians (Written in Egypt during the Years 1833–1835).* London: Ward, Lock, 1842.

———. *Arabic-English Lexicon.* 8 vols. 1863; Beirut, 1968.

Laskier, Michael M. *The Jews of Egypt, 1920–1970: In the Midst of Zionism, Anti-Semitism, and the Middle East Conflict.* New York: New York University Press, 1992.

Lassner, Jacob. *Demonizing the Queen of Sheba: Boundaries of Gender and Culture in Postbiblical Judaism and Medieval Islam.* Chicago: University of Chicago Press, 1993.

Lazar, Moshe, ed. *Joseph and His Brethren: Three Ladino Versions.* Culver City, Calif.: Labyrinthos, 1990.

Lazarus-Yafeh, Hava. *Intertwined Worlds: Medieval Islam and Bible Criticism.* Princeton: Princeton University Press, 1992.

———. "Judaism and Islam: Some Aspects of Mutual Cultural Influences." In *Some Religious Aspects of Islam: A Collection of Articles,* 72–89. Leiden: Brill, 1981.

———. "Judeo-Arabic Culture." In *Encyclopedia Judaica Yearbook 1977/1978,* 101–10. Jerusalem: Keter, 1979.

———. *Mivḥar tekstim le-toldot parshanut ha-qur'an.* Jerusalem: Hebrew University Press, 1979.

———, ed. *Muslim Authors on Jews and Judaism: The Jews among Their Muslim Neighbors* [Hebrew]. Jerusalem: Zalman Shazar Center, 1996.

Leibowitz, Nehama. *ʿIyunim be-sefer bereishit: be-ʿiqvot parshaneinu ha-rishonim veha-aḥaronim.* Jerusalem: ha-Histadrut ha-Tsiyonit, 1966.

———. *Torah Insights.* Jerusalem: Eliner Library, The Joint Authority for Jewish Zionist Education Department for Torah and Culture in the Diaspora, 1995.

Levenson, Alan T. "Christian Author, Jewish Book? Methods and Sources in Thomas Mann's *Joseph.*" In *Agendas for the Study of Midrash in the Twenty-First Century,* ed. Marc Lee Raphael, 123–36. Williamsburg, Va.: College of William and Mary, 1999.

Levenson, Jon. "The Scroll of Esther in Ecumenical Perspective." *Journal of Ecumenical Studies* 13, no. 3 (1976): 440–51.

Lewis, Bernard. *The Jews of Islam.* Princeton: Princeton University Press, 1984.

Macdonald, J. "Joseph in the Qurʾan and Muslim Commentary: A Comparative Study." *The Muslim World* 46 (1956): 113–31, 207–24.

Mach, Rudolf. *Der Zaddik in Talmud und Midrasch.* Leiden: Brill, 1957.

Maimonides, Moses. *The Guide of the Perplexed.* Trans. Shlomo Pines. Chicago: University of Chicago Press, 1963.

Malti-Douglas, Fedwa. *Woman's Body, Woman's Word: Gender and Discourse in Arabo-Islamic Writing.* Princeton, N.J.: Princeton University Press, 1991.

Mann, Thomas. *Joseph and His Brothers.* Trans. H. T. Lowe-Porter. Middlesex, England: Penguin, 1978.

Margoliouth, D. S. *The Relations between Arabs and Israelites Prior to the Rise of Islam.* London: Oxford University Press, 1924.

Marx, Alexander. *Bibliographical Studies and Notes on Rare Books and Manuscripts in the Library of the Jewish Theological Seminary.* Ed. Menahem H. Schmelzer. New York: Jewish Theological Seminary, 1977.

Masᶜūdī, Abū al-Ḥasan ᶜAlī b. Ḥusayn al-. *The Meadows of Gold: The Abbasids.* Trans. Paul Lunde and Caroline Stone. London: K. Paul, 1989.

McGaha, Michael D. *Coat of Many Cultures: The Story of Joseph in Spanish Literature, 1200–1492.* Philadelphia: Jewish Publication Society, 1997.

———. *The Story of Joseph in Spanish Golden Age Drama.* Lewisburg, Penn.: Bucknell University Press, 1998.

McKeithan, Daniel Morley, ed. *Traveling with the Innocents Abroad: Mark Twain's Original Reports from Europe and the Holy Land.* Norman: University of Oklahoma Press, 1958.

Midrash bereishit raba. Ed. Julius Theodor and Chanoch Albeck. 2nd printing (with corrections). Jerusalem: Wahrmann, 1965.

Midrash David Ha-Nagid—Genesis. Ed. Abraham I. Katsh. Jerusalem: Mosad Ha-Rav Kook, 1964.

Midrash ha-gadol on the Pentateuch: Genesis. Ed. Mordechai Margaliot. Jerusalem: Mosad Ha-Rav Kook, 1956.

Midrash Pesiqta Rabbati (with Traditional Commentaries). Tel Aviv: n.p, 1963.

Midrash Rabbah (with Traditional Commentaries, 2 Vols.). Jerusalem: Pe'er Torah, 1970.

Midrash Rabbah. Trans. H. Freedman and Maurice Simon. 3rd. ed. London: Soncino, 1983.

Midrash Tanchuma: Ein agadischer Commentar zum Pentateuch von Rabbi Tanchuma ben Rabbi Abba; zum ersten male nach Handschriften aus den Bilbiotheken zu Oxford, Rom, Parma und München herausgegeben; kritisch bearbeitet, commentirt und mit einer ausführlichen Einleitung [auf Hebräisch] versehen. Ed. Solomon Buber. 2 vols. Vilna: Romm, 1885 [reprinted Vilna (1912); New York (1946); Jerusalem: Ortsel (1963–64)].

Midrash tanḥuma (S. Buber Recension): Translated into English with Introduction, Indices, and Brief Notes. Trans. John T. Townsend. 3 vols. Hoboken, N.J.: Ktav, 1989.

Midrash tanḥuma on the Pentateuch with the commentaries of ᶜEtz yosef and the ᶜAnaf yosef. Ed. Ḥanokh Zundel. 3 vols. Jerusalem: Levin-Epstein, 1969–70.

Midrash Tanhuma-Yelammedenu: An English Translation of Genesis and Exodus from the Printer Version of Tanhuma-Yelammedenu with an Introduction, Notes, and Indices. Ed. Samuel A. Berman. Hoboken, N.J.: Ktav, 1996.

Mir, Mustansir. "The Qurʾānic Story of Joseph: Plot, Themes, and Characters." *Muslim World* 76, no. 1 (1986): 1–15.

Moreen, Vera Basch, ed. and trans. *In Queen Esther's Garden: An Anthology of Judeo-Persian Literature.* New Haven: Yale University Press, 2000.

Morris, James. "Dramatizing the Sura of Joseph: An Introduction to the Islamic Humanities." *Journal of Turkish Studies: Annemarie Schimmel Festschrift* 18 (1994): 201–24.

Nagel, Tilman. "Die Qiṣaṣ al-anbiyāʾ; ein Beitrag zur arabischen Literaturgeschichte." Doctoral dissertation, Rheinischen Friedrich-wilhelms-Universität, 1967.

Najjār, ʿAbd al-Wahhāb al-. *Qiṣaṣ al-anbiyāʾ*. Cairo: Mu'assasat al-Ḥalabī, 1966.

Nemoy, Leon. "ʿAnan ben David: A Reappraisal of the Historical Data." In *Karaite Studies,* ed. Philip Birnbaum, 309–18. New York: Hermon, 1971.

Nestor the Priest. *The Polemic of Nestor the Priest:* Qiṣṣat Mujādalat al-Usquf *and* Sefer nestor ha-komer. Ed. Daniel J. Lasker and Sarah Stroumsa. Jerusalem: Ben-Zvi Institute for the Study of Jewish Communities in the East, 1996.

Nettler, Ronald L. "Early Islam, Modern Islam, and Judaism: The *Isrāʾīliyyāt* in Modern Islamic Thought." In *Muslim-Jewish Encounters: Intellectual Traditions and Modern Politics,* ed. Ronald L. Nettler and Suha Taji-Farouki, 1–14. Netherlands: Harwood Academic Publishers, 1998.

Neubauer, Adolf. *Aus der Petersburger Bibliothek: Beiträge und Documente zur Geschichte des Karäerthums und der karäischen Literatur.* Leipzig: O. Leiner, 1866.

Newby, Gordon D. "The Drowned Son: Midrash and Midrash Making in the Qurʾān and Tafsīr." In *Studies in Islamic and Judaic Traditions,* ed. William M. Brinner and Stephen D. Ricks, 19–32. Atlanta: Scholars Press, 1986.

———. *A History of the Jews of Arabia: From Ancient Times to Their Eclipse under Islam.* Columbia: University of South Carolina Press, 1988.

———. *The Making of the Last Prophet: A Reconstruction of the Earliest Biography of Muhammad.* Columbia: University of South Carolina, 1989.

———. "Tafsir Isra'iliyyat." *JAR Thematic Issue* 47 (1979): 685–97.

Niehoff, Maren. *The Figure of Joseph in Post-Biblical Jewish Literature.* Leiden: Brill, 1992.

Noy, Dov. *Folktales in the Talmud and Midrash* [Hebrew]. Jerusalem: Akademon, 1968.

Obermann, Julian. "Koran and Agada: The Events at Mount Sinai" 58 (1941): 23–48.

Otzar midrashim. Ed. J. D. Eisenstein. New York: Eisenstein, 1915.

Patai, Raphael, and Robert Graves. *Hebrew Myths: The Book of Genesis.* New York: McGraw-Hill, 1966.

Pauliny, Ján. "Some Remarks on the *Qiṣaṣ al-Anbiyāʾ* Works in Arabic Literature." In *The Qurʾan: Formative Interpretation,* ed. Andrew Rippen, 313–26. Aldershot, Hampshire: Ashgate, 1999. Originally published in German as "Eingige Bemerkungen zu den Werken Qiṣaṣ al-Anbiyāʾ in der arabischen Literatur" trans. Michael Bonner, *Graecolatina et Orientalia* 1 (1969): 111–23.

Philo. "On Joseph (De Iosepho)." In *Philo,* 137–271. London: William Heinemann; Cambridge, Mass.: Harvard University Press, 1935.

Pirke De Rabbi Eliezer. Trans. Gerald Friedlander. New York: Sefer Hermon, 1981.

Polliack, Meira. "Genres of Judeo-Arabic Literature in the Cairo Genizah" [Hebrew]. In *ʿEver and ʿArav: Contacts between Arabic Literature and Jewish Literature in the Middle Ages and Modern Times,* ed. Yosef Tobi, 9–26. Tel Aviv: Afikim, 1998.

———, ed. *Karaite Judaism: A Guide to Its History and Literary Sources.* Leiden: Brill, 2003.

———. *The Karaite Tradition of Arabic Bible Translation: A Linguistic and Exegetical Study of Karaite Translations of the Pentateuch from the Tenth and Eleventh Centuries* CE. Leiden: Brill, 1997.

Popper, William. *Egypt and Syria under the Circassian Sultans, 1392–1468 AD: Systematic Notes to Ibn Taghri Birdi's* Chronicles of Egypt. Berkeley: University of California Press, 1955.

Qiṣṣat yōsef ha-tzadīq. Tunis: Sion Uzan, 1910.

Qiṣṣat yūsuf al-ṣiddīq. Baghdad: Maṭbaʿat al-Waṭaniyyah al-Isrāʾīliyyah, 1914.

Quṭb, Muḥammad al-. *Yūsuf wa-imraʾat al-ʿazīz*. Cairo: Maktabat al-Qurʾān, 1984.

Rabghūzī, al-. *The Stories of the Prophets: Qiṣaṣ al-Anbiyāʾ: An Eastern Turkish Version*. Trans. H. E. Boeschoten, M. Vandamme, and S. Tezcan. 2 vols. Leiden: Brill, 1995.

Rabin, Haim, Joshua Blau, and Haim Blanc. "A Scholars' Forum: Jewish Languages—The Shared, the Unique, the Problematic" [Hebrew]. *Peʿamim* (Spring 1979): 40–66.

Raeder, S. "Die Josephsgeschichte im Koran und im alten Testament." *Evangelische Theologie* 26 (1966): 169–90.

Rāzī, Fakhr al-Dīn Muḥammad ibn ʿUmar al-. *Al-Maḥṣūl fī ʿilm uṣūl al-fiqh*. Ed. Ṭāhā Jābir Fayyād ʿAlwānī. 2nd ed. 6 vols. Beirut: Muʾassasat al-Risālah, 1992.

———. *ʿIṣmat al-anbiyāʾ*. Ed. Muḥammad Ḥijāzī. Cairo: Maktabat al-Thaqāfah al-Dīnīyah, 1986.

Redford, Donald B. *A Study of the Biblical Story of Joseph*. Leiden: Brill, 1970.

Reeves, John C., ed. *Bible and Qurʾan: Essays in Scriptural Intertextuality*. Leiden: Brill, 2004.

Renard, John. "Reprise: Joseph of the Seven Doors." In *Seven Doors to Islam: Spirituality and the Religious Life of Muslims*, 259–72. Berkeley: University of California Press, 1996.

Rendsburg, Gary. "Literary Structures in the Qurʾanic and Biblical Stories of Joseph." *Muslim World* 78, no. 2 (Apr. 1988): 118–20.

Resnick, David. "Esther's Bulimia: Diet, Didactics, and Purim Paideia." Unpublished article.

Richler, Benjamin. *Guide to Hebrew Manuscript Collections*. Jerusalem: Israel Academy of Sciences and Humanities, 1994.

Riḍḍā, Muḥammad Rashīd. *Tafsīr sūrat yūsuf*. Ed. Muḥammad Bahjat Bayṭār. Egypt: Maṭbaʿat al-Manār, 1936.

Rizq, Muḥammad Ṭulbah. *Yūsuf al-ṣiddīq*. Cairo: Dār al-Maʿārif, 1966.

Rosenberg, Joel. "When Midrash Is Right: Rabbinic Exegesis and Biblical Literary Criticism." Paper presented at the American Comparative Literature Association, Brandeis University, Mar. 1989.

Rosenblatt, Samuel. "Rabbinic Legends in Hadith." *Moslem World* 35 (1945): 237–52.

Rosenthal, Franz. "The Influence of the Biblical Tradition on Muslim Historiography." In *Historians of the Middle East*, ed. Bernard Lewis, 35–45. Oxford: Oxford University Press, 1962.

Rosenthal, Ludwig A. "Die Josephsgeschichte, mit den Büchern Ester und Daniel Vergleichen." *Zeitschrift für die alttestamentliche Wissenschaft* 15 (1895): 278–90.

Rosen-Zvi, Ishay. "Bilhah the Temptress: *The Testament of Reuben* and 'The Birth of Sexuality.'" *Jewish Quarterly Review* 96, no. 1 (2006): 65–94.

Rubin, Uri. *Between Bible and Qurʾan: The Children of Israel and the Islamic Self-Image*. Princeton: Darwin, 1999.

———. "Prophets and Progenitors in the Early Shīʿa Tradition." *Jerusalem Studies in Arabic and Islam* 1 (1987): 41–65.

Sachedina, Abdulazīz. "Early Muslim Traditionists and Their Familiarity with Jewish Sources." In *Studies in Islamic and Judaic Traditions II*, ed. William M. Brinner and Stephen D. Ricks, 49–59. Atlanta: Scholars Press, 1989.

Said, Edward. "Reflections on Exile." In *Out There: Marginalization and Contemporary Cultures,* ed. Russell Ferguson, Martha Gever, Trin T. Minh-ha, and Cornel West, 357–66. New York: New Museum of Contemporary Arts, 1990.

Samarrai, Q. al-. *How a Western Scholar Interprets Islamic Prophetic Tales.* Leiden: Brill, 1979.

Samuell, R. *Seven, the Sacred Number: Its Use in Scripture.* London: 1887.

Sarna, Nahum M. *Understanding Genesis: The World of the Bible in the Light of History.* New York: Schocken, 1966.

Schäfer, Peter, ed. *The Talmud Yerushalmi and Graeco-Roman Culture.* Tübingen: Mohr Siebeck, 1998.

Schapiro, Israel. *Die haggadischen Elemente im erzahlenden Teil des Korans.* Leipzig: H. Itzhowski, 1907.

Schimmel, Annemarie. *And Muhammad Is His Messenger.* Chapel Hill: University of North Carolina Press, 1985.

Schur, Nathan. *Toldot ha-kara'im.* Jerusalem: Mosad Bialik, 2003.

Schussman, Aviva. "An Iraqi Judaeo-Arabic Version of *Maᶜaseh Avraham:* Some Literary and Linguistic Features." In *Genizah Research after Ninety Years: The Case of Judaeo-Arabic,* ed. Joshua Blau and Stefan C. Reif, 126–37. Cambridge: Cambridge University Press, 1992.

———. *Stories of the Prophets in Muslim Tradition* [Hebrew]. Jerusalem: Hebrew University, 1984.

Schwarzbaum, Haim. *Biblical and Extra-Biblical Legends in Islamic Folk Literature.* Walldorf-Hessen: Verlag für Orientkunde Dr. H. Vorndran, 1982.

———. *The Folkloristic Aspects of Judaism and Islam* [Hebrew]. Tel Aviv: Don, 1975.

———. *Jewish Folklore between East and West.* Ed. and intro. Eli Yassif. Beersheva: Ben-Gurion University, 1989.

———. *Studies in Jewish and World Folklore.* Berlin: Walter de Gruyter, 1968.

Seale, M. S. Qur'an and Bible: *Studies in Interpretation and Dialogue.* London: Croom Helm, 1978.

Sefer pirqei rabi eliᶜezer (with Traditional Commentaries, Warsaw Edition). Jerusalem: n.p, n.d.

Sefer ha-yashar. Ed. Joseph Dan. Jerusalem: Mosad Bialik, 1986.

Sefer ha-zikhronot: hu divrei ha-yamim li-yeraḥmi'el. Ed. and intro. Eli Yassif. Ramat Aviv, Israel: Tel Aviv University, 2001.

Shāhīn-i Shīrāzī, Mowlānā. *Sefer Sharḥ-i Shāhīn ᶜal ha-torah.* Ed. Shimᶜon Ḥakam. Jerusalem: N.p., 1902–05.

Shāhīn-i Shīrāzī, Mowlānā. "Jacob and the Wolf" (selection from Shāhīn's *Bereshit-nāmah*). In Moreen, *In Queen Esther's Garden,* 38–55.

Shamir, Shimon, ed. *The Jews of Egypt: A Mediterranean Society in Modern Times.* Boulder: Westview, 1987.

Shamy, Hasan M. el-. *Folk Traditions of the Arab World: A Guide to Motif Classification.* 2 vols. Bloomington: Indiana University Press, 1995.

Shupak, Nili. "The Joseph Story: Legend or History" [Hebrew]. In *Texts, Temples, and Traditions: A Tribute to Menahem Haran,* ed. Michael V. Fox et al., 125–33. Winona Lake, Ind.: Eisenbrauns, 1996.

Sidersky, D. *Les Origines des Legends Musulmanes dans le Coran y dans les Vies des Prophetes.* Paris: Paul Geuthner, 1933.

Sivan, Hagith. "Rabbinics and Roman Law: Intermarriage in Late Antiquity." *Revue des Études Juives* 156 (1997): 59–100.

———. Review of Ross Shepard Kraemer, *When Aseneth Met Joseph. A Late Antique Tale of the Biblical Patriarch and His Egyptian Wife Reconsidered.* In *Bryn Mawr Classical Review 98.12.02,* 1998.

Sklare, David Eric, *Ben Ḥofni Gaon and His Cultural World: Texts and Studies.* Leiden: Brill, 1996.

Sklare, David Eric, and Haggai Ben-Shammai. *Kitvei ha-yad be-ʿarvit-yehudit be-osfei firqovitsh.* Jerusalem: Ben-Zvi Institute, 1997.

Smith, Barbara Herrnstein. "Narrative Versions, Narrative Theories." In *On Narrative,* ed. W. J. T. Mitchell, 209–32. Chicago: University of Chicago Press, 1981.

Smith, Jonathan Z. "What a Difference a Difference Makes." In *"To See Ourselves as Others See Us": Christians, Jews and "Others" in Late Antiquity,* ed. Jacob Neusner and Ernest S. Frerichs, 3–49. Chico, Calif.: Scholars Press, 1985.

Speiser, E. A. *Genesis.* Garden City, N.Y.: Doubleday, 1964.

Speyer, Heinrich. *Die biblischen Erzählungen im Qoran.* Georg Olms Verlag, 1977.

Spiegel, Shalom. *The Last Trial: On the Legends and Lore of the Command to Abraham to Offer Isaac as a Sacrifice: The Akedah.* Trans. Judah Goldin. Woodstock, Vt.: Jewish Lights, 1993.

Spiro, Socrates. *An Arabic–English Vocabulary of the Colloquial Arabic of Egypt.* 1st edition. Cairo: al-Mokattam Printing Office, 1895.

Stern, David. *Midrash and Theory: Ancient Jewish Exegesis and Contemporary Literary Studies, Rethinking Theory.* Evanston, Ill.: Northwestern University Press, 1996.

Stern, M. S. "Muhammad and Joseph: A Study of Koranic Narrative." *Journal of Near Eastern Studies* 44, no. 3 (1985): 193–204.

Stern, S. M., ed. *Muslim Studies (Muhammedanische Studien).* 2 vols. London: George Allen and Unwin, 1971.

Sternberg, Meir. *Hebrews between Cultures: Group Portraits and National Literature.* Bloomington: Indiana University Press, 1998.

———. *The Poetics of Biblical Narrative: Ideological Literature and the Drama of Reading.* Bloomington: Indiana University Press, 1985.

Stillman, Norman. *The Jews of Arab Lands: A History and Source Book.* Philadelphia: Jewish Publication Society, 1979.

——— *The Jews of Arab Lands in Modern Times.* Philadelphia: Jewish Publication Society, 1991.

The Story of Joseph in Arabic Verse: The Leeds Arabic Manuscript 347. (Ed. with a trans. and notes by R. Y. Ebied and M. J. L. Young.) Leiden: Brill, 1975.

Stowasser, Barbara Freyer. "The Chapter of Zulaykha." In *Women in the Qur'an, Traditions, and Interpretation,* 50–56. New York: Oxford University Press, 1994.

Swartz, Merlin L. *Ibn Al-Jawzi's* Kitab Al-Qussas Wa'l-Mudhakkirin. Beirut: Dar el-Machreq, 1971.

Swartz, Michael D. *Scholastic Magic: Ritual and Revelation in Early Jewish Mysticism.* Princeton: Princeton University Press, 1996.

Ṭabarī, Abū Jaʿfar Muḥammad b. Jarīr al-. *The Children of Israel.* Trans. William M. Brinner. Vol. 3, *The History of al-Ṭabarī,* Albany: State University of New York Press, 1991.

———. *The Commentary on the Qurʾān, Being an Abridged Translation of* Jamʿ al-bayān ʿan taʾwīl al-Qurʾān *with Introduction and Notes by J. Cooper.* Ed. W. F. Madelung and A. Jones. Oxford: Oxford University Press, 1987.

———. *General Introduction and from the Creation to the Flood.* Trans. Franz Rosenthal. Vol. 1, *The History of al-Ṭabarī.* Albany: State University of New York Press, 1989.

———. *Prophets and Patriarchs.* Trans. William M. Brinner. Vol. 2, *The History of al-Ṭabarī.* Albany: State University of New York Press, 1987. Originally published in Arabic as *Taʾrīkh al-rusul w'al-mulūk (Annales*), ed. M. J. De Goeje (Leiden: Brill, 1964).

———. *Qiṣaṣ al-anbiyāʾ.* 1st ed. Cairo: al-Dār al-Miṣriyyah al-Lubnāniyyah, 1994.

———. *Tafsīr al-Ṭabarī: Jāmiʿ al-bayān ʿan taʾwīl al-Qurʾān.* Cairo: Dār al-Maʿārif, 1955.

Tadmor, Hayim. "Was the Biblical *Sārîs* a Eunuch?" In *Solving Riddles and Untying Knots: Biblical, Epigraphic, and Semitic Studies in Honor of Jonas C. Greenfield,* ed. Seymour Gitin, Ziony Zevit, Michael Sokoloff, 317–25. Winona Lake, Ind.: Eisenbrauns, 1995.

Taji-Farouki, Suha. "A Contemporary Construction of the Jews in the Qurʾān: A Review of Muhammad Sayyid Tantawi's *Banū isrāʾīl fī al-Qurʾān w'al-sunna* and ʿAfīf ʿAbd al-Fattāḥ Tabbara's *Al-yahud fī al-Qurʾān."* In *Muslim-Jewish Encounters: Intellectual Traditions & Modern Politics,* ed. Ronald L. Nettler and Suha Taji-Farouki, 15–37. Netherlands: Harwood Academic Publishers, 1998.

"The Testament of Joseph" (from the *Testaments of the Twelve Patriarchs*). In *The Old Testament Pseudepigrapha,* ed. James H. Charlesworth, 819–25. New York: Doubleday, 1985.

Thaʿlabī, Aḥmad b. Muḥammad al-. *ʿArāʾis al-majālis fī qiṣaṣ al-anbiyā', or "Lives of the Prophets."* Trans. William M. Brinner. Leiden: Brill, 2002. Originally published in Arabic as *Qiṣaṣ al-anbiyāʾ, al-musammā ʿarāʾis al-majālis* (Beirut: al-Maṭbaʿah al-Thaqafiyyah, n.d.).

Thompson, S. *Motif Index of Folk-Literature.* Bloomington: Indiana University Press, 1966.

Torat ḥayim. Ed. Mordekhai Breuer, Yosef Kafaḥ, and Mordekhai Leyb Katsenelenbogen. Jerusalem: Mosad ha-Rav Kook, 1986.

Torrey, Charles Cutler. *The Jewish Foundation of Islam.* New York: Bloch, 1933.

Trimingham, J. Spencer. *Christianity among the Arabs in Pre-Islamic Times.* London: Longman, 1979.

Tritton, A. S. *The Caliphs and Their Non-Muslim Subjects: A Critical Study of the Covenant of ʿUmar.* 1930; London, 1970.

Vajda, G. "Isrāʾīliyyāt." In *Encylopedia of Islam.*

VanderKam, James C. *The Book of Jubilees.* Sheffield: Sheffield Academic Press, 2001.

Waldman, Marilyn Robinson. "New Approaches to 'Biblical' Materials in the Qurʾān." In *Studies in Islamic and Judaic Traditions,* ed. William M. Brinner and Stephen D. Ricks, 47–64. Atlanta: Scholars Press, 1986.

Wasserstrom, Steven M. *Between Muslim and Jew: The Problem of Symbiosis under Early Islam.* Princeton: Princeton University Press, 1995.

———. "Jewish Pseudipigrapha in Muslim Literature: A Bibliographical and Methodological Sketch." In *Tracing the Threads: Studies in the Vitality of Jewish Pseudepigrapha,* ed. John C. Reeves, 87–114. Atlanta: Scholars Press, 1994.

———. "Recent Works on the 'Creative Symbiosis' of Judaism and Islam." *Religious Studies Review* 16 (1990): 43–47.

Wegner, Judith Romney. "The Image and Status of Women in Classical Rabbinic Judaism." In *Jewish Women in Historical Perspective,* ed. Judith Reesa Baskin, 73–100. Detroit: Wayne State University Press, 1998.

Wehr, Hans. *A Dictionary of Modern Written Arabic.* 4th ed. Ed. J Milton Cowan. Wiesbaden: Otto Harrassowitz, 1979.

Weiner, Alfred. "Die Faradj Baʿda Shidda Literatur." *Der Islam* 4 (1913): 270–98, 387–420.

Wensinck, A. J. *A Handbook of Early Muhammadan Tradition.* Leiden: Brill, 1971.

Werblowsky, R. J. Zwi, and Geoffrey Wigoder. *The Oxford Dictionary of the Jewish Religion.* New York: Oxford University Press, 1997.

Wheeler, Brannon M. *Prophets in the Quran: An Introduction to the Quran and Muslim Exegesis.* London: Continuum, 2002

Wildavsky, Aaron B. *Assimilation Versus Separation: Joseph the Administrator and the Politics of Religion in Biblical Israel.* New Brunswick, N.J.: Transaction, 1993.

Wills, Lawrence M. *The Jewish Novel in the Ancient World, Myth and Poetics.* Ithaca: Cornell University Press, 1995.

Yahuda, A. "A Contribution to Qurʾān and Ḥadīth Interpretation." In *I. Goldziher Memorial Volume,* 294–95. Budapest: Globus, 1948.

Yalquṭ midreshei teiman. Ed. Avraham Yosef Wertheimer. 2 vols. Jerusalem: Ketab Yad wa-Sepher, 1988.

Yalquṭ shimʿoni ʿal ha-torah le-rabeinu Shimʿon ha-darshan. Ed. Yitzhaq Natan Lehrer, Arthur B. Hyman, and Yitzhaq Shiloni. Jerusalem: Mosad ha-Rav Kook, 1973–91.

Yassif, Eli. *The Hebrew Collection of Tales in the Middle Ages* [Hebrew]. Tel-Aviv: Ha-Kibbutz ha-Meʾuḥad, 2004.

———. *The Hebrew Folktale: History, Genre, Meaning.* Trans. Jacqueline S. Teitelbaum. Bloomington: Indiana University Press, 1999.

———. "Introduction." In *The Golem of Prague and Other Tales of Wonder* by Yehudah Yudl Rosenberg [Hebrew], 7–72. Jerusalem: Mosad Bialik, 1991.

Yohannan, John D. *Joseph and Potiphar's Wife in World Literature: An Anthology of the Story of the Chaste Youth and the Lustful Stepmother.* New York: New Directions, 1968.

Zeligs, Dorothy F. "The Personality of Joseph." In *Psychoanalysis and the Bible: A Study in Depth of Seven Leaders,* 59–90. New York: Bloch, 1974.

Zohar, Zvi. "Lowering the Barriers of Estrangement: Rabbanite-Karaite Intermarriage in Twentieth-Century Egyptian Halakha." In *The Jews of Egypt: A Mediterranean Society in Modern Times,* ed. Shimon Shamir, 143–68, 1987.

Zolondek, Leo. *Book XX of Ghazzālī's* Iḥyāʾ ʿulūm al-dīn. Leiden: Brill, 1963.

Zucker, Moshe. "The Problem of *ʿIsma*—Prophetic Immunity to Sin and Error in Islamic and Jewish Literatures" [Hebrew]. *Tarbiz* 35 (1966): 149–73.

Index

ᶜAbbasids and ᶜAbbasid period, 9, 268n. 23
ᶜAbdallāh b. Salām, 11, 268–69n. 25
Abraham (biblical patriarch): casting into the furnace of, 61n. 38; on God's testing of, 203; informed by God of future exile, 176, 279n. 24; Judeo-Arabic tale of, 5; as a model for Muḥammad, 2, 5–6, 33; in the Qurʾān and Bible, 39, 142, 252, 265n. 2
Adam (first man), 38, 142, 245
Aggadah, 42
ahl al-kitāb, 7
Alexander Romance, 12
Allāh, Sheikh Walī, 278–79n. 19
Alter, Robert, 29, 139, 141–42, 159–60, 179, 214, 246, 248
Amichai, Yehudah, 280–81n. 34
ᶜAnan ben David, xvi–xvii, 265n. 3
Antiquities of the Jews (Josephus), 57n. 17, 65n. 62, 141–2, 145–46, 178–79, 200, 223, 281n. 37, 281n. 39, 283n. 20, 284n. 24
"anxiety of influence", 9–10, 174–75
Apocrypha, 32
ᶜaqeidah (Binding of Isaac), 177
Arabic language, 49–52
Aramaic language, 52, 53, 276n. 11
"artifacts": cultural and literary, xiii, 1, 31–32, 47, 265n. 1
Asenath (wife of Joseph), 240, 241–42, 285nn. 53–54
Asher (son of Jacob), 140
ᶜAṣṣ, ᶜAmr b., 76n. 128
Assembly of Ladies motif, 229–35, 285n. 43
Avot de-rabi natan, 276n. 15
ᶜAzīz, al- (Potiphar): cross-cultural borrowing in Islamic characterizations of, 214–15; depiction of in QSYTunis, 80n. 143; motif of sexual ambivalence of, 215–17; political demise of, 217; purchase of Joseph, 208; as ruler of Upper Egypt, 85n. 180; on title, 282n. 3; variations in the name of, 80n. 143, 208–09. *See also* Potiphar

Baba batra (talmudic tractacte), 162
Bach, Alice, 283n. 12
Banū Qaynuqā tribe, 268n. 25
Baron, Salo, 7
Baskin, Judith, 286n. 1
Baṭanūnī, Ibn al-, 240
Bathsheba (wife of King David) 38
Bayḍāwī, ᶜAbdallāh ibn ᶜUmar al-: on Assembly of Ladies, 234, 235; on caravan, 196, 282n. 42; collation of exegetical traditions, 4; on "false blood," 187; on identity of brother who protected Joseph, 192; on feminine guile (*kayd*), 236–37; on Jacob's dream of wolves, 185; on Joseph, sexual restraint of, 228–29; on Joseph's name, etymology of, 38; on Joseph 166; life and works of, 266n. 5; on Muḥammad's conversion

Bayḍāwī (*continued*)
of Jews, 37; *Anwār al-tanzīl wa-asrār al-taʿwīl* (Qurʿān commentary), 4; on revelation of Joseph surah as response to challenge of Jewish sages, 36; on superiority of Joseph narrative in Qurʿan, 34; on thievishness of Joseph, 198; on women's cunning, 236–37
beauty. *See* physical beauty
Bedouin, tale of the, 84n. 173
Benin, Joel, 269n. 27
Benjamin (son of Jacob), 82n. 161, 149–150, 201–2, 204, 275n. 3
Ben-Sasson, Menahem, 273n. 2
Ben-Shammai, Haggai, 273n. 2
Berakhot (Talmudic tractate), 169
Bereishit (*Genesis*) *raba*, 21, 57n. 17, 61n. 38, 62n. 41, 89n. 194, 97n. 236, 102n. 262, 117n. 353, 119n. 364, 125n. 395, 126n. 405, 126n. 406, 143, 147, 148–9, 153, 159, 160–61, 164, 180, 181, 190, 191–92, 194, 195–96, 210, 218, 225, 226, 244, 277n. 21, 277–78n. 6, 281n. 39, 282n. 8, 283n, 15, 285n. 53, 287n. 12
"Betrothal at the Well," 246–47, 286n. 3. *See also* "type scene"
biblicist material, adoption and adaptation of, 6–11, 27
Bilhah (slavegirl of Rachel), 140, 163, 278n. 11
Blau, Joshua, 50, 51, 54, 274n. 5
Bloom, Harold, 268n. 24
Bohak, Gideon, 275, n.1
Boyarin, Daniel, viii, 41, 265n.
Braun, Martin, 240
Brinner, William M., 269n. 27
Brothers of Joseph: ambiguity in traditions over treatment of Joseph, 183–84; basis for sibling rivalry between Joseph and, 150, 158–67; birth order, importance of, 159–63; characterization of Joseph as thief by, 156; initial love for Joseph, 172, 183; Joseph's test for, 201–2, 204; metaphorical connection between Joseph's relations with Zulaykhā and his relations with his, 243–47; presentation of Joseph's garments to Jacob, 188; remorse of, 202; repressed memories of, 199–201; as righteous, 153; setting of dogs on Joseph, 191–92; view of fraternal connection with Joseph, 182–83, 193, 202; as virtuous, 183. *See also names of individual brothers*

Cain and Abel (sons of Adam), 200–201
Cairo, xi, 4, 76n. 128
Cairo Genizah, 273–74n. 3
Chronicles, Book of, 31, 164, 249
Chronicles of Yeraḥmiʾel, The, 231
Copts, 99n. 248
cross-cultural influences, Jewish-Islamic, xii-xv, 1–12, 138–39, 253–55
Culler, Jonathan, 272n. 45

darshan, or *magīd*, 3
David (biblical king), 23, 38; Judeo-Arabic tale of, 5
Day of Atonement, 180, 280n. 27
dhimma, ahl al-dhimma, 7–8
Dinah (daughter of Jacob), 178, 242, 249, 280n. 25, 285n. 53
Douglas, Mary, 248, 249, 250
dreams: of Joseph, 154, 159, 166–67, 168–69, 171; pattern of repetition in Joseph tales, 170–71; as a reflection of God's plans, 172, 188, 299n. 19; single vs. double, in Joseph tales, 170–74

Egypt, 54, 76n. 128, 207
Elkin, Zeev, 273n. 2
Ephraim (son of Joseph), 29
Eros, 240
Esau (son of Isaac) 140–41, 278n. 9
Esther, Book of, 249–50, 286n. 7; Judeo-Arabic tale of, 5
Eve (first woman), 151, 245–46
Even-Zohar, Itamar, 265n. 2

Fāṭimids, 76n. 128
Feldman, Louis, 275n. 7
Fenton, Paul, 48, 273–74n. 3
Ferguson, Charles, 274n. 8
Firdawsī, al-, 271n. 37
Firestone, Reuven, 6, 275n. 1
Firkovich, Abraham, Firkovich Collection, 12, 48, 273n. 2
folk author, 5, 40
Frye, Northrop, 26

Gabriel (archangel), 227
Gad (son of Jacob), 140
Gan, Moshe, 286n. 7
Geiger, Abraham, 232
Genesis: digressive character of Joseph tale in, 139–41; fertile co-wife posting a threat to the preferred but barren wife motif in, 161, 277–78n. 6; importance of birth order in, 159–60; Joseph and Potiphar's Wife pericope, 211–12; literary merit of Joseph story in, 29–30; narrative structure of, 139–43; prominence of Joseph cycle in, 1–2; redemption for Diaspora Jews motif in, 250–51; role of dreams in developing narrative tension in, 167; sibling rivalry in, 160–65, 166; "slowing-down" narrative time technique, 141–42; translation of, 49. *See also names of individual personages and events*
Ginzberg, Louis, 152–53, 232
Goitein, S. D., 232, 267n. 17, 280n. 31
Goldman, Shalom, 275n. 1
Great Story of Our Master the Messenger Moses, The, 47, 271n. 40
Grünbaum, Max, 61n. 38, 232

ḥadīth, 9, 11, 43, 148
ḥagigah (talmudic tractate), 184
Ha-Gaᶜon, Saᶜadya, 49, 140, 196
Ha-Levi, Joseph, 47, 273n. 2
ḥanān Collection, 48
Hary, Benjamin, 287n. 10
Hebrew language, use of, in Judeo-Arabic texts, 53–54
Heller, Bernard, 232
hendiadys, 145–46
Hippolytus, 239–40
Horovitz, Joseph, 272n. 47
Hubā, 245–46

Ibn Taymīya, 9
ᶜIram dhāt al-ᶜimād, 208, 282b, 2
impotence, motif of, 247
infertility, motif of, 161, 247, 277–78n. 6
intertextuality, xiv–xv, 27–28, 137–38
Isaac (son of Abraham), 33, 140, 151, 280n. 33
Ishmael(son of Abraham), 39
Ishmaelites, 195–97, 281–82n. 41
Islam: claims of ownership and authenticity of Joseph narrative, 35–40; divergent processes of textual formation in, 44; expansion and integration of foreign elements within canon of, 41; process of adoption and adaptation of Jewish scriptures, 6–7, 8–10–11, 36; the *Sunnah,* 43; treatment of sibling rivalry in literature, 160, 165–67; view of biblicist figures as prophets, 43. *See also* Qurᶜān
isrāᶜīliyyāt: ambivalence of *ᶜulamāᶜ* toward, 41; credibility of, 11; description of, 8, 9; Jewish and Christian sources of, 4–5, 33; as pejorative term, 9, 10;
Issachar (son of Jacob), 140

Jacob: ambivalence towards Joseph, 174–75, 177–78, 186–87; concern with protecting Joseph, 176, 186, 189; elaborate preparations in Egypt made to welcome, 129n. 413; encounter of the Bedouin with, 84n. 173; exile of, 279n. 24; favoritism of Joseph, 144–46, 150, 158–59; favoritism of Rachel, 144–45, 146; fear for Brothers, 178–79; fears of a wolf

Jacob (*continuing*)
devouring Joseph, 185; forbearance and patience of, 24; hubris of, 176–77; identical mark on head as Joseph, 127n. 406; insistence that his bones be brought out of Egypt, 251; link between Joseph's beauty and, 148–49, 151; loss of prophecy, 179, 188, 189; mourning of Joseph, 179–82, 238; as passive actor in mandrake episode between wives, 163; prophecy of, 23, 189; protest to Laban, 276–77n. 16; reaction to Brothers' tale of Joseph's demise, 179, 186–87; reaction to Joseph's second dream, 167–68, 176; relationship with Esau, 140; relationship with Reuben, 163–64, 194; religious faith of, 39; return of sight and prophetic powers, 128n. 409, 180–82; special treatment of Benjamin, 150; submission to God's will, 203

Jawzī, al-, 37–38, 228

Jews: conversion to Islam, 7, 268–69n. 25; exilic condition, anxiety over, 29, 247–53; history of life in Arabo-Islamic world, xi, xv, 6, 7, 8, 137–38, 254–5; linguistic and cultural barriers in Arabian Peninsula for, 53. *See also* Judaism

Job (biblical and quranic prophet), 203

Jonah (biblical and quranic prophet), 265n. 2

Joseph (son of Jacob): advice to Reuben, 193; age of, 170; ambivalent portrayal of chasteness of, 225–29; blessings bestowed on masters, 207, 208; Brothers' animosity for, 150, 160–65; Brothers' initial love for, 183; centrality of in Jewish and Muslim tradition, 1–2; connection with Muḥammad, 2, 151; cross-cultural influence, 2, 137–39; descent and arrival into Egypt, 30–31, 75n. 118, 206–8; dreams as defensive tack for essential insecurity, 169; dreams of, as source of Brothers' jealousy and anger, 159, 166–67, 168; encounter with the Bedouin, 84n. 173; as envious of Brothers, 171; forbearance and patience of, 24, 203; grievance at treatment in Canaan and Egypt, 276–77n. 16; identical mark on head as Jacob, 127n. 406; imprisonment of, 220–23; "ill report," brought by, 243–44; insensitivity to Brothers and self-absorption of, 167–172; insistence that his bones be brought out of Egypt, 251; interrogation of Brothers, 119n. 364; as Jacob's favorite son, 144–45, 147–50, 158–60, 161–64, 166–67, 174; *ketonet pasim*, 158–59, 188, 248; lineage of, 139–152; linguistic origins of name of, 38–39; linkages between two main subplots of Joseph cycle, 243–247; link to the Patriarchs, 166; marriage to Zulaykhā, 217–18, 239; metaphorical death of, 199–201; as model for Muḥammad, 33; murder of Zulaykhā by, 242; omission from tale of scene with Potiphar's Wifes' male servants, 283n. 12; Persian versions of tale of, 271n. 37; physical beauty of, 144–51, 215, 218, 224, 244–45, 283n. 16; as a political model of leadership based on accommodation, 251–52; portrayal of, in Bible, 29–32, in Qurʿān, 32–35; positive transformations in Egypt due to presence of, 207; Potiphar's trust of, 212–13, 216; prominence in Jewish and Islamic tradition, 1–2; reference to, as a prophet, 23; refusal to sell Egyptians grain until they undergo circumcision, 117n. 351; relationship with Asenath, 240, 285n.

54; relationship with Benjamin, 150; religious faith of, 23, 39; retraction of the legitimacy of his dreams, 156, 175, 277n. 24; revelation of identity to Brothers, 203; Righteous vs. Veracious, theme of: ambiguity of term *ṣiddīq*, 146, 152–156, 229; sale of, 70n. 87, 83n. 170, 190, 206, 207–8; second dream of, 167–68, 170; sibling rivalry between Brothers and, 158–67, 171, 174; "Solicitous Brother" motif, 189–93; as "stolen" or "stealing" motif, 197–99; Swahili version of story of, 233–34; tale of Zulaykhā and, as an allegory depicting the love affair between God and His believers, 238; test for Brothers, 201–2, 204; transfer of rights of the firstborn from Reuben to, 164; Turkish versions of tale of, 271n. 37; unquestioning obedience to Jacob's will, 177–78; use of knots in waistband, 224, 284n. 23; Zulaykhā's accusations against, 214, 283n. 12; Zulaykhā's attempted seduction of, 211–13, 218–21, 223

Joseph and Aseneth, 32, 102n. 262, 218

Josephus, Flavius: on affection between Jacob and Rachel, 146; on Brothers' vow of silence, 281n. 37; on God's interrogation of Cain, 200; on Jacob's decision to send Joseph after Brothers, 178–79; listing of Esau's progeny, 142; on Reuben's intercession in treatment of Joseph, 65n. 62; story of Joseph and of Exodus from Egypt, 141; treatment of Jewish heroes, 145

Jubilees, 32, 32, 101n. 258, 108n. 300, 180, 212, 283nn, 16, 20, 285n. 53

Judah (son of Jacob): as bearer of "good news" to Jacob, 128n. 409; birthmother of, 140; Joseph's warning to, 70n. 91; as not doing enough to prevent Joseph's mistreatment, 193; persuasion of Brothers not to kill Joseph, 182–83, 190, 191, 192–93; Tamar and, 206, 210–11; temper of, 126n. 401

Judaism: claims of ownership and authenticity of Joseph narrative, 35–40; critique of biblical heroes within, 44; languages of, 49; link between Joseph tale in Genesis and the realization of Jewish peoplehood, 141. *See also* Jews

Judeo-Arabic: language, use of by Jews, 49–54; popular tales, 5

Kaʿb al-Aḥbār, 11, 37, 148, 183, 269n. 25

Karaites, xi, 11–12, 53, 175 and n. 430 there.

Karaite Collection of Judah L. Magnes Museum, 11, 47, 273nn. 1–2

Kasher, Menahem, 281n. 36

kayd (or *makāyid) al-nisāʿ* ("women's guile") motif, 234, 236–38, 240

Ketubot (talmudic tractate), 283n, 18

Khuzāʿī, al-, 22, 66n. 66, 196–97, 206; attempts to remove crown from Joseph's head,207–8

Kisāʿī, Muḥammad b. ʿAbdallāh al-: on "bearer of good news," 128n. 409; on beauty of Joseph and Rachel, 148, 150; on brother held by Joseph as ransom, 122n. 379; on cupbearer and baker, names of, 109n. 301; on greatness of Joseph story, 36; identity of, 266n. 7; on identity of caravan, 196; on Jacob, 128n. 409, 168–69, 189; on Jacob's wives, 143–44; on Jews' challenge to Muḥammad to name stars in Joseph's dream, 37; on Joseph's auction, 206; on Joseph's early history, 144; on Jew's suppression of Joseph story, 37;, on Joseph, 150; on Joseph and Benjamin as twins, 150; on Joseph's age at

Kisāʿī, Muḥammad b. ʿAbdallāh al- (*continued*)
time of dreams, 170; on Joseph's calling Egyptian people to Islam, 40; on Joseph's deed of sale, 203; on Joseph's dreams, 57nn. 16–17, 167–68; on Joseph's shirt, 128n. 409; mark on Joseph's head identical to Jacob's, 127n. 406; *Kitāb badʿ (khalq) l-dunyā wa-qiṣaṣ al-anbiyāʾ*, 4; on Ladies of the Assembly, 235; on name of caravan leader, 66n. 66; on the sale of Joseph, 69n. 86, 70n. 87, 71n. 97; on scene at Rachel's tomb, 74n. 110; tale of Namrūd, 61n. 38; on thievishness of Joseph, 198; on wolf, 63n. 50, 189; on Zulaykhā becomes Joseph's bride, 130n. 416
Kister, M. J., 9
Kodsi, Mourad el-, 273n. 1
Kohen, ḥākhām Abraham, 273n. 1
Kohl, Rita, 265n. 1
Kraemer, Ross Shepard, 275n. 1
Kugel, James L., 153, 229–32, 265n. 3, 274–75n. 1, 282n. 1

Laban (father of Leah and Rachel), 160–61, 276–77n. 16
Lacan, Jacques, vii
Ladies of the Assembly, 229–35, 285n. 43
Lassner, Jacob, 265n. 1, 275n. 1
Lazurus-Yafeh, Hava, 270n. 35
Leah: relationship with Rachel, 160–65, 172; role in Brothers' learning of Joseph's second dream, 173; role in tricking Jacob into consummating their marriage, 160–61, 187; "soft eyes" of, 275–76n. 9; sons of, 140
Leiberman, Joseph, xvii–xviii
Levenson, Jon, 250
Levi (son of Jacob), 140, 183, 193, 194, 281n. 39
Lewis, Bernard, 267–68n. 19
Lilith, 245

Maḥazor Vitry, 231
Maimonides, Moses (Rambam), 280n. 27
Malti-Douglass, Fedwa, 236
mamlūk, 69n. 86
Manasseh (son of Joseph), 29, 126n. 401
Mann, Thomas (*Joseph and His Brothers),* 40, 240–41, 243, 252
McGaha, Michael D., 24, 26, 270–71n. 36, 275n. 1
Megilah (talmudic tractate), 159, 278n. 11
Midianites, 195–97, 281–82n. 41
Midrash and "midrashic mode," xi–xii, 2–5, 21, 40–
Midrash ha-gadol, 216, 281n. 36, 282n. 8
Midrash haggadot, 61n. 38
Midrash tanḥuma, 21, 108n. 299, 125n. 395, 142, 157, 191, 194, 195, 232, 253, 276n. 15, 277n. 17, 284n. 36, 287n. 12
Midrash tehilim, 183, 276n. 15
Mir, Mustansir, 34–35
Morris, James, 285n. 38
Moses: Israelite rebellious towards, 145, 280n. 30; as leader, 44, 141, 251; as a model for Muḥammad, 2, 33
Muḥammad, Prophet: on beauty of Rachel and Joseph, 148; biography of (*Sīrah*) 43; in connection with biblical prophets, 32–33, 37, 42–43; connection with Joseph, 33, 151; conversion of Jews to Islam, 7; evidence of prophethood of, 269n. 25; as the ideal of human perfection, 43; on the narration of biblical stories, 9; physical appearance of, 152; in Yathrib, 4, 267n. 10
Mutanabbi, al-, 235, 285n. 46

Nahmanides, Moses (Ramban), 282n. 9
Naphtali (son of Jacob), 140
"narrative expansions" of scriptural tales, 2–3, 265n. 3
Nidah (talmudic tractate), 286n.1
Niehoff, Maren, 275n. 1

Nimrod, 61n. 38
Noah (biblical and quranic prophet) 142, 265n. 2
Numbers raba, 276–77n. 16

Onkelos, 148, 276n. 11

Pact of ʿUmar, 8
Peʾah (tractate of Jerusalem Talmud), 165
Pesaḥhim (talmudic tractate), 191, 277n. 23, 281n. 36, 281n. 38
Phaedra, 239–40
Pharaoh, 112 and n. 321 there
physical beauty: as basis for connection between Joseph and Muḥammad, 151; as basis for Zulaykhā's jealousy of Joseph, 244–45; of Jacob and Joseph, 148–49, 151; of Joseph, 215, 218, 283n. 16; link to moral attributes in Joseph tales, 145; of Rachel and Joseph, 145–46, 147–48, 149
Pirqei de-Rabbi Eliʿezer, 57n. 17, 61n. 38, 147, 276n. 15
Polemics, Jewish-Islamic, xiv–xv; 3, 5–11; 35–40
Potiphar: adoption of Asenath, 285n. 53; ambiguities in description and behavior of, 213–14; depiction of in QSYTunis, 80n. 143; as a eunuch, 80n. 143, 213, 237, 247; intentions towards Joseph, 216, 217; names in Islamic tradition, 209; purchase of Joseph, 83n. 170, 208, 211; trust placed in Joseph, 212–13, 216. *See also* ʿAzīz, al-
Potiphar's Wife: attempts to seduce Joseph, 211–13, 218–19, 220, 238; charge of sexual assault against Joseph, 214, 283n. 12; invitation to Assembly of Ladies to view Joseph, 230–31, 232–33, 235; as Joseph's punishment for vanity and primping, 225; juxtaposition of beauty of, with that of Joseph, 224; linguistic treatment of name of, 209–10; link between Joseph's beauty and attention from, 215, 218, 283n. 16; as symbolic of the threat to Jewish identity, 249; as "vicious beast," 244. *See also* Zulaykhā
Potiphera (father of Asenath), 216–17, 240, 242
prophets: ethereal glow (nimbus) surrounding, according to Muslim tradition, 76n. 129; infallibility of (ʿ*isma*), 11–14, 43–44; reasons for stories about, 32–33
Pseudepigrapha, 32
Pseudo-Ben Sira (*The Alphabet of Ben Sira*), 245
Purim mitzrayim, 251

Qidushin (Talmudic tractate), 276n. 12
Qudsi, Moses ben Abraham al-, 273n. 2
Qurʿa, al-, 208
Qurʾān: on adultery, 21–22; didactic function of Joseph tale in the, 33–34; incorporation of biblicist material into the, 6, 10, 27, 33; Joseph as Muslim, 39; narrative structure of Joseph tale in the, 34–35, 143; prominence of Joseph tale in the, 2; religious tolerance in the, 8; sibling rivalry in the, 150, 166; single vs double dreams in the, 171, 173–74; solicitous brother, 192; on uncontrollable sexuality of womankind, 236, 237; Western scholars' views on Joseph story in the, 35. *See also names of individual personages and events*
quṣṣas, 3

Rachel: anachronous allusion to in Joseph's dream, 155–56; Arabic name of, 209; competition between Jacob and Joseph for affection of, 175; death of, 160; descent from sufficient cause for Joseph's murder, 149–150;

Rachel (*continued*)
link between Joseph's beauty and, 145–46, 147–48, 149; rivalry between Leah and, 160–65, 172; sons of, 140; special status of, 144–45, 146; thievery of, 198
Ramban (R. Moses), 282n. 9
Rashi (R. Shelomoh Yitzḥaqi), 142, 170, 175, 243–44, 283n, 13
Rebecca, 249, 280n. 33
"relief after adversity" (*al-faraj baʿda al-shiddah*) genre, 13, 246, 270n. 30
Renard, John, 12, 35–36, 275n. 1
"repressed memories" motif, 199–201
retellings (of scriptural narrative), xii, 41–42, 254
Reuben (son of Jacob): chastisement of Brothers for lack of remorse, 206; loss of rights as Jacob's firstborn son, 164; offer to safely transport Benjamin to Egypt, 194; persuasion of Brothers not to kill Joseph, 183, 190–93, 199; sexual relations with Bilhah as retribution against Jacob, 163–64, 278n. 11; words to Joseph in the pit, 24
romance: stages of, 26–27, 157–58
Rosenbaum, Gavriel, 91n. 204
Rosen-Avi, Ishay, 285n. 49
Rosenthal, Ludwig A., 286n. 7
"Rubbish Theory," 31–32

ṣabr, al-, xvi
Samaritans, 31, 278n. 15
Samuel (biblical prophet), 37
Sanhedrin (talmudic tractate), 164, 279n. 23
Sarah (wife of Abraham), 151, 249
Schechem, 242, 285n. 53
Schwarzbaum, Haim, 232, 272n. 47
Sefer ha-yashar, 24, 58n. 19, 61n. 38, 75n. 119, 168, 206, 209, 232
Sekhel ṭov, 192
Septuagint, 278n. 12
Seraḥ(daughter of Asher), 180–81
Shabat (talmudic tractate), 159, 163, 184, 277n. 1
Shechem, 279–80n. 25
Sheiveṭ musar, 61n. 38
Sifrei, 277n. 23
Simeon, son of Jacob, 122n. 379, 140, 183, 193–4, 281n. 39
Smith, Jonathan Z., vii
Song of Songs, 285n. 52
ṣoṭah (talmudic tractate), 102n. 262, 217, 226, 253, 282n. 6, 283n, 20, 285n. 53
Source criticism, 246
"Stories of the Prophets, The," (*qiṣaṣ al-anbiyāʾ*), xii, 4, 137, 156
Story of Our Master Joseph the Righteous, The: agon phase in, 27; ambivalent portrayal of Joseph's chasteness in, 227–29; ambivalent portrayal of Zulaykhā in, 238–42; *anagnorisis* phase in, 27; Assembly of Ladies, 229–32, 235; *basmallah* in, 23, 270n. 35; the Brothers' deception of Jacob, 187–89; the Brothers' repressed memories, 200–01; capital city of Egypt in, 76n. 128; on caravan in two parts, 196; on descent into pit as metaphor for death, 199–200; didactic purpose of, 13–14; circulation of, 5; dreams in, 167–68, 173, 175–76; duplication of chase scene, 220–23; on exposure of Joseph's circumcision, 203; feminine guile (*kayd*) motif in, 237–38; five magnificent houses in, 223–24; on heredity of Joseph's traits, 144-45, 149–50; on identity of Brother who protected Joseph, 192; on identity of leader of caravan, 196–97; incorporation of Jewish and Islamic traditions in, 5–6, 21–24, 27–28, 40–41, 44, 254–55; independence of, 27–28; Jacob's fear for Brothers, 178–79; Jacob's mourning over Joseph, 179–81;

Joseph as stolen or stealing, 197–99; Joseph's descent into Egypt and his sale, 206–208; language used in, 5–6, 22–24, 27–28, 49, 53–54; linkages between two subplots, 244–45, 247; liquor and food motif in, 232; on "murder" of Joseph, 201; Muslim elements in, 21–24; narrative of homosexuality undercurrent in, 215; narrative plots in, 15–21; narrative structure of, 14–15, 25, 139, 205; nomenclature in, 22; other versions of tale referred to in translation of, 48–49; *pathos* phase in, 27; plot synopsis of, 15–21; poetry in, 22–23; on precariousness of exilic condition, 248, 251; reasons for Brothers' hatred, 159; relationship between Joseph and Brothers, 182–85; "relief after adversity" as a motif in, 246; Righteous vs. Veracious, theme of: ambiguity of term *ṣiddīq*, 153–56; role of dreams in developing narrative tension in, 167; as a romance, 26, 27; single vs. double dreams in, 173; solicitous brother motif in, 190–91; superiority of Joseph to Benjamin, 150; surrendering to God's will motif in, 24, 203–4; *tasbīḥ* in, 12–14; testing of Brothers, 202–04; versions of, 11–12, 47–49; on wolf, scene of, 187–88. *See also names of individual personages and events*

*Story of Yusuf, Son of Ya*ᶜ*qub, The:* 24–27, 137, 173, 183, 185, 206, 284n. 23

Sufi account of Joseph and Zulaykhā, 267n. 8

Sufi interpretations of "The Stories of the Prophets," 43, 266n. 8

Ṭabarī, Abū Jaᶜfar Muḥammad ibn Jarīr al-: on beauty of Joseph and his mother, 147–48; on caravan leader's identity, 196; on Jewish source of Potiphar's command to his wife to care for Joseph, 214; on Joseph's reasons for abstaining from sexual intercourse with Zulaykhā, 226–28; on Joseph's denial of dream, 58n. 22, 277n. 24; on Joseph's dream, 173; on Joseph's imprisonment, rationale for, 222; life and works of, 265–66n. 4; *Tafsīr* of, 4; on tale of Nimrod, 61n. 38; *Ta*ᶜ*rīkh al-rusul w*ᶜ*al-mulūk*, 4; on thievishness of Joseph, 198

taḥrīf and *tabdīl* ("falsification" and "alteration" of revelation), 6, 11

Tafsīr, 4

Tamar, 210–11

Tanḥuma. See Midrash tanḥuma

Tanna de bei Eliyahu, 61n. 38

targūm, 276n. 11

Targum Pseudo-Jonathan, 58n. 19, 178

tasbiḥ: as establishing theme of truthfulness, 153; in *Joseph,* 12–14; purpose of, 14–21

Test motif, 201–04

Testament of Joseph, The, 32, 96n. 233, 220, 240, 277n. 17, 283n, 20, 285n. 53

Testament of Reuben, The, 237

Testament of Simeon, The, 145

Testament of the Twelve Patriarchs, The, 192

Testament of Zebulon, The, 281n. 40, 192

Thackston, Wheeler M., 61n. 35, 285n. 54

Thaᶜlabī, Abū Ishāq Aḥmad al-: on angels who come to Joseph in the well, 62n. 40; on Benjamin's name, 82n. 161; on brother held by Joseph as ransom, 122n. 379; on the caravan coming from Midian, 65n. 63; on caravan leader, 66n. 66, 68n. 76, 75n. 118, 196; on casting Joseph's food to dogs, 67n. 70; on drawing of lots by Brothers to determine who will remain behind in Egypt, 195; on Gabriel's rebuke of Joseph, 115n. 337; on identity of Brother

Thaᶜlabī, Abū Isḥāq Aḥmad al- (*continued*) who protected Joseph, 192-93; on the importance of matrilineal affiliation, 149–150; on *ᶜIram dhāt al-ᶜimād,* 282n. 2; on Jacob's dream of wolves, 185–86, 189; on Jacob's examination of Joseph's shirt, 63n. 45; on the Jews' suppression of Joseph story, 37; on Joseph's beauty and comparison to Muḥammad's, 150–52; on Joseph as truthful interpreter of dreams (*ṣiddīq*), 229; on Joseph's age at time of dreams, 170; on Joseph's being thrown in well, 59n. 26; on Joseph's brothers, 166–7; on Joseph's double usurpation of al-ᶜAzīz, 217; on Joseph's dreams, 57n. 16, 171–72, 279n, 21; on Joseph's fear of being killed by Brothers, 69n. 84; on Joseph's garment, 76n. 126; on Joseph's reasons for abstaining from sexual intercourse with Zulaykhā, 284n. 27; on Joseph's sale in Egypt, 83n. 170; on Judah, 65n. 62; *Kitāb ᶜarāᵓis al-majālis fī qiṣaṣ al-anbiyāᵓ*, 4; on lamb slaughtered by Brothers, 199; on Leah as discloser of Joseph's dream to Brothers, 173; life and works, 266n. 6; on linguistic origins of Joseph's name, 38–39; on Mālik ordering Joseph to wash himself, 76n. 124; on men as tales, 47; on Muḥammad's conversion of Jews, 37; on not placing a woman in trust of young man, 205; on old woman who reveals to Joseph's burial site, 280n. 30; on pact among Brothers, 65n. 61, 67n. 69; on reasons for stories about the prophets, 32–33; on relationship between al-ᶜAzīz and his wife, 85n. 179, 215–16; on the sale of Joseph to caravan, 70n. 87, 71n. 99; on Satan's drawing together Joseph and Zulayhā, 100n. 250; on scene at Rachel's tomb, 74n. 110; on superiority of quranic version of Joseph tale to the biblical, 36, 37; on tale of Nimrod, 61n. 38; on wolf, 63n. 53; on Zulaykhā's idol, 97n. 236
Thompson, Michael, 272n. 45
Thousand and One Nights, The, 236
Tirmidhī, Abū ᶜĪsā al-, 152, 277n. 19
tzimtzum, 32
type-scene, 246, 278n. 7. *See also* "Betrothal at the Well

Umayyads and Umayyad period, 9, 268n. 23
umm al-kitāb, 6
Uriah, 38

Wahb ibn Munabih, 11, 25, 170, 269n. 25
Wasserstrom, Steven, 267n. 17, 269n. 26
Wegner, Judith Romney, 286n. 1
Wildavsky, Aaron B., 287n. 11
Women: deceptiveness of, motif of, 236–38; as repository of national or familial pride, 249; as representative of the dominant culture and its threat to the minority culture, 248

yahūdiyyah al-, 49
Yalquṭ shimᶜoni, 181, 194
Yassif, Eli, 267n. 12
Yathrib, 4, 267n. 10
Yelamdeinu (in *Yalquṭ torah*) 108n. 299, 193, 284n, 25

zāwiyah, 221, 283–84n. 22
Zebulon (son of Jacob), 140, 149, 183, 192, 194
Zeligs, Dorothy, 277n. 2
Zilpah (slavegirl of Leah), 140
Zohar, 146, 169, 187, 243, 282n. 8
Zulaykhā (wife of al-ᶜAzīz): alienation between al-ᶜAzīz and, 216; attempts to seduce Joseph, 219–21, 223; beauty of, 224; bribing of Joseph's

jailer, 111n. 309; contrast between mores of Joseph and, 154; as a devouring animal, 244–45, 247; dualist portrayal of, 238–42; "fear of the feminine," 245–46; jealousy of Joseph's beauty, 244–45; Joseph's killing of, 130n. 416; 238–42; linguistic treatment of name of, 209–10; marriage to Joseph, 217–18, 239; physical suffering of, 238–39; rationale for building a house for Joseph, 92n. 210; rejection of Joseph, 240; role in purchase of Joseph, 208; suicide threats of, 225, 285n. 43; as threat to Joseph and the continuity of Israel's sacred history, 248–49; as threat to relationship between master and trusted servant, 237; violent death of, at the hands of Joseph, 242; virginity of, 224, 239; as a well, 246–47. *See also* Potiphar's Wife

www.ingramcontent.com/pod-product-compliance
Lightning Source LLC
Chambersburg PA
CBHW050551170426
43201CB00011B/1656
* 9 7 8 0 8 1 4 3 2 5 6 6 7 *